Multinational Firms in the World Economy

Multinational Firms in the World Economy

Giorgio Barba Navaretti and Anthony J. Venables

With Frank G. Barry, Karolina Ekholm, Anna M. Falzoni, Jan I. Haaland, Karen Helene Midelfart and Alessandro Turrini

Princeton University Press
Princeton and Oxford

Copyright © 2004 by Princeton University Press

Published by Princeton University Press,
41 William Street, Princeton, New Jersey 08540

In the United Kingdom: Princeton University Press,
3 Market Place, Woodstock, Oxfordshire OX20 1SY

Second printing, and first paperback printing, 2006
Paperback ISBN-13: 978-0-691-12803-0
Paperback ISBN-10: 0-691-12803-0

The Library of Congress has catalogued the cloth edition of this book as follows

Barba Navaretti, Giorgio, 1960–
    Multinational firms in the world economy / G. Barba Navaretti and A. J. Venables ;
with F. Barry ... [et al.].
        p.   cm.
    Includes bibliographical references and index.
    ISBN 0-691-11920-1 (cl. : alk. paper)
    1. International business enterprises. 2. International trade. I. Venables, Anthony.
    II. Barry, Frank, 1956– III. Title.

HD2755.5.B368 2005
338.8′8—dc22   2004050592

British Library Cataloguing-in-Publication Data is available

This book has been composed in Times and typeset by T&T Productions Ltd, London

Printed on acid-free paper. ∞

pup.princeton.edu

Printed in the United States of America

10 9 8 7 6 5 4 3 2

Contents

Preface

Depending on your point of view, multinational enterprises (MNEs) are either the heroes or the villains of the globalized economy. Governments compete fiercely for foreign direct investment by multinational firms, but complain when firms go global and move their activities elsewhere. MNEs are seen by some as threats to national identities and wealth and are accused of riding roughshod over national laws and of exploiting cheap labour. However, the debate on MNEs and foreign direct investment is rarely grounded in sound economic arguments.

This book brings clarity to the debate on MNEs. It assesses the determinants of MNEs' actions, investigating why their activity has expanded so rapidly, and why some countries have seen more MNE activity than others. It analyses their effects on countries that are recipients of inward investments, and on those who see MNEs moving jobs abroad. The arguments are made using modern advances in economic analysis, a country case study, and by drawing on the extensive empirical literature that assesses the determinants and consequences of MNE activity.

The volume combines original contributions with a review of the literature. This literature has grown considerably over the past decade, thanks to recent advances in theoretical and empirical tools. On the theory side, new trade theory and the theory of the firm have created tools enabling rigorous analysis of the causes and consequences of multinational activity. The organizational choices of MNEs are being usefully analysed by applying recent developments of contract theory. On the empirical side, new firm-level datasets and the econometric techniques for handling these data have come into use.

Our target audience includes advanced undergraduate and postgraduate students in economics, and policy makers with a good background in economics. Our writing is guided by two principles. One is to focus on issues rather than techniques. The other is to synthesize, producing a common framework within which different contributions can be located and assessed. Technical material is developed, but generally in a way that is 'ramped', so chapters progress in complexity. We have also provided overview chapters and extensive references to the literature.

The multiple authorship of the volume reflects its genesis from two EU funded research networks on foreign direct investment. This co-authorship has proved invaluable in assembling a pool of knowledge much wider and deeper than that of any of the authors individually. We stress that this volume is not a collection of papers, but instead a fully integrated work in which all contributors have had input into all chapters, under the coordination of the two leading authors. The main contributors of chapters of the book are as follows:

- Chapters 1 and 2: Giorgio Barba Navaretti and Anthony J. Venables;
- Chapters 3 and 4: Anthony J. Venables;
- Chapter 5: Alessandro Turrini and Anthony J. Venables;
- Chapter 6: Karolina Ekholm and Karen Helene Midelfart;
- Chapter 7: Giorgio Barba Navaretti;
- Chapter 8: Frank G. Barry;
- Chapter 9: Giorgio Barba Navaretti and Anna M. Falzoni;
- Chapter 10: Jan I. Haaland;
- Chapter 11: Giorgio Barba Navaretti and Anthony J. Venables.

Thanks are due to several organizations and individuals. The European Commission provided support for the networking involved in the project under the TMR network, 'Foreign Direct Investments and the Multinationals: New Theories and Evidence', contract no. ERBFMRX980215, and under the research project, 'Labour Market Effects of Foreign Direct Investments', contract no. HPSECT1999-0001.7. Parts of the work were produced under the auspices of the Globalisation Programme, funded by the UK ESRC, at the Centre for Economic Performance at LSE; the research programme of the Centro Studi Luca d'Agliano; the Global and Regional Economic Performance Programme at SIOS, Norwegian School of Economics and Business Administration. The Centre for Economic Policy Research (CEPR) provided background organization for many of the meetings among the authors.

Emma Taverner provided excellent editorial support. Magnus Blomström was kind enough to make his review on spillovers of foreign direct investments in host countries available to us as a background to Chapter 7. Davide Castellani provided important inputs to Chapter 9. Alessandra Tucci and Riccardo Sarais have been invaluable research assistants. Various people provided very useful comments on preliminary drafts, which enabled us to improve this final version: Paolo Epifani, Sara Formai, Fabrizio Onida, Gianmarco Ottaviano, Stephen Redding, Michele Santoni, Alessandro Sembenelli and three anonymous referees.

Finally, a disclaimer. The opinions expressed in this book by the authors do not necessarily reflect those of the institutions they are affiliated with. Alessandro Turrini contributed to the book while he was at the University of Bergamo and before joining the European Commission.

Contributors

Giorgio Barba Navaretti
University of Milan and the Centro Studi Luca d'Agliano

Giorgio Barba Navaretti is Professor of International Economics at the University of Milan and Scientific Director of the Centro Studi Luca d'Agliano. He has been a consultant for several international organizations and the Italian government. He has published extensively on the economics of multinational firms, on the link between trade, foreign direct investments and technology diffusion, on international economic policy and on firms' dynamics in developing countries. He writes a column in *Il Sole 24 Ore*.

Frank G. Barry
Department of Economics, University College Dublin

Frank G. Barry is a lecturer in economics at University College Dublin, from where he received his BA degree. He holds an MA from the University of Essex and a PhD from Queen's University, Ontario. His publications are in the fields of open-economy macroeconomics and international trade and he has worked extensively on issues of Irish economic development. He has also served as an economic consultant and advisor in Latin America, Africa, Asia and, increasingly in recent times, in the transition economies of Central and Eastern Europe.

Karolina Ekholm
Stockholm School of Economics and CEPR

Karolina Ekholm is Associate Professor at the Stockholm School of Economics. Her research deals mainly with multinational firms and international trade. She has been involved in several studies using firm-level data on Swedish multinationals to address issues about the effects of their foreign expansion.

Anna M. Falzoni
University of Bergamo, CESPRI–Bocconi University and
Centro Studi Luca d'Agliano

Anna M. Falzoni is Associate Professor of Economics at the University of Bergamo. She is also a member of the Board of Directors of CESPRI (Centre for Research on

Innovation and Internationalisation) at Bocconi University and fellow at the Centro Studi Luca d'Agliano. She has an MSc in Economics from the University of Southampton (UK) and a PhD in Economics from Bocconi University. Her main fields of interest are international trade, multinational firms and foreign direct investments.

Jan I. Haaland
Norwegian School of Economics and Business Administration (NHH) and CEPR

Jan I. Haaland is Professor of International Economics at the Norwegian School of Economics and Business Administration (NHH). He is also Research Fellow at the CEPR in London, and a member of the scientific committee of the European Trade Study Group (ETSG). His research fields include international trade and trade policies, foreign direct investments and multinational firms, and general equilibrium modelling of global and regional economic integration.

Karen Helene Midelfart
Norwegian School of Economics and Business Administration and CEPR

Karen Helene Midelfart is Professor Scholar, Norwegian School of Economics and Business Administration and Research Affiliate, CEPR. She received her doctorate from the Norwegian School of Economics and Business Administration (NHH) with a dissertation on economic geography, industry location and trade in 1996. Her main research areas are international economics, economic geography and economic policy, and she has published in journals such as the *Journal of International Economics* and the *Journal of Public Economics*. From 1999 to 2003 she was the research director of the Centre for International Economics and Shipping at NHH. She has served as a consultant for the EU Commission and as a member of government-appointed commissions in Norway preparing reforms of the tax system and of public R&D policy.

Alessandro Turrini
European Commission, Directorate General of Economic and Financial Affairs, CEPR and Centro Studi Luca d'Agliano

Alessandro Turrini is currently working as an economist at the Directorate General of Economic and Financial Affairs. He is also affiliated to CEPR and Centro Studi Luca d'Agliano. Previously, he worked as an assistant professor at the University of Bergamo. He is the author of several articles, published in international academic journals, on trade policy, multinational firms, and the links between international trade and the labour market.

Anthony J. Venables
London School of Economics

Anthony J. Venables is Professor of International Economics at the LSE and directs
the International Trade research programme at the Centre for Economic Performance. Previous experience includes work as research manager of the trade group
in the research division of the World Bank. He has published extensively on international trade issues, including work on trade and imperfect competition, economic
integration and economic geography, including *The spatial economy: cities, regions
and international trade*, with M. Fujita and P. Krugman (MIT Press, 1999).

Multinational Firms in the World Economy

1

Facts and Issues

Multinational enterprises (MNEs) are key players in globalized economies. Foreign-owned MNEs employ one worker in every five in European manufacturing and one in every seven in US manufacturing; they sell one euro in every four of manufactured goods in Europe and one dollar in every five in the US (OECD 2001b).

The general public and policy makers around the world have mixed feelings about MNEs: they see them as either welcome bearers of foreign wealth and knowledge or unwelcome threats to national wealth and identity. Policy makers want MNEs to invest in their country, take pride when their firms rank high in Fortune's list of the largest firms in the world, but are unhappy when national firms close down domestic activities and open up foreign ones, or when foreign brands compete successfully with national ones. The Dr Jekyll and Mr Hyde perception of MNEs stems more from the ambiguous feelings often directed towards large market players with no national identity than from rigorous economic analysis. Indeed, the debate on MNEs is rarely grounded in economic arguments and there is little understanding of what MNEs are, and what the sound reasons for liking or disliking them are.

MNEs are often different from purely national firms and some of the concerns raised are legitimate.[1] They are relatively large, they have competitive power in the market place and bargaining power in the policy-making arena, particularly in smaller developing countries. They are global players who can circumvent national regulations and policies more easily than can national firms. They are footloose, able to move activities between their plants at relatively low cost, removing benefits as rapidly as they deliver them. They mass-produce standardized products, jeopardizing national product variety.

However, these very features of MNEs also explain why countries compete fiercely to attract them. They often bring scarce technologies, skills and financial resources. They are quick to take advantage of new economic opportunities and thus to contribute to the creation of national wealth. They are bound by international stan-

---

[1] We will use the term 'national firm' to mean a firm that produces in a single country, in contrast to a multinational.

dards and market competition and they often offer better employment conditions and product qualities than national firms.

Moreover, MNEs are not just giant corporations like Microsoft or Coca-Cola. Many small and medium enterprises, firms with limited market power in domestic and foreign markets, have one or more foreign subsidiaries. Investing abroad and thus becoming an MNE is a strategy open to and followed by many types of firms.

This book addresses the concerns surrounding MNEs and brings clarity to the debate. It provides a thorough assessment of what MNEs are, of why and where they arise and of their economic impact on home and host economies. We conclude that, although none of these concerns have straightforward answers, the balance bends in favour of MNEs: they are a fundamental feature of modern economies and there is no evidence that their actions are generally less beneficial to home and host economies than are the actions of national firms.

1.1   Multinationals: What Are They and How Are They Measured?

Since multinationals are the subject of this book, the first task is to define them. MNEs are firms that own a significant equity share (typically 50% or more[2]) of another company (henceforth subsidiary or affiliate) operating in a foreign country. MNEs include modern corporations such as IBM, General Motors, Intel and Nike, and also small firms such as Calzaturificio Carmens, a shoemaker employing 250 workers divided between Padua (Italy) and Vranje (Serbia).

The activities of MNEs are best measured by firm-level data, such as the number of people they employ and the size of their sales. Unfortunately, these data on firm-level activities are not widely available. Even when aggregated across firms, there are many gaps in the data and they are not always standardized across countries. Instead, the researcher often has to rely on data on flows of foreign direct investment (FDI). These are recorded from balance-of-payment statistics and they are available across time, industrial sectors and for many receiving and sending countries. According to IMF/OECD definitions (IMF 1993; OECD 1996), FDI is an investment in a foreign company where the foreign investor owns at least 10% of the ordinary shares, undertaken with the objective of establishing a 'lasting interest' in the country, a long-term relationship and significant influence on the management of the firm. FDI flows include equity capital, reinvested earnings and other direct investment capital. In other words, they comprise the financing of new investments, retained earnings of subsidiaries, inter-firm loans and cross-border mergers and acquisitions.

---

[2]More precisely, according to OECD and IMF recommendations, the foreign firm can be defined as a subsidiary if the foreign investor controls more than 50% of the shareholder's voting power or has the right to appoint or remove a majority of the members of this enterprise's administrative, management or supervisory body. Otherwise, it can be defined as an associate enterprise if the foreign investors own between 10 and 50% of the voting shares. See the appendix to the book for statistical definitions.

They are different from portfolio investments, which can be divested easily and do not have significant influence on the management of the firm. Thus, to create, acquire or expand a foreign subsidiary, MNEs undertake FDI. The total direct capital owned by non-residents in a given country each year constitutes the stock of FDI. (See the appendix to the book for a discussion of the statistical definitions of FDI stocks.)

Despite their conceptual differences, we will sometimes use the terms FDI and MNE as if they are synonyms, both acting as a label for the phenomenon studied in this book. We note that other terms are used in the literature—for example, transnational corporation—but we restrict ourselves to terms that have standard usage and exact counterparts in the collection of data.

1.2 The Facts: Empirical Overview

Before embarking on an analysis of MNEs, it is helpful to review the stylized facts about the role of MNEs in the world economy.

Fact 1. FDI grew dramatically in the last 15 years of the twentieth century, far outpacing the growth of trade and income, and then stabilized between 2001 and 2005.

The period 1986–2000 saw an enormous growth of activity by multinational enterprises, as measured by flows of foreign direct investment. As shown in Figure 1.1, inflows of FDI grew much faster than either trade or income; whereas worldwide real GDP increased at a rate of 2.5% per year between 1985 and 1999 and worldwide exports by 5.6%, worldwide real inflows of FDI increased by 17.7%. This compares strikingly with pre-1985 data, when real world GDP, exports and FDI were following closer trends. Between 1970 and 1984, real FDI grew at an average yearly rate of 4.2%, worldwide real GDP by 3.1% and world exports by 5.2%.[3] Since 2001, the rise of world FDI was reversed, and real world inflows were back to their 1998 level. This decline is explained by a series of contingent factors: 1999 and 2000 values were anomalous peaks, partly due to the rise of intra-EU investments following the implementation of the single currency and to the rise of share prices (much FDI takes place through acquisitions in the stock exchange); in 2001, the collapse of share prices and the slowing down of the economy reduced the value and the pace of cross-border mergers and acquisitions.

Despite their rapid growth, FDI flows remain much smaller than trade flows. In 2001 world exports were 7666 billion US$, whereas world FDI inflows were 823 billion US$. However, the picture changes if we revert to the activities of MNEs, activities based on the stock of capital rather than the flow of investment. The sales of

---

[3]The data mentioned come from a special extract of the UNCTAD FDI/TNC Database and from the World Bank, World Development Indicators.

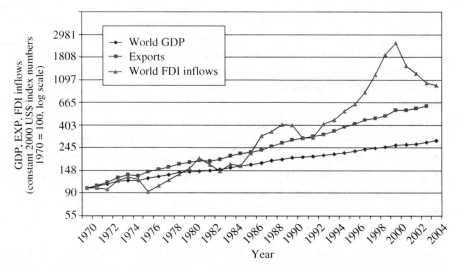

Figure 1.1. Trends in world GDP, exports and FDI inflows, which are index numbers set equal to 100 in 1970 and transformed into a logarithmic scale. *Source:* authors' calculations on World Bank WDI and UNCTAD data.

foreign subsidiaries are in many instances much larger than trade flows. For example, sales of manufacturing products of US subsidiaries in the EU are approximately 3.8 times larger than EU imports from the US and sales of EU subsidiaries in the US are 3.6 times larger than EU exports to the US (US Department of Commerce, Bureau of Economic Analysis and Eurostat). Furthermore, a very large share of world trade is conducted by MNEs. Some commentators have estimated that multinationals— parents and subsidiaries combined—are responsible for 75% of the world's commodity trade (Dunning 1993). According to figures from UNCTAD (1998, 1999a,b, 2000), around one-third of world trade is intra-firm, i.e. between subsidiaries based in different countries or between the subsidiaries and the headquarters of MNEs.

The scale of multinational operations and the role they play in the process of globalization is best gauged by looking at their shares in economic activity. Table 1.1 reports the share of foreign subsidiaries in total manufacturing employment and sales for the G5 countries.[4] These are large, generally above 10% with peaks around 30% for sales in France and the UK. In the US, UK and France they also grew considerably between 1994 and 2001. Note, however, that these shares vary across the five countries analysed. Japan's economy is virtually closed to foreign MNEs, which account for less than 1% of manufacturing employment; in Germany, MNEs account for a lower share of manufacturing employment and output than in the other

---

[4]These statistics are compiled from OECD data. Similar ones are provided by the UN and included in the World Investment Report. The two sets of figures are generally consistent, although for some countries there are differences in the values of the shares.

Table 1.1. Share of foreign subsidiaries in total manufacturing activities (%).

	US 1994 2001	Japan 1994 2001	UK 1994 2001	Germany 1994 2001	France 1994 2001
Employment	12.24 13.27	0.8 1.2	18.1 17.8	7.2 5.8	23.1 30.8
Sales*	15.8 19.74	1.4 2.6	30.6 31.4	13.1 8.3	28.7 35.9

Source: OECD 2003b; OECD STAN Database, 2005, Release 05.

Note: Data for the United States refer to minority and majority foreign-owned firms, while data for Japan, Germany, France and the United Kingdom refer to majority-owned foreign affiliates only.

*USA: turnover (foreign subsidiaries) / production (total manufacturing).

large EU countries, a share that even declined between 1994 and 2001. As discussed in what follows, countries' characteristics and policies play a very important role in explaining the geographical distribution of the activities of MNEs.

MNEs are important in services as well as in manufacturing, although data on service activity are limited. In the UK, the share of foreign subsidiaries in service sector employment in 1998 was 8.4% in utilities and construction, 6.7% in trade, repairs, hotels and restaurants, and 8% in finance, insurance and business services (OECD 2001b), levels somewhat less than half that in manufacturing.

Fact 2. FDI originates predominantly from advanced countries.

Where does FDI come from? As shown in Table 1.2, the predominant source of supply of FDI is the advanced countries.[5] Between 2002 and 2004, 90.8% of outward flows originated in an advanced country. Developing countries had increased their share of outward flows through the 1970s and 1980s to a peak of 15.3% of world flows in the mid 1990s, to see it declining again in the late 1990s. Among individual countries, the US is the world's largest foreign investor. The EU *as a whole* accounted for 71.2% of all outward stocks, a share that has risen sharply partly because of the rise in intra-EU investments[6] associated with deepening integration in the EU and following the creation of the Single Market in 1992. Notice that the EU's FDI is exaggerated relative to the US's, as intra-US investments are classified as domestic investments.

---

[5]We classify countries in this section according to UNCTAD with minor changes. Advanced countries include the 15 countries of the European Union in 2003 (Austria, Belgium, Denmark, Finland, France, Germany, Greece, Ireland, Italy, Luxembourg, The Netherlands, Portugal, Spain, Sweden, United Kingdom), Gibraltar, Iceland, Norway, Switzerland, Canada, the US, Australia, New Zealand, Japan and Israel. Developing countries comprise the rest of the world, including the transition economies of Central and Eastern Europe, Russia and the former CIS countries, Malta, Cyprus and Turkey, as well as South Africa; UNCTAD classifies the transition economies as a separate group and South Africa among the advanced countries.

[6]Intra-EU FDI account for approximately half of all FDI inflows into the EU.

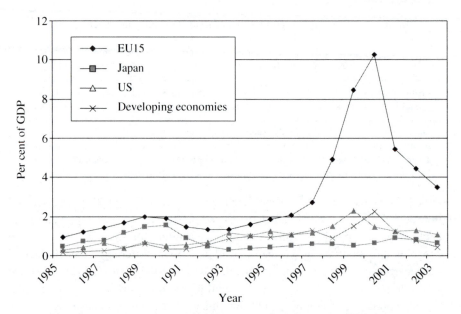

Figure 1.2.   Sources of outward FDI. *Source:* UNCTAD FDI/TNC database.

In the developing world, only the Asian countries (especially China, Hong Kong, Taiwan, South Korea and Singapore) supply a significant share of world flows by the mid 1990s. Most of these investments took place within Asia and therefore declined drastically in the aftermath of the Asian crisis in 1997. The data reported do not yet pick up the recent surge in outward investment from China and India.

Yet, most of the difference between the advanced and developing countries is accounted for by sheer economic size, and the difference in outflows relative to GDP is perhaps less than might be expected. Figure 1.2 maps out the time series of FDI outflows relative to source country GDP (detailed shares are reported in Table 1.8). In the mid 1990s outward flows ranged from an average of 1.3% of GDP for the advanced countries to an average of 0.9% for the developing countries. The noticeable exception is the EU, which moved from a share of 1.3% in the early 1990s to 5.4% in 1997–2003, thus raising the average share of the advanced countries to 2.9%. As argued above, much of the EU increase is driven by intra-EU investments. Although it has declined since 2001, the FDI share of GDP remains higher for the EU than for the other regions of the world.

Fact 3. FDI goes predominantly to advanced countries, but the share of developing countries has been rising.

Turning to the destination of FDI, Table 1.3 shows that most goes to the advanced industrial countries. As will be discussed in Chapters 2, 3 and 6, this is not surprising,

Table 1.2. FDI outflow, % share by area of origin.

Area of origin	1970–73	1974–78	1979–83	1984–88	1989–91	1992–94	1995–97	1998–2001	2002–04
Advanced countries									
USA	48.84	41.96	29.76	17.87	15.12	26.24	21.94	16.08	24.19
Europe	41.33	43.63	48.55	52.78	55.60	47.04	50.56	66.66	54.42
Japan	4.76	6.53	7.84	15.20	18.49	6.70	5.81	3.09	4.60
Oceania	0.92	0.89	1.36	3.71	1.37	1.66	1.20	0.53	2.04
Total advanced countries	**99.61**	**98.05**	**95.62**	**94.26**	**93.11**	**84.43**	**83.55**	**90.02**	**90.34**
Developing and transition countries									
Latin America	0.20	0.69	1.69	0.77	1.42	2.52	3.22	4.11	1.64
Africa	0.19	0.63	1.04	0.27	0.50	0.74	0.71	0.09	0.22
Asia	−0.01	0.60	1.62	4.68	4.94	11.83	12.01	5.42	6.13
Oceania	0.00	0.00	0.01	0.00	0.01	0.03	0.00	0.00	0.00
Central/Eastern Europe and the CIS	0.00	0.03	0.02	0.02	0.02	0.45	0.50	0.34	1.57
Total developing and transition economies	**0.39**	**1.95**	**4.38**	**5.74**	**6.88**	**15.56**	**16.43**	**9.96**	**9.57**
World (%)	100	100	100	100	100.00	100	100	100	100
World (yearly average, million US$)	17 562	29 966	46 748	106 112	223 219	245 400	413 593	945 161	666 454

Source: UNCTAD.

Table 1.3. FDI inflow, % share by area of destination.

Area of origin	1970–73	1974–78	1979–83	1984–88	1989–91	1992–94	1995–97	1998–2001	2002–04
Advanced countries									
USA	8.74	13.10	27.39	39.36	24.96	17.52	20.18	23.19	11.22
Europe	42.79	41.89	30.96	29.23	46.83	34.90	31.25	46.15	47.81
Japan	0.67	0.42	0.56	0.30	0.35	0.59	0.29	0.76	1.17
Oceania	5.99	4.94	4.45	5.33	4.32	3.36	2.80	0.86	3.55
Total advanced countries	**73.42**	**72.76**	**68.42**	**78.95**	**79.51**	**59.30**	**57.37**	**74.83**	**65.82**
Developing and transition countries									
Latin America	12.39	13.54	12.93	7.32	5.85	10.05	12.82	9.41	8.26
Africa	5.91	4.37	2.50	2.26	1.97	2.32	1.82	1.26	2.46
Asia	7.36	8.90	15.68	11.26	11.33	24.14	22.95	11.47	17.07
Oceania	0.66	0.20	0.23	0.11	0.28	0.12	0.14	0.03	0.01
Central/Eastern Europe and the CIS	0.00	0.03	0.05	0.02	0.80	3.82	4.74	2.88	6.21
Total developing and transition countries	**26.33**	**27.05**	**31.40**	**20.97**	**19.43**	**40.45**	**42.47**	**25.04**	**34.01**
World (%)	100	100	100	100	100	100	100	100	100
World (yearly average, million US$)	16 023	27 303	55 597	101 814	187 292	218 800	407 295	1 003 910	665 624

Source: UNCTAD.

given that MNEs often seek large and growing markets. The advanced countries' share of world FDI inflows has fluctuated between 58 and 78%. Notice, however, that they account for a lower share than they do as sources of FDI. Among advanced countries, the picture is similar to that for outward investments, with the largest share concentrated in the EU, although the US is the largest individual country of destination.

As for developing countries, the share of worldwide FDI received by the developing and transition economies jumped from 24.6% in the period 1988–93, to more than 40% in the period 1992–97. It then fell back to 21.33%, following the Asian crisis and grew again to 34% in 2002–04. These flows go overwhelmingly to Asia and Latin America, and China alone took around one-quarter of the total. Indeed, China accounts for much of the increase in flows to developing countries, with its share of world total FDI flows rising from 4.6% for the period 1988–93, to 8.4% for 2002–04.[7] The share of world investment going to sub-Saharan Africa remains low, although has increased somewhat, from around 1.1% between 1988 and 1993 to around 2.5% between 2002 and 2004.

The increase of FDI flows to developing countries reflects the growing importance of FDI as a source of financing of these economies. Figure 1.3 reports FDI inflows relative to the GDP of the host economy (detailed shares can be found in Table 1.9). During the five years from 1986 to 1990, advanced countries received FDI inflows at an average annual rate of 0.9% of their GDP, while the average for developing and transition countries was 0.8% of their GDP. By 1997 to 2003, the inflow rate for the advanced countries had increased to 2.5% of GDP, while that of developing and transition countries as a whole had more than trebled to 3.1% of GDP, with Asia and Latin America taking the lion's share. This finding is not surprising: developing countries lack sufficient domestic resources and they need foreign capital to finance their investments. FDI accounted for a share of roughly 61% of the total financial flows going from OECD to developing countries in 2001 (OECD 2003a).

Fact 4. Mergers and acquisitions account for the dominant share of FDI flows, especially to high-income countries.

The establishment of a foreign subsidiary may take place in one of two ways. Either as a 'greenfield investment', where a new plant is set up from scratch, or as a merger with or acquisition of an existing firm (M&A). As shown in Table 1.4, the majority of FDI takes place through M&A activity rather than through greenfield investments, and the share of M&A has increased steadily since the mid 1980s from 66.3 to

---

[7] In nominal dollar terms, inward direct investment to China increased fro $3.2 billion in 1988 to $60 billion in 2004. The source of all these flows, about 3.7% of China's GDP in 2004, remains hotly debated. The main sources are considered to be Chinese business groups resident in Asia, Chinese businesses resident in China that send their money out and then bring it back to get certain benefits available to foreign investors (the so-called 'round trippers'), and investors from the advanced industrial economies.

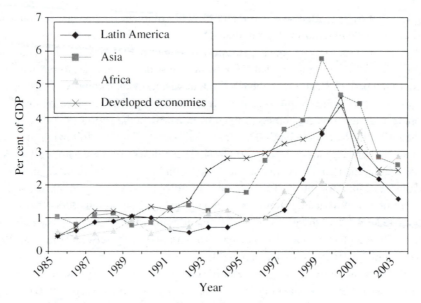

Figure 1.3. Hosts of inward FDI. *Source:* UNCTAD FDI/TNC database.

Table 1.4. Cross-border M&A investments as a percentage of FDI inflows to the host countries.

	1987–91	1992–94	1995–97	1998–2001	2002–04
World	64.80	44.10	58.80	75.59	52.45
Developed economies	77.12	63.05	86.95	91.94	68.37
Developing countries and transition economies	11.84	12.79	15.84	20.51	17.40

Source: UNCTAD, FDI/TNC Database.

76.2% in the period 1998–2001. Since 2001 it has, however, declined back to 52.4% in 2002–04, probably as a consequence of the fall in share prices in 2001. The share of M&A is much smaller in developing than in advanced countries: 17.4% against 68.4% in 2002–04. This reflects the role of FDI in financing new investment projects in developing countries, as well as the scarcity of takeover targets in these countries.

Fact 5. Most FDI is concentrated in skill- and technology-intensive industries.

The most noticeable trend in the sectoral distribution of FDI stocks in the *OECD countries* is the increase in the share of services (from 41.2% in 1982–86 to 61.4% in 1998–2002) and the parallel decline of the primary sector (from 15.1% to 4.3%) (see Table 1.10). This trend reflects the overall shift of world GDP from the primary sector and agriculture towards services. The share of manufacturing in FDI, approximately

Table 1.5. World FDI inward stock by industry, 2003.

Industry	Share of world FDI inward stock (%)
Total	100
Manufacturing	33.3
Food, beverages and tobacco	2.8
Textiles, clothing and leather	0.7
Wood and wood products	1.1
Publishing, printing and reproduction of recorded media	0.7
Coke, petroleum products and nuclear fuel	0.9
Chemicals and chemical products	6.0
Rubber and plastic products	0.5
Non-metallic mineral products	0.8
Metal and metal products	2.1
Machinery and equipment	1.9
Electronic and electronic equipment	3.2
Precision instruments	0.4
Motor vehicles and other transport equipment	3.4
Other manufacturing	9.0
Services	59.8
Trade	10.7
Transport, storage and communications	5.2
Finance	1.0
Business activities	14.9
Other services	11.0
Primary sector	6.9

Source: UNCTAD 2005.
Note: Shares are only reported for a selected number of industries.

40%, is larger than the share of manufacturing in world GDP, which is approximately 30%.

If we look at the distribution of *world* FDI inward stocks in 2003 (Table 1.5), the share of services is 59.8%, that of manufacturing is 33.3% and the primary sector accounts for the remaining share of 6.9%. Within manufacturing, the largest shares are in chemicals, electrical and electronic equipment, transport equipment, etc. Even more revealing is the analysis of the share of employment of foreign subsidiaries in total national employment for the US, UK, Germany and France, the world's largest recipients of FDI (Table 1.6). This indicator relates the activities of MNEs to national activities by sector. Consistent with the sectoral distribution of FDI stocks, we see that foreign subsidiaries account for a larger share of employment in industries like chemicals, machinery and transportation equipment.

The broad sectors in which the presence of MNEs is greatest are characterized by large investments in research and development, a large share of professional

Table 1.6. Share of foreign subsidiaries in total manufacturing
employment by industry (manufacturing).

Sector (2001)	France	Germany	UK*	USA
Food, beverages, tobacco	20.70	3.50	25.90	10.13
Textiles, clothing, leather, footwear	15.00	4.00	9.03	3.08
Wood products	19.90	7.40	1.80	2.69
Paper, printing and publishing	30.90	3.10	11.80	4.45
Chemical products	45.60	24.90	26.10	35.81
Rubber and plastic products	33.70	5.60	18.40	16.09
Non metallic mineral products	32.10	4.30	13.70	28.30
Basic and fabricated metals	28.80	4.60	13.00	8.06
Machinery, total	40.60	6.60	29.00	20.55
Electrical and electronic equipment	33.90	6.60	30.30	21.55
Scientific instruments	30.40	7.30	19.00	—
Transportation equipment	28.80	8.00	34.60	19.22
Other manufacturing	24.20	2.30	9.00	—
Total manufacturing	**30.80**	**5.80**	**20.40**	**13.27**

Source: OECD 2003b; STAN Database for Industrial Analysis, Vol. 2005, Release 05.
*UK data refer to the year 1999.

and technical workers, and the production of technically complex or differentiated goods. These assets provide 'services' to all the operations of the firm and they do not need to be expanded at the same rate as output. Thus, these services generate firm-level economies of scale, in that they can be used at low cost by the foreign plants of the MNEs. As will be discussed in Chapters 2, 3 and 6, firm-level economies of scale are important determinants of FDI.

Fact 6. MNEs are larger and sometimes more productive than national firms.

MNEs are generally large companies compared with national firms, both in home and host countries. Foreign subsidiaries of MNEs are on average larger than national firms in host economies (Griffith and Simpson 2001; Fabbri et al. 2002; Barba Navaretti et al. 2003). The home activities of MNEs are also, in general, larger than those of national firms with no foreign subsidiaries (Fabbri et al. 2002). A crude measure of this gap in host countries can be gauged by comparing the average size of foreign subsidiaries with that of all manufacturing firms in the largest G5 countries (Table 1.7). We find that foreign subsidiaries are relatively large when size is measured in terms of the number of employees, turnover and value added.

   Table 1.7 also shows that the labour productivity of foreign subsidiaries is above average, both when measured by turnover and value added per employee. This find-ing, which will be extensively discussed in Chapter 7, is partly due to the sectoral composition of FDI, which is different from that of the economy as a whole. As

Table 1.7. Comparing average size and labour productivity of foreign affiliates and all firms in manufacturing for the G5 countries.

Year (2001)	France		Germany		Japan		UK*		USA	
	Foreign affiliates	All firms	Foreign affiliates	All firms	Foreign affiliates	All firms	Foreign affiliates	All firms	Foreign affiliates	All firms
Number of employees per firm	302.38	142.36	241.45	170.68	379.58	28.90	231.73	24.99	782.50	52.90
Turnover per firm (millions US$)**	71.70	28.96	74.06	34.55	210.52	8.10	86.72	5.29	234.60	10.70
Value added per firm (millions US$)	18.28	7.41	—	11.99	41.97	2.21	25.45	2.09	66.20	3.80
Turnover per employee (millions US$)**	0.24	0.16	0.31	0.20	0.55	0.28	0.37	0.21	0.30	0.20
Value added (millions US$)/employees	0.06	0.05	—	0.07	0.11	0.08	0.11	0.07	0.08	0.07

*UK data refer to the year 1999.

**US: turnover for all firms proxied by value of production. US data refer to the year 1997.

Source: OECD 2003b; STAN Database for Industrial Analysis, Vol. 2005, Release 05.

argued earlier, MNEs tend to operate in more capital-intensive sectors. However, econometric studies that have carried out rigorous comparisons of labour and total factor productivity (which measures the efficient use of all the factors of production), controlling for size and sectoral effects, have invariably found that foreign-owned subsidiaries are more productive than firms with no foreign affiliates (Barba Navaretti et al. 2003; Criscuolo and Martin 2003; Griffith and Simpson 2001). Recent studies in the UK and the US have found that the home activities of MNEs are also more productive than those of national firms (Criscuolo and Martin 2003; Doms and Jensen 1998).

Fact 7. *Multinational firms are increasingly engaged in international production networks.*

The growth of international production networks, in which different stages of the production of a good takes place in different countries, is now well documented. Chapters 2, 4 and 6 deal extensively with this issue. There are many examples, such as the 'American' car for which

> 30% of the car's value goes to Korea for assembly, 17.5% to Japan for components and advanced technology, 7.5% to Germany for design, 4% to Taiwan and Singapore for minor parts, 2.5% to the UK for advertising and marketing services and 1.5% to Ireland and Barbados for data processing. Only 37% of the production value is generated in the United States.

> WTO 1998

This is sometimes referred to as 'vertical specialization' reflecting countries' production of different stages of a good and the consequent trade in intermediate products. (This is also referred to as 'fragmentation', 'disintegration of production' and 'intra-product specialization'.)

The concept of vertical specialization has no direct counterpart in the trade data that are collected, so attempts to measure its level and growth have inevitably had to use indirect methods. One approach has been to identify trade in parts and components, using highly disaggregated bilateral trade data. The best-known study of this type is by Yeats (1998), who establishes that the share of world trade that is in commodities, classified as parts and components, has been increasing steadily, and now accounts for around 30% of world trade in manufactures. East Asian global exports of components grew faster than any other major product group over 1984–96, increasing by 15% a year (compared with 11% for all products (Ng and Yeats 1999)). An alternative approach is to use input–output data to calculate the share of imports in the total inputs used in production. Campa and Goldberg (1997) find that this share increased substantially from the early 1970s to the early 1990s, doubling for the US, and for the UK approaching a share of one-third in electrical equipment and machinery and transportation equipment. Hummels et al. (2001) work with a different measure, the share of imports in a country's exports. Using input–output data this is measured as the value of imported goods that are embodied in the exports of a particular sector and country. They find that for 10 OECD countries this share increased from 16% in 1970 to 21% in 1990. Furthermore, trade in intermediates accounted for 30% of the growth of total exports of OECD countries between 1970 and 1990. Much, although by no means all, of this trade takes place within multinational firms. Several authors have argued that an increasing share of multinational activity is now of this form. This is evidenced by data on the foreign subsidiaries of US firms, showing that these subsidiaries are becoming less oriented to supplying local markets and more oriented to exporting. Both their imported inputs and exported outputs have increased as a percentage of their overall activity (Hanson et al. 2001).

1.3 The Issues

The stylized facts on MNEs and on FDI outlined above raise a set of issues that are essential to the understanding of MNEs. In the remainder of this introductory chapter, we pose some of the main questions that will be addressed in detail in later chapters of this book.

Issue 1. Why do firms become multinational?

For the purposes of this volume we take as given the existence of large corporations, often with well-known brand names and complex operations ranging across different activities. Yet, the fact that these corporations are large does not mean that they have extensive multinational operations. As we have seen above, small firms are generally less likely to be multinational, yet many—such as the Paduan shoemaker referred to above—are.

There are two quite distinct aspects to multinationality. The first is *the geographic dispersion* of the firm's activities; multinationals have operations in many countries, although the nature of these operations varies widely, from raw materials processing to final product assembly. The other is the concentrated *ownership*, or *internalization*, of these activities. A firm that decides to operate in a foreign country can do it in different ways, for example, by opening a subsidiary or by subcontracting to local firms. Multinationality occurs when the foreign activity is not outsourced to a local firm, but instead undertaken by a subsidiary of the firm itself. An understanding of the trade-offs that firms face in choosing between these two distinct decisions is the essential building block in any analysis of multinationals. It is necessary if we are to understand, for example, what sorts of activities are located in what countries, how multinationals impact on host economies, and how responsive they are to government policy decisions.[8]

We preview in a non-technical way the analytical issues underlying these choices in Chapter 2, and address them in formal economic models in Chapters 3–5. Chapter 3 deals with the international location of firms' downstream activities, focusing on the product market and supply to final consumers. Chapter 4 looks in detail at more upstream activities (the intermediate stages of production), focusing on factor markets and on input costs. Chapter 5 switches to the internalization decision, investigating the costs and benefits of keeping activities internal to the firm, rather than using external contractors and dealing with them through market transactions. The theories developed in these chapters suggest a number of testable hypotheses regarding the determinants of FDI, and in Chapter 6 we see the extent to which they are supported by the data.

Issue 2. Why do MNEs go to some countries and not to others?

We saw above that multinational activity is very unevenly distributed across countries, and also that the geographical pattern of investments has changed in recent years. Why do some countries attract more investments than others? Answering this question is important to the understanding of how some developing countries have been able to grow fast on the basis of successful integration into the world economy, while others appear to have been marginalized. If countries are to be able to design policies to attract investments, then clearly it is necessary that they understand the forces shaping these locational choices.

Many of the forces in play have effects which are not straightforward and that should be carefully assessed. A good example is national legal systems. A legal system that protects the property rights of foreign investors is unambiguously a plus. However, a legal system that protects intellectual property rights might create confidence in the use of independent subcontractors, while in the absence of good protection the firm might keep activity in-house. Multinationality can then be a response to weaknesses in some elements of the legal system, as well as to strengths in other areas. Other aspects of the location choice are also more complex than seems immediately apparent. For example, access to a large market is likely to raise the potential profitability of investments, but it will do so for local firms as well as for multinationals. Taking into account the response of these local competitors to the entry of foreign firms, what can be said about the effect of market size on investment flows? Distance between parts of the firm's operation is important, but again not in

---

[8] The first comprehensive framework to analyse the location and the internalization choices of MNEs was by Dunning (1977a,b, 1981). Markusen (2002) shows how the choices of MNEs can be incorporated into the general equilibrium theory of trade. A full survey of these contributions will be reported in the analytical chapters of this book.

a clear-cut way. Local production is a way of overcoming trade costs in supplying remote markets, but such markets may also face high costs of imported inputs and difficult communications and management problems. Finally, the availability of cheap factors of production, like labour, may attract foreign investors, but not necessarily if local workers are unskilled and unreliable and the local market is small.

These issues are addressed in the theoretical modelling of Chapters 2–4, and come up again in our review of empirical material (Chapter 6) and the case study looking at the recent experience of Ireland (Chapter 8).

Issue 3. What is the effect of MNEs on host economies?

Many commentators regard MNE investments as a source of benefit, bringing inflows of capital and technology and creating new job opportunities. Others see multinational activity as undermining local firms, threatening economic instability and undermining local government. As usual, careful economic modelling and empirical work is needed to form a judgement about the importance of these effects, and we analyse them in Chapters 3 and 4.

There are several aspects to this evaluation. First, a counterfactual needs to be specified. For example, in the absence of an inward investment would the country instead have been served by imports or local production? Second, the potential channels of welfare gain need to be identified, bearing in mind that investments that simply crowd out similar local activities yields no net economic gain. What are these channels?

In the product market, the entry of a multinational firm might simply crowd out national firms, competing away their market shares. However, benefits can arise through several different channels. One is that the investment makes the market more competitive, eroding monopoly power of local firms. Another is that the investment might raise the productivity of local firms through some sort of spillover effect. This will happen if increased competitive pressure induces firms to reduce internal inefficiencies, or if there are direct knowledge spillovers or learning effects. For example, the presence of foreign firms might enable local firms to learn about new technologies, management methods and market opportunities.

In the labour market, the value of job creation by an FDI project obviously depends on what would have happened in the absence of the project. Is there a net increase in employment, or simply crowding out of some jobs by others? It may also depend on job characteristics. Will there be an increase in the demand for skills? Also, foreign firms may have different hiring and firing costs than national firms and react differently to wage and output shocks in the host economy. They have plants in different locations and may find it relatively easy to switch activities between plants. The welfare effects of this can go either way. On the one hand, it may make the labour market more competitive, reducing monopoly power of trade unions. On the other, if it creates volatility and (uninsurable) uncertainty, it will be welfare reducing.

In addition to the mechanisms above, it may simply be the case that the total FDI inflow to an economy is large enough, relative to the rest of the economy, to change prices, bidding up wages and improving the economy's terms of trade. In this case there can be gains even if there are no imperfections or externalities in the host economy. We study this in some detail in our Chapter 8 on the Irish miracle. Chapter 7 provides a thorough review of the evidence on the effects of MNEs in host economies.

Issue 4. What is the effect of MNEs on home economies?

FDI also affects the investing economy (the source or home economy of the MNE). The issue is equally controversial. Countries may benefit from being the home of large MNEs, but question the effects of their firms transferring part of their activities to another country. Once again, we will undertake both theory modelling (Chapters 3 and 4), and review and extend the empirical literature (Chapter 9).

As with host country effects, the researcher has to identify the channels through which the economy is affected. Shareholders typically gain, as the investment is made to raise profits. Direct employment effects are negative, as activities are transferred to other countries. However, the full impact on the level of home country employment depends on the benefits that the firm receives from the investment. If the relocation lowers the firm's costs, then it may lead to an expansion of its overall production (or prevent a fall in its production), this causing home country employment levels to be higher than they otherwise would have been. The firm may benefit from technology transfer (if, for example, the outward FDI takes the form of setting up R&D facilities in Silicon Valley) and from improved access to foreign markets. Once again, to evaluate the effects of any job creation or destruction from the project, the counterfactual has to be specified: what would have happened in the absence of the investment?

As well as changing aggregate employment levels, FDI may also change the skill composition of employment, and perhaps also the stability of employment. One of the main criticisms of those opposed to MNE activity is that it has led to a deterioration of employment conditions, particularly for unskilled labour in advanced countries. We analyse these effects in Chapter 9.

Issue 5. What are the implications for policy?

The link between MNEs and policy is multifaceted, and the issues will be taken up in Chapter 10. The presence of MNEs may change the effectiveness of domestic policies and may create incentives for new policy measures. The effect of MNEs on the effectiveness of policy is illustrated by corporate taxation. MNEs may be able to circumvent tax policy by relocating their activities to lower tax countries. Even if they do not relocate, they may be able to engage in transfer pricing which moves their reported earnings to operations based in low-tax countries. Trade policy also operates differently in the presence of MNEs, as rents from protectionist trade policies get transferred to foreign shareholders rather than national citizens. The general point here is that the response of MNEs to policy may be different to that of national firms. Since they span jurisdictions they may be less accountable to national policy makers and regulators. Their ability to relocate activities makes countries' tax bases more volatile. And their sheer size may give them a powerful bargaining position in dealing with national tax and regulatory authorities.

Policies may also be designed explicitly to attract (or discourage) MNE activity. Many areas of policy—from taxes through trade policy, labour market regulations and the legal system—alter the attractiveness of a country as a host for inward investment. New policies can be specifically designed to attract FDIs. The case of Ireland, discussed in Chapter 8, shows very clearly how the targeted activities of the Ireland Development Agency were instrumental to the Irish FDI boom in the 1990s. Ireland is not unique: many countries or local authorities provide large subsidies, tax waivers or exemptions from regulations in order to attract FDI. Although these policies have sometimes proven successful in attracting investments, it is not clear that they have been good value for public money. For example, in the early 1990s, Portugal gave a financial incentive of more than 250 000 dollars per job created in a car plant (UNCTAD 1996). Policy competition between jurisdictions raises the question of international policy coordination. Is it desirable to prevent countries (or regions) competing in the conditions they offer MNEs? The answer is specific to the policy variable considered—competition to give subsidies may be undesirable, but competition to provide a better legal framework may be beneficial. International policy coordination could also be useful in order to harmonize and ensure transparency of a country's regulations governing FDI and to create commitments against the adoption of domestic policies which are distorting and driven by interest groups. That international agreements are useful is demonstrated by the more than 2000 Bilateral Investment Treaties that are currently in effect. However, it has proved extremely difficult to move to a multilateral regulatory framework, largely because of the asymmetries between developing countries (which are on the receiving side of FDI) and high-income countries (which are on both the receiving and the investing side). All major efforts to agree on a common international framework for FDI policies, such as the OECD-sponsored Multilateral Agreement on Investments (MAI) and the WTO agreement on investments, have so far failed.

Another dimension of international policy coordination which is often taken up by the globalization debate is whether firms should also be the subject of international regulations. The recent multinational scandals of Enron and Parmalat show that national bodies are often unable and do not have the authority to oversee international transactions. Although within regions there are already effective regulatory bodies (e.g. the competition authority of the European Union), there is much discussion as to whether multilateral institutions should be set up ruling on issues as diverse as competition, the environment, labour conditions. Again, this is an area where defining a global framework for consensus is extremely difficult. In Chapter 10 we also provide a cursory discussion of this problem.

1.4   Guide to the Book

This book revolves around the issues outlined above. Chapter 2 gives an overview of the theoretical issues and the main empirical results. The next part of the book focuses on theory. Chapters 3 and 4 discuss the determinants and the impact of MNEs, looking at horizontal and vertical FDI respectively. Chapter 5 deals with the choice of the mode of supplying a foreign market, whether internalized through a foreign subsidiary or outsourced through a market transaction with another firm. Readers not interested in formal economic theory can get the main theoretical insight from Chapter 2, skip Chapters 3–5 and move directly to the empirical chapters. Indeed, the rest of the book is devoted to empirical issues. Chapter 6 reviews the available evidence on the determinants of FDI. Chapter 7 looks at host country effects of MNEs and Chapter 8 is a case study of Ireland, the country which has been most successful in attracting FDI and in using FDI to boost its economic development. Chapter 9 examines the home country effects of FDI. Chapter 10 discusses the main policy issues and Chapter 11 reports the main conclusions and outlines potential areas for future research.

Statistical Appendix

In this appendix we report details of the areas of origin and destination of FDI flows and of the distribution by industry of inward FDI stocks in OECD countries.

Table 1.8. Outward current FDI by area of origin (% of GDP).

	1970 –75	1976 –80	1981 –85	1986 –90	1991 –93	1994 –96	1997 –2003*
Advanced countries							
USA	0.73	0.74	0.31	0.49	0.80	1.13	1.43
Europe	0.68	0.70	0.80	1.70	1.32	1.94	5.49
Japan	0.30	0.27	0.42	1.22	0.57	0.44	0.68
Oceania	0.23	0.25	0.60	1.62	0.90	0.99	1.48
Total	**0.65**	**0.66**	**0.54**	**1.14**	**0.97**	**1.32**	**2.90**
Developing countries and transition economies							
Latin America	0.02	0.04	0.08	0.12	0.31	0.37	1.51
Africa	0.05	0.11	0.40	0.28	0.35	0.43	0.23
Asia	0.01	0.03	0.11	0.52	0.90	1.47	1.18
Oceania	0.00	0.10	0.08	0.14	0.16	0.02	−0.21
South-East Europe and CIS	0.00	0.09	0.01	0.01	0.02	0.08	0.77
Total	**0.02**	**0.05**	**0.14**	**0.32**	**0.53**	**0.89**	**1.20**
World	0.48	0.49	0.41	0.93	0.87	1.21	2.54

Source: UNCTAD.

*For 1997–2003 European data include the new members of the European Union (Cyprus, Czech Republic, Czechoslovakia, Estonia, Hungary, Latvia, Lithuania, Malta, Poland, Slovakia, Slovenia).

Table 1.9. Inward current FDI by area of destination (% of GDP).

	1970 –75	1976 –80	1981 –85	1986 –90	1991 –93	1994 –96	1997 –2003*
Advanced countries							
USA	0.14	0.31	0.52	1.07	0.49	0.85	1.76
Europe	0.67	0.54	0.49	1.08	0.94	1.20	4.42
Japan	0.04	0.02	0.03	0.01	0.04	0.01	0.16
Oceania	1.45	1.13	1.30	2.78	1.89	2.40	2.16
Total	**0.45**	**0.44**	**0.46**	**0.92**	**0.62**	**0.85**	**2.54**
Developing countries and transition economies							
Latin America	0.96	0.82	0.87	0.95	1.49	2.23	3.97
Africa	0.81	0.32	0.54	0.69	0.85	1.33	2.27
Asia	0.25	0.26	0.90	0.95	1.80	2.65	2.77
Oceania	4.99	1.56	3.02	2.77	2.28	2.64	1.49
South-East Europe and CIS	0.00	0.08	0.04	0.03	0.59	1.50	2.41
Total	**0.58**	**0.45**	**0.82**	**0.82**	**1.42**	**2.28**	**3.09**
World	0.44	0.41	0.50	0.85	0.76	1.13	2.65

Source: UNCTAD.

*For 1997–2003 European data include the new members of the European Union (Cyprus, Czech Republic, Czechoslovakia, Estonia, Hungary, Latvia, Lithuania, Malta, Poland, Slovakia, Slovenia).

Table 1.10.   Inward FDI stocks in OECD countries:
distribution by industry (% of total shares).

Sector	1982–86	1987–91	1992–94	1995–97	1998–2002
Primary	15.15	12.77	10.15	6.33	4.35
Manufacturing	39.83	38.65	34.75	35.69	28.52
Services	41.21	45.53	54.44	56.46	61.41
Unallocated	2.89	4.99	2.42	0.72	5.72
Total	**100**	**100**	**100**	**100**	**100**

Source: OECD Direct Investment by Industrial Sector, Vol. 2001, Release 01,
and OECD International Direct Investment Statistics.

Note: Percentages are based on values in current US dollars.

2

The Multinational Enterprise: an Overview of Theory and Empirical Findings

This chapter provides an introduction to and a non-technical summary of the issues analysed in the book. What are the determinants of firms' choices to become multinational? What determines where they locate? What are their effects on host and home economies?

A firm's international activities may take many forms: importing inputs, exporting output, using foreign licensees or subcontractors, and operating foreign subsidiaries. Multinationality has a number of defining features, the first of which is that production is split between several countries. We start, therefore, in Section 2.1 with a discussion of the costs and benefits to the firm of splitting production. (We shall use terminology from manufacturing, although most analysis applies to service activity as well as to manufacturing.) These costs and benefits depend on characteristics of the firm or industry, and on characteristics of the host and home countries. Theory modelling identifies the key trade-offs and suggests a number of hypotheses that are, by and large, confirmed by empirical work.

We then turn, in Section 2.2, to the question of whether these foreign activities are internal to the firm or outsourced to independent operators. This is the classical issue of the boundary of the firm. Is production internalized within a multinational, or outsourced to an independent local firm? Should technology be controlled within a wholly owned subsidiary or licensed to a local firm? Answers depend on comparative costs and on the importance of contractual incompleteness in each sector and country.

Section 2.3 looks at the effects of multinational activity on the host and home countries. How do MNEs affect local firms and workers in each country? Is FDI a complement or a substitute for international trade? Effects operate through many channels and analysis of each of them requires careful thought about the counterfactual. We overview theory and empirical work, concluding that the effects of multinational activity are, on balance, generally positive.

As we address each of these issues we seek to introduce and motivate some of the key concepts, outline the trade-offs that arise, and present some of the evidence. Fuller development of all the issues discussed is contained in the remaining chapters of the book. In this chapter we give just a few of the key references to the literature, with fuller details given in later chapters. However, it is important to mention at this stage that the analytical approach in this book rests on two building blocks developed in earlier theoretical contributions. The first is the OLI framework developed by John Dunning (1977c, 1981), which states that firms decide to invest abroad if

- they have market power given by the *ownership* of products or production processes (O);
- they have a *location* advantage in locating their plant in a foreign country rather than at home (L);
- they have an advantage from *internalizing* their foreign activities in fully owned subsidiaries, rather than carrying them out through arm's-length agreements in the market (I).

The second building block has been termed the 'knowledge-capital model' by James Markusen (2002), and encompasses different works that have developed the OLI approach into a consistent and formalized analytical framework. These include Markusen (1984, 1997), Ethier (1986), Helpman (1984, 1985), Horstmann and Markusen (1987a,b, 1992), Brainard (1993), Ethier and Markusen (1996) and Markusen and Venables (1998, 2000).

2.1   National and International Production

A firm controls a set of assets—technology, reputation and brand name as well as physical capital—and faces demands for its output in a number of countries. What is the profit-maximizing way for this firm to organize its activities?

2.1.1   *Geographical Concentration and Dispersion*

Firms' activities can be concentrated in a single country or dispersed between several, and each pattern has costs and benefits. Production in a foreign country can be commenced in two ways. 'Greenfield investments' occur when firms invest in new physical plant and productive assets. Alternatively, firms can grow through merger and acquisition (M&A) activity, buying existing assets in a foreign country, or merging with a foreign firm. There are a number of important differences between these cases that we pick up at various points below, but they both share the common structure that a firm's production activities become more spatially dispersed.

The costs of geographical dispersion: economies of scale foregone

A firm is considering splitting off some of its activity from an otherwise integrated production process in the home country. What, in terms of the efficient use of factors of production, are the costs of the split? Evidently, this depends on how the overall activities of the firm are split, and we must first do some classification of the possibilities.

At one extreme, we might imagine the firm simply duplicating all its activities in another country: it splits into two identical parts. Such a strategy is typically not followed, and for the good reason that some of the firm's assets have a 'public good' character and their benefits, once developed, can be spread (in a non-rival way, at no cost) firm wide. These 'firm-level assets' are therefore a source of firm-level increasing returns to scale, and to duplicate them would be wasteful.

Firm-level activities include the headquarters staff of the firm, finance operations, R&D expenditures and brand development. Many of the assets created by these expenditures are intangible, having no direct physical manifestation. They include 'knowledge capital' (scientific know-how, patents and management skills) as well as reputation and brand name. For many large firms intangible assets are perhaps the most important. Real-world examples are common: the image of Coca-Cola, the know-how of Bayer and IBM, the reputation of McKinsey and Goldman Sachs, and so on. Scientific know-how or management skills that are applied in one part of the firm can also be applied in another part, so these and other intangible assets provide 'services' to all operations of the firm, both domestic and foreign. Other firm-specific assets are tangible, for example, headquarters buildings, but are still sources of firm-level economies of scale—doubling the output of the firm may not require that the scale of headquarters operations doubles. These firm-level assets—intangible and tangible—are sometimes referred to as the basis of firm-level economies of scale. This refers to the fact that if the firm expands by replicating plants, possibly in different countries, then it encounters economies of scale, since the firm-level assets do not also need to be replicated. In the case of merger rather than greenfield investments, it is likely to be these activities that the firm seeks to 'rationalize' in order to gain economies of scale.

A second possible way that the firm can split geographically is by duplicating just a subset of its activities, for example, setting up a foreign plant in addition to a home plant for some part of the production process. This is referred to as '*horizontal*' investment, as the same (horizontal) stage of the production process is duplicated. A good example is the development of a new assembly plant to serve a foreign market. This duplication of activity means that some economies of scale are foregone, but they are just those at the level of the plant, not the firm. The magnitude of these plant-level economies of scale may be substantial, and can be measured.

The distinction between firm- and plant-level economies of scale is important. Large economies of scale at the level of the firm suggest that the firm will be large, and therefore tend to have sales in many countries. However, large economies of scale at the level of the plant suggest that the firm will not want to split production into many separate units. Therefore, multinationality is most likely to occur when there

Table 2.1. Average firm- and plant-level size of US manufacturing firms, 1987.

	Plant size (A)	Firm size (B)	Plants per firm (ratio B/A)
Chemicals	132	1120	8.5
Transport equipment	663	4190	6.3
Food, beverages and tobacco	157	832	5.3
Paper, printing and publishing	125	610	4.9
Rubber and plastic	130	507	3.9
Electrical equipment	293	1123	3.8
Textiles	279	1056	3.8
Furniture	182	659	3.6
Machinery	172	615	3.6
Apparel	175	526	3.0
Miscellaneous manufactures	120	264	2.2
Leather	178	340	1.9
All industries	177	852	4.8

Note: Size is measured by average number of employees. The sample only includes multi-unit firms, defined as firms with plants in at least two different locations.

Source: Elaborations on the US Bureau of Census Company Statistics can be found in Kim (1998).

are *high* firm-scale economies combined with relatively *low* plant-scale economies. A simple measure of this is to look at firm size compared with plant size in different industries. Table 2.1 presents data on the size (measured by employment) of US firms and plants. Firm size depends on, among other things, firm-level economies of scale, and we see that it is on average quite large in transport and electrical equipment and in chemicals, and small in leather and miscellaneous manufactures. Plant size depends on plant-level economies of scale, and is also large in equipment sectors. Looking at the ratio of firm to plant size gives a crude measure of the relative importance of the two sorts of economies of scale. We see that these are highest in chemicals and transport equipment, and lowest in leather. Industries where this ratio is high forego relatively little of their overall economies of scale by splitting production between plants, as revealed in the high number of plants per firm. It suggests that the costs of duplicating plants through FDI may be quite low in these industries. The presumption that MNEs are more likely to occur in industries with large firm-level economies of scale is supported by the comparison between Table 2.1 and Table 1.6 of the previous chapter, where we reported the shares of foreign subsidiaries in total manufacturing employment by industry: the rank correlation between this share and the ratio of firm to plant size is 0.89.

The costs of geographical dispersion: economies of integration foregone

A third possible way for a firm to split its activities is by function. It might decide, for example, to put all of its production of a particular component part in a separate foreign plant. This type of split is called a '*vertical*' division, referring to the breaking of the value-added chain. It may lead to a technical efficiency loss, but this loss is not to do with the foregoing economies of scale (since the plant might handle the firm's entire production of that function or process so is not duplicating activities), but rather with loss of economies of integration.

A simple example of these economies of integration is steel production, where, from the blast furnace through the rolling mills, steel is kept hot. Disintegrating the process means the steel cools and has to be reheated. More generally, what are the sources of disintegration costs when activity is split across international borders? We will refer to them as 'trade costs', and note that they include packaging and freight costs, costs of time in transit, import tariffs on goods that cross borders, and a whole package of penalties associated with having to manage geographically separate operations.

In many activities trade costs are very substantial. While freight charges on densely used routes may only be around 5% of the value of goods shipped, looking worldwide they are much higher. For example, the median freight charge between all country pairs for which data are available is 28% of the value of goods shipped.[1] Of course, trade volumes are much higher on routes where trade costs are low than on routes where they are high, so freight charges on US imports amount to an average of just 3.8% of the value of imports (Hummels 1999, from US customs data).

An important element of the costs of disintegration is the time it takes to ship products between plants. Empirical work by Hummels (2000) estimates that the cost of time in transit is around 0.5% of the value of goods shipped *per day*. A small part of this is the interest charge on the goods. Another part is the fact that goods depreciate or become obsolescent in transit; for example, computer chips of a given design depreciate in value rapidly as technology creates new and faster chips. Perhaps the most important element is the fact that modern production techniques require synchronization of activities, and shipping goods over long distances introduces an inevitable uncertainty about delivery, making production planning more complex. Thus, just-in-time management techniques attach high value to proximity of component suppliers (see Harrigan and Venables 2004). An alternative way to get a handle on the magnitude of trade costs is to ask what they must be for international trade to be as small as it is, relative to trades that take place within countries. Using this approach Anderson and van Wincoop (2003) estimate that trade costs in many cases exceed 100% of the FOB value of goods shipped.

---

[1]CIF/FOB ratios from IMF Direction of Trade Statistics. (CIF is cost, insurance and freight, i.e. the cost of a good delivered to the importing country; FOB is free on board, i.e. the cost of a good, excluding insurance, freight and payments for other services involved in moving the good from the exporting to the importing country.)

To summarize, the main costs of horizontal FDI (HFDI) are plant-level economies of scale foregone, while the costs of vertical FDI (VFDI) are economies of integration foregone. Of course, not all divisions of production can be neatly packaged into horizontal and vertical. Duplication of assembly plants is typically regarded as horizontal, but if components have to be shipped to the plant, then disintegration costs will be incurred as well as loss of plant-level economies of scale. A vertical investment may not involve exactly 100% of a firm's production of some component moving to another plant, in which case there will be some horizontal duplication of production of the component. Nevertheless, the distinction between horizontal and vertical investments is useful, and we will make much of it throughout this book. It enables us to distinguish between investments as different as Japanese automobile plants in Europe, designed to produce for the European market, and investments in call centres in India to service the worldwide activities of American or European airlines or insurance companies.

The benefits of geographical dispersion: market access and competition

Disintegration costs on internal transactions within the firm are a force for the spatial concentration of activity, as we saw above. But if the final consumers of the firm's output are dispersed across countries, then the costs of reaching them are a force for dispersion of production. Local production avoids transport costs and trade barriers that might be incurred in supplying the market by imports. Thus, we expect that trade costs on the firm's final output will encourage the firm to undertake horizontal investments in the downstream stage of its activity, for example, the construction of assembly plants to meet local demand in each market. The plants of Japanese car manufacturers, like Honda, Nissan and Toyota in the UK, are good examples of investments made to serve the European market and avoid tariffs and other trade barriers.

Jumping trade costs is not the only source of gain to be had from proximity to markets. The firm may be better able to shape its final product to local tastes and respond to changes in local market conditions if it has a presence in the market. The following statement from Unilever's website summarizes this concept well: 'Many of our brands have international appeal, while others are leaders in local markets. It is our keen understanding of cultures and markets that allows us to anticipate consumers' needs and to provide them with what they need, when they need it' (Unilever.com).

Furthermore, a presence in the local market may be important in shaping the firm's interaction with other competitors in the market. The equilibrium prices and sales volumes of firms typically depend on the marginal costs of all firms supplying the market. An investment that saves on trade costs (compared with serving the market through imports) reduces the marginal cost of supplying the market. This will, in standard models of market competition, cause the firm with the lower marginal cost to expand and may also reduce the sales volumes and prices of other firms. Thus, an FDI project that reduces the marginal costs of supplying the market will have a strategic effect, since it causes a change in the behaviour of rival firms that is in the interest of the investor: rivals cut their sales. This change in market shares may occur with the total number of firms in the market staying constant, or it may actually lead to the exit of some competitors, reinforcing still further the benefit derived by the multinational from its presence in the market. These gains in market power will be even greater if the investment takes the form of a merger or acquisition, directly eliminating one potential rival. Market power considerations are a major motivation behind both domestic and international M&A activity.

The benefits of geographical dispersion: factor costs

The costs of primary inputs vary across locations, and access to low-cost inputs is a major reason for dispersion of the firm's activity. The most extreme example of this is, of course, FDI in primary and resource-based industries—the mine goes where the minerals are. More generally, MNEs will gain from moving unskilled-labour-intensive activities to countries where unskilled wages are low, R&D-intensive activities to places where scientists are relatively cheap, and so on. The expansion of EU investments in Central and Eastern European countries, US investments in Mexico, and the investments in software companies in Bangalore are all driven by the aim of reducing costs of production.

Several remarks are required about these statements. First, factor prices have to be adjusted for the quality of the factor input. The evidence shows that FDI rarely goes to the lowest-wage economies, going in preference to countries that have abundant labour with basic education. Second, firms look at the cost of labour, not its abundance. However, in equilibrium there is likely to be a relationship between the two, so it is generally correct to say that R&D-intensive activities will take place in countries where scientists are relatively abundant, and so on. Third, primary factor costs are a higher share of total costs (and possibly also higher relative to transport costs) in the more upstream stages of production. Thus, while factor costs are important for all activities, they will be relatively more so for upstream production than for downstream stages. Finally, the potential for benefiting from international variation in factor costs evidently depends on the extent to which there is variation in the factor intensity of different (separable) parts of the firm's production process. If all stages of the activity have the same factor intensities, then there is no factor cost saving from geographically dispersing them.

2.1.2 *Resolving the Trade-Offs: Determinants of FDI*

A short summary of the costs and benefits we have outlined is given in Table 2.2, distinguishing between the cases of horizontal and vertical investment. The main trade-offs are, for HFDI, between returns to scale foregone and the benefits of access to markets, and for VFDI, between disintegration costs and the benefits of producing in countries with low factor costs.

Table 2.2 summarizes costs and benefits but how are these trade-offs resolved, and what testable hypotheses are derived? Full analysis of the equilibrium outcomes resulting from these trade-offs is contained in Chapters 3 and 4. Table 2.3 summarizes some of the predictions concerning which firms are more likely to become multinationals, and which are the countries they are more likely to invest in.

First, the analysis of why firms go multinational offers predictions about the sectors in which multinational activity should be observed. We expect to see it where firm-specific assets (such as knowledge capital and reputation) are important relative to plant-level economies of scale. For VFDI, the important factor will be the extent to which firms can fragment production processes into stages with different factor intensities. Trade costs also vary across industries, but their impact will be different for horizontal and vertical FDI. We expect to see HFDI in industries where final goods have high transport costs, but conversely expect to see VFDI in sectors where trade and other disintegration costs are low.

The second issue concerns the location of multinational activity, and here too there are quite different predictions for horizontal and vertical FDI. Horizontal FDI will tend to be drawn to locations with good market access, where sales will be large enough to cover plant-level fixed costs. Market access may be good because the country itself has a large high-income population, or because the country is well-located to access to such markets. By contrast, vertical investment will be drawn to locations with lower factor costs. Trade costs are particularly important for VFDI where products at different stages of the production process may cross borders many times. Low-wage locations with good transport and trade links to other parts of the corporation will therefore be the favoured locations. This explains the presence of such activities in areas such as Mexico and Eastern Europe.

2.1.3   Determinants of FDI: Empirical Evidence

What empirical evidence do we have on the factors affecting the decision to invest abroad? Is it consistent with the predictions summarized in Table 2.3? We expect horizontal and vertical FDI to respond to different sets of motives, yet the data will typically contain both types, making identification of determinants difficult. Therefore, before assessing the role of specific determinants, it is important to size up the relative importance of the two types of investment.

Horizontal or vertical FDI?

The horizontal and the vertical models are not competing theories seeking to explain a given multinational activity; their predictions apply to different types of investment

Table 2.2. Benefits and costs to the firm of horizontal and vertical FDI.

	Horizontal	Vertical
Costs	Returns to scale foregone Disintegration costs	Disintegration costs
Benefits	Market access: Saving trade costs Strategic advantage	Factor cost saving

Table 2.3. Determinants of FDI: theoretical predictions.

Determinants	Prediction by type of investment	
	Horizontal	Vertical
Determinants relate to types of firms or industries		
Firm-level economies of scale	+	+
Plant-level economies of scale	−	?
Product-specific trade costs	+	−
Costs to disintegrate stages of production	−	−
Difference in factor intensity between stages of production	?	+
Determinants relate to types of countries		
Trade costs (distance, trade barriers, etc.)	+	−
Market size	+	?
Factor cost differentials	?	+

projects and to different sets of investing and receiving countries. Until recently there has been consensus that the overwhelming proportion of FDI is horizontal rather than vertical. This is as would be expected, given that most FDI flows are North–North, as shown in the previous chapter (Tables 1.2 and 1.3). Empirical tests in a framework that seeks to encompass both types of investment (such as Markusen's 'knowledge-capital model') generally show that the location of foreign subsidiaries is mostly driven by factors consistent with the horizontal model, such as the size of the host market and the similarity between host and home factor endowments (Markusen and Maskus 2002).

Ideally, the researcher would like to be able to separate the data into investments that are horizontal and those that are vertical. Conceptually, this is difficult, as the distinction is not always clear-cut, and practically it is very demanding of the data. It requires firm-level information on the sales and on the purchases of inputs by foreign subsidiaries. Sales need to be classified according to their destination (sales to the local market, export to the home country, export to other countries), and inputs according to whether they are used for further reprocessing or for resale in the local market. Such data are generally not directly available. Exceptions are the data on US multinationals, which report the extent to which subsidiaries export back to the US, as compared with supplying local or third countries. It can reasonably be assumed that plants exporting a large share of their output back to the US are VFDI, while those selling locally or exporting to third countries are HFDI. Analysis based on these US data suggests that there are growing flows of VFDI; furthermore, these investments mostly take place between countries with different factor endowments, as predicted by the theory of VFDI (Hanson et al. 2001; Slaughter 2003).

In conclusion, although HFDI still accounts for the largest share of FDI flows, the share of VFDI is larger than sometimes suggested, and it is a share that has been increasing since the early 1990s.

Firm- and plant-level economies of scale

The trade-off between firm- and plant-level economies of scale is found to be an important factor affecting a firm's decision to invest abroad. Most studies find that firms or sectors in which firm-level economies of scale are important are more likely to serve foreign markets through subsidiaries than through exports (see, for example, the studies of both US and Swedish FDI by Brainard (1997) and Ekholm (1998)). Firm-level economies of scale may be captured by indirect measures, such as the number of non-production workers relative to production workers. Alternatively, they may be captured directly, by measuring firm- or industry-specific features that generate such economies, such as investments in intangible assets like R&D and advertising. These measures are found to be consistently positively correlated with the extent of multinational activities.

The role of plant-level economies of scale depends instead on the features of the investment. In general terms, they are found to discourage foreign investments and favour the concentration of production activities. However, for VFDI, they some-times favour the fragmentation of production, as firms concentrate one production stage in one location, not necessarily at home, and serve all assembly plants from there.

Country determinants of FDI

The cross-country pattern of FDI is quite well approximated by the 'gravity' relationship (Ekholm 1998; Shatz 2003). This links bilateral FDI between countries to the income of each country, the distance between them, and possibly also other 'between-country' factors such as sharing a common language or border.[2] Thus, a

---

[2]Gravity models are extensively used for bilateral trade flows, and have also been used for other interactions such as cross-border equity holdings. Anderson (1979) was the first to provide a theoretical

large share of FDI takes place between nearby countries, following regional patterns. There are many examples of these types of investments: intra-EU FDI, US investments in Mexico and Canada, EU investments in Central and Eastern Europe, Japanese investments in other Asian countries. While the gravity relationship provides a useful benchmark, very similar relationships hold for almost all sorts of spatial economic interactions, for example, trade flows, telecommunications, cross-border equity holdings, and technology transfer. It is therefore important to move beyond the gravity relationship and identify the determinants of FDI relative to other forms of international interactions, such as trade.

Trade costs. Trade costs are a very important determinant of FDI, and studies take into account a variety of components of such costs including transport costs, distance, and trade policy barriers. Theory predicts that these costs can affect FDI either way, depending on the type of investment considered. When looking at aggregate flows (dominated by HFDI), studies typically look at alternative modes of supplying a foreign market: exports and sales of foreign subsidiaries. They find that sales of foreign subsidiaries become more important *relative to trade* the higher are trade costs (Brainard 1997; Carr et al. 2001; Yeaple 2003). This is especially true for MNE activity between industrialized economies. In contrast, where vertical investments can be identified, the evidence is that VFDI is discouraged by higher trade costs (Hanson et al. 2001). In line with theory, trade barriers, transport costs and distance discourage vertical investments as they increase the cost of trading components between production units.

Size of the market. The size of the market is also found to be a fundamental factor of attraction for MNEs (Brainard 1997; Carr et al. 2001; Markusen and Maskus 2002). Most FDI flows towards large markets. We have shown in Chapter 1 that the largest share of FDI inflows is accounted for by the US and the EU. Market size affects FDI inflows and imports alike, and various studies show that both flows respond to a similar extent as the size of the host market expands. As investing in a given country implies large fixed costs, firms are willing to afford it if prospective sales are sufficiently large. Trade barriers and the market size interact in affecting a firm's investment decision. The creation of the Single Market in Europe is a good example of this. It reduced the cost of trading in the region and consequently expanded the internal market. This made Europe more attractive to foreign investments from the US or Japan that wanted to bypass the EU's external trade barriers to gain access to the whole European market. Indeed, the EU attracted extremely large flows of new

---

foundation for the gravity model of international trade. The relationship between neoclassical and new trade theory has more recently also been subject to analysis by Deardorff (1998) and Feenstra et al. (2001).

FDI, and it accounted for much of the striking increase in world FDI flows in the 1990s.

Factor cost differentials.   VFDI is expected to take place especially between countries with different factor endowments and factor costs. Indeed, the surge of North–South regional investments in the 1990s, between the US and Mexico or between the EU and Central and Eastern European countries, confirms this prediction. These investments are part of the broader pattern of fast-growing North–South outsourcing activities, taking place both within MNEs, and also through arm's-length agreements between independent producers.

Assessing the effect of factor cost differentials on FDI flows is not easy. We expect them to be important for VFDI, yet most studies analyse average investment flows, where HFDI is predominant. Also, North–South FDI to developing countries is relatively new, as it really grew in the 1990s, and thus it is not picked up by studies based on earlier data. A further problem is that differences in factor endowments and in factor costs may be offset by differences in factor productivity which are difficult to measure for the researcher; in contrast, producers know exactly how long it takes to produce a T-shirt in Timisoara, in Naples or in Beijing, and there are large differences across locations. Finally, factor endowments are also difficult to measure. For example, accurate statistics on the skill composition of the labour force in a given country are rarely available. However, although for all these reasons the importance of differences in factor endowments is likely to be underestimated, some recent econometric studies are starting to find evidence that investments are also driven by factor cost differences (Hanson et al. 2001; Yeaple 2003).

Tax differentials and policies.   Many countries provide generous incentives, such as direct subsidies, tax rebates and other active policies, to attract FDI. These subsidies reduce the fixed or operating costs of setting up a foreign subsidiary. To what extent are MNEs' investment and location decisions affected by such policies? Various recent studies find that tax differentials influence an MNE's decision on where to locate its activities, although they do not seem to affect the decision to invest. For example, differences in the average tax rate influence the choice by US MNEs of where to locate in Europe, conditional on them having already decided to invest in Europe (Devereux and Griffith 1998, 2002). Also there is not complete consensus on how strong the tax effect is, although, according to Hines (1999), an elasticity of FDI with respect to taxes of minus 0.6 is a typical result in much of the literature.

The case of Ireland is an example of a deliberate and successful policy effort to attract MNEs. But Ireland became known as the Celtic Tiger not just because it offered the lowest tax rates in Europe: it was a doorway to the EU market, it was able to attract and expand a highly skilled, English-speaking and relatively cheap labour force, and it made major infrastructure improvements. Probably, on balance, subsidies are rarely sufficient to attract investments, decisions also being taken on labour force, infrastructure and market access. Certainly, subsidies should not be considered by developing countries as a shortcut to bypass other structural constraints hindering inflows of FDI.

2.2 Internalization and the Boundary of the Firm

Horizontal and vertical divisions of the firm are essentially geographical, and we now turn to the organizational form of the firm. When expanding to new markets, does the firm prefer to keep its functions internal or choose to rely on market relations? FDI is to do with firms choosing to keep activities inside the firm, operating wholly owned foreign subsidiaries. However, under some circumstances, firms may choose instead to simply buy components from a foreign supplier or to license their know-how or brand image to a foreign party.

McDonald's restaurants are all franchised to local partners, whereas Gap's 4000 single-brand stores are all fully owned. Even within the same company, foreign plants are sometimes organized in different ways. Pirelli, an Italian multinational manufacturing tyres and cables, produces its most innovative tyres in its wholly owned plants abroad and its most innovative cables through a foreign licensee. Why so? What factors influence a firm's decision to keep some activities internal while others are outsourced to external producers?

The trade-off faced by firms between internalizing and relying on market transactions is usually thought of in the following way. Internalizing may bring a direct cost penalty, but avoids problems of contractual incompleteness in dealing with outside agents.

The cost penalty of internalization is based on the fact that the firm undertakes the activity itself, rather than seeking out the lowest-cost local supplier. The local supplier may have better information about local conditions (labour skills, demand conditions or administrative procedures) that means it can produce more cheaply than the MNE. It may be highly specialized with particular expertise in the activity. It may also be a local firm in a sector with significant plant-level economies of scale, in which case expanding the production of the local firm may be lower cost than setting up a new plant owned by the MNE.

On the other side of the equation, the costs of using the market, as opposed to keeping activities within the firm, are determined by transaction costs, imperfect information, and contractual incompleteness. Multinationals may find it difficult to protect their firm-specific assets, and difficult or expensive to motivate independent local firms to act in the best interests of the multinational.

In Chapter 5 we discuss three sets of issues that may affect market transactions between MNEs and local producers in host economies: the hold-up problem, emerging because of incomplete contracts; the risk of dissipating intangible assets owned by the MNE to the benefit of their local counterparts; the agency costs of monitoring local counterparts when there is asymmetric information. Throughout this book we focus on the extreme alternatives between wholly owned subsidiaries and external arm's-length agreements. We do not address intermediate forms of internalization, like joint ventures in which foreign investors hold a share of a foreign company in partnership with other foreign investors and/or with locals. Although several studies specifically analyse the problems involved in the joint ownership of assets, most of the issues are similar to those involved in the dichotomous alternative between wholly owned subsidiaries and external arm's-length contracts (Grossman and Hart 1986; Hart and Moore 1990; Hart 1995).

We now briefly discuss the hold-up problem, the risk of dissipation of intangible assets and the agency problem.

The hold-up problem

Firms may prefer not to outsource activities, but to keep them internal, in order to avoid inefficiencies related to the so-called *hold-up problem* that arises in the presence of incomplete contracts. This problem can occur when it is not possible to write contracts covering all possible contingencies affecting the relationship between the firm and an input supplier. The supplier may then fear that after having made the necessary investment to produce the input, the MNE will deny the due payment claiming that some contingencies uncovered by the contract have occurred. The contract then has to be renegotiated, and if the investment is specific to the relationship (i.e. has no other use), then the supplier's bargaining position will be weak. Fearing this, the supplier's initial investment is likely to be suboptimal. This inefficiency reduces the total return from outsourcing, making it more likely that investments will be undertaken by wholly owned subsidiaries.

This may explain the decision of some firms, after many years of outsourcing production to foreign companies, to start manufacturing in wholly owned subsidiaries. As a possible example, consider Ikea, the Swedish retailer of home furnishing. Its core competencies are represented by its design capability and its distribution and retail network, which enable Ikea to offer well-designed items at bargain prices. Until recently Ikea had no manufacturing facilities, and it was a pioneer in international procurement. Its items are designed and engineered in Sweden and produced by external subcontractors based in more than 70 countries, generally with cheap labour and close proximity to raw materials and reliable access to distribution channels. Independent suppliers must adapt quickly to the changing needs of Ikea designers and engineers and strictly follow their specifications. This requires investments that are specific to very particular products or product lines. Although Ikea provides technical and financial assistance to help the suppliers to cope with its requests and their activities are strictly monitored, hold-up problems can easily arise. Indeed, Ikea has recently opened a manufacturing subsidiary, Swedwood, which has acquired the control of several previously independent Eastern European producers (Beamish 1996; see also http://www.ikea.com).

Dissipation of firm-specific assets

Local production involves application of some of the firm-specific assets, and the firm may wish to keep these assets internal to itself, rather than transferring them to local agents. This is likely to be particularly true when these assets consist of knowledge capital.

One reason for internalization is that it may simply be too costly to transfer to third parties (for instance, through license agreements) the know-how required to perform the activities. This occurs especially when the knowledge capital of the MNE is embodied in the human capital of the MNE's employees, as in the case of skill-intensive service sectors such as banking or consulting. Paradoxically, internalization is also likely if knowledge is too easily transferred, so vulnerable to theft. If the firm-specific know-how of the MNE can be easily appropriated by a foreign licensee (e.g. through learning-by-doing), the possibility arises that the licensee can start production on its own, competing with the MNE. In order to avoid that, the MNE has two alternatives. The first is to share some of its monopolistic rents with the licensee by asking for a low licence fee. The second is that the MNE keeps its knowledge capital internal, operating through a subsidiary.

The fact that technological know-how and knowledge capital are easily appropriable provides a rationale for Pirelli's investment choices discussed earlier. Pirelli has developed a revolutionary technology to build tyres, the Modular Integrated Robotized System (MIRS), which is a completely computer-managed production process that requires no labour input. It is also cost saving and reduces the variability in product quality, providing an important source of competitive advantage for the company. Plants based on MIRS technology will be opened in Pirelli's three main foreign markets (Germany, UK and the US) as greenfield investments in wholly owned subsidiaries. According to interviews with Pirelli's managers, the main rationale for this strategy is to protect proprietary knowledge in the MIRS technology. In contrast, Pirelli will probably license to independent firms the production of Afumex, an innovative low-cost power cable which guarantees much higher safety standards in case of fire than traditional cables. In this case, Pirelli does not seem to be concerned with knowledge dissipation and its aim is rather to achieve a pervasive and fast market penetration. Cables is a low margin and very competitive mature sector. The basic technologies are widely available, whereas the innovative components of Afumex are protected by patents which are quite difficult to bypass (http://www.pirelli.com, http://www.just-auto.com, http://www.automotriz.net, *The Economist*, 22 April 2000).

A firm's specific assets include reputation as well as technical know-how. In this case, the problem is not that of spillovers, but rather the fact that the foreign party may have too few incentives to maintain the stock of goodwill of the MNE. A typical case is that of franchising. Franchisees of well-known firms (e.g. McDonald's) gain customers thanks to a strong brand image, but they have an incentive to behave as free-riders by not contributing enough to the maintenance of these firms' reputations. The alternatives for the MNE are again either to leave enough rents to franchisees to discourage free-riding behaviour, or to operate through wholly owned subsidiaries. This explains McDonald's and Gap's diverging strategies. McDonald's products are simple and standardized and quality is easy to monitor. The risk of the franchisee spoiling McDonald's image is limited. In contrast, coordination and quality control of fashion stores is more difficult to achieve. Products are not standardized, they change often and store layout is a key marketing strategy. This is probably why clothing retailers like Gap, with stores worldwide, prefer to exert direct quality control and own their retail outlets. This argument is even more compelling for top fashion designers like Armani or Gucci, who always own their stores (http://www.gapinc.com; Jackson and Shaw 2001; Bruce 1987).

Agency costs

A further set of costs incurred in relying on contracts with foreign parties goes under the heading *agency costs*. These are costs associated with monitoring employees and motivating managers, and arise because the actions of employees cannot be perfectly observed. When firms expand their activities internationally, the sources of informational asymmetries are likely to increase, and the agency problems become more acute. For instance, relying on local sales agents to serve foreign markets may involve significant costs to the firm, associated with the fact that the agent can easily manipulate information on the state of the market in order to extract a surplus. When agency costs are particularly relevant, organizing sales through owned subsidiaries can be a preferred alternative.

An example of this is given in a case study of Rowntree's South Africa Branch (FitzGerald 1995). Now part of the Nestlé group, Rowntree is a well-known British producer of chocolate and confectionary, which since the early twentieth century has expanded in foreign markets, particularly those formerly belonging to the British Empire. Rowntree started exporting to South Africa in 1900. By 1925, because of the rise of tariff barriers, Rowntree decided to license production to a newly formed joint venture where the majority share of capital and managerial control were in the hands of one of its former importing agents. The partnership worked until divergent views concerning the marketing and advertising strategies emerged. The local shareholder was not willing to implement the aggressive marketing strategy which Rowntree had applied worldwide, and was instead pursuing a lower-effort

Table 2.4. The costs of external (market) transactions.

Type of transaction	Type of FDI	Problem	Consequence
Transferring intangible assets	• Horizontal • Vertical	• Imperfect appropriability of knowledge • Imperfect appropriability of reputation	• Dissipation of proprietary knowledge • Dissipation of goodwill
Carrying out one stage of production	• Vertical	• Hold-up with incomplete contracts • Agency with incomplete information	• Underinvestment • Inefficient scale of production/sales

and lower-cost strategy. It exploited Rowntree's brands to cash in high returns on the initial capital investments. Because of this, in 1950 Rowntree decided to acquire the majority control of the joint venture and consequently strengthen its control over the subsidiary.

Table 2.4 summarizes the main costs of using the market for particular activities and implicitly the reasons for internalizing them, distinguishing between horizontal and vertical FDI. In the case of HFDI the motives for internalization will be mainly related to the necessity of protecting a firm's intangible assets (preventing imitation and dissipation of knowledge capital or brand image). These problems may also arise with vertical investments, but are less likely to. In the case of VFDI the main advantage of internalization is avoidance of transaction costs due to incomplete contracts and asset specificity. In both cases, the major costs of internalizing activities come from not using the comparative advantage of a local producer. By not relying on specialized agents (upstream as input suppliers, or downstream as assemblers or distributors), average costs for supplying final output are increased. Moreover, opening a wholly owned subsidiary generally involves paying plant-specific fixed costs that can be saved by relying on market relations.

2.3 Effects of FDI

Much of the policy and popular concern about MNEs arises from perceptions of their effects on host and home economies. These effects are frequently difficult for the researcher to identify, because of the myriad channels through which they occur, and because of the difficulty of specifying the counterfactual; what would have happened in the absence of the FDI project?

2.3.1 Transmission Mechanisms

The effects of FDI on host (receiving) and home (sending) countries are transmitted through different channels that can be organized into three groups: product market effects, factor market effects, and 'spillover effects'. The importance of these effects depends on the form of the investment—for example, whether it is horizontal or vertical—and the characteristics of the countries. We organize our overview of these issues under three headings.

Product market effects

Undertaking an FDI project may cause the firm to change the quantities of goods that it buys and sells in the host and home country market. The most obvious example of this is horizontal foreign direct investment, the point of which is to replace imports by local production in order to better supply the host country market. What is the effect of this on local consumers and firms? If local firms were previously producing close substitutes, then it is quite possible that the effect of the investment is simply to crowd out local supply. Consumers are then no better off, and some local firms have been forced to reduce sales (or forced out of the industry) by the presence of the MNE.

This is a central case, and there are other cases in which real income in the affected country can either fall or rise. If the MNE enters by merging or acquiring an existing supplier, then the effect may be anti-competitive, harming consumers. Alternatively, the MNE may increase competition in the market, and perhaps also increase variety or quality, tending to raise consumer welfare. If the MNE has higher productivity than local firms, then some of this benefit may be passed on as a price reduction. One motive for entry may be 'tariff jumping', in which case government may lose tariff revenue as a consequence of the investment.

Factor market effects

Factor market effects can arise in both capital and labour markets. While MNEs may raise some of their funds on local capital markets, there is generally capital inflow, augmenting local supplies of capital. The more important impact is in labour markets, where several issues arise. The first is on the overall demand for labour: does the presence of MNEs raise employment, and, conversely, does outward investment by FDI reduce labour demand at home? The second is on the skill composition of the demand for labour: does the presence of MNEs raise the demand for skills in host economies, and does the expansion of activities abroad raise the demand for skills at home? And given these changes in factor demands, what happens to factor prices?

One prediction from theory is that, in an extreme case, FDI will continue to the point where factor prices are equalized across countries. This should take the form of upwards pressure on wages (particularly unskilled wages) in developing countries, accompanied by downward pressure on unskilled wages in advanced countries as jobs relocate. The positive effects of FDI on wages in some of the more successful developing and middle-income countries has been clear, and we discuss it more in our case study of Ireland (Chapter 8). However, effects are generally more complex. Wage effects depend on the relative skill intensity of the activities carried out by MNEs and on the relative skill abundance of the countries where they operate. If an MNE based in the US transfers its labour-intensive activities to a country abundant in unskilled labour, say Mexico, the relative demand for skills may rise in both countries. In the US, because unskilled-labour-intensive activities are moved away; in Mexico, because the unskilled-labour-intensive activities transferred from the US require more skills than the average Mexican firm (Feenstra and Hanson 1996, 1997). These issues are addressed in Chapters 3 and 4.

Spillovers

It is often argued that the most important benefits to accrue from FDI are a variety of 'spillovers', which may be technological or pecuniary externalities. The former arise when FDI imposes costs or benefits that are not directly transmitted through markets. The latter arise when effects transmitted through markets are not fully paid for, so parties to the transaction may receive economic surplus.

Technological externalities include technology transfer, learning about markets and acquisition of labour skills. They can arise in many different ways as, for example, employees working in MNEs move to national firms bringing specific technological and managerial knowledge, or as suppliers of intermediates to the MNE acquire the technological specifications and procedures used by the MNE.

One source of pecuniary externality arises when both national firms and MNEs use intermediate products from a local industry. There may then be complementarities between the MNE and local firms, as the MNE strengthens local supplier industries, thereby benefiting other local firms that use these products. The mechanism is illustrated by case study evidence from developing East Asia. Hobday (1995) finds many situations in which initial multinational investments in developing East Asia created backward linkage effects to local suppliers. Examples from Taiwan include computer keyboards, personal computers, sewing machines, athletic shoes and bicycles. Initial foreign investments created demand for local firms to supply components or assembly services to multinational firms. This backward linkage effect led to entry of local firms as well as to improvements in quality, productivity and product diversity. The growth of productive intermediate-goods suppliers in turn created a forward-linkage effect to the final-goods producers, drawing in more multinationals and domestically owned firms. There then followed a second-round backward linkage effect and so forth. In some cases (e.g. bicycles, computers), local

Table 2.5.   Summary of effects of MNEs in home and host countries.

Where do the effects arise?	Effects	
	Host	Home
Product markets		
	Productivity differences	Productivity differences
	Competition and market supply	Output levels
Factor markets		
	Employment and wages	Employment and wages
	Skills	Skills
	Volatility	Volatility
Spillovers		
	Transmission of technology	Technological sourcing
	Transmission of intangible assets	
	Pecuniary externalities	

firms eventually displaced the original multinational entrants. We develop these ideas theoretically in Chapter 3.

These effects are summarized in Table 2.5, which also separates out host and home country impacts. The next section summarizes some of the empirical findings.

2.3.2   Effects of Multinationals on Home and Host Economies: Empirical Literature

The ultimate aim of the empirical literature on the impact of MNEs is to understand how these firms contribute to national income in both host and home countries, and how they affect national welfare more generally. The obvious starting point, then, is the analysis of whether MNEs perform better than national firms, using resources more efficiently. We then examine if they behave differently in factor markets, and finally the extent to which they generate spillovers for home and host economies.

Differences in performance

The possibility that MNEs perform better than national firms is well rooted in theory. The ability to exploit ownership advantages and firm-level economies of scale through HFDI, or access cheap factors of production through VFDI, should boost performance. Indeed, the overwhelming evidence for MNEs both operating abroad (foreign subsidiaries) and at home (headquarters and home plants) is that they perform better than fully national firms (i.e. firms with no foreign operations). The analysis of firm-level data for the UK, the US, Italy and various other developed and developing countries reports that average labour productivity in foreign subsidiaries of MNEs is between 30 and 70% higher than in national firms and for the home activities of MNEs it is approximately 30% higher (Griffith 1999; Griffith and

Simpson 2001; Benfratello and Sembenelli 2002). These results are consistent with the aggregate evidence provided by the OECD and reported in Table 1.7. However, these firms do not perform better just because they are MNEs. They do so because MNEs also have many other characteristics, combining bundles of inputs and other features which national firms do not have. MNEs are larger, they do more R&D, they use more capital, they employ more skilled labour, they have different products from those produced by national firms, and so on. Once we control for these other factors, the efficiency gap is considerably reduced, to a range varying between 1 and 7%.

Even having controlled for these other characteristics, the question remains as to the extent to which the better performance is a consequence of being multinational. If foreign subsidiaries are acquired through M&A, foreign investors are quite likely to cherry pick the best performers. Equally, those national firms that become foreign investors by opening a foreign subsidiary are the best performers anyway. Various studies use econometric techniques to control for this selection issue. Essentially, they benchmark MNEs in host and home countries to a hypothetical counterfactual: how would these very firms perform if they were still nationally owned or if they had not invested abroad? When these analyses are implemented, in various instances the evidence of a favourable productivity gap still holds. Although some studies do not find significant positive effects, none find a significant negative effect of multi-nationality. In other words, MNEs are never found to perform worse than national firms, even when the most rigorous econometric procedures are performed (Griffith 1999; Benfratello and Sembenelli 2002; Conyon et al. 2002; Barba Navaretti and Castellani 2003).

This finding has important implications. Policy makers should be reassured by the evidence that when a national firm transfers part of its production to cheap-labour countries or is bought out by foreign investors, its performance is generally better than if the firm had not invested abroad or had stayed national. Moreover, MNEs often have features (size, R&D investments, brands, etc.) that national firms do not have and which in themselves are important, as they enrich the domestic production structure and they improve its average performance.

Employment and output effects in home countries

Policy makers are also concerned that when national firms invest abroad they divert resources and jobs to foreign countries. Even though outward investment strengthens and improves performance at home, the size of home activities could still decline, as employees get laid off and domestic plants are downsized or even closed down.

Theoretical predictions are ambiguous here: domestic and foreign employment and output could be either complements or substitutes. This relationship is therefore tested by several empirical studies (Head and Ries 2001; Brainard and Riker 1997a; Blonigen 2001). The main finding emerging from studies focusing on employment is that VFDI generally complements domestic activities, whereas HFDI sometimes substitutes for them. Consistent results are achieved when the relationship between exports from home plants and output of foreign subsidiaries is analysed. VFDI, by fragmenting the production chain, is found to enhance exports from home plants. In contrast, HFDI reduces exports from home plants. These results contrast with the general belief that investments in cheap-labour countries weaken home activities, whereas those in other advanced economies enhance the national presence in foreign markets. The reason is probably that vertical investment reduces production costs for the MNE as a whole, therefore raising output and employment of complementary activities at home or at least preventing them from declining.

Wages and skills

An issue that keeps coming up in the globalization debate is whether MNEs are good or bad employers. Whether they pay higher or lower wages for a given level of skills than national firms in host countries is central to this debate. We will see in Chapter 7 that most arguments predict that MNEs pay higher wages than national firms. There is indeed overwhelming evidence that this is the case, both in developed and developing countries.

Evidence on this issue for advanced countries is mostly based on US and UK data. The wage premium paid by MNEs in these countries varies between 6 and 26%, depending on the study (Lipsey 1994; Griffith and Simpson 2001). In a sample of UK establishments that change ownership status, it is found that wages increase by 3.4% after the acquisition of national firms by foreign investors, and decline by 2.1% after the acquisition of foreign-owned companies by domestic investors (Conyon et al. 2002). The evidence on developing countries also reports that MNEs pay higher wages than national firms. Plant-level studies on Cote d'Ivoire, Indonesia, Morocco and Venezuela report wage premiums, which vary widely, between 10 and 260% (Aitken et al. 1996).

Another important issue is whether MNEs employ more skilled personnel than national ones. This issue concerns both domestic and foreign MNEs. As for home effects, firm-level studies conducted on Japanese, Swedish and UK MNEs find that skill intensity at home increases as a consequence of foreign investments, particularly when firms invest in developing countries (Slaughter 2000; Head and Ries 2002). This pattern is consistent with the presumption that VFDI relocates unskilled-labour-intensive stages of production to countries where this type of labour is relatively abundant.

As for whether foreign MNEs employ more skilled workers than do local firms in host countries, the evidence available is not conclusive and fails to provide clear-cut answers. According to theory, the relative demand for skilled labour depends on the factor intensities of the home and host activities of the MNEs and on the relative factor endowments of home and host economies. One pattern that emerges from studies using industry-level data is that the gap in skill intensity between MNEs and national firms is larger in developing countries, like Mexico, than in advanced countries, like the US (Feenstra and Hanson 1997; Blonigen and Slaughter 2001).

Employment volatility

Do people working in MNEs face a higher risk of losing their jobs—higher employment uncertainty—than faced by people working in locally owned firms? Although this issue is equally important for foreign and domestic MNEs, we concentrate on the effect of foreign MNEs in the host country (in Chapter 7). There may be two reasons why employment could have a different degree of volatility in MNEs than in national firms. The first is that MNEs have a different degree of exposure to international shocks than do national firms. The second is that, by being organized to operate several plants, they have lower costs of relocation than national firms. Furthermore, these lower costs of relocation make MNEs less accountable to national authorities and regulations than fully national firms.

The evidence on this matter, based on the analysis of a panel of firms operating in 11 European countries, does not support this prediction. Employees of MNEs are less likely to lose their jobs than workers in national firms, although MNEs adjust employment more rapidly than national firms. Thus, while shocks to the demand for labour cause MNEs to adjust faster than national firms, the magnitude of this adjustment, as measured by the wage elasticity of labour demand, is smaller than for national firms. Thus, for any given shock, fewer people lose their jobs (Barba Navaretti et al. 2003).

Technological sourcing

As technological knowledge is concentrated geographically, MNEs could locate their plants in knowledge-intensive areas to acquire new technologies and skills. Technological sourcing is of increasing importance for MNEs: high-tech firms often locate research labs in areas like Silicon Valley, Cambridge, UK, or Cambridge, MA, where they can interact with other R&D-intensive firms and research labs. These investments are expected to enhance technology and productivity at home. Few studies have addressed this issue, and some of them find some evidence that technological sourcing has indeed enhanced both R&D activities and productivity in home plants (Braconier et al. 2001; Pottelsberghe de la Potterie and Lichtenberg 2001).

Effects on productivity of national firms in host economies

In addition to their own performance, MNEs may have an effect by changing the performance of local firms. As we saw earlier, these effects can be transmitted through markets (product and labour markets and also markets for knowledge and technology); market transactions may sometimes be associated with pecuniary externalities (when economic surplus arises on the transactions); or effects may be transmitted directly, as pure technological externalities (e.g. unintended knowledge spillovers between firms).

The external effects of MNEs have been widely studied in the literature (see Chapter 7 and also Görg and Greenaway (2001) for a survey), and is probably the single issue to which empirical work on MNEs has devoted the most attention. Studies use different methodologies and types of datasets, and produce an array of results that are far from conclusive. Recent studies on the UK find robust evidence of spillovers from MNEs. The magnitudes of these spillovers can be computed: a 10% increase in the share of MNEs in the activities of a UK industry raises the total factor productivity (TFP) of that industry's domestic plants by about 0.5% (Haskel et al. 2002; Griffith et al. 2003).

However, many studies do not find general positive effects of MNEs on domestic efficiency. Transmission of spillovers depends on a host of country- and industry-specific conditions. The most important factor is what has been defined as the absorptive capacity of national firms, their technological proximity to MNEs. External effects do not take place in a vacuum, but only if national firms effectively interact with MNEs and if they are able to actively take part in the learning process. Thus a generalized finding is that absorptive capacity must be above a minimum threshold for technological spillovers to take place.

Consistently across studies, spillovers are found to have limited effects in poor countries. The available evidence shows that MNEs start being beneficial to domestic activities from middle-income countries onward. Few local firms in the poorest countries are in direct competition with foreign MNEs, and few of these countries possess the technical skills needed to absorb modern technologies. This evidence has the important implication that FDI has little impact on transforming domestic industry in the least advanced countries.

Across industries, spillovers are larger in industries where MNEs are widely present and when local firms are able to interact with them. In software, good and abundant engineers are a key factor favouring technological spillovers from MNEs in Bangalore, Dublin and Silicon Valley alike. A further important factor affecting spillovers is the existence of vertical linkages between MNEs and national firms. Various studies find that upstream national firms are especially likely to benefit from their role of input suppliers to MNEs. MNEs are found to deliberately support suppliers in various ways: by helping them in setting up production facilities; by providing technical assistance to raise product quality; by assisting them in purchasing raw materials; by training employees and managers.

Effects on competition in local markets

Finally, another important issue is the effect of MNEs on competition in local markets. On the one hand, MNEs could have pro-competitive effects, by reducing price-cost mark-ups. If MNEs are the best performers, they could force the best among national firms to increase efficiency and the worst ones to leave the market, thus raising the average efficiency of the industry. If efficient MNEs fully replace inefficient national firms, this is a favourable effect for national welfare. On the other hand, if the market becomes more concentrated, mark-ups could then rise, notwithstanding the improvement of average efficiency.

From the empirical point of view, disentangling technological spillovers from pro-competitive effects is not easy, as gains in efficiency and increases in competition have opposite effects on profit margins. For example, if we observe an increase in profit margins of national firms, it is not clear whether this is due to gains in efficiency or increased market power. In fact, there are very few studies focusing on the pro-competitive effect of MNEs. A recent study on Spain finds that the entry of MNEs dampens the profit margins of national firms in the short run, but it then generates long-term gains in efficiency and therefore a long-term reversal of the decline in profit margins (Sembenelli and Siotis 2002).

2.4 Conclusions

In this chapter we have given an overview of the basic conceptual issues that arise in the analysis of FDI and multinational firms. We also summarized the main empirical findings and discussed how far they fulfil theoretical predictions. The first part of the chapter dealt with the determinants of FDI. A number of points can be made. First, those firms that find it profitable to organize themselves as multinationals (i.e. to undertake FDI and operate wholly owned subsidiaries) are likely to be characterized by intangible firm-specific assets from which firm-level economies of scale originate. Second, the main motives for FDI are access to foreign markets (prevalent in the case of HFDI) or reducing production costs (prevalent in the case of VFDI). When FDI is horizontal, the main trade-off faced by firms is one between increased sales and foregone economies of scale. In the case of vertical investment the trade-off is between lower input costs and increased trade costs. The empirical evidence shows that both horizontal and vertical FDI are important components of investment flows and that these theoretical predictions are generally supported by the empirical evidence.

FDI is not the only way in which firms can organize themselves as transnational entities. Relying on market relations with foreign third parties (e.g. through licensing or outsourcing agreements) is also an alternative. Firms will choose to internalize their activities via owned subsidiaries when contractual problems give rise to transactions costs in vertical relations (the hold-up problem), allow dissipation of firm-specific assets (technical knowledge or reputation), or create incentive problems with foreign partners (agency costs).

Effects of MNEs on both host and home economies are transmitted in a number of ways, though product markets, factor markets and by spillovers to national firms. On average the effects of MNEs are found to be favourable, enhancing economic activity and the long-term income prospects of both home and host economies.

3

Horizontal Foreign Direct Investment: Product Market Access

As we saw in Chapter 2 (and summarized in Table 2.1), there are two distinct sets of reasons for firms to split their production activities geographically. In this chapter we focus on market-oriented investments and develop the theory of horizontal foreign direct investment (HFDI). Firms undertake investments in order to gain some advantage in supplying local or regional markets, even though they may incur other costs in so doing. As suggested in Chapter 2, such investment is probably the predominant type of FDI between high-income countries, and has also been a reason for investment flows to developing countries, particularly those which employed import substitution development strategies, so creating an incentive for 'tariff jumping' inwards investment.

We address two sorts of questions in this chapter. The first is, under what circumstances will HFDI occur? Firms typically have a choice of supplying a foreign market through exports or through local production. What circumstances will be conducive to the firm choosing local production, i.e. becoming multinational? We undertake a theoretical investigation of this question in Sections 3.1 and 3.2, with a view to providing empirically testable hypotheses; empirical results on these hypotheses are discussed in Chapter 6. The second sort of question we address is, what are the effects of HFDI on firms and consumers in the host economy? This is analysed in the remaining sections of the chapter. Here too, the theory seeks to inform empirical work, and also to provide a basis for formulating policy towards FDI. These themes are developed further in Chapters 7 and 10.

3.1 A Model

The key decision that we want to model is: will a firm choose to supply a market through exports or by setting up local production? This is a choice between different modes of supply, so is typically non-marginal. This is because the prices charged and quantities sold in the market will be different according to which mode of supply is chosen, and the decision has to be taken on the basis of an evaluation of profits in each situation. The way to analyse such a choice is to formulate behaviour and analyse outcomes in a two-stage game. At the second stage a market game takes place; given the chosen mode of supply—and hence numbers of firms of each type (national, multinational and foreign exporters) who are supplying the market—prices and quantities are determined, and firms earn profits. Before this, at the first stage of the game, firms choose mode of supply (whether or not to become multinational), knowing—from having thought through the second stage of the game—what profits they would earn from each mode.

The rest of this section is devoted to analysing the second-stage (or market) game, and Section 3.2 turns to the first-stage choice of entry mode. We develop the theory in a way that requires the minimum amount of technical apparatus, the background detail being filled in in Section 3.3. The models we develop draw most directly on Markusen and Venables (1998, 2000), but have earlier antecedents in Horstmann and Markusen (1992), Smith (1987) and Brainard (1997), as well as other extensions that we cite as we go through the chapter.

3.1.1 The Market Game and Operating Profits

The analysis in this chapter will be set in partial equilibrium, i.e. will focus simply on interactions in a single industry or sector, ignoring general equilibrium effects (although in Section 3.4.3 we extend this to two closely related sectors). As we build this model we will usually work with just two countries; generalization to many countries is conceptually straightforward, but complicates development of the main ideas. In some contexts it is best to think of a host region rather than a host country; for example, it is best to think of the EU as a whole, rather than of a particular country within it.

The first task is to specify the profits that a firm makes in a single market in which it is operating. We label country-specific variables with subscripts, and will look at a firm's operations in country i. Total expenditure on the industry in this country is denoted E_i, which we take to be exogenous (it will be endogenized in Section 3.3). There are a number of firms active in the industry, each producing its own variety of product. Individual firms (and varieties) are labelled with superscripts, so p_i^k and x_i^k are the price and quantity of firm k in the country i market. Production in each firm takes place at constant marginal costs, the level of which for firm k is c_i^k. The operating profits of this firm are then

$$\pi_i^k = (p_i^k - c_i^k)x_i^k. \tag{3.1}$$

The firm chooses a price (or quantity) to maximize this, given the demand function for its variety. We look at the details of this choice later, and for now it is sufficient to note that the first-order condition for this problem is the equality of marginal revenue to marginal cost,

$$p_i^k(1 - 1/\varepsilon_i^k) = c_i^k, \tag{3.2}$$

where ε_i^k is the firm's perceived elasticity of demand, i.e. the proportionate fall in output that firm k expects to experience following a proportional price increase. Using this, operating profits can be rewritten as

$$\pi_i^k = p_i^k x_i^k / \varepsilon_i^k = s_i^k E_i / \varepsilon_i^k, \tag{3.3}$$

where s_i^k is defined as the firm's market share, $s_i^k \equiv p_i^k x_i^k / E_i$. We will assume that each firm's perceived elasticity of demand, while depending on demand parameters, is firm specific only through dependence on the market share of the firm, $\varepsilon_i^k = \varepsilon(s_i^k)$. Typically, a higher market share s_i^k is associated with a lower perceived elasticity, ranging from monopoly (when $s_i^k = 1$) to perfect competition (when $s_i^k = 0$ and price equals marginal cost). Operating profits earned by firm k in market i are then

$$\pi_i^k = s_i^k E_i / \varepsilon(s_i^k). \tag{3.4}$$

Of course, we have not yet done the analysis to know what the firm's market share is or how it depends on costs, but expression (3.4) will be a useful building block in what follows.

3.1.2 *Countries and Firm Types*

We assume that there are just two countries, so E_1 and E_2 are market sizes (expenditures) in the industry under study in countries 1 and 2. The key to analytical tractability is to group the firms that supply these markets into different types. Thus, instead of all firms being potentially different from each other, we assume that they are divided into multinational firms that produce in both countries, and national firms that produce in a single country and export to the other.[1] Each of these types is further divided according to their location or, for multinationals, the location of their headquarters, giving four firm types. The number of multinational firms headquartered in countries 1 and 2 will be denoted m_1 and m_2 and the number of national firms in each country, n_1 and n_2.

This grouping is possible only if there is symmetry of firms in each type, both with respect to their costs and their demand functions. On the demand side, we shall simply assume that all firms in a market face the same demand functions. This means that the products they produce, while possibly differentiated, are symmetric in the sense that if two firms charge the same price, then they will have the same level of demand and hence the same market shares.

On the cost side, production costs vary only according to where production takes place. Thus, all firms have the same technology and constant marginal costs. (The implications of relaxing this strong assumption are discussed in Section 3.5.) However, international differences in factor prices might cause the level of the costs to

---

[1] Of course, it is possible that under some circumstances a multinational produces a good locally and also imports the same good (see, for example, Rob and Vettas 2003).

vary across countries, so the unit costs of producing in each country will be denoted by c_1 and c_2. Costs of supplying the market consist of these production costs together with transport and distribution costs; these include the transport costs, tariffs and other costs incurred in supplying the market through imports rather than through local production. These take the iceberg form, meaning that to ship one unit of good from one country to the other requires that τ units be shipped. Thus, the marginal cost of a firm in 1 of supplying country 2 is $c_1\tau$; similarly, the marginal cost of a firm in 2 supplying market 1 is $c_2\tau$. The costs incurred by each type of firm in supplying each market are summarized in the first two columns of Table 3.1. Market 1 is supplied either by local production, which has costs c_1 whether it is undertaken by a national firm or a multinational, or by imports with unit costs $c_2\tau$. Notice that this formulation assumes that multinationals undertake all stages of production in the country of sale, so the only intra-firm trade is in headquarters' services. An alternative would be to assume that some upstream activities (e.g. component production) remained in the home country and only downstream activities (e.g. assembly) moved to the host. We explore in detail the possibility of fragmenting the production process in this way in the next chapter.

Much of the analysis will focus on the firms' market shares. All firms with the same costs in a market will have the same prices and hence the same market shares, so we no longer need to distinguish between such firms. We therefore write the market share of a single country i firm in its home market as s_i (dropping the superscript k). Multinationals producing in country i have the same marginal costs as national firms, and hence exactly the same market share, s_i. Imports, however, have different unit costs both because they are produced with the other country's factor prices, and because they are subject to transport costs. We therefore define $s_i\varphi_j$ as the market share in country i of an importer from country j, i.e. of a firm with costs $c_j\tau$ as compared with the costs of local production, c_i. φ_j will be smaller the higher is τ and the higher is c_j relative to c_i. We will usually think of $\varphi_j \leqslant 1$, because of trade costs, although this could be overturned if c_j were much smaller than c_i. The magnitude of φ_j will also depend on demand elasticities and strategic behaviour, and we analyse this more explicitly in Sections 3.3 and 3.5. For present purposes we will treat φ_j as a parameter, and refer to it as the freeness of trade (terminology employed by Baldwin et al. (2003)), noting that it is larger the lower are trade costs. This discussion is summarized in columns four and five of Table 3.1, indicating that multinationals operate plants in both countries.

As outlined in Chapter 2, there may be increasing returns at the level of the plant and at the level of the firm. We shall assume that these arise because of plant- and firm-level fixed costs, modelled in the simplest possible way. Thus, the fixed cost of running headquarters in country i is denoted $c_i H$, and the costs of setting up a plant, $c_i F$. Assuming all firms have access to the same technology means that the

Table 3.1.   Costs and market shares.

	MC1	MC2	MS1	MS2	Fixed costs
National in 1, n_1	c_1	$c_1\tau$	s_1	$s_2\varphi_1$	$c_1(H+F)$
National in 2, n_2	$c_2\tau$	c_2	$s_1\varphi_2$	s_2	$c_2(H+F)$
Multinational in 1, m_1	c_1	c_2	s_1	s_2	$c_1(H+F)+c_2F$
Multinational in 2, m_2	c_1	c_2	s_1	s_2	$c_2(H+F)+c_1F$

MC1, marginal cost of supplying country 1; MC2, marginal cost of supplying country 2; MS1, market share in country 1; MS2, market share in country 2.

input requirements in these fixed costs F and H are the same for all firms; however, since the costs are incurred in different countries they face different local factor prices, captured by the factors c_1 and c_2. These fixed costs are summarized in the final column of Table 3.1.

This provides the building blocks needed to determine the profits that firms will earn, dependent on the mode of supply that they choose. We look at these profit levels for multinational and then for national firms.

Multinational firms

A multinational that is headquartered in country 1 has fixed costs comprised of two elements. In its home market it incurs $c_1(H+F)$, the fixed costs of headquarters and of operating one plant. In its foreign market it incurs a fixed cost c_2F, the cost of operating a plant in country 2. Its marginal operating costs in each market are c_1 and c_2, with associated market shares s_1 and s_2. Total profits—operating profits in the two markets minus fixed costs—are

$$\Pi_1^{M} = s_1 E_1/\varepsilon(s_1) + s_2 E_2/\varepsilon(s_2) - (H+F)c_1 - Fc_2. \tag{3.5}$$

There are m_1 of these firms, and there are m_2 multinationals headquartered in country 2 with profits

$$\Pi_2^{M} = s_1 E_1/\varepsilon(s_1) + s_2 E_2/\varepsilon(s_2) - (H+F)c_2 - Fc_1. \tag{3.6}$$

Notice the force of the assumption that all firms that produce in a country have the same marginal costs (as well as facing the same demands). Multinationals from both countries 1 and 2 therefore have the same share in each market, and hence make the same operating profits. However, their fixed costs may differ because of different levels of fixed costs in countries 1 and 2.

National firms

Let us now derive the analogous expressions for national firms, looking first at a national firm in country 1. Such a firm incurs fixed costs of $c_1(H+F)$, the headquarters' costs and the fixed costs of one plant. Production takes place in country 1 at marginal cost c_1 giving it a market share of s_1 and hence earnings in this market of $s_1 E_1/\varepsilon(s_1)$, the same as multinational firms producing in country 1. All national firms are able to export, and their marginal cost in supplying market 2 is $c_1 \tau$ giving a market share of $s_2 \varphi_1$ as shown in Table 3.1. The profits of a single country 1 national firm are therefore

$$\Pi_1^N = s_1 E_1/\varepsilon(s_1) + s_2 \varphi_1 E_2/\varepsilon(s_2 \varphi_1) - (H + F)c_1. \qquad (3.7)$$

We denote the number of such firms n_1. There are n_2 country 2 national firms, whose profits can be written analogously as

$$\Pi_2^N = s_2 E_2/\varepsilon(s_2) + s_1 \varphi_2 E_1/\varepsilon(s_1 \varphi_2) - (H + F)c_2. \qquad (3.8)$$

Market shares

To complete the characterization of the equilibrium of the market game, we need only determine market shares. Because of their definition as shares, this is easy. The number of firms that supply country 1 by local production is $n_1 + m_1 + m_2$, each with market share s_1; in addition, n_2 firms supply market 1 through trade, and their market share is $\varphi_2 s_1$. Since market shares sum to unity we have equation (3.9 a), while (3.9 b) gives the analogous expression for market 2:

$$1 = (n_1 + m_1 + m_2)s_1 + n_2 \varphi_2 s_1, \qquad (3.9\,a)$$

$$1 = (n_2 + m_1 + m_2)s_2 + n_1 \varphi_1 s_2. \qquad (3.9\,b)$$

Our analysis will turn on values of s_1 and s_2 derived from these equations and then used to evaluate the profits of different firm types. Pulling together these profit statements (equations (3.5)–(3.8)) for the four different types of firms, we have

$$\left.\begin{aligned}
\Pi_1^M(n_1, n_2, m) &= s_1 E_1/\varepsilon(s_1) + s_2 E_2/\varepsilon(s_2) - (H + F)c_1 - Fc_2, \\
\Pi_2^M(n_1, n_2, m) &= s_1 E_1/\varepsilon(s_1) + s_2 E_2/\varepsilon(s_2) - (H + F)c_2 - Fc_1, \\
\Pi_1^N(n_1, n_2, m) &= s_1 E_1/\varepsilon(s_1) + s_2 \varphi_1 E_2/\varepsilon(s_2 \varphi_1) - (H + F)c_1, \\
\Pi_2^N(n_1, n_2, m) &= s_2 E_2/\varepsilon(s_2) + s_1 \varphi_2 E_1/\varepsilon(s_1 \varphi_2) - (H + F)c_2.
\end{aligned}\right\} \qquad (3.10)$$

Notice that we have written the functional dependence of profits on the number of firms of each type, having defined the total number of multinationals by $m = m_1 + m_2$. The dependence is transmitted via market shares and, since m_1 and m_2 only enter (3.9) additively, they only enter profits through their sum, m. Furthermore, if costs are the same in both countries, then multinationals earn the same profits regardless of where they are located. At some points in what follows we will make this assumption, and then just work with multinationals in aggregate, m, rather than separated out by location of headquarters, m_1, m_2.

3.2 National versus Multinational Supply

We now turn to the first stage of the game. Comparing profit levels, what mode of supply will firms choose? To answer this we make one further simplification. This is that the mark-up, $\varepsilon(s)$, is constant, and we denote this constant value σ. This assumption will be relaxed in Section 3.5.

3.2.1 Greenfield Investments

The first question we pose is the following. Suppose that there are n_1 and n_2 national firms in each country, and m multinationals. Will it be profitable for one of the country 1 national firms to switch status and become multinational? This is answered by comparing $\Pi_1^N(n_1, n_2, m)$, the original profits of a firm in country 1, with $\Pi_1^M(n_1 - 1, n_2, m + 1)$, the profits it receives when it becomes multinational given that there is now one less national firm and one more multinational. Notice that this is a greenfield investment, in the sense that n_2 is unchanged: instead of taking over or merging with a country 2 national firm, one more plant is constructed in country 2. Thus, the total number of firms, $n_1 + n_2 + m$, is held constant.

Switching from being a national firm to a multinational changes the second-stage market equilibrium, and all the information we need is captured in the change in the firms' market shares. These changes affect only market 2, not market 1. In the initial situation, a firm producing in market 2 had share s_2 solved from equations (3.9) as

$$s_2 = \frac{1}{n_2 + m + n_1 \varphi_1}. \tag{3.11}$$

After the change its market share becomes

$$s_2 = \frac{1}{n_2 + (m + 1) + (n_1 - 1)\varphi_1}. \tag{3.12}$$

The new value is smaller than the original, providing $\varphi_1 < 1$. To find out the change in profits, we use expressions (3.11) and (3.12) in the expressions for Π_1^N and Π_1^M (equations (3.10)); we shall denote the change in profits from this greenfield investment by a country 1 firm, given initial firm numbers n_1, n_2, m, by $\Delta_1^G(n_1, n_2, m)$. Thus

$$\Delta_1^G(n_1, n_2, m) \equiv \Pi_1^M(n_1 - 1, n_2, m + 1) - \Pi_1^N(n_1, n_2, m)$$
$$= \frac{E_2}{\sigma}\left[\frac{1}{n_2 + (n_1 - 1)\varphi_1 + (m + 1)} - \frac{\varphi_1}{n_2 + n_1\varphi_1 + m}\right] - Fc_2. \tag{3.13}$$

The firm becomes multinational if this expression is positive. Going multinational means the disadvantage of having to operate two plants and bear the additional fixed cost of Fc_2. Against this is a change in operating profit, given by the term

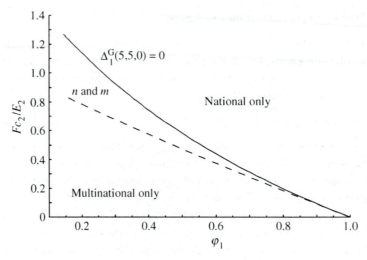

Figure 3.1.   Greenfield MNEs.

in square brackets. What do we know about this term? If $\varphi_1 = 1$, then it is zero; switching the source of supply to country 2 has no effect, since the costs of supply are unchanged. But if $\varphi_1 < 1$, as will be the case if $c_1 < c_2\tau$, the term is certainly positive. Operating profits are increased because of the lower unit cost of supply, and the consequent change in the equilibrium of the market game. As would be expected, the term in square brackets is decreasing in φ_1, indicating that the value of becoming multinational is greater the greater the cost disadvantage of being an exporter. Notice too that the whole of the term in square brackets is multiplied by E_2, the size of the market that the firm is entering.

As increasingly many country 1 firms become multinational, so the value of becoming multinational decreases, because the term in square brackets is decreasing as m rises and n_1 falls. Thus, the more firms that have switched to being multinational, the lower the return to a further firm switching. Figure 3.1 illustrates this, by plotting loci of $\Delta_1^G(n_1, n_2, m) = 0$, i.e. values of Fc_2/E_2 on the vertical axis at which $\Delta_1^G(n_1, n_2, m)$ equals zero for each value of φ_1 on the horizontal. The upper line is drawn when $n_1 = n_2 = 5$ and $m = 0$, and the lower when $n_1 = 1$, $n_2 = 5$ and $m = 4$. Above the lines it is not worthwhile to become multinational, while below it is. Thus, if we consider situations with different parameter values, the following pattern emerges. In the upper right area there are no multinational firms; the fixed costs of entry are too high relative to the size of the market and the small marginal cost advantage of local production. Moving down and to the left, multinationals emerge, and become an increasing share of the total population of firms, until the point is reached where all firms are multinational.

This analysis gives three simple hypotheses. The number of multinationals operating in a particular country or product market, relative to the number of national firms, will be greater the higher are trade barriers (high τ giving low φ_i), the lower are plant-level fixed costs, $c_i F$, and the larger is the host country market, E_i. The first of these seems hard to reconcile with the observation that FDI has grown rapidly during a period in which many trade barriers have fallen. However, offsetting this, the fixed costs of producing in foreign markets may have fallen more rapidly than trade costs, and market size has grown. We will see in Chapter 6 that, looking at cross-sections of industries and host countries, there is considerable empirical support for these hypotheses.

3.2.2 Mergers and Acquisitions

As we saw in Chapter 1, a very high proportion of FDI takes the form of M&A activity—an existing firm taking over, or merging with, a foreign firm. What are the gains to becoming multinational through a merger, and how do they compare with those from a greenfield investment?[2] This can be modelled as a country 1 national firm switching to become a multinational based in country 1, together with the takeover (and disappearance) of a country 2 firm. The return to this merger is denoted $\Delta_1^A(n_1, n_2, m)$; it is given by the profits of the multinational in the new situation, minus the profits of both the national firms of which it is composed:

$$\Delta_1^A(n_1, n_2, m) \equiv \Pi_1^M(n_1 - 1, n_2 - 1, m + 1) - \Pi_1^N(n_1, n_2, m) - \Pi_2^N(n_1, n_2, m). \tag{3.14}$$

In the new situation there is one more multinational and one less national firm in each country, and the profits foregone are those of both the merging firms—a national firm from each country. In the case of acquisition the same equation can be interpreted in a slightly different way: the first two terms on the right-hand side are the increase in operating profits of firm 1, from which must be subtracted the price firm 1 pays for firm 2, which is equal to its profits. Notice that in this formulation the merger or acquisition involves loss of a firm and of a product variety; the merged firm closes down one of the brands.[3]

Evaluation of the profit levels involves using the appropriate numbers of firms in the market share equations, (3.9). Doing this and inserting the results into the profit

---

[2] The literature on M&A is small compared with that on greenfield investments. Horn and Persson (2001) use cooperative game techniques to explore equilibrium ownership structures of firms. Policy towards international mergers is studied by Horn and Levinsohn (2001).

[3] We assume that one firm disappears with loss of its variety. If it were to remain, then so too would its plant-level fixed cost and there would no effect whatsoever. Loss of operating profit due to merger is sometimes called the 'merger paradox'. Generally, the result depends on the form of oligopolistic interaction between firms (see Salant et al. 1983).

equations (3.10) and thence (3.14) yields

$$\Delta_1^A(n_1, n_2, m) = \frac{E_1}{\sigma} \left[\frac{1}{n_1 + (n_2 - 1)\varphi_2 + m} - \frac{1 + \varphi_2}{n_1 + n_2\varphi_2 + m} \right]$$
$$+ \frac{E_2}{\sigma} \left[\frac{1}{n_2 + (n_1 - 1)\varphi_1 + m} - \frac{1 + \varphi_1}{n_2 + n_1\varphi_1 + m} \right] + c_2 H.$$
$$(3.15)$$

How does this differ from the case of a greenfield investment? First, there is now a fixed cost *saving*; the number of plants operating is unchanged, but costs are saved by closing the headquarters' operations in country 2, $c_2 H$. The cost of the M&A is loss of market share, as two sources of supply (one from each of the previously independent national firms) are merged into a single source of supply (the multinational). Thus, in the case of M&A, the new merged firm saves fixed costs and loses market share, relative to the sum of their initial positions. (Although, of course, in the case of acquisition, the *acquiring* firm incurs larger fixed costs and larger sales, while those of the acquired firm go to zero.)

Further implications of this can be seen if we go to the special case in which costs are the same and the numbers of national firms are the same, $c_1 = c_2$, $\phi_1 = \phi_2$ and $n_1 = n_2 = n$. Then

$$\Delta_1^A(n_1, n_2, m) = \frac{E_1 + E_2}{\sigma} \left[\frac{1}{n(1 + \varphi) + m - \varphi} - \frac{1 + \varphi}{n(1 + \varphi) + m} \right] + cH. \quad (3.16)$$

The term is square brackets is negative if $\varphi > 0$, and increasing in absolute value the larger is φ. Thus, merger occurs if $c_2 H$ is large, or φ is small (meaning that initial trade and consequent loss of market share are small). This is illustrated in Figure 3.2, which gives the freeness of trade on the horizontal axis and the cost saving (relative to market size) on the vertical. The lines give loci along which returns are zero, and above these lines merger occurs. As in Figure 3.1, the returns to multinationality are decreasing in both the freeness of trade and the number of multinational firms. These properties give the upwards slope of the lines and the zones in which different combinations of firm types are operational.

Comparing the cases of greenfield investments and M&A activity, we see that high trade costs are conducive to both types of investment. However, whereas greenfield investments are deterred by high plant-level fixed costs relative to market size, M&A activity is promoted when firm-level fixed costs are large relative to combined market size. These points are drawn out somewhat further in Figure 3.3, which reports the most profitable form of activity. The horizontal axis is, as before, the freeness of trade, and the vertical gives the market size of country 1 relative to that of markets 1 and 2 together. In the region marked *national only*, no multinational activity at all is profitable; in the other regions, the most profitable type of HFDI is that marked. We

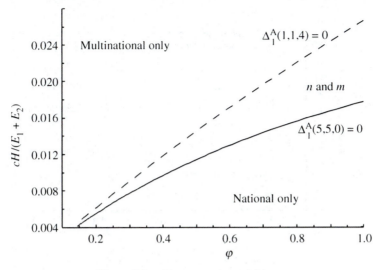

Figure 3.2. Mergers and acquisitions.

learn several things from the figure. First, the importance of market size in attracting greenfield investments. It is worth paying the fixed cost to establish production in country 1 the larger is this market, this accounting for the region in which greenfield investment by a country 2 firm (so in country 1) is most profitable. Mergers and acquisitions do not have this market size bias, as production in both countries is going on before and after the merger. Furthermore, they are relatively more profitable the higher are trade costs (the less free is trade).

It is worth emphasizing that Figure 3.3 does not yield firm predictions as to outcomes. In many of these regions both greenfield investments and M&A are profitable. The figure says which is most profitable, but either could occur. Furthermore, the comparison made is between the status quo and one action (greenfield investment or M&A). In reality more complex combinations are possible. For example, if an M&A does not occur, one firm may proceed with a greenfield investment; the profitability of the M&A should then be assessed not relative to the status quo, but relative to what profits would be after the greenfield investment. Multi-stage games have been modelled by various authors to explore these possibilities (see, for example, Horstmann and Markusen 1992; Motta 1992; Markusen 2003, Chapter 3).

3.2.3 Free Entry

We now move from situations in which the total number of firms is fixed to situations where the number of firms is endogenously determined in response to profit opportunities, i.e. from looking at oligopolistic industries to those in which entry is sufficiently free to make them monopolistically competitive. If there is free entry

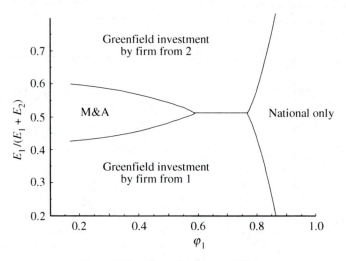

Figure 3.3.   Greenfield versus M&A.

and exit, then the number of active firms is determined by zero-profit conditions. We continue to analyse HFDI as a two-stage game, but the first stage now takes the following form. There are very many potential firms of each type, and at the first stage they choose whether or not to enter, given the entry decisions of all other firms. At the second stage they produce and supply to each market as in the preceding sections. Second-stage profits are given as above (equations (3.9) and (3.10)).

The equilibrium conditions for the first stage are that profits are non-negative for all firms that have entered, and non-positive for all potential firms that have chosen not to enter. We write these equilibrium conditions as follows:

$$\left.\begin{array}{ll} \Pi_1^N(n_1, n_2, m_1 + m_2) \leqslant 0, & n_1 \geqslant 0; \\ \Pi_2^N(n_1, n_2, m_1 + m_2) \leqslant 0, & n_2 \geqslant 0; \\ \Pi_1^M(n_1, n_2, m_1 + m_2) \leqslant 0, & m_1 \geqslant 0; \\ \Pi_2^M(n_1, n_2, m_1 + m_2) \leqslant 0, & m_2 \geqslant 0. \end{array}\right\} \tag{3.17}$$

Expressing them this way assumes that the numbers of firms are measured by continuous variables. Each pair of inequalities holds with complementary slack, so the first says that if there is a positive number of country 1 national firms active, then their profits are zero; and, conversely, if their profits are negative, then the number of active firms of this type is zero. Our task is now to show how equilibrium configurations of $\{n_1, n_2, m_1, m_2\}$ are determined, and how they depend on parameters of the model.

The easiest first case is if the two economies are identical, so the conditions for non-negative profits of national firms and for multinationals, (3.10), can be expressed as

$$\left.\begin{array}{l} \varPi^N = sE(1+\varphi)/\sigma - (H+F)c \leqslant 0, \\ \varPi^M = sE2/\sigma - (H+2F)c \leqslant 0, \end{array}\right\} \quad (3.18)$$

where, since countries are identical, subscripts have been dropped. Conceptually, these equations determine the numbers of firms; algebraically, the only endogenous variable in the equations is market share, s, linked to numbers of firms by equations (3.9). Since there is only one endogenous variable in these two equations generally, only one of them can hold with equality, the other holding with inequality. Solving the first equation in (3.18) for s and then using this value in the second and rearranging we see that both national and multinational firms will coexist (both the equations (3.18) hold with equality) only if parameters satisfy the equation

$$\tfrac{1}{2}(1-\varphi) = \frac{F}{H+2F}. \quad (3.19)$$

There are multinationals and no national firms if the right-hand side of this is less than the left—either because of high firm-level fixed costs relative to plant-level fixed costs, H/F, or high trade costs, τ (low φ). On the other side of the inequality, there are national firms only.

Several comments are in order. The presence of multinationals depends on trade costs and fixed costs, as it did in previous cases. Once again, high trade costs increase the likelihood of HFDI. Fixed costs no longer enter relative to market size, essentially because the number of firms in the industry is proportionate to market size. Instead, the crucial parameter is the *ratio* of plant-level fixed costs to overall firm-level fixed costs. HFDI is more likely the greater is H to relative to F. The model therefore generates the hypothesis that multinationals will be prevalent in industries where firm-level economies of scale are important relative to plant-level economies of scale. We will see empirical support for this hypothesis in Chapter 6.

The fact that national and multinational firms only coexist on a knife edge in parameter space is a somewhat artificial consequence of some of the modelling simplifications we have made, and arises for two reasons. First, firms within each type are assumed to all be homogeneous; obviously, if firms had varying degrees of efficiency, then we would expect to see an equilibrium with some combination of the most efficient national firms and the most efficient multinationals. (This is explored in recent work by Helpman et al. (2004) and we discuss it more fully in Section 3.5.) And, second, even with the homogeneity assumption, coexistence could occur if more variables were endogenous. As it is, firms compete in two product markets; changes in the number of firms affect profits only through their effects on shares in each market, and since there are only two of these variables, there are only two types of firm at equilibrium. If, however, factor prices are also endogenous, then changes in the mix of firms affects profits through changes in

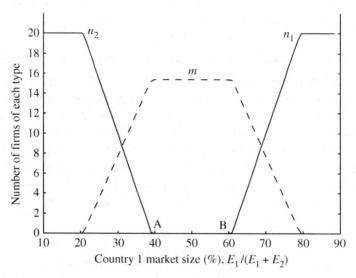

Figure 3.4.   Free entry.

market shares and factor prices (a four-dimensional space, not a two-dimensional one), so coexistence ceases to be a knife-edge property.

Country differences

The equilibrium configuration of national and multinational firms depends on country characteristics, as well as on technology. For what country configurations will multinationals replace national firms? The first experiment is to consider differences in market size, maintaining the assumption that costs are the same in both countries, in which case location of the multinational's headquarters is unimportant and we can work with $m = m_1 + m_2$.

The horizontal axis of Figure 3.4 gives country 1 expenditure as a percentage of total expenditure, and the vertical gives the equilibrium number of firms of each type. It is derived by computing solutions of (3.17) with (3.10) and (3.9). The figure illustrates that when market 1 is very small the only active firms are national firms in country 2 and vice versa. It is when countries are relatively similar in size that multinationals replace national firms (doing so completely when $E_1 = E_2$, providing the right-hand side of (3.19) is less than the left). The intuition comes from the 'home market effect' that operates in models of this type. A large market attracts disproportionately many firms, so country 1 national firms do well when the country 1 market is large. It is when this home market effect is weak that entry of firms producing in both markets—multinationals—is profitable. Notice that there is now a region in which both multinationals and national firms from one country coexist.

Analytical results can be obtained by finding the edges of these regimes. For example, suppose that there are only multinationals, as when market sizes are approximately equal, so $n_1 = n_2 = 0$. In that case $s_1 = s_2 = 1/m$ (equations (3.9)), and the profits of a multinational firm and a (potential) country 2 national firm and are, from equations (3.10),

$$\Pi^M = \frac{1}{\sigma m}(E_1 + E_2) - (H + 2F)c, \qquad \Pi_2^N = \frac{1}{\sigma m}(E_1 + E_2 \varphi) - (H + F)c,$$

$$(3.20)$$

respectively. Setting $\Pi^M = 0$ we can solve for m, and use this in Π_2^N to find the point at which it just becomes profitable for entry by country 2 national firms to commence (point A in Figure 3.4). Eliminating m we obtain that entry by country 2 national firms is not profitable if

$$\frac{E_1(1 - \varphi)}{E_1 + E_2} > \frac{F}{H + 2F}.$$

$$(3.21)$$

This is a natural generalization of (3.19). The analogous exercise can be undertaken to find point B in Figure 3.4, and combining them we find that, providing

$$\frac{2F}{H + 2F} < 1 - \varphi,$$

there is an interval of values of $E_1/(E_1 + E_2)$ within which the only firms operating are multinationals. The interval is wider the higher is H/F or higher is τ (lower φ).

A similar experiment can be done if expenditure in the two countries is assumed equal, but production costs in each vary because of international differences in factor prices. Outcomes are very similar to those illustrated in Figure 3.4, but with market size difference replaced by cost difference on the horizontal axis. If country 2 has the cost advantage, then all production is undertaken in country 2, i.e. by country 2 national firms, and vice versa if country 1 has the cost advantage. It is when costs are similar in the two countries that multinational production occurs. Intuitively, this says that national production and international trade occurs when there are large comparative advantage gains to be made, due to differences in costs. When these gains are more modest, FDI takes over. These results have collectively been termed a 'convergence hypothesis' (Markusen and Venables 1996), as they suggest that it is when economies are similar—in either size or comparative costs—that horizontal multinational activity is most likely to be seen.

Pulling the results from this free-entry case together, the model suggests three main hypotheses. HFDI is more likely if trade costs are high; if firm-level economies of scale are important relative to plant-level economies of scale; and if the countries under study are relatively similar in factor costs and in market size. The analysis presented here is based on just two countries, but it is conceptually easy to extend it to a larger number. One aspect of this extension merits discussion. Suppose that initially one 'country' comprises a number of different regions (or countries) with high trade costs between them (think of this as the EU, with the other country the US). It is then possible that the market in each of these regions is too small to attract FDI from the other country. Economic integration reduces or removes these barriers, turning the separate small regions into a single large economy. Establishing an affiliate in one of these regions may now be profitable, as it can serve as an export platform to other parts of the integrated economy. This 'export platform' investment will be discussed again in Chapter 8 on the Irish economy. The point is that economic integration can bring about an effective convergence of market size (e.g. between the US and the EU) that promotes FDI. Notice therefore that low trade barriers within a region (e.g. the EU) and high trade barriers between regions (EU and US) are both conducive to HFDI between these blocs.

3.3 Demand and Firm Behaviour

Our modelling to this point has used the minimum possible amount of analytical apparatus, but to proceed further more apparatus is needed. This section develops the demand and market behaviour that underlies the model so far, and that will be used explicitly in the remainder of the chapter.

Modelling is based on the Dixit–Stiglitz model of monopolistic competition and its multi-market extensions (Dixit and Stiglitz 1977; Helpman and Krugman 1985; Fujita et al. 1999). We continue to focus on a single industry, and expenditure on this industry in country i is denoted, as before, E_i. This expenditure is divided between varieties of differentiated product and, following Dixit–Stiglitz, it is assumed that each firm produces its own single variety. Consumer utility over these varieties is given by a constant elasticity of substitution (CES) utility function. For country i this utility is denoted X_i and given by

$$X_i = [\Sigma_k (x_i^k)^{(\sigma-1)/\sigma}]^{\sigma/(\sigma-1)}, \tag{3.22}$$

where σ is the elasticity of substitution between varieties and x_i^k is the quantity of the kth firm's product supplied to country i. Dual to this utility function is a unit expenditure function, or price index, denoted G_i and given by

$$G_i = [\Sigma_k (p_i^k)^{(1-\sigma)}]^{1/(1-\sigma)}. \tag{3.23}$$

Given these preferences and the expenditure levels E_i, the demand functions for each product can be found; the partial derivative of the expenditure function with respect to price gives the compensated demand function (by Shephard's Lemma). Firm k therefore has country i sales given by demand curve (or inverse demand curve)

$$x_i^k = (p_i^k)^{-\sigma} G_i^{(\sigma-1)} E_i \quad \text{or} \quad p_i^k = (x_i^k)^{-1/\sigma} X_i^{(1-\sigma)/\sigma} E_i. \tag{3.24}$$

σ, the elasticity of substitution between varieties, is also the compensated price elasticity of demand for a single variety. Notice that the product of the price index and utility is total expenditure, $G_i X_i = E_i$. The share of the firm in the market follows directly from (3.24) as

$$s_i^k \equiv p_i^k x_i^k / E_i = (p_i^k / G_i)^{1-\sigma}. \tag{3.25}$$

Up to this point total expenditure on the products of the industry in each country, E_i, has been treated as exogenous. However, consumers choose how much to spend on this industry as a function of their total income, Y_i, and the price index for these products, G_i. We represent this choice by a quasi-linear indirect utility function, with price elasticity η, $\sigma > \eta$.[4] Overall consumer utility, V_i, is therefore

$$V_i = \frac{\bar{E}_i G_i^{1-\eta}}{\eta - 1} + Y_i. \tag{3.26}$$

The first term is the consumer surplus derived from the industry under study (where $\bar{E}_i$ is a constant), and the second is total income in country i. Utility is, of course, decreasing in the price index, so if income Y_i is unchanged, the price index can be used as a measure of welfare change.[5] By Roy's identity $X_i = \bar{E}_i G_i^{-\eta}$, so $E_i = \bar{E}_i G_i^{1-\eta}$. Using this in (3.24), the demand function for the sales of a single firm is now

$$x_i^k = (p_i^k)^{-\sigma} G_i^{\sigma - \eta} \bar{E}_i. \tag{3.27}$$

Applying this to the context of this chapter, we note several things. First, the pricing rule of equation (3.2) depends on the perceived change in demand as each firm changes its price. From demand function (3.27) the perceived elasticity, $\varepsilon(s_i^k)$ is equal to the constant σ if each firm takes the price index G_i as a constant in its profit-maximization decision. This is the 'large group' assumption, meaning that a single firm's price is a small enough element in the price index (equation (3.23)) for a change in price to be perceived to have only a negligible effect. In Section 3.5.1 we discuss the effects of relaxing the large group assumption, and instead looking at oligopolistic interaction between firms in the industry.

We have up to now asserted that variation in market shares depends on variation in marginal costs (including trade costs) without giving an explicit equation for this dependence. This dependence is now clear from the demand equations in (3.25). If one firm has marginal costs and prices that are higher than that of another by a factor $c_j \tau / c_i$, then its market share will be smaller by a factor

$$\varphi_i = (c_j \tau / c_i)^{1-\sigma} = (p_j \tau / p_i)^{1-\sigma} = p_j \tau x_j / p_i x_i.$$

---

[4] η is the elasticity of the quantity index X with respect to the price index G. $\sigma > \eta$ implies that the elasticity of demand for a single variety is greater than the elasticity of demand for products of the industry as a whole.

[5] A unit elastic demand is given by $V_i = E_i \ln(G_i) + Y_i$.

As would be expected, the sensitivity of market shares to cost differences is greater the higher is the price elasticity of demand.

3.4   The Effect of FDI on the Host Economy

We now turn from the determinants of HFDI to its consequences. What is the effect on the host country of entry by a foreign multinational? There are three main mechanisms on which we will focus. The first is in the product market. Changing supply from multinational and foreign firms will affect consumers, possibly making them better off; at the same time, the change in competition will have an effect on national firms' sales and profits, possibly causing a change in the number that operate. We will call these the 'product market effects'. Second, multinational activity will impact on the factor market, changing demand for local factors of production—the 'factor market effect'. Finally, there may be 'linkage effects' of various types, as multinationals raise activity levels in related areas of the economy. The next three subsections investigate these mechanisms. The analysis does not seek to be comprehensive, but merely to explore the way the mechanisms operate, illustrate possibilities and point to key factors that are important in making a full assessment of effects.

We concentrate on the effects on a single host economy (country 1). This country is supplied by n_1 local firms, each setting price p_1; by m multinationals with price p_m (these multinationals have headquarters located in the foreign country); and by n_2 foreign firms that have price p_2 in their home market and consequently price $p_2\tau$ on their exports to market 1. The corresponding quantities consumed are x_1, x_m, x_2. Since firms in each of these three groups are symmetric, the price index, level of expenditure and demand functions in market 1 are

$$\left.\begin{aligned}
G_1 &= [n_1 p_1^{1-\sigma} + n_2(p_2\tau)^{1-\sigma} + mp_m^{1-\sigma}]^{1/(1-\sigma)}, \\
E_1 &= n_1 p_1 x_1 + n_2 p_2\tau x_2 + mp_m x_m, \\
x_1 &= p_1^{-\sigma} G_1^{\sigma-\eta} \bar{E}_1, \\
x_2 &= (p_2\tau)^{-\sigma} G_1^{\sigma-\eta} \bar{E}_1, \\
x_m &= p_m^{-\sigma} G_1^{\sigma-\eta} \bar{E}_1.
\end{aligned}\right\} \qquad (3.28)$$

Looking first at the price index, for each group of firms that have the same price, the summation of equation (3.23) is, in equation (3.28), simply the number of firms in the group times the common value of their price, raised to the power $1 - \sigma$. Expenditures on the three groups add to total expenditure on the industry, and the demand functions for a representative variety from each group are given in the last row.

3.4.1 *Product Market Competition and Consumer Welfare*

Horizontal FDI is designed to supply the host country product market, and it is to product market effects that we look first. The direct effect of the entry of multinationals is twofold. First, there is the direct change dm in the number of multinationals, each of which sells output of value $p_m x_m$ on the country 1 market. Second, multinational entry will typically be a direct replacement of other firms' supply. If, for example, a foreign firm changes its supply mode, then creation of a multinational is removal of a foreign national importer, so $dn_2 = -dm$. In the case of merger or acquisition, there is also loss of a domestic firm, so $dn_1 = dn_2 = -dm$. In addition to these direct effects, there may also be indirect effects, as the market equilibrium changes. If there is free entry and exit of local firms, this will take the form of an endogenous response in the number of these firms, giving a further change dn_1.

To start analysing the implications of these changes, consider first the effect of multinational entry on the country 1 price index, G_1. Differentiating the price index from (3.28) gives

$$\frac{dG_1}{dm} = \frac{G_1^\sigma}{1-\sigma}\left[p_1^{1-\sigma}\frac{dn_1}{dm} + (p_2\tau)^{1-\sigma}\frac{dn_2}{dm} + p_m^{1-\sigma}\right]$$

$$= \frac{G_1^\eta}{\bar{E}_1}\frac{p_m x_m}{1-\sigma}\left[\frac{p_1 x_1}{p_m x_m}\frac{dn_1}{dm} + \varphi\frac{dn_2}{dm} + 1\right], \qquad (3.29)$$

where the second equation also uses the demand functions of equations (3.28). Notice that in this differentiation we have assumed that costs and prices are unchanged, assumptions that we will relax later on. φ now measures the sales of an importing foreign firm relative to local production by a multinational $\varphi = p_2 x_2 / p_m x_m$, and we will assume from now on that $\varphi \leqslant 1$. If the multinational and local firm have the same marginal costs, then $p_1 x_1 / p_m x_m = 1$, although we now allow for the possibility that these costs, sales and market shares differ.

Suppose first that there are no induced changes in the number of local firms. For a greenfield investment, in which multinational entry replaces an importer, $dn_2/dm = -1$ and $dn_1/dm = 0$. The term in square brackets becomes simply $1 - \varphi$, meaning that $dG_1/dm < 0$ (since $\sigma > 1$ and $\varphi \leqslant 1$). As a consequence, consumers gain from the entry of multinationals, essentially just because the price of the variety of the foreign firm that becomes multinational falls. However, in the case of M&A investment the multinational replaces a foreign importer and a local firm, so $dn_1/dm = dn_2/dm = -1$. Sales of the multinational are less than the total sales of the foreign and local firm it replaces, so $dG_1/dm > 0$.[6] Consumers suffer a welfare loss as the merger means loss of a variety.

---

[6] In (3.29) $|-p_1 x_1 / p_m x_m - \varphi + 1| < 0$ or $p_m x_m < p_1 x_1 + p_2 x_2$.

In addition to these direct effects, we expect to see an endogenous response in the number of local firms. This is the 'product market competition' effect, indicating the extent to which local firms may be crowded out of the industry by competition from multinationals. In models of this type firms make zero profits if they hit a particular level of sales (a level determined by technology and the price-cost mark-up and which we will denote $\bar{x}$), making positive profits if they exceed it and losses if they fall short.[7] Surviving firms' sales must therefore be the same before and after multinational entry. However, we also know that demand for each firm's output is given by equation (3.28) as $x_1 = p_1^{-\sigma} G_1^{\sigma-\eta} \bar{E}_1$. It therefore follows that national firms continue to break even only if G_1 remains constant. Turning the argument around, to hold $x_1 = \bar{x}$ the number of local firms must adjust to keep G_1 constant, meaning that, from (3.29) with $dn_2/dm = -1$,

$$\frac{dn_1}{dm} = (\varphi - 1)\frac{p_m x_m}{p_1 x_1} \leqslant 0. \tag{3.30}$$

This gives the extent to which local firms are crowded out of the industry. If $\varphi = 0$, then in the initial situation the foreign firm was not supplying any imports, so once it becomes multinational all of its domestic sales are additional supply to the market, crowding out a local firm one-to-one. At the other extreme, if $\varphi = 1$, then switching from importing to local production gives no increase in supply, and causes no crowding out. In the case of M&A the expression in (3.30) gives the net effect of FDI on local firms; that is, one firm is lost in the merger, but this raises profits inducing entry to return the local industry to zero profits.

What is the effect of multinational entry on host country welfare in this case? Providing some local firms remain in the industry, the price index is unchanged, and so therefore is consumer utility. While this provides the benchmark case, we immediately make some qualifications. The first is that this depends on all local firms being identical; if they are heterogeneous, then multinational entry will tend to force out the least efficient national firms; the remaining more efficient firms will survive at a lower level of the price index, bringing a consumer welfare gain. The second is that this result must be qualified if there are other distortions present in the host economy, such as an import tariff. For example, if imports were subject to a tariff, then multinational entry would also cause a loss of tariff revenue, this leading to a reduction in domestic welfare.[8] Thus, 'tariff-jumping' FDI that causes contraction of imports that are subject to a tariff is welfare reducing.

---

[7] Suppose that local firms sell only in the country 1 market, making zero profits when

$$(p - c_1)x_1 - (H + F)c_1 = [x_1/(\sigma - 1) - (H + F)]c_1 = 0,$$

where the second equation comes from using the pricing rule $p_1/(1 - 1/\sigma) = c_1$. This equation makes it clear that zero profits are attained only if firms sell output $x_1 = (H + F)(\sigma - 1)$.

[8] Tariff revenue enters the income term in the indirect utility function, (3.26).

What we learn from this analysis of the product market effects is then that HFDI is likely to lead to a crowding out of local production. In the central benchmark case the magnitude of crowding out is exactly that at which HFDI has zero welfare effect. To make a case for or against HFDI, it is therefore necessary to look to further effects, such as other market distortions, or reasons why crowding out is incomplete or selects a biased mix of firms.

3.4.2 Factor Demand

Many countries see inwards investment as a source of employment. Factor market effects are studied in more detail in the next chapter, but we can briefly outline some of the employment implications of HFDI here. Suppose that the shares of labour in the costs of country 1 local firms and multinationals are λ_1 and λ_m, respectively. These factor intensities might differ, for example, because the multinational is relatively highly dependent on imported inputs, or because it uses a different technology. Unit cost functions of the two types of firms are therefore

$$c_1 = w^{\lambda_1} I^{1-\lambda_1}, \qquad c_m = w^{\lambda_m} I^{1-\lambda_m}, \tag{3.31}$$

where w is the wage rate and I is the price of other inputs. Denoting country 1 employment in the sector by L, the value of labour demand from local firms' and multinationals' local operations is

$$wL = \lambda_1 n_1 c_1 (x_1 + H + F) + \lambda_m m c_m (x_m + F). \tag{3.32}$$

Holding prices and output levels per firm constant, the change in labour demand associated with entry of a multinational is

$$w\,dL = \lambda_1 c_1 (x_1 + H + F)\,dn_1 + \lambda_m c_m (x_m + F)\,dm. \tag{3.33}$$

However, the change in the number of local firms is determined by product market crowding, as given by equation (3.30), so

$$\frac{w}{p_m x_m} \frac{dL}{dm} = \lambda_1 (\varphi - 1) \left(\frac{c_1 (x_1 + H + F)}{p_1 x_1} \right) + \lambda_m \left(\frac{c_m (x_m + F)}{p_m x_m} \right). \tag{3.34}$$

The second term on the right-hand side of this expression gives the employment creation in multinationals. The first term is negative, giving loss of employment in local firms crowded out. Overall, the expression may be positive or negative. It is more likely to be positive the higher the share of costs and labour in the multinational's revenue, and the greater is φ, indicating that the FDI is largely replacing imports and therefore has a small crowding-out effect.

3.4.3   Linkages and Spillovers

Many arguments have been made suggesting that there are beneficial spillovers from multinational firms to various activities in the host economy. We review these arguments and the empirical evidence behind them in Chapter 7. One mechanism that has received particular prominence in the policy literature (see Chapters 8 and 10) is that there may be demand and supply linkages between MNEs and local firms. These linkages can generate a positive effect between multinational and domestic production which can offset or overturn the crowding-out argument made above. The story is that multinational entry can lead to improvements in local industries supplying intermediate inputs (backwards or demand linkages). These in turn may benefit other users of these inputs (forward or cost linkages), so that multinational entry may actually promote local production in the same sector, as well as related ones. There is then a complementarity between multinational and local firms; intermediate demand from multinationals expands the intermediate sector, which in turn benefits local firms in the downstream industry.

We can model this using the ingredients that we already have, and drawing on Markusen and Venables (1999) (see also Rodriguez-Clare 1996). Suppose that both local and multinational firms operate in a 'downstream' industry, using intermediate products from a local 'upstream industry'. The shares of these intermediates in the costs of local and multinational firms are μ_1 and μ_m, respectively, i.e. unit cost functions are $c_1 = w^{\lambda_1} I^{\mu_1}$ and $c_m = w^{\lambda_m} I^{\mu_m}$, where I is now the price index for locally produced intermediates. Exponents sum to less than or equal to unity and any other inputs have price one. To create the complementarity the upstream intermediate goods industry must have some form of increasing returns to scale. To capture this suppose that this industry is monopolistically competitive, and characterized by a simplified form of the Dixit–Stiglitz apparatus that we have already developed. Intermediate products are differentiated, and the price index for intermediates is a CES function similar to (3.23); this means that downstream firms benefit from having a wide range of specialized inputs available, and the extent to which they value this is captured by the elasticity of substitution between different varieties of intermediates, denoted $\theta > 1$. To make things as simple as possible, each variety is offered at price equal to 1 and can be produced only in quantity 1. Denoting the number of varieties of intermediate good that are produced by v, then the price (I) and quantity (J) indices for intermediates take the form,

$$I = v^{1/1-\theta}, \qquad J = v^{\theta/\theta-1}, \tag{3.35}$$

and expenditure on intermediates is $IJ = v$. These price and quantity indices are analogous to (3.23) and (3.22), where the term v enters because of the sum over the prices or quantities (each taking value unity) of the v varieties. Notice that increasing the size of the industry reduces the price index, $dI/dv < 0$, because $\theta > 1$.

Since intermediates are a proportion μ_1 of local firms' costs and a proportion μ_m of multinationals' costs, the value of intermediates used is

$$v = \mu_1 n_1 c_1 (x_1 + H + F) + \mu_m m c_m (x_m + F) \qquad (3.36)$$

(analogous to (3.32), noting that the price of each intermediate variety is unity). We are now in a position to capture the forward and backward linkages between the upstream and the downstream industry. Setting the wage at unity and using the intermediate price index (3.35) in the expressions for unit cost, we have $c_1 = v^{\mu_1/(1-\theta)}$ and $c_m = v^{\mu_m/(1-\theta)}$, and hence also $c_m = c_1^{\mu_m/\mu_1}$. Since $\theta > 1$, the cost equations say that expanding the number of upstream varieties lowers costs in the downstream industry—a forward or cost linkage. Using these expressions to eliminate v from equation (3.36) gives

$$(c_1)^{(1-\theta-\mu_1)/(1-\theta)} = \mu_1 n_1 (x_1 + H + F) + \mu_m m (x_m + F)(c_1)^{(\mu_m - \mu_1)/(1-\theta)}. \quad (3.37)$$

This equation, which we will refer to as the *cost equation*, summarizes the forward and backward linkage between the downstream and upstream industries. It is highly non-linear but, by inspection, it is clear that (at least in the simple case where $\mu_1 = \mu_m$) increasing downstream activity (such as an increase in n_1) reduces costs in the downstream industry. The mechanism is entry of upstream firms, this improving the range of upstream varieties on offer, lowering their price index, and meaning that the downstream industry is better served by its supply industry.

This relationship has to be linked to the product market effects studied earlier. Local firms in the downstream industry break even if they sell $\bar{x}$. Sales are given by the demand function, (3.28):

$$\bar{x} = p_1^{-\sigma} \bar{E} G_1^{\sigma-\eta} = p_1^{-\sigma} \bar{E} [n_1 p_1^{1-\sigma} + n_2 (p_2 \tau)^{1-\sigma} + m p_m^{1-\sigma}]^{(\sigma-\eta)/(1-\sigma)}$$

$$(3.38\,a)$$

or

$$\bar{x} = c_1^{-\sigma} \bar{E} \left(\frac{\sigma}{\sigma - 1} \right)^{-\eta} [n_1 c_1^{1-\sigma} + n_2 (c_2 \tau)^{1-\sigma} + m c_1^{(1-\sigma)\mu_m/\mu_1}]^{(\sigma-\eta)/(1-\sigma)}.$$

$$(3.38\,b)$$

Equation (3.38 b) replaces prices by costs, using the fact that they are always proportional to each other. We will refer to this as the *breakeven equation*; it captures product market competition, and says that increasing supply to the market (an increase in the term in square brackets, for example, an increase in m) is consistent with local firms maintaining zero profits only if they are accompanied by a reduction in costs, c_1. This relationship also gives a decreasing relationship between c_1 and n_1, but now reflecting product market competition.

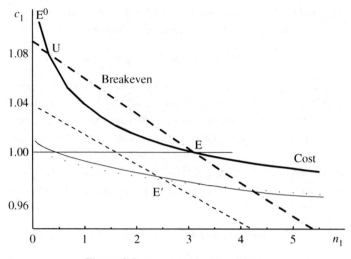

Figure 3.5.   Equilibria with linkages.

The two relationships (3.37) and (3.38) are illustrated by the bold lines in Figure 3.5, which has on the horizontal axis the number of host country national firms, n_1, and on the vertical the price they charge, c_1. The lines are constructed with the numbers of foreign firms held constant and, on the bold lines, the number of multinationals equal to zero, $m = 0$. The curve labelled *cost* traces out the effect of varying n_1 on costs and hence prices (equation (3.37)), and it is downward sloping because of the linkages we have outlined. The curve *breakeven* is the zero-profit condition for local firms (3.38): below it firms would make a profit, and above it they make a loss—large numbers of firms with high costs do not attain the levels of sales needed to break even.

The presence of increasing returns creates a potential for multiple equilibria and, as drawn, there are three possible equilibrium outcomes. At point E the local industry is relatively large. This large number of firms can survive because the large industry supports a large local supply industry, producing a wide range of specialist intermediate goods; this gives a low price index for intermediates, I, and hence low costs. Point U is also an equilibrium, although it is unstable, in the following sense. If n_1 were to increase slightly from this point, firms could survive only by charging a lower price (along the *breakeven* line). However, linkages are sufficiently strong that actual costs and prices fall by more than this, so profits become positive; the industry would then expand to point E. The third equilibrium is at point E^0, where no local firms are active. Since there are no multinationals either, there is no local supply industry, and it is not profitable for any local firm to enter. This is a low-level equilibrium trap in which a coordination failure means that it is not profitable for the downstream industry to develop given the absence of supply of intermediates:

and it is not profitable to produce intermediates, given the absence of local firms in the downstream industry.

Clearly, the configuration of equilibria depends on the positions of the curves in Figure 3.5. We now turn to analysing the way in which entry of multinationals shifts the curves, changing outcomes and possibly also changing the number of equilibria. Suppose that the economy is at initial equilibrium E. Multinational entry shifts both the curves, but we can see what happens by considering a borderline case in which entry leaves c_1 unchanged. Evidently, there is no change in costs if output in the upstream industry is unaffected, i.e. v is unchanged. From (3.37), this is true if

$$\mu_1 c_1 (x_1 + H + F)\, dn_1 + \mu_m c_m (x_m + F)\, dm = 0. \tag{3.39}$$

What about the breakeven line? If costs and prices are unchanged, then local firms continue to break even if the term in square brackets in (3.38) is unchanged, which is true if

$$p_1 x_1\, dn_1 + (1 - \varphi) p_m x_m\, dm = 0. \tag{3.40}$$

This is exactly as in our earlier analysis of product market effects (equation (3.30)), and corresponds to a leftwards shift of the breakeven line (since a positive dm requires a negative dn_1 if remaining local firms are to break even). Combining (3.39) and (3.40) gives the condition for multinational entry to leave costs and price unchanged:

$$0 = \mu_1 (\varphi - 1) \left(\frac{c_1 (x_1 + H + F)}{p_1 x_1} \right) + \mu_m \left(\frac{c_m (x_m + F)}{p_m x_m} \right). \tag{3.41}$$

Interpretation is straightforward. The left-hand side is the intermediate demand created directly by the multinational, while the right-hand side is that associated with the change in the number of local firms. In the benchmark case in which cost is unchanged these effects are equal; taking into account product market crowding out, multinational entry causes no additional backward linkage, so has no further effects. In terms of Figure 3.5 the new equilibrium is at some point along the horizontal line to the left of E.

If the right-hand side of (3.41) is larger than the left, then multinational entry will expand intermediate production, reducing the price index I, and will also reduce the price index of final goods, G_1, leading to an increase in welfare. This case is illustrated by the light lines of the figure, where the equilibrium is shifted to point E'. The expansion of upstream production has reduced cost and prices in the downstream industry, also raising welfare in the economy.

Expression (3.41) is clearly analogous to the change in labour demand given in equation (3.34), and is more likely to be positive the higher is use of domestic intermediate goods by the multinational, and the more the multinational activity replaces imports. When the expression is non-zero it changes production in the upstream industry, and this now has a feedback effect on the downstream, by changing the number of intermediate goods supplied and hence their price index and costs in the downstream industry.

One further interesting possibility arises from this example. Suppose that the initial equilibrium is at E^0 rather than at E. Then multinational entry, shifting the curves downwards to the equilibrium at E', has the effect of eliminating this equilibrium. Thus, multinational entry, which creates a demand for some locally produced intermediates, has the effect of destroying the low-level equilibrium. It creates an upstream industry, and hence also a local downstream industry. This then is a case of extreme complementarity between multinational investment and local firms in the same industry. In Chapter 2 we discussed some empirical examples of this phenomenon in Asia, and Chapter 7 will report further empirical work on the role of such forward and backward linkages. Policy implications of a reduced-form version of this model are pursued further in Chapter 10.

Finally, we should stress that the model outlined above simply illustrates how one possible spillover from multinational firms to domestic industry may work. Other mechanisms are also possible, such as direct technological externalities or technological spillovers arising through outsourcing supply of intermediates to local industry (see Pack and Saggi 2001). We return to these issues in the empirical discussion of Chapter 7.

3.5   Extensions

The results in this chapter have been derived under a number of very strong assumptions, and we now outline ways in which some of these can be relaxed. We focus on three assumptions. First, up to this point we have assumed that price-cost mark-ups are constant, so that changing the mix of firms has no effect on the intensity of competition in the market. Relaxing this assumption means that, given marginal costs, multinational entry can change the equilibrium prices charged by other firms. Second, we have (except in Section 3.4.3) worked with constant marginal costs for firms of each type. In particular, we have ignored the fact that larger firms may have lower marginal costs, for example, because their scale induces them to undertake more R&D, which in turn gives them lower marginal cost. And third, we have assumed not only that costs are constant, but also that they are uniform amongst types of firms. In reality, firms are heterogeneous, with different costs and different scales, and it is difficult to do empirical work that does not take this fact on board. In the following subsections we discuss relaxing each of these assumptions in turn.

3.5.1   Strategic Behaviour and Price-Cost Mark-ups

The standard Dixit–Stiglitz apparatus uses the assumption that firms all set a constant mark-up of price over marginal cost. As we saw above, this is based on the idea that there are sufficiently many firms in the industry for each to be able to ignore the effect of its actions on the industry aggregates—the 'large-group' assumption. The alternative is to model oligopolistic interaction, i.e. to look for the Nash equilibrium of a game between firms.

One possibility is that firms' strategic variables are quantities, so they compete as Cournot oligopolists. Under this hypothesis the price-cost mark-up is an increasing function of the share of the firm in the market, and the precise form of this relationship, derived in the appendix, is given by

$$\frac{1}{\varepsilon(s_i^k)} = \frac{1}{\sigma} + \left(\frac{1}{\eta} - \frac{1}{\sigma}\right)s_i^k. \tag{3.42}$$

The first term on the right-hand side, $1/\sigma$, measures each firm's monopoly power over its own variety of product. The second term derives from the fact that, given the sales of other firms, each firm also perceives the effect of its action on the industry aggregate quantity index, (3.22), and the magnitude of this effect depends on both the demand elasticities, and on the size of the firm in the market, as measured by its share, s_i^k. Thus, if $s_i^k = 0$, then $\varepsilon(s_i^k) = \sigma$, the elasticity of demand for a single variety, while if there is a monopolist, then $s_i^k = 1$ and $\varepsilon(s_i^k) = \eta$, the elasticity of demand for the industry output in aggregate. The analogous expression for price competition (Bertrand competition) takes the form $\varepsilon^B(s_i^k) = \sigma + (\eta - \sigma)s_i^k$ (see Appendix 3.2).

Analysis is now complicated by simultaneity between mark-ups and market shares. However, there is one important and simple case. Suppose that there is Cournot competition and products are perfect substitutes, so $\sigma \to \infty$. In this case $1/\varepsilon(s_i^k) = s_i^k/\eta$, so the profits made by firm k in market i are, from equation (3.4), $(s_i^k)^2 E_i/\eta$. The equations for profits of firms of different types are therefore (rewriting equations (3.10))

$$\left.\begin{aligned}
\Pi_1^M(n_1, n_2, m) &= s_1^2 E_1/\eta + s_2^2 E_2/\eta - (H + F)c_1 - Fc_2, \\
\Pi_2^M(n_1, n_2, m) &= s_2^2 E_2/\eta + s_1^2 E_1/\eta - (H + F)c_2 - Fc_1, \\
\Pi_1^N(n_1, n_2, m) &= s_1^2 E_1/\eta + (s_2\varphi_1)^2 E_2/\eta - (H + F)c_1, \\
\Pi_2^N(n_1, n_2, m) &= s_2^2 E_2/\eta + (s_1\varphi_2)^2 E_1/\eta - (H + F)c_2.
\end{aligned}\right\} \tag{3.43}$$

There is now a single price in each market, and firms with higher marginal costs have a narrower price-cost margin, smaller market share, and higher perceived demand elasticity, $\varepsilon(s_i^k) = \eta/s_i^k$. φ_i once again measures the market share effect of different marginal costs, and is a function of the cost difference and demand elasticity, although now it also depends on market share (see the appendix).

Qualitatively, these equations are very similar to equations (3.10), essentially with market share replaced by market share squared. Intuitively, the increased sensitivity of profits to market share comes from the fact that small market share is associated with small sales *and* low price-cost mark-up. The equations can be analysed in conjunction with the market share equations, (3.9), in a manner similar to the analysis of Section 3.2, and yielding qualitatively similar results. For full analysis of this case see Markusen and Venables (1998).

3.5.2   Varying Marginal Costs

The analysis has been greatly simplified by assuming that firms' marginal costs are constant. What happens if they are variable? One possibility is that they vary with the volume of production in the industry as a whole. We have already seen this in Section 3.4.3, where linkage effects mean that expanding the industry reduces costs. And in the next chapter we will see general equilibrium factor market effects, under which factor prices respond to factor demands. However, another possibility is simply that the technology is such that each firm's marginal costs are a (non-constant) function of the firm's own output.

Intuitively, this seems an important mechanism. Firm-level fixed costs may include choice variables such as the level of R&D expenditure, and (in the case of process R&D) this will yield a return in terms of lower marginal costs. (For product innovation see Baldwin and Ottaviano (2001).) It will then turn out that firms that are larger (for example, because of multinationality) will choose a higher level of R&D, and have lower marginal costs. Although we are not aware of any papers that model multinationals in this way, it is easy to see what its implications are. The size differences between single- and multi-plant firms that we have seen in this chapter become amplified, as multi-plant firms undertake more R&D and become even larger. However, despite this quantitative difference, qualitative outcomes are likely to be very much as in the analysis of this chapter. No new issues of principle are introduced by the fact that there is a functional relationship (internal to the firm) between the firm-level fixed cost and the level of marginal cost.

3.5.3   Cost Heterogeneity

We have drawn heavily on the assumption that firms all have the same technology and so, at equilibrium, can be grouped into types—national and multinational—within which they are identical. This is a powerful simplifying assumption, but is obviously at variance with reality. What happens if firms are in some way heterogeneous, such as having different technology? This is perhaps the most important extension to make, and work on it is now underway by Helpman et al. (2004).

The first point is that heterogeneity allows the coexistence of different firm types at free-entry equilibrium. Helpman et al. (2004) analyse a free-entry model in which all firms have the same fixed costs but different marginal costs. They show that if there are fixed costs to exporting, then low-productivity firms will not engage in any international activity at all, just serving their domestic market. If the fixed costs to becoming multinational exceed those for exporting, then, at equilibrium, only the most productive firms are multinational, and those with lower productivity levels serve the domestic market and export (are national firms in our terminology). The intuition is exactly as expected from the trade-off between fixed and marginal costs that we have studied in this chapter. The higher fixed costs of multinational activity can be recouped only if there are large sales volumes, and these are attained only if marginal costs are sufficiently low. A further implication of their model is that there will be more MNE activity, relative to exports, in industries in which there is a wide dispersion of productivity across firms.

The second point concerns the welfare economics of trade and multinational activity. Entry of relatively efficient multinational firms crowds out less efficient national firms, so raising average productivity in the industry and bringing welfare gain. Thus, whereas in our analysis of Section 3.4.1 the consumer price index G_1 remained constant when some local firms were crowded out (absent linkage effects), with heterogeneous firms we would expect this price index to fall, as it is high cost/price firms that exit. Consumers then gain, as multinational entry raises productivity, and reduces average costs and prices in the market.

3.6 Conclusions

The models of this chapter have investigated market seeking or HFDI, so have focused on interactions between firms in the product market. Clear hypotheses are derived about the characteristics of firms and industries that are likely to be engaged in this sort of FDI and about the types of countries between which this FDI is most likely. Investigation of the effects of FDI is less complete, but demonstrates the effects that the researcher needs to identify—market crowding out, employment effects and linkage effects—and shows how these can generate real income costs or benefits. The chapter also makes clear that there is considerable scope for further research, in particular introducing heterogeneity between firms, and allowing multinationals to compete on more fronts, for example, through R&D as well as just through price.

Throughout this chapter we maintained the assumption that multinationals exported headquarters' services to the affiliate, while the affiliate undertook all stages of the production process for local supply. In reality, of course, a wider range of activities than just headquarters may remain in the home country; for example, all components may be produced in the home country and then exported for assembly in the host. In the next chapter we turn to looking at ways in which the production process may be split between countries. Fundamentally, however, the next chapter looks at cases in which the affiliate supplies not just the local market (national or regional) but also exports its output to the rest of the world, including back to the home country.

Appendix 3.1. Parameters Underlying Figures

Figure 3.1: $E_1 = E_2 = 50$; $\sigma = 5$, $c_1 = 1$; $c_2 = 1$; $F = 1.5$; $H = 0.3$.
Figure 3.2: $E_1 = E_2 = 50$; $\sigma = 5$, $c_1 = 1$; $c_2 = 1$; $F = 1.5$; $H = 0.3$.
Figure 3.3: $\sigma = 5$, $c_1 = 1$; $c_2 = 1$; $F = 2.0$; $H = 0.3$.
Figure 3.4: $\sigma = 5$, $c_1 = 1$; $c_2 = 1$; $F = 1.0$; $H = 0.3$.
Figure 3.5: $\sigma = 5$, $\theta = 8$, $\eta = 2$, $\mu_1 = \mu_m = 0.3$, $\bar{E} = 4.4$.

Appendix 3.2. Section 3.5.1

Derivation of perceived elasticity of demand, equation (3.42). From equation (3.27), the inverse demand curve can be written as

$$p_i^k = (x_i^k)^{-1/\sigma} X_i^{(\eta-\sigma)/\eta\sigma} (\bar{E}_i)^{1/\eta}.$$

Logarithmically differentiating and using $\hat{\ }$ to denote a proportional change gives

$$\hat{p}_i^k = -\hat{x}_i^k/\sigma + \hat{X}_i(\eta - \sigma)/\eta\sigma.$$

Differentiating the quantity index with respect to a proportional change in the quantity of a single variety and using the demand function gives $\hat{X}_i = s_i^k \hat{x}_i^k$. Together, these equations give the elasticity (3.42). The Bertrand elasticity can be found analogously by logarithmically differentiating demand function

$$x_i^k = (p_i^k)^{-\sigma} G_i^{\sigma-\eta} \bar{E}_i,$$

where a single price and quantity changes.

   In the homogenous product Cournot model of equations (3.43), there is a single price in each market and the equality of price to marginal revenue (in market 2, for example) takes the form

$$p_2(1 - s_2\varphi_1/\eta) = c_1\tau_1, \qquad p_2(1 - s_2/\eta) = c_2.$$

These relationships implicitly define the equilibrium value of φ_1 given by

$$s_j\varphi_i = s_j(c_i\tau/c_j) + \eta(1 - c_i\tau/c_j)$$

rather than by $\varphi_i = (c_j\tau/c_i)^{1-\sigma}$.

4

Vertical Foreign Direct Investment: Input Costs and Factor Prices

We saw in Chapters 1 and 2 that there are increasing volumes of 'North–South' FDI. Some of this takes place because firms have geographically fragmented their production, outsourcing (geographically if not organizationally) parts of the production process. These stages may be the production of components or stages of the manufacturing process, and are also increasingly service activities—the outsourcing of customer support services, call centres and information technology support. The main force driving these changes is very simple; firms move different stages of the production process to countries with lower costs. This chapter presents a systematic analysis of the determinants of this production fragmentation, and of some of its effects. (For previous analyses of fragmentation see Jones (2000) and articles in Arndt and Kierzkowski (2001).)

Firms fragment production as it enables them to benefit from lower production costs, but other costs are incurred—the disintegration costs discussed in Chapter 2. The first task of this chapter is to investigate the trade-off between these forces (Section 4.1). Using a partial equilibrium framework we illustrate the different forms that the international organization of multi-stage production can take, depending on factor price differences and on these disintegration costs. For some values of these variables there is no FDI; for other values there is HFDI, and, for yet others, VFDI. As the organization of production changes, so too does the volume of trade. It is quite possible that a steady reduction in trade and disintegration costs may bring intervals in which trade volumes fall as well as intervals in which they rise; where HFDI occurs investment is a substitute for trade, and where VFDI occurs it is a complement.

The second task of the chapter is to investigate the effects of VFDI. There are economic benefits from this sort of investment, but who are the recipients of these benefits? Working in partial equilibrium enables us to outline possibilities, showing how gains may be divided between consumers, factors of production in the home country, and factors of production in the host (Section 4.2). We also discuss the possibility that international investment flows may be associated with 'wage gradients'—the wage declining as we move from central economic regions to peripheral ones—and show how trade and disintegration costs determine maximum wage rates that remote locations can pay.

To go beyond outlining possibilities requires a full general equilibrium model, and this is constructed in Section 4.3. The basic model is a simplified version of that of Helpman (1984), which adds VFDI to a Heckscher–Ohlin model of international trade. There are two countries, two factors of production, and initially two tradeable goods. Vertical FDI creates a third tradeable good—the components used in production of one of the final goods—and fragmentation of production is the way in which this additional trading possibility is used. This model suggests that VFDI will tend to lead to factor price equalization across countries. In Section 4.4 we extend these results (in the spirit of work by Feenstra and Hanson (1996)) to show that other outcomes are possible. A full analysis of the factor price effects of VFDI requires careful specification of the alternative uses to which the factors would have been put in the absence of the investment.

Throughout this chapter we work with models of perfect competition and constant returns to scale, in which there is no natural concept of a firm. This may seem odd for a book about multinationals, but the value of these assumptions are that they allow us to focus on the way in which cost differences shape production. The models in this chapter apply not just to multinational activity, since the outsourcing described could be undertaken through arm's-length relationships with independent firms. The firm's decision to conduct business internally or with independent local firms is our topic in Chapter 5.

4.1 Cost-Minimizing Locations

When will a firm choose to split its production process between several locations and make a vertical investment (VFDI)? To answer this question we dispense with increasing returns to scale and look simply at the cost-minimizing locations of a firm in which production involves two distinct stages, c and a, referring to component production and assembly, respectively. Adding more inputs and more stages of production is conceptually straightforward, although this would make exposition more cumbersome. We suppose that both stages use two primary inputs, labour and capital, with country i prices w_i and r_i. The inputs are probably best thought of as unskilled labour and skilled labour (i.e. human capital abundant labour), but we stick with the traditional terminology of trade theory, referring to labour and capital.

Both component production and assembly operate with constant returns to scale, so the costs of primary factors used at each stage to eventually produce one unit of final output can be described by unit cost functions $c(w_i, r_i)$ and $a(w_i, r_i)$. Production of a unit of final output involves a fixed number of components (which we can set equal to 1), so there is no possibility of technical substitution between primary factors and components. This means that the two elements enter total costs additively. Trade costs are incurred on shipping final products, and trade or disintegration costs are incurred on shipping components. We write the cost of a unit of output delivered to country k, given that the components are produced in country i and the final assembly takes place in country j, as B_{ijk}:

$$B_{ijk} = [c(w_i, r_i)\tau_{ij}^c + a(w_j, r_j)]\tau_{jk}^a. \tag{4.1}$$

τ_{ij}^c and τ_{ij}^a are the ad valorem trade cost factors for upstream and downstream products, respectively, with $\tau_{ii}^c = \tau_{ii}^a = 1$ and, for $i \neq j$, $\tau_{ij}^c, \tau_{ij}^a \geqslant 1$.[1] To interpret this, suppose that components are produced in country 1, assembled in 2 and then shipped back to 1 for consumption (B_{121}). The cost of component production in 1 is $c(w_1, r_1)$, and this is marked up by τ_{12}^c, the costs of shipping to 2 or the disintegration cost. Additional primary factor input for assembly in 2 costs $a(w_2, r_2)$. If the product is shipped back to country 1 for final consumption, then further trade costs τ_{21}^a are incurred on the whole product. Notice that components incur trade costs twice if they are produced in one country, exported for assembly, and then exported again embodied in the final good.

Under what circumstances will the firm fragment production, producing in two different locations, $i \neq j$? The remainder of this section addresses this question in a simple partial equilibrium framework in which factor prices are held constant. General equilibrium issues will be addressed in Section 4.3.

Trade costs and disintegration costs

There are two countries, 1 and 2, and country 1 has higher wage—it is the 'Northern' economy. Trade costs are the same in both directions ($\tau_{ij} = \tau_{ji}$) and can be written τ^c and τ^a, dropping the subscripts. We anchor discussion by making two assumptions about the pattern of comparative advantage in the product. The first is that country 1 has a comparative advantage in the product as a whole; that is, if the two stages have to be done in the same location ($\tau^c = \infty$) and final product trade is free ($\tau^a = 1$), then country 1 is the cheaper place to produce. The second is that assembly is labour intensive, so that if fragmentation occurs, it is assembly that moves to country 2, while component production stays in 1. The other case, where components are labour intensive, is covered in the appendix. With this reference point, how do the location of production and the pattern of trade depend on τ^c and τ^a?

Figure 4.1 illustrates outcomes. The horizontal axis is the shipping cost for components (or disintegration cost) τ^c, and the vertical axis is the trade cost for final assembled products, τ^a. The zones correspond to different production patterns, and

---

[1] The trade costs are modelled as ad valorem, but there would be no qualitative difference if they were instead specific, so $B_{ijk} = c(w_i, r_i) + \tau_{ij}^c + a(w_j, r_j) + \tau_{jk}^a$.

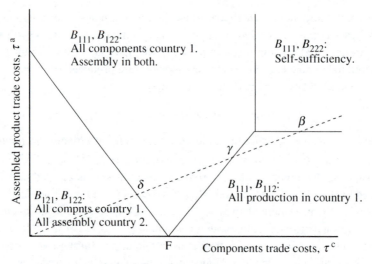

Figure 4.1. Assembly labour intensive; country 1 high wage.

in each we give the sourcing of products for final consumption in market 1, B_{ij1}, and for final consumption in market 2, B_{ij2}. For example, B_{211} indicates that consumption for market 1 is met by component production in country 2 and final assembly in country 1.

The lower right regime, $\{B_{111}, B_{112}\}$, corresponds to an initial position in which it is relatively cheap to trade in the assembled product but disintegration costs are sufficiently high that both stages of production take place at the same location. In line with assumed comparative advantage, the good is produced entirely in country 1. Of course, if there were also high barriers to trade in the assembled product, then no trade at all would occur, giving the upper right region $\{B_{111}, B_{222}\}$, in which both countries are self-sufficient in the product. The line dividing these cases is the locus of trade costs at which country 2 can be supplied at the same cost from either location, $B_{112} = B_{222}$. Using equation (4.1), this is simply

$$[c(w_1, r_1) + a(w_1, r_1)]\tau^a = [c(w_2, r_2) + a(w_2, r_2)]. \tag{4.2}$$

Factor prices are fixed (until Section 4.3), so the borderline between these cases is just the fixed value of τ^a illustrated by the horizontal line.

The bottom left region is where trade costs on both components and assembled products are low enough that fragmentation occurs, with all component production taking place in country 1 and all assembly in country 2, $\{B_{121}, B_{122}\}$. As assembly moves to the low-wage country (country 2) so the mode of supplying both countries changes, and at point F on the figure two things happen. Country 1 is now supplied by products assembled in 2 rather than in 1, so $B_{121} = B_{111}$, i.e.

$$[c(w_1, r_1)\tau^c + a(w_2, r_2)]\tau^a = [c(w_1, r_1) + a(w_1, r_1)]. \tag{4.3}$$

Similarly, it becomes profitable to supply country 2 with products assembled in 2 rather than in 1, so $B_{122} = B_{112}$, i.e.

$$[c(w_1, r_1)\tau^c + a(w_2, r_2)] = [c(w_1, r_1) + a(w_1, r_1)]\tau^a. \tag{4.4}$$

When $\tau^a = 1$ these two relationships are identical, giving the value of τ^c that is marked by point F. For $\tau^a > 1$, they are different relationships, corresponding, respectively, to the downwards and upwards sloping lines in Figure 4.1. In the upper central area above these lines the pattern of production is that all components are produced in country 1, but τ^a is large enough for assembly to take place in the same location as consumption, giving regime $\{B_{111}, B_{122}\}$.

This analysis is based entirely on cost-minimizing location decisions in a world of constant returns to scale and perfect competition. It illustrates however, that both VFDI and HFDI can arise. While the lower left corner of the figure illustrates VFDI, the upper central area is observationally equivalent to HFDI: all component production is occurring in country 1, and assembly is taking place in the country of final consumption.

To complete this simple analysis we illustrate the value of trade, and also summarize, in Figure 4.2, information on the location of production. The horizontal axis of this figure gives trade costs corresponding to the dashed line in Figure 4.1, i.e. variation in both τ^a and τ^c along this ray. For illustrative purposes the figure assumes that country 1 consumes two units of the final product and country 2 one unit, regardless of price. The solid lines give value added in production in each country. When trade costs are high both countries are self-sufficient and, given levels of consumption, country 1 has more production than country 2. Reducing trade costs to point β causes all production to concentrate in country 1, the country with comparative advantage in the product as a whole. Reducing trade costs further, at point γ assembly for market 2 moves to country 2, and finally full fragmentation occurs (point δ), with value added in each country as illustrated. In each step to the left along this diagram the total value of resources used in the industry (the sum of the two solid lines) diminishes, as reducing trade costs promotes efficiency in the world location of production. However, we see non-monotonic behaviour of value added in each country. Initial trade liberalization causes concentration of production in country 1 and loss of production in 2, and this is reversed with further liberalization. Essentially, the changing pattern of trade costs means that at first only country 1's comparative advantage (in the product as a whole) can be exploited, while at lower costs country 2's comparative advantage (just in assembly) comes into play.

The dashed line gives the corresponding value of trade. Notice that as HFDI starts (point γ) so the value of trade falls: country 2 imports components rather than fully finished products and investment is a substitute for trade. However, where VFDI commences (point δ) the value of trade increases, and exceeds world value added

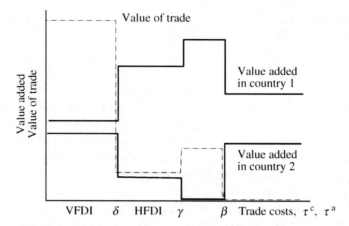

Figure 4.2. Assembly labour intensive; country 1 high wage.

in production of the good. VFDI is complementary with trade because some components are traded twice—shipped from country 1 to country 2, and then returned to country 1 embodied in final output. (And trade is measured gross, not by value added, so includes this type of double counting.)

The general points that come from this analysis are then that both production and trade are non-monotonically related to trade costs. In this example, reductions in trade costs initially 'deindustrialize' country 2, as all production of the product moves to country 1. However, further reductions in trade costs enable production to relocate in line with the factor intensities of each stage of the production process; this expands country 2 production as it comes to undertake all assembly. Similarly with trade volumes. Falling trade costs over some ranges increase trade volumes, but it is also possible that, in some range, lower trade costs are associated with a reduction in trade volumes. The increases in trade volumes occur as lower trade costs enable production to move in line with comparative advantage, either in the product as a whole (point β) or in particular parts of the production process (VFDI at point δ). The reduction in trade volumes (point γ) occurs as HFDI substitutes for trade, in line with the analysis of the preceding chapter.

4.2   Fragmentation and Factor Prices

The focus in the preceding section was on the implications of trade and disintegration costs for the organization of production. We now switch emphasis to the effects of VFDI, while remaining in this simple partial equilibrium framework.

In the previous chapter we organized effects into three broad headings: product market, factor market and spillover. For VFDI we will say very little about the product market. Essentially, we assume that the VFDI brings new activities, not

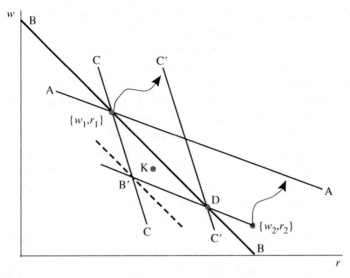

Figure 4.3. Iso-cost lines. $p = a(w_1, r_1) + c(w_1, r_1)$; BB: $p = a(w, r) + c(w, r)$; AA: $p = a(w, r) + c(w_1, r_1)$; CC: $p = a(w_1, r_1) + c(w, r)$; C'C': $p = a(w_2, r_2) + c(w, r)$.

competing with existing firms, and that the output is sold in an integrated world market or exported back to the parent, rather than just being sold in the local market. Spillover arguments may be important as there may be complementarities with other domestic activities. These may be similar to those discussed in Chapter 3, and we discuss them further in Chapter 7. Our emphasis here is just on the factor market. What are the implications of VFDI for factor demands and hence for factor prices?

A first pass at this question can be made by using the same apparatus as in the preceding section, but with attention now turned to factor prices rather than trade costs and disintegration costs. Thus, Figure 4.3 has factor prices, w and r, on the axes, rather than trade costs. The lines on the figure are iso-cost curves for production of one unit of the good; line BB is for integrated production; line AA is for assembly, given component costs; and line CC is for components, given assembly costs. For simplicity these are constructed for fixed coefficient technologies, hence giving straight lines.

Suppose that initially fragmentation is impossible, and that the industry operates only in country 1, in which factor prices are given at $\{w_1, r_1\}$. The world price is equal to country 1 unit costs, so $p = [c(w_1, r_1) + a(w_1, r_1)]$. The iso-cost line BB is the locus of factor prices $\{w, r\}$ at which integrated production has costs equal to p; it has slope equal to the ratio of capital to labour on integrated production. If there are no trade costs on final products, $\tau^a = 1$, then all other countries' factor prices must lie on or above line BB; otherwise it would be profitable to start up production in a lower-cost country.

Now suppose that fragmentation is possible, and let there be no disintegration costs, $\tau^c = 1$. Then two new iso-cost lines become relevant. Line AA is the locus of factor prices below which assembly is profitable, given that the goods price stays at p and component production remains in country 1 at factor prices $\{w_1, r_1\}$. Its gradient is the capital–labour ratio in assembly, and we draw it for the case of assembly being labour intensive. Line CC is the analogous line for component production, given that assembly continues to take place at factor prices $\{w_1, r_1\}$ and the good's price stays at p. The equations defining the lines are given in the figure.

Assume that component production continues to take place in country 1 and ask, will assembly relocate? And if so, what are the consequences for factor prices? This fragmentation will occur if some country has factor prices below AA (so assembly is profitable) but above BB (it is not profitable for the integrated production to move). As drawn, country 2 with factor prices $\{w_2, r_2\}$ lies in this region.

If fragmentation occurs and assembly moves to country 2, what happens to prices and profitability in the industry? There are three possibilities, although in our partial equilibrium setting we cannot say what combination of them will actually occur. The first possibility is that the movement of assembly to country 2 bids up factor prices there, as illustrated by the arrow from $\{w_2, r_2\}$. If the output price p and factor prices $\{w_1, r_1\}$ are unchanged, then $\{w_2, r_2\}$ will be bid up to the line AA (so the new unit cost equals the initial price). However, the arrow's squiggliness indicates the fact that we do not know the exact combination of changes in w_2 and r_2, an ambiguity that we show how to resolve in Section 4.3. Notice that there is a real economic gain from fragmentation; the allocative efficiency of world production has increased, and in this case the gains are captured by factors of production in the lower-wage country.

The second possibility is that benefits accrue to factors of production in country 1. Along $C'C'$ component production breaks even at initial price p and with the unit cost of assembly equal to $a(w_2, r_2)$. (To see this it may be helpful to note that $a(w_2, r_2) = a(w_D, r_D)$, where w_D, r_D are factor prices at point D. The equation of $C'C'$ is therefore also $p = a(w_D, r_D) + c(w, r)$.) Factor prices in country 1 can therefore change to lie on $C'C'$, as indicated by the arrow through $\{w_1, r_1\}$. In this case the efficiency gain from fragmentation is captured by factors in the high-wage country, although this partial equilibrium framework does not contain enough information to predict how this is divided between w_1 and r_1.

The third possibility is that the output price falls, given factor prices in each country. The new price would then be $p' = a(w_2, r_2) + c(w_1, r_1)$, $p' < p$. The dashed line through B' parallel to BB is the locus of factor prices at which integrated production could compete with fragmented production at these factor prices $\{w_2, r_2\}$ and $\{w_1, r_1\}$. In this case the efficiency gains are passed on to consumers of the product.

While Figure 4.3 delineates possibilities, the exact outcome depends on the full general equilibrium, to be looked at in Section 4.3. One further point can, however, be made from Figure 4.3. It is often suggested that the alternative to a country losing some stages of production (fragmentation) is that it loses the whole of the activity to foreign competition. We can see this by considering another country, k. This country initially has factor prices lying above BB. However, for some exogenous reason they change, moving to the point marked K in the figure. Following this change, but without fragmentation, country k would acquire the entire industry (since costs are below line BB). However, with fragmentation, if the price falls to $p' = a(w_2, r_2) + c(w_1, r_1)$, then it acquires none of it, since K lies above the new iso-cost lines. The point is that fragmentation allows country 1 to retain more of the industry than it otherwise would have. It is only by moving assembly to country 2 that country 1 is able to retain any presence in the industry whatsoever, given the incipient competition from country k.

Wage gradients

A common feature of VFDI, at least for some products, is its propensity to locate close to large centres of economic activity, for example, Mexico and Eastern Europe serving the US and Western Europe, respectively. This is a natural consequence of the role of trade costs, and also depends on levels of wages in these countries. Indeed, the analysis that we have developed suggests a 'wage gradient' from central to more peripheral regions.

For example, consider the point at which it is just worthwhile for a low-wage country to start importing components and undertaking assembly for export to a high-wage country. In terms of Figure 4.2 this is at a point such as δ on the boundary where $B_{121} = B_{111}$, so equation (4.3) holds:

$$[c(w_1, r_1)\tau^c + a(w_2, r_2)]\tau^a = [c(w_1, r_1) + a(w_1, r_1)]. \tag{4.5}$$

We now read this equation in the following way. If trade costs and factor prices w_1, r_1, r_2 are exogenous, then the relationship implicitly defines w_2 as a function of these factor prices and trade costs.

Now consider the following thought experiment. Suppose that there are many different countries at varying distances from a large central location (country 1, 'North'), and more remote locations have higher costs of trading with the centre, τ^c and τ^a. How low must wages be in each of these economies if they are to be just at the margin of hosting VFDI? The simplest thought experiment is to hold factor prices in country 1 constant, and also hold $r_2 = r_1$ constant (think of this as internationally mobile capital). Differentiating (4.5) with respect to transport costs and country 2 wages, we can derive a 'wage gradient', saying how wages must fall to compensate for the costs of distance. It takes the form

$$\frac{\mathrm{d}w_2}{w_2} = -\frac{1}{\lambda}\left[\frac{1}{\alpha}\frac{\mathrm{d}\tau^{\mathrm{a}}}{\tau^{\mathrm{a}}} + \frac{1-\alpha}{\alpha}\frac{\mathrm{d}\tau^{\mathrm{c}}}{\tau^{\mathrm{c}}}\right], \qquad (4.6)$$

where α is the share of assembly in the total cost of production $\alpha \equiv a(w_j, r_j)/B_{ijk}$ (and the share of components is $1 - \alpha = c(w_i, r_i)\tau^{\mathrm{c}}/B_{ijk}$), and λ is the share of labour in the value added of assembly, $\lambda \equiv (\partial a(w_j, r_j)/\partial w_j)(w_j/a(w_j, r_j))$.

The main point about this equation is that, if assembly is to be profitable, quite small trade costs must be compensated for by relatively steep wage gradients. For example, if the share of assembly in total costs and the share of labour in assembly (α and λ, respectively) both take value 1/2, then a 10% increase in both trade costs (e.g. going from free trade where they take value unity to value 1.1) is associated with a 60% reduction in the critical wage. Intuitively, there are two reasons why the required wage reduction is so large. The first is that trade costs squeeze value added from two sides. Trade costs on final assembled products reduce the price that local producers receive for the assembled product, and trade costs on components increase the prices of their inputs. The second is that immobile factors have to absorb all of this squeeze on value added. If r_2 is the price of an internationally mobile factor, such as capital, then it is likely to be at least as high in a developing country as in an advanced country, i.e. $r_2 \geqslant r_1$. The wage, w_2, then absorbs the reduction in value added, and the reduction will have to be larger the smaller is the share of labour in value added, this explaining the $1/\lambda$ term in the equation.

Equations (4.5) and (4.6) are not, of course, full equilibrium relationships, since they merely describe wages at which VFDI becomes possible. Economies at remote locations may have a higher wage rate than the one satisfying these equations, but then such economies will not become hosts for VFDI. If wage rates are lower than those from the equations, then it is strictly profitable to undertake VFDI, this tending to bid up wages in such economies. Furthermore, VFDI can occur in many sectors, each with different transport costs and different technologies (including parameters α and λ), and hence with different wage gradients. These gradients will be relatively flat for products with low transport costs and a high share of labour in costs, suggesting (given a distribution of wage rates across countries) that these products are the ones most likely to engage in VFDI.

Further analysis of these possibilities requires a full general equilibrium model in which both factor prices and goods' prices are endogenously determined. Venables and Limao (2002) construct such a model (although focusing on trade rather than FDI), and show how production patterns are determined by the interactions of goods' factor intensities and goods' transport intensities with countries' factor endowments and transport costs.

4.3 Fragmentation in General Equilibrium

To make further progress we need to move to a general equilibrium setting, in which goods and factor prices, as well as the location of production, are made endogenous. The standard framework for doing this is a two-country, two-good, two-factor model. Helpman (1984, 1985) and Helpman and Krugman (1985) showed how the Heckscher–Ohlin model of trade could be extended to include FDI, and in this section we set out a version of their analysis. We ask two questions. Under what circumstances does FDI occur? And what is the effect of FDI on factor prices in the host and the home country? Endogenizing factor prices makes the analysis richer in some ways but, in order to remain tractable, simplifications need to be made in other directions. The most crucial one is to assume from now on that final products are all completely freely traded ($\tau^{a} = 1$), and that components are either not traded at all ($\tau^{c} = 4$) or are perfectly freely traded ($\tau^{c} = 1$).

The two economies have endowments of labour and capital denoted L_1, K_1, L_2, K_2. Manufacturing has production as described above, and we shall refer to it as the M-sector. Furthermore, we will assume that the production function in this sector has fixed factor intensities, an assumption that will sometimes simplify exposition but is not necessary for the main results. Factor usages in this sector in each country are denoted L_1^{M}, K_1^{M}, L_2^{M}, K_2^{M}. The rest of the economy, the Y-sector, we take to be the numeraire. It employs the entire endowment, minus factors employed in the M-sector, so output levels in this sector and market clearing factor prices are given by

$$
\left.
\begin{aligned}
Y_i &= Y(L_i - L_i^{M}, K_i - K_i^{M}), \\
w_i &= \frac{\partial Y(L_i - L_i^{M}, K_i - K_i^{M})}{\partial L_i}, \\
r_i &= \frac{\partial Y(L_i - L_i^{M}, K_i - K_i^{M})}{\partial K_i}.
\end{aligned}
\right\}
\tag{4.7}
$$

Incomes in each country are the sum of the returns to the two factors, $w_i L_i + r_i K_i$, $i = 1, 2$.

Turning to the demand side, factor income is received by consumers with identical homothetic preferences who demand the M and Y goods. Since goods' prices are the same in both countries (both final products are freely traded), these assumptions ensure that both countries consume the two goods in the same proportions; net trades therefore arise because of international differences on the supply side, not in demand.

Before looking at fragmentation, we first set out the benchmark case where fragmentation is impossible. The equilibrium of the world economy can be illustrated by using a device that was employed by Dixit and Norman (1980), although this has antecedents (see Krugman (1995) for a discussion). This consists of finding

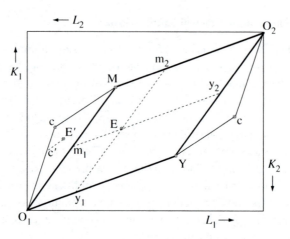

Figure 4.4. Production and FPE.

the 'integrated equilibrium' of the world economy, and then working back to see what happens when this integrated economy is split into countries. The analysis utilizes a world box diagram to illustrate factor supply and factor demands, and this is illustrated in Figure 4.4. The dimensions of the box are the *world* endowment of labour (horizontal) and capital (vertical), and the endowments of countries 1 and 2 are measured from origins O_1 and O_2, respectively. A point such as E represents the division of the world endowment between countries, with country 1's endowments measured on the coordinate system from O_1 and country 2's from O_2. Thus, at point E, country 1 is somewhat smaller than country 2, and more capital abundant, since E lies above the main diagonal of the box.

The first step of the argument is to suppose that the world constitutes a single integrated economy, with no barriers to trade in goods or factors. Given the technologies of goods M and Y and the preferences of consumers, the general equilibrium can be found: goods' prices, factor prices, techniques of production and quantities produced and consumed. In particular, it is possible to derive the quantities of capital and labour used in production of each of the goods; the vector O_1M gives the quantities of capital and labour used in the M-industry, and O_1Y gives the corresponding quantities used in the Y-industry. Since there is full employment of both factors at equilibrium, these vectors sum to the world endowment (hence the parallelogram O_1MO_2Y). As illustrated, the M-industry is the more capital intensive.

Now consider dividing the world into two countries that can trade goods freely, but have distinct and non-tradeable endowments, represented by a point such as E. Can free trade reproduce the integrated equilibrium? Providing the endowment point E lies inside the parallelogram O_1MO_2Y the answer is yes. Country 1 uses endowment vector O_1m_1 in the M-industry and endowment vector O_1y_1 in the Y-industry, these two vectors adding up to point E. Correspondingly, country 2 uses O_2m_2 and O_2y_2 in each sector. These input quantities secure full employment of both factors in both countries and produce exactly as much output of each good as did the integrated equilibrium; no prices need change.

Different endowments in the parallelogram are associated with different structures of production in each country, but the same levels of world output. Consider the effects of relocating some of country 2's labour endowment to country 1. Point E tracks horizontally to the right, and we see that country 1's employment in the labour-intensive industry expands (O_1y_1) and in capital-intensive (M) industry contracts (O_1m_1)—a proposition known to trade theorists as a Rybczynski effect. Opposite changes occur in country 2, so world employment and output levels in each sector remain unchanged.

The parallelogram O_1MO_2Y is known as the factor price equalization set (FPE set), because within the set both countries have the same factor prices (those of the integrated equilibrium), so $w_1 = w_2$, $r_1 = r_2$. What happens if the endowment point lies outside this set? To the northwest, country 1 uses some of its endowment in manufacturing, but some is left over (recall that manufacturing has fixed coefficients), this residual being very capital abundant with $(K_1 - K_1^M)/(L_1 - L_1^M)$ greater than the gradient of O_1M and much greater than the gradient of O_1Y. It is used in Y production, but Y-sector producers will choose a technique this capital intensive only if the wage–rental ratio w_1/r_1 is higher than at the integrated equilibrium. As expected then, outside the FPE set the more capital abundant country has the higher wage–rental ratio.

Fragmentation

What is the effect of allowing M production to fragment into components and assembly? The total factor usage in manufacturing (at the integrated equilibrium) is vector O_1M, and we now suppose that this is made up of two distinct elements. One is vector O_1c, factor usage in component production, and the other is vector cM, assembly. Since there are, by assumption, no disintegration costs, these vectors sum exactly to O_1M. They are illustrated in Figure 4.4 for a configuration in which component production is the more-capital-intensive stage; assembly, while labour intensive relative to components, is capital intensive relative to Y production. We look at an alternative configuration in Section 4.4.

Is there any incentive to fragment production, operating the two stages in different countries? Inside the FPE set the answer is evidently no; since there are no factor price differences between countries, there is no incentive to split production. However, outside the FPE set there are international differences in factor prices, this creating the incentive to fragment. To see what happens we use the same analytical trick as before, constructing the integrated equilibrium, now allowing for the possibility of fragmentation. The effect of allowing fragmentation is to increase the area of the FPE set to the shape O_1cMO_2cY. This set is constructed by summing the vectors of factor usage in the integrated equilibrium, just as was the original FPE set. Now, however, there are three activities, and their input vectors (O_1c, cM and O_1Y) are ordered according to their factor intensity at the integrated equilibrium factor prices.

Consider point E'. This is outside the original FPE set O_1MO_2Y, but is inside the new enlarged FPE set; country 1 and country 2 can now fully employ their factor endowments at the integrated equilibrium factor prices because of the extra opportunities created by fragmentation. For example, if country 1 employs vector O_1c' of its endowment in component production and the remainder, vector $c'E'$, in assembly, then the integrated equilibrium can be reproduced. Country 2 undertakes all of Y production, as well as some assembly and a small amount of component production. Notice, however, that the precise production pattern is now indeterminate. There are infinitely many combinations of the three activities that fully employ both countries' endowments at the integrated equilibrium factor prices. Helpman (1984, 1985) assumed that, other things being equal, it would be advantageous to locate assembly and component production in the same place. The outcome is then the one that we have illustrated (by point c') as this minimizes the amount of manufacturing that is disintegrated.

In summary then, this analysis tells us several things. First, VFDI occurs only if endowments are sufficiently different; inside the original FPE set there is no reason to fragment, and it occurs only outside this set. Second, in the enlarged FPE set VFDI occurs, and its effect is to eliminate international factor price differences. Wage–rental ratios move in opposite directions, so at point E' in Figure 4.4, FDI causes the wage–rental ratio in country 1 to fall and that of country 2 to rise.

However, the analysis is somewhat restrictive in its scope. It assumes that there are no trade or disintegration costs; we saw in Section 4.2 how important these can be (see also Norman and Venables (1995) for a general equilibrium analysis). It also focuses almost exclusively on the FPE sets, with and without FDI. We now turn to looking in more detail at what happens outside these areas.

4.4 Factor Price Convergence?

The formation of the North American Free Trade Area in 1994 was associated with a substantial increase in FDI inflows into Mexico. Much of this is vertical; for example, frames for automobile seats being made in the US, shipped to Mexico for covers to be stitched on, and then shipped back to the US for assembly in the automobile. At the same time as this surge in FDI was occurring there was a marked increase in the skill premium (the ratio of wages of skilled workers to unskilled workers) in both the US and Mexico. Of course, there were many other changes occurring

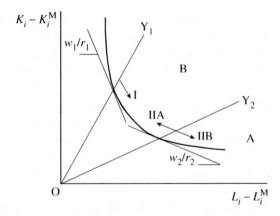

Figure 4.5. Relocation and factor prices.

in these countries at the same time, but could VFDI have been part of the story? The analysis of the previous section would suggest not, since it indicates that VFDI tends to bring factor price convergence, this being associated with factor price ratios moving in opposite directions in the two countries. It suggests that we should expect to see skill premiums increasing in the US, but declining in Mexico, as demand for the abundant factor (unskilled labour) increases. However, it was pointed out (first by Feenstra and Hanson 1996) that many of the production activities that relocated across the border were unskilled labour intensive by US standards, but skilled labour intensive compared with most activities in the Mexican economy. The analysis of the preceding section needs to be enriched to analyse such cases.

Figure 4.5 illustrates some possibilities. The isoquant represents the technology of 'the rest of the economy', the Y-sector of Section 4.3. The slope of line OY_1 is country 1's capital–labour endowment *net* of factor usage in the M-sector, so is $(K_1 - K_1^M)/(L_1 - L_1^M)$, while the analogous line OY_2 gives the same information for country 2. The factor price ratios in countries 1 and 2 are measured by the slope of Y-sector isoquants as they cross these rays. Thus, as the figure is drawn, the initial situation does not have factor price equalization (similar to point E' of Figure 4.4, before fragmentation). Full employment is achieved with some factor usage in manufacturing, and the remainder being used in the 'rest of the economy' (the Y-sector) with very different factor intensities and hence factor prices. Country 1 is the high-wage economy.

Suppose that fragmentation is possible, and that some stage of manufacturing production relocates from country 1 to country 2. One possibility is that this stage of production is highly labour intensive, with capital–labour ratio lying below lines OY_1 and OY_2, i.e. in interval A. Then country 1 has *lost* some labour-intensive M-sector activity, so its Y-sector must become more labour intensive to employ the resources released: this is illustrated by the arrow I, implying that the wage–rental ratio in country 1 must fall. (This is like the US skill premium rising as unskilled intensive jobs move to Mexico.) For country 2, the activity gained is labour intensive relative to the factor intensity of the rest of the economy (interval A lies below OY_2, the slope of which is $(K_2 - K_2^M)/(L_2 - L_2^M)$), so the Y-sector, employing the rest of the economy's endowment, must become more capital intensive, moving as indicated by the arrow IIA. This is the case of convergence, and we see wage–rental ratios moving in opposite directions in the two countries. If enough activities with techniques of production in region A relocated, then factor price equalization would be achieved, as in the previous section.

Alternatively, suppose that the activity that relocates has factor intensity given by a ray in the range B. Once again, this is labour intensive relative to country 1, which moves along arrow I. However, this activity is capital intensive relative to activity in 2, so the mix of factors remaining in country 2's Y-sector becomes more labour intensive. This is a shift in direction IIB, reducing the wage–rental ratio in country 2. As in the NAFTA case, vertical investment can reduce the returns to one of the factors (w_i, unskilled labour) in *both* countries. Evidently, the likelihood of this case arising is greater the wider is the difference between countries' factor endowment ratios—the larger is area B relative to A.

How does this relate to the analysis of the preceding section? The main point is simply that both the initial and the new situation are outside the FPE set. A general comparison of factor prices outside the FPE set (original and new) is complex. It depends on the technologies in the two production sectors in quite detailed ways, and analysis is complicated by the fact that fragmentation can change all factor prices and goods' prices (as we saw in the discussion of Figure 4.3 in Section 3.2). However, it is worth computing an example to show what can happen. The example we develop is one in which the Y-sector is as before, and in which the fragmentation of manufacturing gives one stage (components) that is more capital intensive than the Y-sector (at the integrated equilibrium), while the other stage, assembly, is more labour intensive. Details of parameters used in computing the example are given in the appendix.

Figure 4.6 illustrates the original FPE set (without fragmentation) as O_1MO_2Y. Manufacturing production can fragment into vectors O_1c and O_1a (equal to cO_2 and aO_2, respectively), these summing to O_1M. Y-sector production at integrated equilibrium factor prices is $O_1Y = ac$, and the new FPE set is O_1caO_2ca. Constructing this set requires that the factor usage vectors be added in order of their factor intensity. Thus, moving from O_1 along the upper edge of the new FPE set, the first vector is the most capital intensive; O_1c, component assembly. The second is Y-sector production at integrated equilibrium factor prices, $ac = O_1Y$. The third is the most labour intensive; assembly, aO_2. Stacking the vectors this way maximizes the area

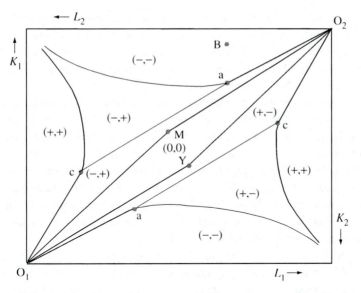

Figure 4.6. Change in wage–rental ratio (country 1, country 2).

of the new FPE set, and this is the correct thing to do, as we seek the set of all possible factor endowments that will give rise to factor price equalization, by means of any combination of activities. (Vectors in Figure 4.4 were stacked according to the same principle, but in that case both assembly and components were more capital intensive than integrated equilibrium Y-sector production.)

The purpose of Figure 4.6 is to illustrate what fragmentation does to factor prices at all points in the endowment box, not just in the extended FPE set. The changes in the wage–rental ratios in country 1 and country 2 are given by the first and second signs in the brackets in each region. As we have already seen, within the original FPE set allowing fragmentation causes nothing to happen, $(0, 0)$. In the extended FPE set wage–rental ratios converge to equality, this involving a fall in the wage–rental ratio in the capital-intensive country and rise in the labour-intensive country.

Moving outside the new FPE set, consider first the $(-, +)$ area in the northwest area of the box. In this area the factor abundance ratios of the two countries are not too different; factor prices are not equalized, but they move in opposite directions towards equality. This is like case A of Figure 4.5. The relocation of activity causes Y-sector production to become more labour intensive in the capital-rich country (country 1) and more capital intensive in the labour-abundant country (country 2).

The region above the diagonal marked $(-, -)$ is where wage–rental ratios fall in both countries. Country 1 gets all of capital-intensive component production, causing its Y-sector to become more labour intensive so reducing w_1/r_1. Country 2 gets assembly, but in this region country 2 is extremely labour abundant. Acquiring assembly (where previously country 2 had no manufacturing activity at all) therefore requires that Y-sector production in 2 become more labour intensive, this reducing the wage–rental ratio w_2/r_2. If w_2/r_2 is the ratio of wages of unskilled to skilled workers, then the Mexico–US example corresponds to a point in this region, such as B, with Mexico being country 2 and the US country 1.

Similar arguments apply to other regions of the figure. In each of the cases where factor price ratios move in the same direction the relocating activity is capital intensive relative to Y-sector production in one country, and labour intensive relative to Y-sector production in the other. (In the language of trade theory, there are factor intensity reversals.) Furthermore, while results illustrated in Figure 4.6 concentrate on factor price ratios, it must also be remembered that goods' prices change. Fragmentation increases world income, although there are cases in which the country exporting manufactures in the initial situation can suffer a welfare reduction from fragmentation, because of a terms-of-trade loss.

The general equilibrium analysis of this section shows how the wage and price effects of fragmentation, discussed in general terms in Section 4.2, can be resolved in a specific model. However, outcomes are quite complex and are also model specific, depending on the configurations of the technologies in various sectors of the economy. There are two general points to take away from the analysis. Wage effects depend first on the factor intensity of the relocating activity relative to the factor intensities of the sectors from which factors are drawn (for the host economy) or the sectors in which factors have to be re-employed (for the home). In our examples these have been tradeable sectors, but they may also include non-tradeables, for example, unskilled workers in advanced countries becoming re-employed in service activities. And, second, goods' prices may also change. For tradeable goods in the world economy these effects are likely to be quite small, but if factors need to be re-employed in non-tradeable services, then these effects could be significant, tending to reduce the wages of factors used intensively in the expanding service activity.

4.5   Conclusions

The material of this and the preceding chapter has outlined the main economic analyses of the determinants and consequences of multinational activity. It suggests what factors are likely to be conducive to multinational activity, and in Chapter 6 we will present the evidence on these relationships. However, the theory also points to the difficulties that will be encountered. If the FDI data are an aggregate of both horizontal and vertical investments, then identifying particular effects will be difficult. HFDI is a substitute for trade and occurs when trade costs (on final assembled products) are relatively high; VFDI is a complement to trade costs, occurring when trade costs are low. As we saw in Section 4.1, this can give rise to non-monotonic relationships between trade costs, levels of FDI and levels of trade.

Analysis of the effects of FDI contains two parts. One is knowing how FDI is different from other activities, in product supply, factor intensity or the creation of spillovers. In Chapters 7–9 we will present a good deal of evidence on these issues. The other is knowing the economy's equilibrium responses to FDI. We have studied these in partial equilibrium (Chapter 3) and in general equilibrium (Chapter 4). Analytically these can be quite complex, and they are hard for empirical researchers to quantify. As we will see in Chapters 7–9, empirical progress in this direction is much more limited.

One element of theory remains to be covered. That is to study the boundaries of the international firm, and ask when international production is organized within a multinational enterprise, and when it is conducted simply through arm's-length trade. This is the subject of the next chapter.

Appendix 4.1. Parameter Values in Figures 4.1 and 4.2

> Fixed coefficient technologies, 1 component per unit final output.
>
> Components: lab input per unit 0.2, capital 0.8.
>
> Assembly: lab input per unit 0.8, capital 0.2.
>
> Factor prices: $w_1 = 1$, $r_1 = 1$, $w_2 = 0.66$, $r_2 = 1.45$.

Appendix 4.2. Parameter Values in Figure 4.6

Preferences are Cobb–Douglas, with expenditure equally divided between M and Y. The Y-sector is Cobb–Douglas, with an L share of 0.55; at the integrated equilibrium all prices are unity and the labour/capital ratio is 0.55. The M-sector has fixed coefficient technology, with one unit of components and one unit of assembly required to produce one unit of output. The labour/capital ratio in components is 0.33 and in assembly is 2.

Appendix 4.3. Components Labour Intensive

Figure 4.7 is analogous to Figure 4.1, but with components labour intensive. If both elements of transport costs are very high, then there is no trade, so B_{111} and B_{222} indicate autarky. If τ^a is low while τ^c is high, then comparative advantage in the good as a whole determines production; thus, in the bottom right all production takes place in country 1, for consumption in both countries. The incentive to fragment arises as components are labour intensive and country 2 has the lower wage. However, this comparative advantage can only be exploited if τ^c is low enough. The dividing line is

$$c(w_1, r_1) = c(w_2, r_2)\tau^c \tag{4.8}$$

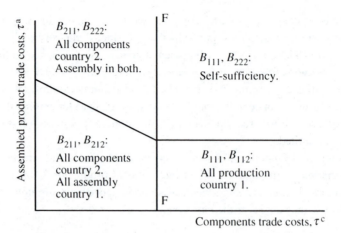

Figure 4.7. Components labour intensive; country 1 high wage.

at which point 2's production cost advantage just offsets the trade cost disadvantage (given that assembly is in 1, so components all have to be shipped). This is marked by the vertical line FF. Along the downward-sloping line firms are indifferent about the location of assembly for supply of market 2, given that components are produced in 2. This has equation

$$[c(w_2, r_2) + a(w_2, r_2)] = [c(w_2, r_2)\tau^c + a(w_1, r_1)]\tau^a. \tag{4.9}$$

Both trade costs enter the right-hand side, and it is this that creates the downward slope of this line segment. Notice that in Figure 4.7, the point at which the labour-intensive activity (components) moves out of country 1 to country 2 depends only on τ^c (at line FF), because components output is shipped, but there are no traded inputs to components. In Figure 4.1 the labour-intensive activity is assembly, and assembly can incur trade costs both in shopping output (τ^a) *and* in shipping the inputs to assembly, (τ^c). Thus, fragmentation could be caused by a reduction in either τ^a or τ^c.

5

Multinationals: the Firm and the Market

The international operations of firms can be organized internally, in wholly owned subsidiaries, or externally, under arm's-length contracts with independent local producers. Multinational enterprises arise when firms choose to internalize their activities, i.e. to own the physical assets used in their operations abroad, even though arm's-length contracts may offer lower set-up costs and greater flexibility. We refer to these two modes of international production as internalization and outsourcing, respectively. While intra-firm trade has grown fast, it has been suggested that an increasing share of international production is now taking place through outsourcing rather than internalized in wholly owned subsidiaries. For example, in the case of North–South production networks in areas such as textiles, automotive products and electronics, a considerable share of labour-intensive activities is outsourced by Northern firms to Southern producers. The share of US imports coming from affiliates of US multinationals has fallen slightly (Hanson et al. 2001), suggesting that foreign outsourcing by US firms might have outpaced the growth of intra-firm trade.

A comprehensive theory of the multinational firm must offer an analysis of the choice between internalization and outsourcing. In a sense, the theory of the multinational firm is a sub-case of the theory of the boundaries of the firm—what is done internally and what is outsourced. (This view is expressed, for instance, in Rugman (1980) and Ethier (1986).) These boundaries are usually set by the interplay of two sorts of factors. One is that outside contractors may have an advantage, relative to the firm, in undertaking various activities; the other is the difficulty that the firm encounters in coordinating and controlling the actions of local contractors. For example, a large integrated firm may have an advantage in its 'core' activities, and relying on local firms may increase the efficiency with which a variety of ancillary activities are carried out. However, a local firm will have its own objectives, generally different from those of the parent company. In principle, objectives can be aligned by writing contracts that reward the local firm for the activities it undertakes; but in practice it might not be possible to write or enforce contracts that fully solve this issue of aligning incentives between firms operating through the market system.

These problems arise for national, as well as multinational, firms. The idea that market relations could be efficiently replaced by the hierarchy of a firm's organization goes back to Coase (1937). In that view, transaction costs are related to inefficiencies in coordinating production activities through the market system in a world of imperfect information. The emphasis in the literature has gradually shifted from coordination problems to the idea that transaction costs are mainly associated with a problem of incentives in an environment of contractual incompleteness and relation-specific investments (Williamson 1979). It is likely that operating in a foreign country exacerbates these problems. Contractual failures are most likely to arise in the presence of imperfect information and when some of the activities involve intangible assets. For example, there may be greater problems in enforcing contractual arrangements when firms operate with partners that are located abroad. Property rights on the knowledge embodied in R&D-intensive products cannot be easily defined and enforced, and when production is carried out abroad proprietary knowledge can easily be dissipated to partners involved in production. Additionally, the agency problems associated with monitoring of the operations of sales agents based abroad are likely to be more severe than those encountered in analogous activities undertaken within national boundaries.

It is difficult to derive a comprehensive taxonomy of the market failures that may arise in the international operations of MNEs and their implications for the choice of the mode of entry in a foreign market. As an illustration, we will therefore consider three types of contractual failure. The first concerns the sort of opportunistic behaviour that may arise if firms on one or both sides of the relationship are called on to make relationship-specific investments. This is the 'hold-up' problem first studied by Williamson (1979), Grout (1984), Grossman and Hart (1986) and Hart and Moore (1990) and is the subject matter of Section 5.2. In Section 5.3 we look at some recent extensions of this work, placing hold-up in a wider model of international industry equilibrium. The second concerns the protection of intangible assets, such as technical knowledge or reputation, and is the subject of Section 5.4. Drawing on the literature, including Rugman (1985, 1986), Horstmann and Markusen (1987b, 1996) and Markusen (2001), we develop analytical frameworks to analyse situations in which the choice of internalization may be dictated by the need to avoid the dissipation of proprietary technical knowledge or of the firm's reputation for providing high-quality goods. Finally, in Section 5.5, we turn to agency problems, addressed in the context of multinational activity by Horstmann and Markusen (1996). However, before turning to these problems of contractual failure we first outline a general framework that will be used throughout the chapter, and set out the benchmark case in which there are no contractual problems.

5.1 An Analytical Framework

The general analytical framework we use to model internalization is to suppose that production involves two activities (or sets of activities), x and y. We need not, at this stage, specify exactly what these activities are, but we assume that revenue, $R(x, y)$, is an increasing and concave function of them both. Activities can be performed either by the multinational (and its affiliates) or by an independent local firm. We label the activities such that the multinational has an advantage in x, and the local firm in y. Thus, if the multinational undertakes x-activity (perhaps in its home country) it costs c per unit. If undertaken in the host country by a local firm, its cost per unit is γc, $\gamma \geqslant 1$. Independent local firms have advantage in y; their cost is a per unit, whereas if this activity is undertaken by the multinational or its affiliate, the cost is αa, $\alpha \geqslant 1$.

In the context of HFDI, x is most naturally thought of as upstream activities, and y in terms of downstream activities. The exact division is, of course, industry specific, so x might be R&D and component production, and y downstream assembly or just sales activity. For VFDI, y might be a particular set of components, production of which is moved abroad.

In the absence of contractual problems, the efficient allocation of tasks is clearly that the multinational performs x and outsources y to the local firm. Joint profits achieve a maximum when x and y are chosen to maximize

$$\pi = R(x, y) - ay - cx \tag{5.1}$$

giving first-order conditions

$$R_x(x, y) = c, \qquad R_y(x, y) = a. \tag{5.2}$$

From the assumed concavity of $R(x, y)$ in both arguments, the first-order conditions imply that the optimal value of x will decrease with c and the optimal value of y will fall as a rises.

The outcome characterized by the first-order conditions in (5.2) could be decentralized between the multinational and the local firm in several different ways. Suppose, for example, that the multinational sells x-activity (components) to the local firm at price q. The local firm is the residual claimant, meaning that it receives the revenue, $R(x, y)$ net of the price of components. Denoting the profits of the multinational and the local firm by Π^M and Π^L, respectively, we have

$$\Pi^M = (q - c)x, \qquad \Pi^L = R(x, y) - ay - qx. \tag{5.3}$$

If both firms are price takers and the price is set at $q = c$, then the decentralized choice of x and y by the multinational and the local firm gives exactly the same outcome as joint profit maximization. (The multinational is indifferent about the quantity of x, which can therefore be set by demand from the local firm.) The multinational outsources y-activity so that production is in line with the advantages of the firms; arm's-length trade takes place, rather than multinational activity. Clearly, the same outcome would be arrived at if the multinational was the residual claimant and purchased y-activity from the local firm at price a. In addition, lump sum transfer payments could be made to redistribute profits. For example, the multinational might charge the local supplier a 'participation fee'; if this fee is set by auctioning the contract to deal with the multinational, then bidding amongst a large number of potential local firms will drive their profits to zero, transferring all profits to the multinational.

This is the benchmark case, but the problems are clear. First, these firms are not price takers in their bilateral trade, and second the objects being traded are often intangible or contain unobservable elements, on which it is difficult to write contracts. The remainder of the chapter is devoted to pursuing the implications of these problems.

5.2 Hold-up

When parties have to invest in assets that are relation specific, and when it is impossible to write complete contracts that cover all the possible issues that may arise in carrying out transactions, parties to the contract have an incentive to engage in opportunistic behaviour. The problem is that each party can claim that the contract has not been met, and use the threat of not trading in order to try and gain a larger share of profits. This threat of 'hold-up' means that the contract may be renegotiated after investments in relationship-specific assets have been sunk. As a consequence parties are unwilling to undertake the amount of investment that maximizes the joint surplus from the transaction.

The impossibility of writing complete contracts comes from the fact that exchange between firms often involves goods and services with specific characteristics not easily verifiable by third parties or a court. Contracts specifying terms of exchange contingent on the realized characteristics of the goods cannot be enforced, since there will be no court able to verify whether the actual characteristics of the goods correspond to those agreed in a contract. Under such circumstances, the terms of trade can only be defined ex-post, after production (and investment) in the activities to be exchanged has taken place and contingencies have realized. A hold-up problem emerges when the activities exchanged between firms are not only non-contractible but also relationship specific. Even if the trading partners can ex-ante choose in a pool of potential competing counterparts, they end up forming an ex-post bilateral monopoly; given expenditures on relationship-specific assets, they have an incentive to trade bilaterally rather than with outside parties. The presence of relation specificity has a major role in defining the ex-post terms of trade between parties entering incomplete contractual arrangements. However, it also means that in deciding about their investments, each party will anticipate that they are 'held-up' in the relationship with their partner. They will then underinvest, as they anticipate that they will not receive the full marginal revenue created by their investment.

Relation-specific investments are typical when an input supplier has to design and manufacture equipment whose characteristics are specific to a buyer's particular order, but of little use to other buyers. These supplies often require large and specific investments. Imagine a supplier of components to a car manufacturer. Large specific plants will have to be set up to supply the technological specifications and the volumes of production required by downstream customers. We will discuss in Chapter 7 the case of MNEs assembling trucks in India and the complexity of their relationship to their input suppliers. These investments can also be relatively important for smaller transactions in traditional sectors. We discussed in Chapter 2 the case of Ikea and its Eastern European furniture suppliers. But consider a small textile producer in India who has to manufacture block printed fabrics for an Italian designer[1]. She will have to prepare and produce blocks according to his/her customer's specifications, train workers, enhance quality controls. Many of these investments may be specific to the relationship with the Italian designer.

Underinvestment outcomes associated with transaction costs and asset specificities have been documented in a number of case studies (Joskow 1977) and in cross-plant studies (Monteverde and Teece 1982; Lyons 1994). Again, take the example of block printing. The Italian designer would probably have a tale to tell about how the initial quality of the Indian block printer was low and how it slowly improved. We tend to consider these as learning processes, but often the initial slackness can simply be explained by the hold-up problem. The Indian block printer invests little in quality, as he is afraid that the initial deal might be renegotiated. When the relationship with the Italian designer builds up with time and reciprocal trust is established, then the block printer will be less concerned about a possible renegotiation and will invest more in quality.

The first formal treatment of the hold-up problem was developed by Grout (1984). In that approach, and the one that we start with here, such problems are assumed to occur in a firm's dealings with other firms, but not internally within the firm. The first application of the hold-up problem to the analysis of FDI and multinational activity was by Ethier (1986), who modelled the issue of internalization on the basis of transaction costs and incomplete contracts. Internalization is assumed to be the only way to deal with uncertain contingencies affecting the technical relations between the MNE and upstream producers that cannot be dealt with using arm's-length contracts. The focus in Ethier (1986) is on characterizing an international equilibrium (in terms of factor prices, trade and FDI flows), where internalization is explicitly modelled. In other papers the framework of incomplete contracting is used to explore the issue of FDI expropriation (Thomas and Worrall 1994; Schnitzer 1999). Matouschek (1999) builds up a microfoundation for FDI spillovers in the host country on the idea of the hold-up problem.

---

[1] Giorgio's mother-in-law.

Using our basic framework, hold-up can be modelled by supposing that neither x nor y are contractible. For example, x might be an investment in the quality of products that are produced by the multinational. The other activity is local sales, and y is an investment in the quality of the sales team. We have already seen the efficient outcome, but in this case it cannot be decentralized between the firms. For example, it might not be possible to contract on the quality of the local sales force. What are the alternatives?

One possibility is that the entire activity is internalized by the multinational (operating with an affiliate): in that case profits are

$$\Pi^{\mathrm{I}} = R(x, y) - a\alpha y - cx, \tag{5.4}$$

where the superscripts 'I' and 'O' will be used to refer to the multinational's profits under internalization and outsourcing, respectively. Activity levels satisfy first-order conditions:

$$R_x(x, y) = c, \qquad R_y(x, y) = \alpha a. \tag{5.5}$$

This is the internalized outcome, but it forfeits the advantage that the local firm has in y-activity. Since $\alpha > 1$ profits are reduced, and the level of y input is also distorted downwards compared with the efficient case.

Alternatively, the activity may be outsourced by the multinational to a local firm, but with contractual incompleteness. Decisions are taken at two stages. First, the multinational and the local firm undertake investments x and y, respectively. Then, at the second stage, they meet and decide how to split the revenue, $R(x, y)$. In the event of disagreement nothing is produced, although x and y investments can be put to some other use (an outside option) to earn r_c and r_a per unit, respectively. Since the activities x and y performed by the multinational and the local firm are assumed to be relation specific, $r_c \leqslant c$ and $r_a \leqslant a$. This means that by selling the product of their own investments to outside parties, neither the multinational nor the local firm can fully recover their investment costs.

The division of revenue is determined according to a Nash bargain in which the multinational's share of rents ('bargaining power') is equal to θ. The multinational therefore has payoff

$$\Pi^{\mathrm{O}} = \theta[R(x, y) - xr_c - yr_a] + xr_c - cx. \tag{5.6}$$

The terms on the right-hand side of this expression say that, in the Nash bargain, the multinational gets the value of its outside option, xr_c, plus share θ of the surplus. This surplus (the term in square brackets) is the revenue earned over and above what would be made if agreement was not reached and both parties had to exercise their outside options. Additionally, the firm has to pay its production costs, cx. Choice of x by the multinational at the first stage is taken knowing that this is the payoff, so the first-order condition is

$$\theta R_x(x, y) = c - (1 - \theta)r_c. \qquad (5.7)$$

Analogously for the local firm, the level of profits is

$$\Pi^L = (1 - \theta)[R(x, y) - xr_c - yr_a] + yr_a - ay \qquad (5.8)$$

and the first-order condition for choice of y gives

$$(1 - \theta)R_y(x, y) = a - \theta r_a. \qquad (5.9)$$

Comparison of first-order conditions (5.7) and (5.9) with the first-best efficient outcome, (5.2), indicates that outsourcing subject to hold-up generally creates an inefficient outcome. Investment levels depend on the outside options available to the multinational and the local firm, respectively r_c and r_a, and the parameter of bargaining power, θ.

The outside options affect the parties' payoffs in two ways: via the size of joint profits (efficiency) and via the ex-post distribution of rents. Concerning the size of joint profits, it is clear from the first-order conditions (5.7) and (5.9) that when $r_c = c$ and $r_a = a$ the outcome of the ex-post Nash bargain replicates the efficient outcome (first-order conditions (5.2)). The reason is that in such a case there is no asset specificity; all the costs of the investment can be recouped by exercising the outside option. Conversely, in the case in which the outside option on an activity is below its production cost ($r_c < c$ or $r_a < a$), then there will be a tendency towards underinvestment in the corresponding activity.[2] The concern of being 'held-up' in the specific relation with its counterpart leads to a reduction in the perceived marginal revenues from the investment and therefore to underinvestment, reducing joint profits.[3]

A second effect of outside options is on the distribution of the payoffs between parties. This effect is easily understood by noting that in expressions (5.6) and (5.8) the outside option of one of the parties reduces the payoff of the other. A bigger outside option, say, for the local firm tilts the outcome of bargaining in its favour, since what it receives from the agreement must always exceed what could be obtained selling activity y elsewhere.

The bargaining power of the multinational is measured by the parameter θ, and underinvestment in activity x will be stronger the lower is θ, while the opposite will hold for activity y. This implies that whenever there is a complementarity relation

---

[2]This is understood from the system of first-order conditions (5.7) and (5.9) compared with the analogous conditions for the efficient outcome (5.2).

[3]The extent of underinvestment also depends on the interaction between the two activities in the revenue function. If activity x and y are complements (which is guaranteed by $R_{xy}(x, y) > 0$), then underinvestment in one activity is aggravated by the underinvestment in the other activity.

between the two activities, overall surplus is maximized for intermediate values of the bargaining power θ. As well as affecting efficiency, the value of θ obviously also determines the distribution of surplus between parties.

The multinational has the choice of internalization or outsourcing. It will choose internationalization if the profits obtained operating with an affiliate Π^{I} (where x and y are given by the solution to equations (5.5)) are greater than the profits Π^{O} achieved by outsourcing to the local firm (where x and y are derived from the solution of the system of first-order conditions (5.7) and (5.9)). The comparison turns on the direct efficiency loss (α), the outside options, and bargaining power.

An example with specific functional forms will make things more concrete. Let us assume the following functional form for revenues: $R(x, y) = x^{\mu\eta} y^{\mu(1-\eta)}$. The parameter η measures the x intensity of revenue, and $\mu < 1$ is the elasticity of revenue with respect to scale (an equi-proportionate change in both x and y). Thus, if there is constant returns to scale in production but a downward-sloping demand curve for output, μ is 1 minus the reciprocal of the price elasticity of demand. We have seen how the choice of x and y depends on outside options and bargaining shares, and using the first-order conditions derived above, the optimized value of revenue can be written as the following function of parameters:

$$R^*(w_x, w_y) = A[w_x^\eta w_y^{1-\eta}]^{\mu/(\mu-1)}, \tag{5.10}$$

where w_x and w_y are measures of the relevant input costs, A is a constant and the function is decreasing in the input prices (see the appendix for derivation).

If production is internalized, then input costs are the actual unit costs faced by the firm, $w_x = c$ and $w_y = a\alpha$, and R^* is evaluated at these values. Profits are revenue minus costs and can be evaluated (see the appendix) as

$$\Pi^{\text{I}} = R^* - xw_x - yw_y = (1 - \mu)R^*. \tag{5.11}$$

Under outsourcing the relevant unit costs of inputs are $w_x = [c - (1 - \theta)r_c]/\theta$, and $w_y = [a - \theta r_a]/(1 - \theta)$ (see equations (5.6) and (5.8)), and the function R^* is evaluated with these values. The profits of the multinational and the local firm, respectively, are (see the appendix)

$$\left.\begin{aligned}
\Pi^{\text{O}} &= \theta[R^* - xw_x - yr_a] = [1 - \mu\eta - \mu(1 - \eta)r_a/w_y]\theta R^*, \\
\Pi^{\text{L}} &= (1 - \theta)[R^* - yw_y - xr_c] = [1 - \mu(1 - \eta) - \mu\eta r_c/w_x](1 - \theta)R^*.
\end{aligned}\right\} \tag{5.12}$$

Equations (5.10)–(5.12) together express the returns to different production modes as functions of the parameters that face the firm, so enable derivation of the effects of parameter changes on modal choice.

Figure 5.1 illustrates the returns as a function of the bargaining power parameter θ. The example is constructed with symmetry in the choice of x and y ($\eta = 0.5$,

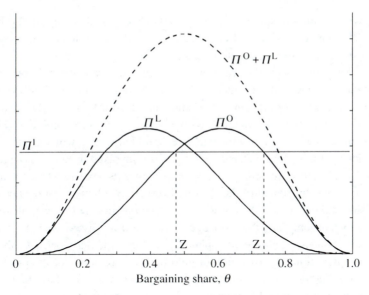

Figure 5.1.   Internalization versus outsourcing.

$a = c = 1$, $r_a = r_c = 0.5$, $\alpha = 2$ and $\mu = 0.8$). While θ does not affect Π^I
its impact on Π^O and Π^L is non-monotonic, with returns to outsourcing relatively
high at intermediate values of θ. Thus, if the internalization choice is made on the
basis of comparison of Π^I and Π^O, we see that internalization occurs for values
of θ above or below the interval ZZ, and outsourcing in the interval. When θ is
high the multinational gets a high share of the surplus, but the total surplus is very
small because incentives for the investing local firm are so weak. When θ is low
the multinational only gets a small share of it, and consequently also has little
incentive to invest. It is at intermediate values of θ—a relatively equal division of
the surplus—that outsourcing to a local contractor is most likely to be preferred to
internalization.

Changing other parameters shifts the curves in Figure 5.1. Thus, if the multinational's outside option (r_c) increases, the Π^O curve shifts upwards, increasing the
likelihood that outsourcing occurs; an increase in the outside option reduces the
severity of the hold-up problem. Increasing the multinational's share in production
(decreasing η, the parameter giving the y share) also increases Π^O; however, it
increases Π^I by more, as the cost disadvantage to the multinational of internalizing
y production, α, now applies to a smaller share of costs.

A further possibility is that the multinational could charge the local firm a participation fee, before any investment is made. If there are many potential local suppliers,
then they will be willing to bid for the right to supply the multinational, so the fee
is set at the level that bids their profits down to zero. Since the multinational now

captures the profits of the local firm, it makes the modal choice on the basis of $\Pi^O + \Pi^L$ relative to Π^I, this obviously increasing the attraction of outsourcing and the range of values of θ in which it occurs.

The above discussion illustrates why, in order to avoid the hold-up problem, multinationals may prefer to internalize their international operations even if this implies a direct loss of efficiency. Grossman and Hart (1986) and Hart and Moore (1990) extend the theory of the firm, recognizing that incentive problems (hold-up) may occur even within an integrated firm. Ex-post bargaining will take place among the various entities (divisions, etc., within a firm) involved in carrying out relation-specific investments. According to this 'property-rights' approach to the analysis of firms' activities, the extent of the hold-up is crucially affected by the allocation of ownership rights between the parties to the relation-specific transactions. Because ownership gives one party the residual control over firms' assets (namely, the power to decide about issues not contemplated in an arm's-length contract), that party will not suffer from the possibility of hold-up. The optimal allocation of property rights should assign more assets to the party whose investment has greater impact on the joint surplus from the transaction. This 'property-rights' view of the firm has recently been developed in an international setting by Antras and Helpman (2004) and Antras (2004).

This generalization can be readily handled in the framework we have developed. Different organizational modes have different outside options and bargaining powers, $\{r_c, r_a, \theta\}$, implying different values of the relevant input prices $\{w_x^O, w_y^O\}$, $\{w_x^I, w_y^I\}$. Plugging these into the revenue function, R^*, and profit statements (as in (5.12)) it is easy to compute the profit levels that are used to choose organizational form. For example, Antras and Helpman suppose that if outsourcing occurs, then the multinational can charge an entry fee, and both the multinational and the local firm have zero outside options. Internalization increases the outside option of the multinational; by internalizing, the multinational is effectively buying the rights to fire the management of its wholly owned affiliate, and to seize the y investment made by this management. It can then produce (i.e. has a positive outside option) in the event of disagreement. This means that the multinational can appropriate a higher fraction of revenue under integration than under outsourcing. Antras and Helpman also add fixed costs to each mode, assuming that these are greater for internalization than outsourcing, $f^I > f^O$.

Figure 5.2 illustrates this configuration of assumptions in an example using the revenue function R^*, equation (5.10). Given other parameters, the returns to each mode are evaluated for different values of η. We see that internalization is more likely the higher is η, this measuring the x intensity of revenue. This says that when the multinational is, technologically, the more important partner, then internalization is chosen in preference to outsourcing. This is in line with Grossman and Hart's

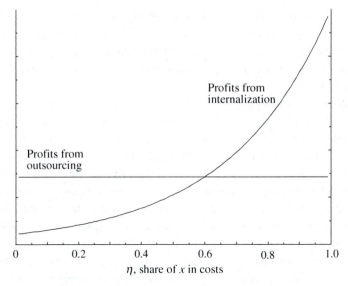

Figure 5.2. Internalization versus outsourcing.

(1986) finding that residual rights should be controlled by the party undertaking the relatively more important investment.

Summarizing, the model of hold-up illustrates how contractual incompleteness and relationship-specific investments can cause firms to reject contracts with independent local contractors in favour of internalization within the multinational. Exact outcomes depend on parameters, and the framework we have outlined can be used with different parameter configurations to explore a wide range of different possibilities. For example, firms often engage in joint ventures and other forms of cost sharing. These ventures vary in the distribution of power between the multinational and the partner. The analysis outlined here provides a general framework within which it is possible to evaluate the effects of different allocations of ownership within the integrated structure, and the contribution of the relation-specific investments of each of the parties.[4]

5.3 Hold-up in Industry Equilibrium

So far, we have looked at the relationship between just two firms, but what determines the number of firms active in the industry, and might it be the case that some

---

[4]Evidence reported in Desai et al. (2002a) shows that over the past two decades US multinationals have shifted from joint ventures to owned subsidiaries to carry out their international operations. These findings may be interpreted in the light of the hold-up problem. The falling communication costs and trade barriers that characterized the 1980s and 1990s may have resulted in higher outside opportunities for parties entering international joint ventures, especially for those that previously had few outside options (e.g. contractors in developing countries).

choose to outsource, while others internalize? Answers to these questions are given in recent work by Grossman and Helpman (2002, 2003), as well as in the papers of Antras (2004) and Antras and Helpman (2004). These papers embed the endogenous determination of outsourcing versus vertical integration in general equilibrium international trade models.

Grossman and Helpman (2002, 2003) develop a series of papers in which the number of firms in the industry is endogenous, and each faces a choice of whether to concentrate activities in a single country or split them internationally, and also whether to internalize activity in the firm or outsource. Here we outline a simplified version of Grossman and Helpman (2002), who use an industry equilibrium framework to study the choice between integration and outsourcing in a single country. A related framework is used in Grossman and Helpman (2003) to analyse the determinants of the alternative between outsourcing and FDI in an international North–South economy. Ottaviano and Turrini (2003) analyse the impact of trade costs on the choice between export and FDI in a setting where FDI activity entails a double-sided hold-up problem both for the investing multinationals and local contractors.

As in the earlier models of this chapter, the benefit of outsourcing is lower marginal costs. These cost levels determine firms' profits and also shape the industry equilibrium; more firms outsourcing increases the competitive pressure on firms that do not outsource. The costs of outsourcing are twofold. Outsourcing involves costs of matching with local firms, and also hold-up in the relationship with these firms. If there is heterogeneity amongst firms, then there may be equilibria in which a proportion of firms outsource, while the remainder internalize all activities.

To model this, the first building block is the industry and market within which multinationals operate. Multinationals produce final products, each firm having a distinct variety, and the number of such firms and varieties is denoted n and endogenously determined. To model demand we use the Dixit–Stiglitz apparatus developed in Chapter 3. Thus, the price of the kth variety is p^k, revenue earned, R^k, is price times quantity, and G and E denote the price index and expenditure, respectively. (To focus on internalization we assume an integrated world market, so do not distinguish these variables by country.) From equations (3.23) and (3.24),

$$R^k = (p^k)^{1-\sigma} G^{\sigma-1} E, \qquad G = \left[\sum_k (p^k)^{1-\sigma} \right]^{1/(1-\sigma)}, \qquad \sigma > 1. \qquad (5.13)$$

As in Chapter 3, we group final goods' producers into types, but the types are now those that outsource (superscript 'O') and those that internalize (superscript 'I'); the proportion of multinationals that outsource is ρ. Prices have a constant mark-up over marginal cost, and we choose units such that firms that outsource set a price of

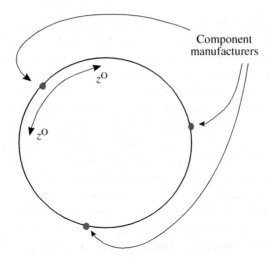

Figure 5.3. Component-specification space.

unity and the integrated firms set a price $\alpha > 1$, reflecting the higher marginal cost of not using a local supplier.

With a price-cost mark-up of $(\sigma - 1)/\sigma$, a firm's operating profits are a constant fraction $1/\sigma$ of revenue. The operating profits of integrated firms and outsourcers are therefore $\Pi^1 = R^1/\sigma$ and $\Pi^O = R^O/\sigma$. Using (5.13) and our price normalizations, these profit levels can be expressed as

$$\Pi^O = \frac{E}{n\sigma[\rho + (1-\rho)\alpha^{1-\sigma}]}, \qquad \Pi^1 = \Pi^O\alpha^{1-\sigma}. \tag{5.14}$$

This says that profits of an outsourcer are lower the more firms there are (the greater is n), and the greater is the proportion ρ of firms using the lower marginal cost technology (outsourcing). A high cost penalty to internalization (high α) increases Π^O but reduces Π^1.

A multinational that outsources gets its components from a local firm. However, each multinational must have its own exact, and firm-specific, component specification. The second building block of the model is to describe the matching of firms and suppliers. Grossman and Helpman suppose that there are infinitely many component specifications, located on the circumference (of unit length) of a circle. The n multinationals have different specifications that are uniformly distributed on this space (with density n, since the length of the circumference is unity). The number of local component manufacturers is endogenously determined and denoted m. As these firms enter they choose a preferred specification, i.e. a point on the circumference, and this results in their being equally spaced around the circle. This is illustrated in Figure 5.3, for the case of $m = 3$.

With this specification some multinationals are 'close' to a component supplier and others are far away. To tailor components to a multinational's exact specification has a cost that depends on this distance. Specifically, to produce a component a distance z away from its own location, component manufacturers incur a modification cost of μz. Because of this modification cost, component manufacturers will generally only serve multinationals within a certain distance, and we denote this (endogenous) distance z^O, as illustrated. This means that each component manufacturer serves $2nz^O$ multinationals. Furthermore, since multinationals outsource only if they are served by a component supplier, it also gives the proportion of multinationals that outsource, $\rho = 2mz^O$; the right-hand side of this is the fraction of the unit circumference that is served by m component suppliers.

With these building blocks, we can now complete the description of the model. Components are relationship specific, and the hold-up problem means that payment for them is negotiated through a Nash bargain in which the multinational's share of surplus is θ. This immediately tells us how z^O is determined. Component manufactures only incur the modification cost if it is less than or equal to the share of surplus they receive, so the marginal specification is

$$\mu z^O = (1 - \theta)\Pi^O. \tag{5.15}$$

We noted above that the number of component manufacturers, m, is endogenous. It is determined by free entry until their profits are zero:

$$2nz^O\left[(1 - \theta)\Pi^O - \int_0^{z^O} \mu z \, dz\right] = 2nz^O[(1 - \theta)\Pi^O - \tfrac{1}{2}\mu(z^O)^2] = F_m. \tag{5.16}$$

Each component manufacturer expects to serve $2nz^O$ multinationals at profits per multinational given by the term in square brackets, their share of surplus minus modification costs. The middle expression performs the integration, and the right-hand side equates these profits to the entry cost, F_m.

Finally, we close the model by determining the number of multinationals. When they enter they do not know whether they will outsource or be integrated. They therefore enter until expected profits are zero:

$$(1 - \rho)\Pi^I + \rho\theta\Pi^O = F_n, \tag{5.17}$$

where the right-hand side is again an entry cost.

This completes description of the equilibrium, and to analyse it we use $m = \rho/2z^O$, $\Pi^O = \mu z^O/(1 - \theta)$ and equation (5.14) to eliminate Π^O, m and n from (5.16) and (5.17) and derive

$$F_m = \frac{E(1 - \theta)z^O(2 - z^O)}{\sigma[\rho + (1 - \rho)\alpha^{1-\sigma}]}, \qquad F_n = \frac{\mu z^O}{1 - \theta}[\rho\theta + (1 - \rho)\alpha^{1-\sigma}]. \tag{5.18}$$

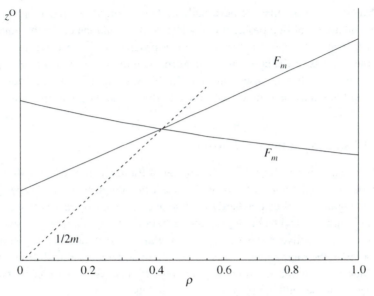

Figure 5.4. Equilibrium outsourcing.

These relationships contain just two endogenous variables, z^O and ρ, and are illustrated in Figure 5.4 (each relationship labelled by its left-hand side parameter). Other endogenous variables can be found—the only one that is particularly transparent being the number of local firms operating, given by $m = \rho/2z^O$.

We learn several things from this analysis. First, an interior solution, in which some firms outsource and others are vertically integrated, $\rho \in (0, 1)$, is possible. This arises because of the heterogeneity of multinational firms—each requires its own specification and may be more or less far away from the specifications preferred by the local firms.

The proportion of firms outsourcing depends on parameters in the following way. Higher component manufactures fixed costs relative to market size, F_m/E, reduces the number of component suppliers, reducing the amount of outsourcing while increasing the number of multinationals each serves. In terms of Figure 5.4 an increase in F_m/E shifts the F_m curve upwards, shifting the equilibrium to a lower value of ρ and higher z^O. An increase in multinational fixed costs, F_n, means fewer of these firms are active, so the remaining firms are larger, making it more worthwhile for component manufacturers to modify their components; there is therefore an increase in the amount of outsourcing. In terms of the figure, an increase in F_n shifts the F_n curve upwards, raising both ρ and z^O. A reduction in modification costs, μ, has a similar effect. Of course, these parameter changes may move the equilibrium to a corner, in which only outsourcing occurs ($\rho = 1$) or only internalization ($\rho = 0$).

Clearly, the model that we have outlined here is highly stylized, but it sets the simple bilateral hold-up problem in a wider context, endogenizing the numbers of firms. It is an example of a currently active programme of research that seeks to integrate models of the boundary of the firm with models of industry equilibrium, and ultimately full general equilibrium. In this way the material in Chapters 3–5 of this volume may be synthesized into a more general theory of the multinational firm.

5.4   Dissipation of Intangible Assets

Another major motive for the internalization of foreign activities by multinationals concerns the exploitation of intangible assets in foreign markets. Property rights over intangible assets can be hard to define and enforce, so local licensees may be able to steal ideas and technology. More generally, it might not be possible to give licensees the incentives to contribute to the maintenance of the stock of goodwill and reputation of the multinational. Internalization of activities within the multinational may then be preferred to arm's-length contracts (licensing) in order to avoid this dissipation of the multinational's intangible assets.

The problem of protecting the intangible assets of multinationals is at the core of the analysis of internalization developed by Rugman (1985, 1986) and formally by Horstmann and Markusen (1987b), Ethier and Markusen (1996) and Markusen (2001). The intangible assets of the MNE may consist either of superior knowledge (related, for instance, to the production process or to the design of a new product) or of a stock of goodwill (associated, for instance, with the reputation for product quality). When the intangible asset consists of superior knowledge, then the optimal organizational structure of multinationals will depend on the degree of transferability of this 'knowledge capital'. This is the idea first developed in Ethier and Markusen (1996), who assume that knowledge is transferred to foreign parties through use. Once knowledge has been transferred the licensee might terminate the deal with the multinational and set up its own production unit. The problem for the multinational is that of designing an optimal licensing contract. However, a contract designed in a way that prevents defection by the licensee may be costly to the multinational, since some rents must be shared with the licensee to make defection unprofitable. The multinational might then prefer to operate with an owned subsidiary in spite of higher operation costs.

When instead the intangible asset of the multinational consists of a stock of goodwill, licensing (for instance, through a franchising contract) could be sub-optimal due to free-riding. This idea is modelled in Horstmann and Markusen (1987b). If quality is not observable to consumers before purchase, the licensee might gain from the reputation of the multinational. Any licensing contract that tries to transfer all the surplus from the licensee to the multinational would be unfeasible: by skimping on quality and providing a product (service) of lower quality the licensee obtains a positive gain. To avoid free-riding the multinational is thus obliged to transfer some rents to the licensee. If quality provision is better monitored in a wholly owned subsidiary, the multinational might prefer to internalize foreign activities even if this entails higher operation costs. In the remainder of this section we outline two simple models of these cases of dissipation of knowledge and dissipation of reputation.

Dissipation of knowledge

It is often the case that the source of the ownership advantage of the multinational is some form of superior knowledge concerning production technology, management techniques or the market and the consumers. In this case, the intangible asset exclusively owned by the multinational is a stock of know-how. The services of this asset may be transferred through licensing, or may be kept internal to the firm. When, for instance, the know-how of the multinational consists of technical blueprints obtained by past R&D, the multinational may choose to serve foreign markets either by selling licences (patents) to local firms, by opening an owned subsidiary, or through an intermediate mode of entry such as a joint venture. Although the sale of patents is most probably the cheapest way to serve foreign markets, we observe many firms that prefer to meet foreign demand by means of their own subsidiaries. The reason is that the transfer of knowledge to third parties is sometimes a very costly alternative.

This has to do with the fact that knowledge is a very particular good. Some types of knowledge are difficult to transfer outside the boundaries of the firm in which it originates. For instance, several forms of know-how are, to some extent, embodied in the human capital of the employees, and human capital cannot be transferred overnight. This occurs especially when knowledge has a 'tacit component', i.e. when it cannot be fully codified for the general user. Examples are management consulting companies or international firms of lawyers, where all the knowledge is in the people working for the companies. In such cases, it can be difficult to transfer know-how without direct personal contacts between contracting parties, lengthy demonstrations and constant involvement. When the cost of transferring know-how is sufficiently high, an internalized solution through FDI may be the only feasible alternative for the multinational. It is a fact that firms selling highly specialized services (consultancy, financial services) normally undertake their foreign operations via wholly owned subsidiaries: the alternative would entail costly training of local employees. Indeed, when moving up the ladder of their careers, the employees of these companies are often made partners or shareholders to share the benefit of the common pool of knowledge, rather than dissipate it by moving to more generous competitors. The intrinsic costs of knowledge transfer by MNEs have been empirically investigated in Teece (1977) and further discussed and documented in Teece (1986).

Consider now the other extreme: types of knowledge that can become available to third parties very easily, instantly, once revealed. In such cases, transfer of knowledge may again be very costly. We are indeed in the presence of the 'fundamental paradox' concerning information as the object of transactions. On the one hand, the buyer is willing to purchase the content of the multinational know-how only if there are guarantees concerning its market value. On the other hand, the multinational cannot fully reveal the content of its know-how before exchange takes place: the buyer may reject the deal because she has in effect already acquired relevant information without costs.

The example of Pirelli and the MIR technology discussed in Chapter 2 illustrate this point. Pirelli builds its wholly owned MIR plants precisely to avoid any dissipation of knowledge about its new technology. This also explains why pharmaceutical companies are so concerned about operating in countries where the protection of intellectual property rights is weak and why most of the time they produce in wholly owned subsidiaries. When knowledge is too 'volatile', contracts between local parties may be impossible to write. A hierarchical organization that internalizes the exchange of know-how is the only alternative in these cases (see Teece (1986) and Markusen (1995) for a discussion of this topic).

So, when knowledge is either very hard or very difficult to transfer to third parties, the multinational is not really free to choose, and must internalize its international expansion. What about intermediate cases, namely, cases in which knowledge spills over to third contracting parties in an uncontrolled, but gradual way? At such intermediate levels of transferability, the multinational chooses between arm's-length contracts and FDI on the basis of a comparison between the costs and the benefits of the two alternatives. We illustrate this case through a model drawing on an idea originally developed by Ethier and Markusen (1996), and subsequently applied in Markusen (2001), Fosfuri et al. (2001) and Glass and Saggi (1999).

To illustrate how this works, we start by considering a simple model in which the multinational's technical knowledge can be stolen by a licensee. To model this we need two time periods. Thus, we restate the present value of profits of the multinational (and its affiliate) if activity is internalized as

$$\Pi^I = R_1 - a\alpha - c + [R_2 - a\alpha - c]/(1 + \delta). \tag{5.19}$$

In this expression a subscript denotes a time period, and we assume that x- and y-activity levels are fixed at a value of 1 in both time periods, yielding fixed revenues R_1 and R_2. δ is the per period interest rate that is used to discount future profits, the term in square brackets. The multinational's unit costs for x and y are c and $a\alpha$, respectively. The two activities can be given different interpretations, but for concreteness we will think of x-activity as component production and y-activity as assembly.

A local host country firm can undertake the y-activity (assembly) at unit cost $a < a\alpha$, so the multinational considers licensing such a firm to undertake this activity. We let this firm be the residual claimant and denote the licence fee in each period s_1, s_2. The multinational then makes profit

$$\Pi^O = s_1 - c + [s_2 - c]/(1 + \delta) \tag{5.20}$$

while the licensee's profits, Π^L, are

$$\Pi^L = R_1 - s_1 - a + [R_2 - s_2 - a]/(1 + \tilde{\delta}), \tag{5.21}$$

where we allow the licensee to have a different discount rate, $\tilde{\delta}$.

The key argument is now to suppose that during the first period the licensee is learning about the technology of its multinational partner. In particular, γ, its cost disadvantage in x-activity (producing components), drops from a prohibitively high level in the first period to $\tilde{\gamma}$ in the second. This captures the idea that, as a result of licensing, know-how on activity x spills over gradually from the multinational to the licensee. It follows that the licensee has the option of breaking its contract at the beginning of the second period, after having 'stolen' the know-how from the multinational. If it does so, it makes profits[5]

$$R_1 - s_1 - a + [R_2 - \tilde{\gamma}c - a]/(1 + \tilde{\delta}). \tag{5.22}$$

Evidently, the multinational can prevent this defection only if its sets its second period licence fee at a lower level than the licensee's production costs, $s_2 \leqslant \tilde{\gamma}c$. This is the incentive compatibility constraint.

From this, we see that the multinational will choose to internalize if profits Π^I from (5.19) are greater than Π^O from (5.20), evaluated with the incentive-compatible value of the second period licence fee, $s_2 = \tilde{\gamma}c$, i.e. if

$$R_1 - a\alpha + (R_2 - a\alpha - \tilde{\gamma}c)/(1 + \delta) > s_1. \tag{5.23}$$

This does not yet offer a complete theory of the multinational's choice, since the right-hand side, s_1, is an endogenous variable yet to be determined. The most natural way to resolve this is to suppose that the multinational invites local firms to bid for the first period licence fee. In this way s_1 will be bid up to the level at which the licensee's profits Π^L (from (5.21)) are zero (the participation constraint). Solving s_1 in this way and using the value in inequality (5.23) yields the following condition for the multinational to internalize:

$$(\tilde{\delta} - \delta)(R_2 - \tilde{\gamma}c) > a[\alpha(2 + \delta)(1 + \tilde{\delta}) - (1 + \delta)(2 + \tilde{\delta})]. \tag{5.24}$$

---

[5]Note that after the defection of the licensee, the multinational may want to license its know-how to a second licensee in the second period. In the present treatment we do not consider this eventuality, which is instead analysed in richer models (e.g. Ethier and Markusen 1996).

From this we see that if $\delta = \tilde{\delta}$ and $\alpha \geqslant 1$ the multinational will always license rather than internalize. Essentially, it is prepared to accept a low licence fee in period 2, $s_2 \leqslant \tilde{\gamma} c$ (satisfying the incentive compatibility constraint) because it can be fully recouped by charging a high first period licence fee, s_1 (by, for example, auctioning the licence to local firms). The multinational is thereby able to extract all of the surplus from the licensee, and therefore chooses licensing over internalization, in order to keep productive efficiency high.

Under what circumstances is the multinational not able to extract the full surplus? One possibility is that there are imperfect capital markets, and that is the reason we allowed the two firms to have different discount rates. Thus, if $\tilde{\delta} > \delta$, the multinational puts more weight on the future than does the local host country firm, i.e. it has access to lower interest rates. We then see that internalization may occur. The reason is that, since the licensee discounts second period profits more heavily, it will be ready to accept the licensing contract only if the first period licence fee is sufficiently low. However, such low first period fees will necessarily imply a loss (transfer of rents) for the multinational. One notes that internalization is more likely to be preferred to licensing the greater the difference in discount rates, and the smaller the multinational's cost penalty, α. Internalization is also more likely when the term $\tilde{\gamma}$ is low, meaning that a higher degree of spillover is associated with a higher transfer of rent from the multinational to the licence fee to avoid defection.

There may be other reasons why the first period licence fee cannot extract all of the surplus. One case, analysed by Ethier and Markusen (1996) involves a double-sided agency problem. That is, not only is it possible that the licensee steals the technology, but also that the multinational might break the terms of the licence by, for instance, licensing the technology to a different firm. This constrains the maximum value of the first period licence fee s_1, so, from (5.23) making it more likely that internalization is preferred to licensing.

In summary, internalization induced by possible dispersion of knowledge is more likely to emerge in firms whose know-how is subject to spillovers, like pharmaceuticals, and that are able to borrow in capital markets at lower cost, like firms based in high-income economies. It is also more likely to occur when the alternative of licensing is with local counterparts that are capable of fast learning and when host countries do not provide strong enforcement of property rights. These findings are broadly consistent with empirical evidence. Mansfield and Romeo (1980) and Mansfield et al. (1980), among others, show that technology transfer activities by US multinational are more likely to occur internally (as opposed to licensing) when the product or the technology is new, so that the losses from knowledge spillovers are potentially high. Smith (2001) presents cross-country empirical evidence on US firms' foreign operations confirming that licensing is a more likely entry mode in markets characterized by stronger protection of intellectual property rights. The harsh debate and bargaining on how to reform the TRIPS[6] agreement to make sure that developing countries can get access to cheap medicines and vaccines in case of epidemics or a threatening spread of diseases, show how concerned pharmaceutical MNEs are about the weakening of intellectual property rights even in peripheral countries.

Dissipation of reputation

A variant on the case of internalization driven by dissipation of intangible assets arises when the multinational's firm-specific asset is reputation. A local firm may not have the same incentive to preserve and enhance reputation as does the multinational itself. We illustrate this idea in a simplified version of a model due to Horstmann and Markusen (1987b). (Earlier models of reputational equilibria include Shapiro (1983) and Allen (1984).)

The industry under study has a large number of local firms producing a low-quality good at constant unit production costs $\bar{a}$ that sells for price $\bar{p} = \bar{a}$. In contrast, the MNE's good is high quality and some consumers are prepared to pay a fixed premium for the good, so it sells to these consumers at price $p > \bar{p}$. In each period of time the number of such consumers is equal to 1. The MNE's technology is such that it can produce the high-quality good at cost αa, with $p > \alpha a$, so that profit can be made. However, if the multinational firm licenses a local firm to produce the good, the local firm has lower cost, $a < \alpha a$, as before.

The efficient outcome is clear. The MNE licenses a local firm to produce the high-quality good. Profits of $p - a$ are made per period and, if there are many local firms competing for the licence, all profits will be transferred to the MNE in the per period licence fee, $s = p - a$. However, by licensing the product, the MNE has handed over to the local firm control of an intangible asset—the technology for producing the high-quality good. Will the local firm manage this in the long-term interests of the MNE?

The reputational story is as follows. Suppose that quality cannot be observed by consumers before purchase, although they can observe that the licensee is using the MNE's brand, known to be high quality. The licensee can continue to supply the high-quality good, or alternatively can switch to selling the low-quality good under the high-quality brand. This is not detected immediately (since quality cannot be detected before purchase), so for some period of time (which we take to be one time period) the licensee is able to sell a low-quality product at a high-quality price. However, at the end of this period the brand reputation is destroyed; we assume that it is destroyed forever, so future sales of the will only fetch price $\bar{p}$.

What is the incentive to cheat in this way? The licensee makes one period gain $a - \bar{a}$, the cost saving from producing low-quality goods rather than high quality. The

---

[6]Trade-Related Aspects of Intellectual Property Rights.

loss is that in all future periods it makes zero profits (selling low-quality products at $\bar{p} = \bar{a}$) instead of making $p - a - s$, profits net of the licence fee. For the licensee not to cheat, the present value of this stream of profits must exceed the gain from cheating, so $(p - a - s)/\delta > a - \bar{a}$, where δ is the interest rate per period (recalling that the length of the period is defined as the length of time taken to detect cheating). This condition is the incentive compatibility constraint. If it is satisfied, then the licensee has the incentive to do what the MNE wants it to do (not destroy the brand's reputation). However, satisfying the condition is costly for the MNE; the licence fee no longer transfers all the surplus to the MNE, as some is left with the licensee, so long as he does not cheat.

Will the MNE license the product or produce it itself? The maximum licence fee it can extract per period is the value of s from the incentive compatibility constraint, and it will license if this exceeds per period earnings it can make itself, $p - \alpha a$. (Notice that we do not allow an upfront fee giving the multinational the present value of all the surplus, as was discussed in the case of the knowledge-dissipation model.) After some rearranging, this yields the following condition for licensing:

$$\alpha - 1 > \delta(a - \bar{a})/a. \tag{5.25}$$

As can be seen, this depends on parameters in the obvious way. The MNE is more likely to license the greater is its cost disadvantage α, the more rapid is detection (low δ), and the lower the cost saving from cheating, $a - \bar{a}$.

More complex contractual arrangements can be developed, and occur in reality, in response to this problem. For example, quite often in a licence contract, MNEs also acquire the right to monitor and inspect the activity of the licensee, in order to ensure the maintenance of the goodwill capital. This contractual form is typical in the provision of standard services for the general public (think, for instance, of the franchising contracts operated by McDonald's or Pizza Hut). By contrast, in the case of specialized enterprise services (e.g. banking), where the provision of high quality requires greater effort and is more difficult to monitor, internalization is more likely than licensing or franchising. We discussed in Chapter 2 how most fashion houses own their shops worldwide, because of their need to control the quality of their product and to preserve their brand image.

5.5 Agency Costs

One activity in which local firms might be expected to have a significant advantage over the multinational is final distribution and sales. Local sales agents are likely to have market knowledge and perhaps also established distribution networks to which the MNE might not have access. Nevertheless, even in this activity, it is often the case that multinationals internalize distribution in preference to the alternative of an arm's-length contract with local sales agents. Zeile (1993) reports that a large fraction of foreign firms prefer to sell on the US market using owned sales branches to control the distribution of their products rather than relying on local agents. Nicholas (1983), from economic history, documents the development of internal rather than outsourced distribution by British multinationals before 1939.

One reason given for this choice is the presence of agency costs. Although an independent local agent may have superior information about the state of the market, it is not necessarily in her interest to reveal it to the multinational firm. The agent is likely to have different objectives from the firm and if her actions are not directly observable, then there is a possibility that she will 'shirk'. The costs of dealing with such an agent might be greater than the cost disadvantage of the firm running its own internalized distribution system.

The classic modelling of this trade-off is the principal–agent problem.[7] This problem can arise in many contexts, but for present purposes we focus on sales and distribution. Suppose that sales in the market depend on the effort put in by the sales force, and that this is not directly observable. Furthermore, it cannot be inferred from the actual levels of sales, since these also have a random component known to the agent but not to the multinational. The multinational therefore cannot distinguish whether a low level of realized sales is attributable to low effort by the agent or to a 'bad' state of the market. An incentive scheme is then needed to induce effort from the sales force but such a scheme creates its own inefficiency. A multinational might then be faced with the following choice: either internalize, by setting up its own sales unit in which, by assumption, effort can be monitored; or outsource to a local firm, getting a direct efficiency advantage but also incurring the agency costs associated with having to induce the firm to supply effort.

This situation has been modelled by Horstmann and Markusen (1996). The simplest version of their model can be set up as follows. Consider a multinational that is willing to sell its good in a foreign market where there are N potential consumers. Each buys one unit, and we set the price charged by the multinational at unity. N is a random variable: with probability β its value is N_H, with probability $1 - \beta$ the value is N_L, where $N_H > N_L$ (high and low states of demand). Both the multinational and the local agent are assumed to be risk neutral. Actual sales do not depend solely on the number of potential customers, but also on the effort, y, provided by the local

---

[7]See, for instance, Mas Colell et al. (1995) for a general treatment of the principal–agent problem. A sub-case of the principal–agent problem is that of moral hazard, which broadly refers to cases in which the pursuit of the agent's individual objectives clashes with the interests of the principal. The term 'moral hazard' comes from the insurance literature and is normally used to describe situations of 'hidden action' in which the agent's behaviour may deviate from the principal's objectives due to fact that her effort is not monitorable. However, the term is also used (e.g. Hart and Holmstrom 1987) when the principal–agent problem originates from the fact that the agent has superior information on some economic variable ('hidden information').

agent in promoting sales. We capture this fact by assuming that the actual amount of sales (the number of buyers, and also the revenue) is $R_i = yN_i$, where $i = $ H, L. Effort is costly, and it is assumed that the cost effort function, $\alpha a(y)$ is increasing and convex in y. As usual, $\alpha > 1$ is a cost penalty to internalization; local agents find it cheaper to exert the effort needed to achieve a particular level of sales.

First, consider a firm that internalizes its sales operation. It observes the state of nature, instructs its workforce how much effort to put in conditional on the state, and makes payments to them. The expected profits are then

$$E\Pi^1 = \beta(R_H - s_H) + (1 - \beta)(R_L - s_L), \tag{5.26}$$

where revenues R_i are directly controlled by the firm (via control of effort) and where s_i denotes the payments made in each state, $i = $ H, L. These payments have to be sufficient to secure participation of the sales force, i.e. to give them income, net of the cost of effort, greater than a reservation utility level, u_0:

$$s_H - \alpha a(R_H/N_H) \geqslant u_0, \qquad s_L - \alpha a(R_L/N_L) \geqslant u_0, \tag{5.27}$$

where we have substituted $y_i = R_i/N_i$ in the expressions for the cost of effort. The firm chooses the payments, s_i, and the revenue levels (equivalent to effort, since $y_i = R_i/N_i$) to maximize profits subject to these constraints. Both the participation constraints (5.27) will hold with equality, so s_i can be substituted directly in the objective, and optimization takes place just with respect to R_i. If $a(y) = y^2/2$, then expected profits are

$$E\Pi^1 = \beta\left(R_H - \frac{\alpha}{2}\left(\frac{R_H}{N_H}\right)^2\right) + (1 - \beta)\left(R_L - \frac{\alpha}{2}\left(\frac{R_L}{N_L}\right)^2\right) - u_0. \tag{5.28}$$

Optimal values of R_i are given by $R_i = N_i^2/\alpha$ and using this back in (5.28) optimized profits can be expressed as a function of parameters,

$$E\Pi^1 = [\beta N_H^2 + (1 - \beta)N_L^2]/2\alpha - u_0. \tag{5.29}$$

The quadratic form of this expression reflects the fact that the state of the market determines revenue directly, and also by causing a higher level of effort to be expended.

What about the case of outsourcing to local sales agents? There is an efficiency gain, since $\alpha = 1$. However, the multinational no longer observes the state of nature, known only to the local agent. It observes the realized level of revenue R_i and can make payment s_i contingent on this. This creates a principal–agent problem in which there is hidden information.

To illustrate the difficulties that arise, suppose that the local agent was confronted with a contract offering the same payments and effort levels as in the internalization case (but derived with $\alpha = 1$) and with these values denoted by a superscript '*'. If state H occurs, what does the agent do? If the agent reports that state H has occurred and puts in the commensurate effort to yield R_H^*, then she would receive payment s_H^* and utility would be just u_0. However, suppose that instead she reports that state L occurred. Revenue R_L^*, and therefore payment s_L^*, can be attained with an effort level strictly less than y_L^*; her utility level is therefore strictly greater than u_0 (which is the utility level she would receive from effort level y_H^* and payment s_H^*). The agent therefore has an incentive to misreport, and this reduces the firm's expected profits; it will never have a good state reported.

The firm can do better by designing a contract such that in state H the agent truthfully reveals that state H occurs, putting in a higher level of effort and receiving a higher payment. This is an example of a result known generally as the revelation principle, which states (loosely) that the principal can never do better than by designing a contract which induces the agent to truthfully reveal the hidden information (see Myerson (1991) for complete analysis). In our context, to induce such truthful revelation the contract has to satisfy the incentive compatibility constraint:

$$s_H - a(R_H/N_H) \geqslant s_L - a(R_L/N_H). \tag{5.30}$$

This says that the levels of payments and revenues (effort) specified in the contract are such that, when N_H occurs, the agent prefers to truthfully reveal that the state of nature is high, taking payment s_H and generating revenue R_H, rather than declare that it is low. In addition, the contract must satisfy the participation constraint, (5.27), although now this constraint binds only in the low state. Pulling this together, the firm chooses s_i and R_i to maximize

$$E\Pi^O = \beta(R_H - s_H) + (1 - \beta)(R_L - s_L) \tag{5.31}$$

subject to

$$s_H - a(R_H/N_H) \geqslant s_L - a(R_L/N_H), \qquad s_L \geqslant a(R_L/N_L) + u_0. \tag{5.32}$$

Once again, optimization is easy as the constraints (holding with equality) can be used to substitute s_i out of the objective. Using the quadratic effort function $a(y) = y^2/2$, expected profits are

$$E\Pi^1 = \beta \left(R_H - \frac{1}{2} \left[\left(\frac{R_H}{N_H} \right)^2 - \left(\frac{R_L}{N_H} \right)^2 + \left(\frac{R_L}{N_L} \right)^2 \right] \right)$$
$$+ (1 - \beta) \left(R_L - \frac{1}{2} \left(\frac{R_L}{N_L} \right)^2 \right) - u_0. \tag{5.33}$$

Maximization with respect to R_i gives first-order conditions $R_H = N_H^2$ and $R_L = N_L^2(1 - \beta)/(1 - \beta(N_L/N_H)^2)$. Maximized profits are

$$E\Pi^O = \frac{\beta N_H^2}{2} + \frac{(1 - \beta)N_L^2}{2} \left[\frac{1 - \beta}{1 - \beta(N_L/N_H)^2} \right] - u_0. \tag{5.34}$$

Comparing this with (5.29), we see that the impact of hidden information on the firm's profits is given by the term in square brackets, which, since $N_L \leqslant N_H$, is less than or equal to unity. Intuitively, designing a contract to meet the incentive compatibility constraint means that the principal has to transfer some surplus to the agent. The transfer occurs only in the low state, and is sometimes referred to as the 'informational rent' that the agent earns from her informational advantage.

The firm makes its choice of mode on the basis of comparing expected profits under the regimes of internalization and outsourcing, equations (5.29) and (5.34). As in previous cases, the direct inefficiency cost of internalization ($\alpha > 1$) reduces profits under this mode. Pulling in the opposite direction is the agency cost of outsourcing, the square bracket in (5.34). This can be interpreted by noting that the square bracket is unity if $N_L = N_H$ or if $\beta = 0$; if $\beta = 1$, the whole term disappears. It is therefore when uncertainty is large ($N_L < N_H$ and intermediate values of β) that the agency cost is large, and multinationals are most likely to arise, internalizing their local operations. A higher degree of risk is associated with a higher likelihood of internalization. The reason is that agency costs (the rents transferred to the agent to induce truth telling) increase with the potential variation in market size, since the incentive not to reveal state H is higher the higher the effort saved by declaring instead L, which in turn is proportional to the ratio N_H/N_L.

This is the benchmark model, but Horstmann and Markusen (1996) extend it to a multi-period setting. The MNE may then optimally choose to use a local agent initially, shifting to internalization in later periods. Sales agents are then used to 'explore new markets'. The MNE will learn the state of the market from the agent, thus avoiding the risk of setting up costly infrastructures in non-profitable markets.

5.6 Conclusions

This chapter provides an analytical framework to understand the circumstances under which the internationalization of activities takes place through the opening up of foreign subsidiaries or through arm's-length agreements. The basic trade-off is between the higher costs involved in setting up and running wholly owned operations and the market failures affecting the contractual relationship with local firms. These market failures generate a rent for these local firms, and reduce profits accruing to the MNE.

We have analysed in detail three types of market failures generating trade-offs between internalized and arm's-length transactions. The first one is the hold-up problem. Transactions become relation specific when the supplier has to carry out investments which are specific to that relationship and when products cannot be sold to third parties without taking large losses. These features emerge frequently in customer supplier relationships, both in more technologically intensive and in traditional types of operations. Because of uncertainty, contracts cannot be complete.

Thus, parties in these captive transactions might wish to renegotiate the terms of the contract ex-post. We show that under these circumstances local suppliers are likely to underinvest, compared with what he/she would do if there were no market failures.

The second problem is the dissipation of intangible assets. According to the knowledge-capital model, MNEs invest abroad in order to exploit their intangible assets. Unfortunately, these assets may well be dissipated by the investment itself. We discuss two types of intangible assets: technology and goodwill. Local counterparts may learn the technology to their own advantage and become competitors in the future. Equally, they could dissipate the MNE's good name and reputation by producing low-quality products under high-quality brands. In both cases the risk of dissipation is lower if the firm carries out the activities with its own subsidiaries. Yet, arm's-length agreements could give cost savings. To avoid dissipation under arm's-length agreements MNEs need to pay locals a rent, providing them with the right incentive not to defect or to cheat. This rent will be higher the higher the risk of dissipation. Thus, the more intangible asset intensive the activity carried out, the more likely is the MNE to internalize it.

The third issue analysed concerns the principal–agency relationship between MNEs and local firms. In this case the relationship can be affected by problems of hidden action or hidden information about the local market. In the case of hidden information many features of the local market might be unknown to the MNE. The local agent could have an interest in reporting that the market is worse than it actually is, to justify his/her poor performance. Once more, to compensate for these information asymmetries and induce the agent to maximize his effort anyway, the MNE must divide its rent with the agent.

The analysis of these market failures provide some understanding on how key variables interact in making one or the other option more profitable. Clearly, opening up wholly owned subsidiaries is deterred by high costs of running them relative to the costs of local firms. Less trivially, we find that for arm's-length agreements to take place requires a balance of incentives. For example, bargaining power should be relatively balanced in order to provide incentives for both parties. Similarly, when we are considering the problem of the dissipation of knowledge, external transactions emerge at intermediate ease of technology transfer. When it is too difficult to transfer, the costs of making locals able to use it is too high. If it is too easily dissipated, MNEs are more likely to protect it, avoiding any unnecessary transfer. Of course, the MNE may also face a wider range of choices than the internalization/outsourcing alternative posed throughout this chapter. Various sorts of joint venture and cost-sharing agreements are possible, although have not been that widely studied.

The empirical literature confirms that the relationship between foreign investors and local firms is especially effective when the asymmetries between them are not too large. Technological spillovers to national firms are found to be larger, either when there is sufficient technological proximity between the parties or when there is an active business relationship between them.

Appendix

Given effective input prices w_x, w_y, maximization of

$$x^{\mu\eta} y^{\mu(1-\eta)} - xw_x - yw_y$$

with respect to x and y gives first-order conditions $\mu\eta R = xw_x$, $\mu(1-\eta)R = yw_y$, where $R = x^{\mu\eta} y^{\mu(1-\eta)}$. Eliminating the optimized values of x and y gives equation (5.10), $R^* = A[w_x^\eta w_y^{1-\eta}]^{\mu/(\mu-1)}$, with $A \equiv [[\mu(1-\eta)]^{1-\eta}[\mu\eta]^\eta]^{\mu/(1-\mu)}$.

6

Determinants of FDI: the Evidence

We have identified two distinct reasons why a firm would want to invest abroad. One is to supply a market directly through an affiliate (horizontal investment (HFDI), as discussed in Chapter 3). The other is to find low-cost locations for parts of the production process (vertical investment (VFDI), as discussed in Chapter 4). In each case a firm faces trade-offs in its investment decision. Avoiding trade costs through HFDI implies foregoing economies of scale, as production is distributed across several plants. Exploiting international differences in factor prices through VFDI means incurring costs of geographically disintegrating production. Theory suggests factors that are important in these trade-offs; some of these factors are firm or industry specific (e.g. the importance of economies of scale), some are country characteristics (e.g. market size or factor prices), and often it is the interaction of these firm and country characteristics. This chapter is devoted to empirically testing the hypotheses suggested by theory and to measuring the quantitative importance of different factors in determining MNE activity.

6.1 A General Framework

Theory comes up with a number of predictions on how firm, industry and country characteristics influence the investment decision. These predictions are summarized in Table 2.3 and derived in Chapters 3 and 4. Some of the main ones are that HFDI will take place when gains in trade costs and strategic advantage are large relative to the fixed cost of setting up a new plant. We therefore expect to find MNEs mainly among firms that can spread assets across several plants at little cost, i.e. when firm-level economies of scale are large relative to plant-level economies of scale. VFDI is predicted to occur when factor cost savings are large relative to the costs of fragmenting activities in several locations. Thus, it is more likely to occur for firms with production processes that can be easily fragmented into several stages characterized by different factor intensities and between countries with different factor endowments. Trade and transport costs will tend to act to encourage HFDI, but discourage VFDI.

Table 6.1. Dependent and independent variables.

Y_{ij}^h	Alternative measures of the extent of operations carried out by industry h firms originating in country i in host country j, e.g. investment flow, firm sales, value added, employment
X^h	Returns to scale at the plant level, returns to scale at the firm level (multiplant economies of scale), factor intensities, R&D intensity, advertising intensity
X_i	Home country market size, factor endowments, trade barriers, tax rates, membership of regional integration agreements
X_j	Host country market size, factor endowments, trade barriers, tax rates, investment promotion policies, membership of regional integration agreements
X_{ij}	Geographical distance, trade costs, similarity in factor endowments, similarity in market size, membership of same regional integration agreement
X_{ij}^h	Transport costs, tariffs, varying across industry and across countries

Before investigating these and other hypotheses in detail, it is useful to set out a general framework that encompasses most of the studies that we will look at. We therefore write the following expression:

$$Y_{ij}^h = f(X^h, X_i, X_j, X_{ij}, X_{ij}^h, X^h \times X_i, X^h \times X_j) + \varepsilon_{ij}^h. \tag{6.1}$$

The dependent variable, Y_{ij}^h, is some measure of the extent of operations performed in host country j by industry h multinationals headquartered in home country i. Explanatory variables are a vector of firm and/or industry characteristics (X^h), of home country characteristics (X_i), of host country characteristics (X_j), and of bilateral relationships between home and host countries (X_{ij}), such as the distance between them. Some of the firm or industry variables may also be country specific, or specific to the bilateral relationship between countries (X_{ij}^h). There may also be interactions between these variables as, for example, when an unskilled-labour-intensive firm is attracted to a country abundant in unskilled labour ($X^h \times X_j$).

An empirical study typically selects specific variables in some or all of the general categories of equation (6.1). Table 6.1 lists specific variables, elements of these vectors, that have been used in empirical studies.

The choice of which variable to use depends partly on the conceptual issues being addressed and partly on data availability. Most of the earlier literature on the determinants of FDI used balance-of-payments data to construct the dependent variable, Y_{ij}^h. However, the theory presented in previous chapters gives predictions on real activity by multinational firms rather than financial flows generated by them.

More recent literature in this area has used data on affiliate production or sales as the dependent variable, which makes it more closely related to the theory.[1]

The conceptually appropriate variable to use depends on the hypothesis being investigated. An important aspect of this is the stage of firm's decision-making process. Referring back to previous chapters, we can think of the firm's decision problem in a two-stage game, where the firm first chooses whether or not to produce in a country and then, if production is established, chooses production levels. The sets of variables listed above may impact on the firm's decisions at these different stages in different ways. For instance, geographical distance may discourage a firm from setting up a foreign plant because countries far away tend to constitute less important markets than countries nearby. But if a plant is established, then the share of affiliate sales in total foreign sales (i.e. affiliate sales plus exports) may very well be higher the further away the host country is, because higher transportation costs will encourage the firm to supply the market through affiliate sales rather than exports.

One implication of the multiple-stage nature of the firm's decision problem is that interpretation of the results from the estimation of a regression equation based on an equation such as (6.1) crucially depends on the choice of dependent variable, Y_{ij}^h. Ideally, an empirical implementation of (6.1) would involve two parts. A discrete choice model (where Y_{ij}^h would indicate whether a firm headquartered in country i has chosen to set up affiliate production in country j) together with an analysis of the scale of affiliate operations, conditional on the observation that affiliate production takes place in country j. Such an implementation would, however, require detailed information about the firm's operations across countries, information that is usually unavailable to the researcher. Instead, many studies are based on data on the scale of affiliate activity at the aggregate industry level. Such studies provide useful information but it should be noted that they really estimate a reduced form equation in the sense that they focus on the outcome of both stages of the firm's decision problem. Some studies have tried to disentangle how different variables impact on different decision stages and we shall indicate so whenever this is the case.[2]

Most of the findings we discuss in this chapter are based on estimating some form of equation (6.1). In Box 6.1 we provide one of the best-known examples of such a regression, drawn from a study that will be referred to frequently in the chapter. This, and the other studies we draw on, are of course multiple regressions, although we organize the discussion around the impact of particular variables in turn. In

---

[1] Some of the earlier studies that in fact use measures of real activity are Horst (1972), Swedenborg (1979) and Lipsey and Weiss (1981).

[2] In most of the discussion in this chapter, the suffix h is used to indicate either industry- or firm-specific variables, depending on context. When we introduce heterogeneous firms within an industry, then the suffix k will indicate firm-specific variables and the suffix h industry-specific ones.

the following discussion, we start by considering evidence on the role played by industry/firm characteristics (i.e. variables of the X^h type, Section 6.2) and then move on to evidence on the role played by home and host countries characteristics (i.e. variables of the X_i, X_j and X_{ij} type, Section 6.3). One key question is whether the data lend more support to the theory of HFDI than to the theory of VFDI. We address this in Section 6.4, and will see that it is not an easy empirical task as both types of investment coexist and are not easy to distinguish in the data. Finally, in Section 6.5 we focus on two specific issues that affect FDI: regional integration agreements and the 'herding' or agglomeration of FDI projects.

Box 6.1. The Proximity–Concentration Trade-Off

We take as an example one of the regressions of Brainard (1997), who seeks to examine the roles of proximity (i.e. trade costs) and concentration (due to scale effects) by estimating a series of equations including

$$\ln\left(\frac{\text{EXP}_{ij}^h}{\text{AS}_{ij}^h + \text{EXP}_{ij}^h}\right) = \alpha_0 + \alpha_1 \ln(\text{firm-scale}^h) + \alpha_2 \ln(\text{plant-scale}^h)$$
$$+ \alpha_3 \ln(\text{tax}_j) + \alpha_4 \ln(\text{pwgdp}_{ij}) + \alpha_5 \ln(\text{freight}_{ij}^h)$$
$$+ \alpha_6 \ln(\text{tariff}_{ij}^h) + \alpha_7 \ln(X_j) + \varepsilon_{ij}^h. \tag{6.2}$$

The dependent variable is, for each industry h, the share of exports in the total sales (exports plus affiliate sales) by country i to country j in industry h. Thus, EXP_{ij}^h is exports from country i to country j in industry h, and AS_{ij}^h is sales by affiliates of firms headquartered in i in country j and industry h. The first two independent variables just vary across industries; firm-scale^h and plant-scale^h are measures of firm- and plant-level economies of scale in industry h. The next variable, tax$_j$, is the average effective corporate tax rate in host country j, followed by a bilateral measure, pwgdp$_{ij}$, the absolute value of the difference in per-worker GDP between countries i and j. The measures of trade costs and barriers, freight$_{ij}^h$ and tariff$_{ij}^h$ vary across sectors and across country pairs. Finally, there are a number of other host country controls, such as language, openness to trade, and political variables, that are summarized in the vector X_j.

   Brainard's sample is outwards investment by the US, so the home country, i, does not vary in the sample. The equation is estimated on 27 host countries and 63 primary and manufacturing sectors for 1989, and results are given in Table 6.2. Noting that the dependent variable is the log of 1 *minus* the share of affiliates, we see that all signs but one are as would be predicted by the theory of HFDI and are significant. The exception is the tax variable, which indicates that higher corporate taxation encourages affiliate sales. Each of these effects, and some of the issues surrounding choice of appropriate variables and data, are discussed in Sections 6.2 and 6.3.

Table 6.2. Estimating the trade-offs affecting FDI: fixed costs and market access.

	Dependent variable Y_{ij}^h: Share of exports in affiliate supply + exports
firm-scale^h	−0.2726 (−4.7)
plant-scale^h	0.1345 (2.7)
tax$_j$	−0.569 (−1.79)
pwgdp$_{ij}$	0.296 (3.75)
freight$_{ij}^h$	−0.2717 (−4.6)
tariff$_{ij}^h$	−0.3707 (−7.4)
Adjusted R^2	0.233
Number of observations	1035

OLS estimates. t statistics in brackets. *Source:* Brainard (1997, Table 1, Column 4).

6.2 Industry and Firm Determinants of FDI

In this section we focus on the empirical evidence on how industry and firm characteristics affect the extent of multinational activities. In so doing, we postpone
discussion of any potential effects stemming from the interaction between indus-
try/firm characteristics and country characteristics (variables of the $X^h \times X_i$ or
$X^h \times X_j$ type).

The broad industrial picture has already been described in Chapter 1, where we
saw that foreign subsidiaries account for a larger share of employment in industries
like chemicals, machinery and transportation equipment. It appears that the presence
of MNEs is greatest in sectors characterized by large investments in research and
development, a large share of professional and technical workers, and the production
of technically complex or differentiated goods. To what extent is this borne out by
econometric studies, containing multiple explanatory variables?

Firm- versus plant-level economies of scale

The hypothesis from theory is that firm-level economies of scale are likely to promote
FDI, while plant-level economies of scale are likely to be detrimental to it, and this
is confirmed by the econometric evidence.

These studies generally consider the alternative between serving foreign markets
through affiliate sales or through exports, so typically take as dependent variable

affiliate sales relative to total foreign sales (exports plus affiliate sales). Box 6.1 gives an example from Brainard (1997). In an industry-level study of outward and inward affiliate sales for the US, she finds fairly consistent evidence that affiliate sales are large relative to trade in industries with large firm-level economies of scale and smaller in industries where plant-level economies of scale dominate. This holds both for the activities of US MNEs in foreign countries and of foreign MNEs in the US.[3]

A key issue is to do with the measurement of firm- and plant-level economies of scale. Brainard (1997) uses the number of production workers in the median plant as an industry measure of plant-level economies of scale, and the number of non-production workers in the average US-based firm as an industry measure of firm-level economies of scale. Brainard's results are supported by a number of other studies using similar types of measures of firm- and plant-level fixed costs (e.g. Ekholm 1998; Norbäck 2001; Yeaple 2003; Helpman et al. 2004).

An alternative is to identify the firm-specific assets that are the sources of firm-level economies of scale. Firm-specific assets include knowledge about product designs or production processes, trade-marks, reputation for high-quality products, and brand image. Although intangible, they are typically generated by observable expenditures made by firms. For example, several studies have used advertising intensity as a measure of brand image and, using industry-level data, find a positive relation between advertising intensity and FDI. Brainard (1997) reports some evidence in favour of the hypothesis that advertising intensity promotes affiliate sales over trade. She finds a positive relation between advertising intensity and the share of affiliate sales in total foreign sales.[4]

Another important source of firm-specific assets is technological knowledge created by R&D activities. Because expenditures for R&D are relatively easy to observe, several studies have examined whether the R&D intensity of the firm or the industry is positively related to the propensity to carry out FDI. Such studies based on industry-level data have generally found a positive relation.[5] Typically, these studies

---

[3] Brainard (1997) uses several different specifications in her study. She runs regressions on the levels of affiliate sales and trade and on the share of trade in total foreign sales. In one of the specifications, she uses a generalized Tobit model to distinguish between the impact of the independent variables on the discrete decision to set up affiliate production, on the one hand, and on the decision of how large a share of total foreign sales should be supplied through affiliate sales, on the other.

[4] However, at the same time she finds a negative relation between advertising intensity and the level of inward affiliate sales, which is contrary to expectations and makes the results somewhat difficult to interpret. According to Brainard (1997), a possible explanation for this result is that advertising intensity is measured with US data, which may poorly capture the industry variation in advertising intensity in other countries.

[5] Some early studies include Horst (1972) and Lall (1980a) and a more recent one is Brainard (1997). A survey of this literature can be found in Pearce et al. (1992). See also Caves (1996, Chapter 1).

find that both the extent to which firms in an industry conduct foreign operations and the share of affiliates in industry output are positively related to the R&D intensity of the industry. Thus, industries in which firms tend to have high outlays on R&D are industries that tend to generate a lot of FDI.

However, this is a context in which the distinction between the two stages of a firm's decision taking—whether to locate abroad, and then how much to produce abroad—is likely to be important. Although high R&D intensity makes it more likely that firms will decide to expand overseas, it is not necessarily the case that, once the investment takes place, the higher the R&D intensity the larger the ratio between the sales of foreign subsidiaries and exports. There is indeed some evidence that R&D investment has a different impact on the two decision stages.

Looking at the first-stage decision, a comparison between Swedish MNEs and national firms in 1998 reveals that R&D expenditures per employee were, on average, about 10 times greater for MNEs than they were for national firms (Ekholm and Hesselman 2000).[6] Moreover, Brainard (1997) in a probit analysis of the probability that firms in different industries in the US had foreign affiliates, finds a positive association with R&D intensity. However, results change when foreign activities are analysed just for samples of MNEs, i.e. *conditional* on firms having already decided to produce abroad. For example, Norbäck (2001) finds that the higher the R&D intensity of Swedish multinationals in manufacturing the lower the share of their affiliates' sales in total foreign sales. Brainard (1997) similarly finds that R&D intensity has a positive effect on the level of US exports as well as US outward affiliate sales; the former effect is larger, with the elasticity of exports with respect to R&D intensity taking value 0.46, compared with an elasticity of affiliate sales with respect to R&D intensity of 0.18. A number of explanations are offered, including costs of technology transfer and interactions between determinants of FDI and of trade. It appears that R&D, as a firm-specific asset, is promoting MNE activity; and in addition, R&D as a source of comparative advantage is driving exports as well as affiliate sales.

Finally, economies of scale will also be important in shaping the activities of affiliates once established. Large plant-level economies of scale promote concentration of activity. Other things equal, a firm will operate fewer plants, the greater the plant-level economies of scale, and this will typically mean that such plants will export as well as just supply local markets. Thus, Hanson et al. (2001) find that US-owned affiliates tend to export a larger share of their production the greater their plant-level economies of scale. In other words, in industries characterized by strong plant-level economies of scale, foreign affiliates tend to serve markets other than just the host country market.

---

[6]The control group of Swedish manufacturing firms without foreign producing affiliates consisted of firms with an export share of at least 10%.

Firm heterogeneity in productivity

Recent work has introduced firm heterogeneity to models of trade and multinational activity, and generated several testable hypotheses. As we saw in Chapter 3, Helpman et al. (2004) have argued that heterogeneity implies that firms in a given industry face different trade-offs in the decision to invest abroad. The fixed cost of investing abroad (which is generally higher than that of exporting) can only be recouped if foreign sales are large and these are attained when marginal costs are sufficiently low. Only the most efficient firms, those with the lowest marginal costs, will choose to supply the foreign market through affiliate sales.

   Helpman et al. (2004) investigate this hypothesis using US data from 1994 which include information about foreign affiliates of US MNEs across industries and host countries. They first estimate a cross-industry regression of the ratio between US exports and US affiliate sales, which includes amongst independent variables a mea-sure of the degree of heterogeneity in firms' productivity. To construct an industry measure of this heterogeneity, they rely on information about the size distribution of firms (utilizing the result in their model that there is a one-to-one mapping between the distribution of productivity and size). They show that different measures of the size dispersion have a positive and significant effect on affiliate sales relative to exports. This would thus imply that industries with a higher degree of heterogeneity in productivity tend to have more affiliate sales relative to exports.

   Switching to the firm level, Helpman et al. (2004) then analyse if their pre-dicted sorting pattern between firms' efficiency and their foreign activities holds. They use firm-level data to rank US firms according to their labour productivity and, controlling for capital intensity and industry, indeed find that the most pro-ductive firms engage in FDI, the least productive do not have any international activity, and those in the middle are non-MNE exporters. The productivity advan-tage of MNEs over exporters is 15%. Their result is consistent with those of other studies comparing MNEs and national firms that will be analysed in Chapters 7 and 9.

6.3   Country Determinants of FDI

The next big question is: what country characteristics are important in determining FDI? Why are some countries more attractive hosts for multinationals—in aggregate, in particular sectors, and from particular home countries—than other countries?

   The first stylized fact to note is that the cross-country pattern of FDI is quite well approximated by the 'gravity' relationship. This links bilateral FDI between countries i and j to the income of each country, the distance between them, and possibly also other 'between-country' factors such as sharing a common language or border.[7] A number of authors including Shatz (2003) and Ekholm (1998), using a variety of different datasets, find that around 60% of the cross-country variation in affiliate activity can be explained by a gravity framework. While this provides a useful benchmark, very similar relationships hold for almost all sorts of spatial economic interactions, for example, trade flow, telecommunications, cross-border equity holdings and technology transfer. The task of empirical work on FDI is therefore to move beyond the gravity relationship and identify the determinants of FDI relative to other forms of international economic activity such as trade.

The early literature in this area did not build directly on formal theory, but was motivated by the ideas associated with the OLI framework (see Chapter 2). With the incorporation of multinational firms into general equilibrium trade models from the mid 1980s and onwards, it became possible to base empirical work on theoretical predictions regarding the relationship between MNE activity and home and host countries characteristics. As already mentioned, there are two distinct reasons why a firm would want to invest abroad. First, it may want to avoid costs associated with cross-border trade by supplying a market directly through an affiliate (HFDI). Second, it may want to exploit international differences in factor prices by splitting its production process geographically (VFDI). These two theories give, in some cases, conflicting predictions, particularly about the effects of some country and between-country characteristics. For example, whereas the theory of HFDI predicts a positive relation between the volume of FDI and the degree of similarity in relative factor endowments between home and host countries, the theory of VFDI predicts a negative relationship. Whereas the theory of HFDI predicts that FDI increases with trade costs, the theory of VFDI predicts that it decreases with trade costs.

This clearly poses problems for the applied researcher and for the interpretation of many of the results in the literature. The literature divides into essentially three approaches. The first is simply to accept that the data contain both sorts of investment, and that any regression is reporting some sort of average effect. This is the larger part of the literature, and inevitably forms the basis of most of the results we report in this section. The second is to try to split the data, using some observable characteristic, between those investments that are horizontal and those that are vertical. This is generally not possible, but we will see some examples of it on US data later in this section. The third approach is to try to estimate a model that encompasses both theories; approaches along these lines will be discussed in Section 6.4.

In what follows we will take up several issues in turn: trade and transport costs, taxation, production costs and factor endowments, and market size.

---

[7]Gravity models are extensively used for bilateral trade flows, and have also been used for other interactions, such as cross-border equity holdings. Anderson (1979) was the first to provide a theoretical foundation for the gravity model of international trade. The relationship between neoclassical and new trade theory has also more recently been subject to analysis by Deardorff (1998) and Feenstra et al. (2001).

Trade costs and barriers

Trade costs and various kinds of trade barrier are crucial variables for explaining the pattern of FDI. The level of these costs varies both across country pairs and across industries—in the framework of equation (6.1) these are X_{ij}^h variables. With regards to the industry variation in trade costs, it is clear that FDI in services such as banking, business services and hotel services arises largely because of sometimes prohibitively high transaction costs associated with cross-border trade in these services.

Several studies analyse the joint effect of a set of variables capturing transport costs, tariffs and non-tariff barriers on the choice of supplying a given market through exports or affiliate sales (e.g. Brainard 1997; Carr et al. 2001; Markusen and Maskus 2001, 2002; Yeaple 2003). These studies are based on industry-level data for the US and they look at the outward activities of US MNEs in foreign markets and at the inward activities of foreign MNEs in the US. They share one common result: that affiliate production tends to increase relative to exports with the level of transport costs and other trade barriers. Brainard (1997) (see Box 6.1) and Yeaple (2000), for instance, find fairly consistent evidence of freight costs as well as tariffs having positive effects on the share of total foreign sales (in the US by foreign firms or in third countries by US firms) accounted for by affiliate sales.[8] These results are in line with the predictions for HFDI.

This is a context in which, once again, it is important to distinguish between the two decision-making stages of investing abroad: the investment decision itself and the level of foreign activities. For example, when Brainard performed a probit analysis on whether or not there are affiliate activities in a particular industry or country, the estimated coefficient of freight costs becomes insignificant or, in the case of inward FDI to the US, significant with the wrong sign. This result is similar to one obtained by Ekholm (1998). Using a measure of trade costs that varies only across industries, she estimates the effect of transportation costs on both the probability of observing any affiliate sales and on the relative importance of affiliate sales in total foreign sales, conditioned on presence of affiliate activity. Transportation costs have a positive effect on the relative importance of affiliate sales, but no effect on the probability of observing affiliate activity. One possible interpretation of these findings is that foreign affiliates are more likely to be set up if their presence in the market through exports has already been established, and once this decision has been made, the more costly it is to supply a foreign market through exports, the greater the relative importance of affiliate sales.

---

[8] In Brainard (1997), freight costs were measured as the ratio of freight and insurance charges to import values as reported by importers to the US Bureau of the Census. Tariffs, measured as ad valorem tariff rates, were collected from a database compiled by GATT (see pp. 526, 527).

One important source of trade costs is artificial trade barriers, and the tariff-jumping motive for FDI has been explicitly examined in a number of recent papers.[9] In general, these studies find that tariff jumping is an important motive for investments in the US and the EU. For example, Barrell and Pain (1999b) examine the determinants of aggregate flows of Japanese FDI into both the European Union and the US in the 1980s. They find that Japanese FDI into a particular country is strongly influenced by the extent of that country's trade protection measures and, in particular, by its extent of antidumping activities. Blonigen and Feenstra (1997) use cross-industry data on Japanese FDI into the US during the period 1980–88 and find that Japanese FDI was highly responsive to both actual antidumping measures and the threat of such measures. They also find evidence of greenfield investment having a negative effect on the threat of introducing protectionist measures in the future, implying that Japanese FDI in the US may have mitigated protectionism against Japanese imports.

Although these studies suffer from the problem of being based on aggregate data, their results are partly confirmed by firm-level evidence.[10] The effect of antidumping measures is studied by Belderbos (1997) and Blonigen et al. (2002b), who match firm-level data on FDI with antidumping cases affecting these firms. Belderbos (1997) focuses on Japanese FDI into the US and the European Union across 36 electronic products and finds that tariff-jumping motives are very important determinants of FDI. Blonigen et al. (2002b) uses a more comprehensive dataset which includes information on FDI by non-Japanese firms and in a wider product range. He finds much smaller effects of US antidumping duties on FDI. Probit regressions indicate that an increase in antidumping duties of 10 percentage points increases the probability of FDI by 0.8 percentage points (from a 12.2% average probability of FDI at the means of the regressors to a 13.0% probability). The difference in results is largely due to the fact that Japanese firms have experience of overseas operations and are therefore more likely to respond with FDI than other firms being affected by antidumping duties.

We have previously noted the opposing predictions on the effects of trade costs on horizontal and vertical investments. The results described up to now are based on data which include both types of investment and which do not discriminate between them. As HFDI accounts for the largest share of FDI flows, particularly into the US, the country most extensively analysed, the pattern observed most likely characterizes the decision of firms carrying out HFDI.

---

[9]We use the familiar definition of tariff jumping to indicate FDI meant to circumvent all types of policy-induced trade barriers.

[10]Aggregate at national level in the case of Barrell and Pain (1999b) and aggregate industry data in the case of Blonigen and Feenstra (1997).

To understand the effects of trade costs on VFDI, it is necessary to work on data that can discriminate between the two types of investment. One way of discriminating is provided by information on the destination of affiliate sales, since HFDI is meant to serve local markets and VFDI to generate exports from host countries. The US data on multinationals provide such information, and has been exploited by several authors.

Markusen and Maskus (2001) decompose overall affiliate sales into sales destined for the local market and sales destined for exports, and consider the different roles of trade costs for each group. They find that host country trade costs are positively related to affiliate sales destined for the local market, which is consistent with the theory of HFDI. To investigate VFDI they look at the effect of trade costs on exports by affiliates. Contrary to expectations, the estimated relationship between the trade costs of the host country and affiliate exports back to the home country (the US) is positive and significant.[11] The complicating factor here is probably export platform FDI; as discussed in Chapter 3 this is essentially horizontal, but into a region rather than a single country. Theory suggests that it will be large if trade costs into the region are large, and trade costs within the region are small. Markusen and Maskus (2001) try to capture this by further splitting their data on US MNEs according to whether affiliates export primarily to the US or to other countries. However, since there is little variation in home country characteristics in this dataset, they are not able to generate any additional results on the effect of home country trade costs.

A comfort to theorists, the expected negative relationship between VFDI and trade costs emerges once data series covering a large part of the 1990s (when VFDI became an important component of FDI flows) are used, once the analysis is carried out at the industry level and once accurate measures of the vertical activities of foreign affiliates are devised. Hanson et al. (2001) isolate two different indices capturing the possible vertical nature of FDI. One is the ratio of affiliate exports to affiliate sales destined for the local market, which they call a measure of *export platform FDI*. The other is the ratio of affiliate imports from parents for further processing to total affiliate sales, which they refer to as a measure *outsourcing* FDI.[12] They find that both these measures are affected negatively by trade costs. The negative effect of transportation costs and host country trade barriers on the index of export platform FDI suggest that higher trade costs make affiliate activity more oriented to local sales rather than to exports, i.e. more likely to be horizontal than vertical. The negative effect on the index of outsourcing FDI means that higher trade costs raise the cost of importing intermediate inputs, and make the affiliates less competitive as suppliers of world and home markets.

---

[11] Markusen and Maskus (2001) use aggregate country data, not looking at separate industry effects.

[12] Hanson et al. (2001) also consider the firms' strategies with respect to whether they choose to engage in distribution activities or production activities in the host country.

Summing up, there is thus a substantial amount of evidence that trade costs, be it transportation costs, trade barriers, or even the threat of trade barriers, induce firms to undertake FDI and serve foreign markets through local production rather than through exports. These findings reflect the fact that world FDI seems to be predominantly horizontal in nature. However, where it is possible to accurately identify FDI that is predominantly vertical, trade costs have the opposite effect on FDI, in line with the predictions of theory.

Tax differentials and policies to attract FDI

Corporate taxation might be expected to have a clear and unambiguous effect on all sorts of FDI, low tax rates encouraging inwards investment. Matters turn out to be much less clear-cut. In theory, tax payments depend not just on average corporate tax rates but on details of the tax system and on the possibility that multinationals can shift profits by transfer pricing and other means. In empirical work we have already seen, in Box 6.1, how Brainard's (1997) study produced a perverse (although insignificant) effect, with high corporate tax reducing exports relative to affiliate sales.

We discuss the issues in detail in Chapter 10, and here just provide the briefest of summaries. While some of the earlier studies in the literature reached the conclusion that tax differentials only had a negligible effect on the pattern of FDI (Brainard 1997; Wheeler and Mody 1992), more recent work—typically with more disaggregate data and more detailed tax information—has attributed greater weight to tax. Hines (1999), in his survey of empirical studies, concludes that 'the econometric work of the last 15 years provides ample evidence on the sensitivity of the level and location of FDI to tax treatments.' He suggests that an elasticity of -0.6 of FDI with respect to taxes is a typical result in the literature. There is also evidence that responsiveness to tax has increased in recent years, as might be expected if VFDI, which is not tied to serving a particular market, has increased in importance.

Devereux and Griffith (1998) point to the fact that differences in taxation mainly influence the choice of where to locate the investment, once the decision to undertake an investment has already been taken. For example, their study of the location choice of US MNEs finds that difference in the effective average tax rate plays a significant role, conditional on the firm having already decided to invest in the EU.

In addition to taxation, a wide range of other policy instruments have been used, with varying degrees of success, to try and attract investment. Irish experience with these policies is reviewed in Chapter 8, and Chapter 10 draws the wider picture.

Production costs and factor endowments

The evidence on the role played by production costs differentials in determining FDI is rather mixed. This is yet another instance where predictions are different for HFDI and VFDI. We expect HFDI to be larger the more similar host and home countries. By contrast, we expect VFDI to increase with differences in factor endowments and factor costs, as this is precisely what investors are looking for.

Empirical studies that explicitly base their specifications on hypotheses derived from general equilibrium models have typically included measures of differences in relative factor endowments rather than production cost differentials. Brainard (1993) uses US data to test whether multinational activity increases with differences in relative factor endowments. Rather, she finds that total volumes of affiliate sales (for the bilateral activity between a pair of countries) are explained by similarities rather than differences in relative factor endowments. In Brainard (1997) (see Box 6.1) the variable $pwgdp_{ij}$ is the absolute value of the difference in per-worker GDP between countries i and j. A large value of this variable captures factor endowment differences, and we see that it has a positive coefficient, being associated with high exports rather than affiliate sales.

However, there is evidence that labour skills have a positive effect. Carr et al. (2001) report that affiliate sales are higher the larger the difference in the relative supply of skilled labour between the home and the host country. Ekholm (1997) similarly finds that foreign production increases with the home country's relative endowment of skilled labour. This approach is extended by Yeaple (2003), who uses an empirical specification similar to these earlier studies to jointly analyse country factor abundance and industry-specific factor intensities, particularly skill intensity (i.e. to study an $X^h \times X_j$ interaction). He finds that the effect of a host country's relative skill abundance on affiliate sales varies across industries: MNEs' investments in skill-abundant countries are in skill-intensive industries, whereas the opposite happens in countries with low skill abundance.

A number of studies have included measures of labour cost differentials as an explanatory factor for FDI (e.g. Braunerhjelm 1994; Hatzius 1997; Kravis and Lipsey 1982; Swedenborg 1979; Wheeler and Mody 1992). Some of these studies find no effect at all from labour cost differentials, while some even find the opposite. One problem affecting some of these studies is that the measure used for labour costs does not control for differences in productivity. This means that a positive effect of labour costs on FDI may still be consistent with firms being attracted by low *unit* labour costs. Moreover, none of these studies are able to distinguish between the labour costs of skilled versus unskilled labour. Even if affiliate activities are likely to be less skill-intensive than parent activities, their skill intensity is unlikely to be at the lowest tail of the overall distribution (cf. Markusen 2002). This means that MNEs are unlikely to engage in affiliate activities in countries with very scarce supplies of skilled labour, which are also the countries with the lowest average labour costs.[13]

---

[13]This interpretation is supported by the results presented by Markusen and Maskus (2001). They find the US outward FDI is attracted to countries with a relative abundance of skilled labour.

Market size

Market size, as suggested by theory, increases MNE affiliate production. The larger the host market the greater the likelihood that MNEs will be able to recoup the fixed cost of their foreign plants. Brainard (1997), Carr et al. (2001), Ekholm (1998) and Markusen and Maskus (2001, 2002) provide various estimates of the elasticity of foreign subsidiaries sales with respect to market size. These elasticities vary, depending on the study and on the market size measure used, but they are invariably large. For instance, Brainard (1997) in her analysis of the foreign activities of US MNEs, estimates an elasticity of foreign affiliate sales with respect to host country GDP of 0.6, while the corresponding elasticity for US exports is estimated at 0.7. Markusen and Maskus (2002) find that the elasticity of affiliate sales destined to the local market with respect to host country GDP is 1.6, whereas the elasticity of affiliate sales destined to exports is 1.1.

According to theory, we also expect that the relative market size of home and host countries matters for FDI. In particular, models of HFDI predict that MNEs tend to replace national exporting firms with multinational firms when national markets are of similar size. This prediction has obtained support in several studies. For instance, Carr et al. (2001) look at the effects of size and size difference. They find an elasticity of foreign affiliate sales with respect to the sum of GDP of the home and host countries of 5.35, implying that a 1% increase in combined real income leads to a 5.35% increase in affiliate sales. There is a robust negative effect of the squared difference between the home and host countries GDPs on real affiliate sales. The degree of similarity in home and host countries GDPs has a positive impact on the volume of multinational activity.

6.4 The Relative Importance of Horizontal versus Vertical FDI

Based on the studies cited in the previous section there is substantial evidence suggesting that getting access to foreign markets through foreign affiliates is a strong motive for FDI. The evidence on the role played by production cost differentials and differences in relative factor endowments is, on the other hand, very mixed. This has led researchers to draw the conclusion that HFDI is more prevalent and important than vertical FDI. Another piece of evidence pointing in the same direction is the fact that the main part of affiliate sales seems to be directed to the local market. That is, foreign affiliate sales are heavily dominated by local sales. UNCTAD reports that the foreign affiliates' export shares, on average, were around one-fifth during the 1980s and 1990s (UNCTAD 1998, Table I.5).

Despite the fact that most actual FDI appears to be horizontal, there is, however, some support for the relevance of factor-market considerations for FDI. It is notable that the bulk of empirical assessments of the empirical assessments of the role of factor costs as determinants of FDI have been based on cross-sectional data for the late 1980s and panel data for the period 1986–94. The boom in FDI inflows to developing countries that occurred from the early 1990s onwards is thus not reflected in these studies. Hanson et al. (2001), who split the analysis of multinational activity according to the dependent variable in order to distinguish between horizontal and vertical FDI, emphasize that FDI patterns in the 1990s were much more diverse than had previously been the case. Moreover, they argue that as most empirical analyses of multinational activity have excluded data for most of the 1990s, they have ignored a period in which factors other than market access came to play a more significant role in the strategies of US multinationals.[14] Hanson et al. (2001) claim that the importance of vertical FDI as a driving force behind multinational activity is increasing and that the observed vertical FDI has a clear regional and industrial dimension. Affiliates of US MNEs are concentrated in North America and various emerging economies, and in industries involving separable high-skill and low-skill tasks.

Other influential papers have sought to estimate a model that encompasses both horizontal and vertical FDI, trying to use the fact that theory predicts that we should observe mainly the one or the other for different values of the independent variables. In doing so, one aims at assessing the relative importance of horizontal versus vertical FDI. Carr et al. (2001) and Markusen and Maskus (2002) both use a panel (1986–94) of cross-country data of the activities of US MNEs and of foreign subsidiaries based in the US to estimate models that integrate both horizontal and vertical motives for FDI. Vertical FDI is expected to occur when home and host countries have different relative endowments of skilled labour. Firms will then have an incentive to split headquarters and plants by locating the headquarters in the country relatively abundant in skilled labour and production plants in the country relatively scarce in skilled labour. In particular, when the relatively skill-abundant country is smaller than the other country, firms headquartered in that country will have incentives to carry out their production in proximity to the large foreign market.

They base their analysis on the estimating equation:

$$AS_{ij} = \beta_0 + \beta_1(GDP_i + GDP_j) + \beta_2(GDP_i - GDP_j)^2$$
$$+ \beta_3(SK_i - SK_j) + \beta_4(GDP_i - GDP_j)(SK_i - SK_j) + \gamma X_{ij} + \varepsilon,$$
$$\text{(6.3)}$$

where AS_{ij} is real affiliate sales, X_{ij} is a vector of independent variables, now including variables such as trade costs, investment barriers and geographical distance, and γ is a vector of regression coefficients.

---

[14]Their evidence on an increased importance of international fragmentation of production is consistent with the findings by Hummels et al. (2001). Hummels et al. estimate that vertical specialization of trade accounts for up to 30% of world exports and that it has grown as much as 40% over the last 25 years.

The first independent variable in equation (6.3) is the sum of home and host countries GDPs, which is expected to have a positive effect on horizontal affiliate activity (i.e. $\beta_1 > 0$). The second variable is the squared difference in home and host countries GDPs, capturing the degree of dissimilarity in country size, which is expected to have a negative effect on horizontal affiliate activity (i.e. $\beta_2 < 0$). None of these variables are predicted to have an effect on vertical affiliate activity which is independent of differences in relative factor endowments. This means that the hypotheses that $\beta_1 > 0$ and $\beta_2 < 0$ can be tested against the alternative $\beta_1 = \beta_2 = 0$ as a test of the horizontal versus the vertical model (Markusen and Maskus 2002). Using data covering both inbound and outbound affiliate activities for the US Carr et al. (2001) and Markusen and Maskus (2001) find that $\beta_1 > 0$ and $\beta_2 < 0$, which is consistent with support for the model of HFDI, but not for the model of VFDI.

The third variable is the difference in relative skill endowments and the fourth is this difference interacted with the difference in GDP. The theory of HFDI predicts that affiliate activity is promoted by similarity in relative skill endowments between the home and host countries ($\beta_3 < 0$), while the theory of VFDI predicts that it increases with the difference in relative skill endowments between the home and host countries ($\beta_3 > 0$).[15]

They find that $\beta_3 > 0$, which is consistent with the model of VFDI. However, when Markusen and Maskus (2001) only use data on outbound affiliate activities, they find that $\beta_3 < 0$, which implies support for the horizontal rather than the vertical model of FDI. These contradictory results have led some researchers to re-estimate the model using different specifications and/or datasets, including country pairs in which the US is neither home nor host country (e.g. Blonigen et al. 2002a; Braconier et al. 2002, 2003). Some of these studies favour the horizontal model, while none of them, however, present results that favour the model of vertical over horizontal FDI.[16]

Markusen and Maskus (2002) carry out a formal test of the so-called knowledge-capital model—integrating both types of motives for FDI—against models of purely horizontal FDI and purely vertical FDI. They find that the integrated model outper-

---

[15] In the horizontal model, affiliate activity is actually not maximized when relative endowments are identical, but when the smaller country is somewhat more skill abundant (see Figure 12.2 in Markusen 2002). However, the most accurate way of translating the model's predictions to testable hypotheses is probably still to posit a positive relationship between affiliate activity and the degree of similarity of relative skill endowments.

[16] Blonigen et al. (2002a) specify differences in relative skill endowments as absolute differences and claim that this enables them to reject the knowledge-capital model in favour of the horizontal model. Braconier et al. (2002) pool data for the US with data on outbound affiliate activity for Sweden, thereby including observations in which the home country is small and abundant in skilled labour. Braconier et al. (2003) use an even larger dataset and somewhat different specifications of the skill and size variables. Their results are more supportive of the knowledge-capital model.

forms a model of VFDI, but not a model of HFDI. They conclude that the model of purely horizontal FDI does as well in explaining the pattern of FDI as the integrated model, whereas the model of vertical FDI is clearly rejected in favour of both the integrated model and the model of purely horizontal FDI.

A few studies have used the strategy of trying to separate out observations that one would expect to be more closely related to VFDI, to test whether the theory of VFDI gets support when using these observations only. Using US data, Brainard (1993) and Markusen and Maskus (2001) get some support for the relevance of factor market considerations as determinants of FDI when they split affiliate production into local sales and exports. In Markusen and Maskus (2001), the results from a regression equation similar to (6.3) show that export sales of foreign affiliates are positively related to differences in relative endowments of skilled labour between home and host countries. Moreover, the proportion of export sales in total affiliate sales decreases with the relative abundance of skilled labour of the host country when they use data for both outbound and inbound affiliate activities for the US.[17] They also find that affiliate production for export is more sensitive to a rise in investment barriers than affiliate production for local sales. A possible explanation for this result is that FDI that is not undertaken to serve a specific foreign market is more sensitive to investment costs because the MNE has the option to choose another location. This result would then imply that affiliate production for exports does indeed reflect vertical rather than horizontal FDI, or, alternatively, that the host country is used as an export platform for a region.

Hence, even though the empirical evidence indicates that VFDI does not account for a significant amount of world FDI, it still suggests that it plays a role, and, most likely, an increasing one. We have already argued in Section 6.2 that it is much more difficult to single out the effects of factor cost differences than of other variables like market size. Thus the importance of VFDI is likely to still be underestimated given the details of the data available for empirical analysis. However, the ongoing and advancing data collection with respect to FDI and MNEs will provide us with more detailed information that enables the construction of a broader range of independent as well as dependent variables. This, in turn, makes it easier to disentangle vertical and horizontal FDI, and to significantly improve our knowledge of the determinants and patterns of vertical versus horizontal FDI in the world economy.

6.5   Other Factors Affecting the Location of FDI

Most of the works analysed in this chapter address the basic determinants discussed in the theoretical models of Chapters 3 and 4. There are, however, other factors that

---

[17] However, as has been mentioned previously, in their analysis of outbound affiliate activity only, they find that affiliate activity increases with the abundance in skilled labour of the host country, both regarding local production as well as production for exports.

have important effects on the trade-offs between the costs and benefits of investing abroad and which are important determinants of the location of FDI. We consider two such factors: regional integration and the agglomeration and 'herding' of FDI projects.

Regional integration

Regional integration provides a very useful and natural example with which to analyse the determinants of the location of FDI. The reduction of internal trade costs associated with regional integration may affect volumes and patterns of FDI both into and within the integrated area. The increase in effective market size that regional integration entails should, according to theory, increase inwards HFDI into the area. However, between countries in the integrated area, reduced trade costs might deter HFDI while encouraging VFDI. Regional integration may also lead nationally segmented markets to become integrated, which may in turn impact on market structure, the organization of firms, and the attractiveness of M&A activity. We might also expect these effects to vary across regional integration schemes. Some of them are between countries with relatively similar economies and factor endowments (the EU) and others between countries with important differences in factor endowments (NAFTA).

A number of studies have addressed these issues in the context of NAFTA. According to Blomström and Kokko (1997b), NAFTA has had significant effects on the location of US multinational activity. In line with what the theory of HFDI would predict, affiliate activities in Canada have become less important relative to exports to Canada as market access has been facilitated through the free-trade agreement. At the same time, FDI into Mexico, which is typically vertical, has increased rapidly.

As for the EU, we observe that the volume of FDI in Europe increased substantially in the 1990s. A brief look at the pattern of FDI in Europe shows that the large European countries—the UK, Germany and France—have attracted the major share. However, as shown by Table 6.3, their dominating role as recipients of FDI has decreased over time, whereas some small countries have experienced large increases in inflows of FDI. In particular, this seems to be the case for the UK and Germany. The UK hosted approximately 34% of total EU FDI in 1980, whereas the corresponding figure for 1999 was around 24%. For Germany, the figure for 1980 was about 20% and for 1999 about 14%. In contrast Belgium–Luxembourg, Ireland and Sweden have become important host countries over the last 10 years, which is reflected both in their share of EU FDI as well as through the ratio of FDI to GDP. Given their access to the regional market, small countries are viable export platforms for external investors, particularly if they have lower factor costs or tax rates than the larger countries in the region. Ireland is the obvious case of a small country which

Table 6.3.   Distribution of inward FDI stocks within the EU.

	1980		1990		1999	
	A	B	A	B	A	B
Austria	4.0	1.7	6.2	1.5	11.2	1.4
Belgium–Luxembourg	5.9	4.0	28.3	8.1	108.3	11.0
Denmark	6.3	2.3	6.9	1.3	20.9	2.3
Finland	1.1	0.3	3.8	0.7	14.5	1.0
France	3.4	12.3	8.4	12.1	17.1	11.0
Germany	4.0	19.9	7.3	15.5	13.7	13.7
Greece	11.3	2.5	16.9	1.9	17.7	1.4
Ireland	19.5	2.0	12.2	0.8	50.7	2.7
Italy	2.0	4.8	5.3	8.1	9.4	6.5
Netherlands	11.1	10.4	23.6	10.3	50.1	13.0
Portugal	12.8	0.6	15.3	0.7	21.2	1.2
Spain	2.4	2.8	13.4	9.1	20.5	6.8
Sweden	2.3	2.0	5.4	1.7	32.7	4.1
United Kingdom	11.7	34.3	20.8	28.3	26.8	23.9
EU 15	5.3	100	11.0	100	22.2	100

A, Inward FDI as a percentage share of GDP; B, Percentage of total EU inward FDI.
Source: UNCTAD (2000, 2001).

has become an important platform for MNEs outside the region (mostly US) to export into the region. A case study of Ireland is the subject of Chapter 8.

A substantial part of the increase in inward FDI in Europe shown in Table 6.3 is, however, due to an increase in intra-EU FDI. This appears to be against what theory would predict, given the FDI we observe is primarily horizontal in nature. But this increase is mainly driven by a substantial rise in the number of cross-border mergers and acquisitions (M&A). Hence, what it reflects is that, following European integration, there has been considerable restructuring of European industries, and this in turn had consequences for the location of economic activity within Europe (see Braunerhjelm et al. 2000).

The empirical literature dealing with the effect of European integration on FDI has primarily focused on FDI from outside Europe. One issue that has been examined is whether the closer integration between the European countries has affected the propensity for non-European MNEs to invest in the area. A number of studies have examined whether the formation of the European Community and the 1992 Single Market Programme has affected US and Japanese FDI into Europe (for a survey of this literature, see Blomström and Kokko (1997b)). Most studies conclude that FDI into Europe was spurred by increased European integration. For instance Barrell and Pain (1999a), who use balance-of-payment data for US FDI into Europe 1978–94, find that the overall level was higher in the period 1989–94 compared with 1978–93. They attribute this to the effect of the Single Market Programme.

There is some evidence suggesting that membership of the European Community led to significant increases in FDI for Ireland, Spain and Portugal, but not for Greece. This has been interpreted as evidence of EU membership interacting with domestic institutions and policies in determining the attractiveness of a particular country for non-European FDI. The same conclusion seems to apply when addressing the effect of MERCOSUR on FDI into Argentina, Brazil, Paraguay and Uruguay. According to Blomström and Kokko (1997b), domestic policies in these countries have been more important in determining FDI inflows than regional integration. This implies that we need to be careful when assessing the effects of regional integration. In fact, integration, in addition to reducing internal trade barriers, also affects the member countries' domestic institutions and policies.

Another aspect of European integration is the ongoing transition of the countries in Central and Eastern Europe (CEE) to market economies and the Eastern enlargement of the European Union. It is evident that there has been a strong increase of FDI into CEE since the mid 1990s, possibly lured by the prospect of stronger integration with Western Europe (see, for example, Braconier and Ekholm 2002; Barba Navaretti et al. 2001). Barba Navaretti et al. emphasize the increased importance of CEE in international production networks, reflecting VFDI into the region.

Agglomeration and herding

FDI is encouraged by proximity to customers or by factor price differentials. However, proximity to other firms may also play a role in the location of FDI. Economists have long recognized the importance of agglomeration benefits for the location of firms. Industrial clusters in which firms benefit from locating close to each other may arise because of knowledge spillovers, thick markets for specialized factors, or forward and backward linkages between customer and supplier firms. Moreover, the new economic geography literature has over the last decade developed microeconomic foundations enabling the study of the impact of agglomeration effects on industrial structures and international trade (Fujita et al. 1999). This has also triggered empirical analysis of the role of agglomeration benefits for the location of firms in general, and, of relevance here, for the location of FDI. We discussed in Chapter 3 how the location of MNEs can give rise to pecuniary externalities. A number of different empirical approaches have been followed.

Among the first contributions to this literature was Wheeler and Mody (1992), who used country characteristics such as the quality of infrastructure, degree of industrialization and the level of inward FDI into the respective market as measures of agglomeration factors. They concluded that these factors appear to be important determinants of US outward FDI. Head et al. (1995, 1999) used a similar approach to that of Wheeler and Mody to examine the location of Japanese manufacturing investment across the US states in the 1980s. In order to take into account the role of agglomeration effects in determining location, they included a variable measuring the number of Japanese firms within the same sector already located in the region. Their estimation yielded a positive coefficient for this variable, which the authors took as evidence for the importance of agglomeration economies for the location of Japanese FDI in the US.

However, as pointed out both by Decoster and Strange (1993) and by Barry et al. (2003b), even in the absence of agglomeration economies, such as knowledge spillovers and market linkages, investors may exhibit a tendency to imitate each others' location. Foreign firms typically face greater uncertainties than domestic firms in the host country, and may therefore have strong incentives to follow previous investors, because the choice of location is interpreted as a positive signal of the attractiveness of the location. In addition to agglomeration economies, firms may seek each others' proximity purely because of 'demonstration' effects. As a result, it may be difficult to disentangle the effect of agglomeration economies from demonstration effects when analysing the determinants of FDI.[18]

This point is emphasized by Barry et al. (2003b), who set out to disentangle real from spurious agglomeration by studying the activities of US-owned firms in Irish manufacturing. Their results suggest that both agglomeration economies and demonstration effects are important, particularly in terms of the signals that the behaviour of US firms transmit to other US firms, while agglomeration effects are more important than demonstration effects for firms in high-tech sectors.

A somewhat different approach to agglomeration and FDI is used by Braunerhjelm and Svensson (1996) and Braunerhjelm et al. (2000). Both studies are based on data on Swedish MNEs for the 1970s, 1980s and 1990s. Braunerhjelm and Svensson examine whether an index measuring the country's degree of specialization in a particular industry affects the propensity of foreign firms belonging to this industry to carry out affiliate production in the country. They argue that such an index captures local support systems and networks within industries, and may also be interpreted as a proxy for intra-industry R&D spillovers. In an empirical analysis which also includes a set of other country characteristics, it is found that the more important the industry of the investing firm in the host country, the higher the probability that a firm has established an affiliate there, and the larger the production of an affiliate there.

Braunerhjelm et al. (2000) proceed along the same line of analysis as they aim at examining the impact of an extensive set of country and industry characteristics

---

[18] Neither the proxy for agglomeration factors chosen by Wheeler and Mody (1992), nor the one chosen by Head et al. (1995, 1999), allows a distinction between agglomeration economies and demonstration effects.

on the localization of the foreign operations of Swedish MNEs. These include both fundamental economic determinants, such as market size and labour costs, as well as policy variables. The study reports strong support for the role of industry-specific agglomeration effects.

The way Braunerhjelm and Svensson (1996) and Braunerhjelm et al. (2000) model agglomeration effects implies that there is less reason to worry about whether the effects picked up are real agglomeration effects or just demonstration effects. However, there may be more reason to worry about whether the proxy really captures agglomeration economies or rather the strength of comparative advantage based on relative factor endowments or technology. Similar criticism applies to a number of other studies, e.g. Barrell and Pain (1999a) and Devereux and Griffith (1998). Devereux and Griffith use industry data on production, demand and R&D to construct agglomeration variables by taking the value of the variable in each industry in a particular country as a proportion of the total for that industry across all countries (i.e. it is measured as the host country's share of that industry's total production, demand or R&D). They find that the estimated coefficients of all three variables are positive and significant. However, possibly with the exception of the variable constructed from data on industry demand, this may be due to the importance of the host country's comparative advantage rather than agglomeration economies in determining FDI.

Related to the analysis of the role of agglomeration economies are studies of technology sourcing. Technology sourcing would be a motive for FDI if the firm invests abroad in order to get access to foreign technologies. There are different ways a firm could source foreign technology through a foreign affiliate. One way would be to set up a foreign affiliate in proximity to foreign firms with advanced technology, i.e. in so-called 'centres of excellence'. The foreign affiliate might then benefit from knowledge spillovers, which, in turn, could be transferred to other parts of the MNE. The alternative would be to directly acquire a foreign firm with advanced technology, in which case knowledge only had to be transferred within the firm. Based on an analysis of Japanese investment in the US, and US and Japanese investment in the EU, respectively, Kogut and Chang (1991) and Neven and Siotis (1995) report that R&D intensity (at the sectoral level) in the host country has a positive impact on FDI. This suggests that technology sourcing may be an important motive. The evidence on the effects of technological sourcing will be taken up again in Chapter 9.

To summarize, there is some evidence that agglomeration economies play a role in determining the location of FDI. However, work is still required to develop well-specified measures of agglomeration economies and to introduce them in such a way that real agglomeration effects can be separated from spurious ones.

6.6 Concluding Remarks

In this chapter we have reviewed the empirical literature on the determinants of FDI. Even though there is a very large literature on this topic, we have focused mainly on relatively recent studies, as there have been substantial developments with respect to generating theoretical prediction, getting access to detailed datasets and econometric methods in the last decade. Still, the scope and need for further research are evident. We shall point to a set of issues that seems particularly important to resolve.

The theoretical predictions have been largely generated from models making a strict distinction between horizontal and vertical motives for FDI. Most of the FDI that we observe, however, is difficult to fit into such a strict taxonomy. Even when an exporting firm decides to locate some of the production destined for foreign markets abroad, there is likely to be a vertical element stemming from the fact that headquarters activities still remain in the home country. Besides, a particular location may be chosen for its low production costs rather than its large domestic market if it is easy to export to third markets, which also introduces a vertical motive along with a horizontal one. It would be useful to have more studies allowing for such a variety of motives for FDI.

The major share of world FDI consists of cross-border M&A. Although most of the theory does not distinguish between greenfield investment and M&A, it seems reasonable to expect that M&A often occur for different reasons than greenfield investment. Not least are purely strategic factors likely to be important in this context. This is an area where more of both theoretical and empirical analysis is needed.

Most of the work on the determinants of FDI focuses on either industry/firm characteristics *or* country characteristics. But in reality, the location of FDI will be determined by multivariate interaction between firm and country characteristics. There are very few studies that explicitly take this into account. There is a growing literature on the determinants of industry location that uses such a framework, and since FDI is one source of changes in industry location a closer integration of these two strands of the literature would be useful.

7

Host Country Effects: Conceptual Framework and the Evidence

Many countries now actively seek inward FDI, although this has not always been the case. The development model of the 1960s and 70s typically led countries to restrict or prohibit inwards investments, and even today full 'national treatment' of foreign firms is the exception not the rule.[1] This chapter is devoted to analysing the economics underlying these attitudes. What do we know about the effects of FDI on the host economy, and are there grounds for believing that the presence of multinationals is beneficial?

One possibility is that there are unemployed (or under-employed) resources in the economy and that multinational investments bring some of these resources into use. This is an important motivation in many developing and transition economies, although less so in economies that generally have full employment. Another is that FDI is of sufficient scale to have general equilibrium effects in the host economy. For example, labour demand is raised sufficiently to bid up wages and improve the economy's terms of trade with the rest of the world. We saw these effects analytically in Chapter 4 and will return to them in our case study of Ireland (Chapter 8). Aggregate effects may also show up in growth performance, and in Section 7.1 we will briefly review some econometric attempts to use cross-country data to identify such effects; generally these cross-country growth regressions have not turned out to be fruitful.

Most of the empirical evidence on which we focus in this chapter is firmly micro-oriented, looking at firms or industries. It seeks to identify the main routes through which FDI may change performance at this level. One possible route is that multinationals may be different, in a number of key aspects, from local firms.[2] If so, there will be a *compositional effect*, as the share of multinationals in the economy changes.

---

[1] 'National treatment' means that foreign and nationally owned firms are treated equally (see Chapter 10).

[2] In this chapter we use the term 'multinational' to refer just to foreign-owned subsidiaries operating in the host country. 'Local' firms are national firms that produce only in the host country and also multinationals headquartered in the host country.

For example, do multinationals have higher productivity or pay higher wages than local firms? If so, increasing the share of multinationals in the economy may raise productivity or wages, by shifting employment from local to multinational firms. Sections 7.3–7.5 are devoted to presenting the evidence of these effects. There are, however, a number of tricky conceptual issues that have to be clarified before any useful conclusions can be drawn. Section 7.2 lays these out, thereby providing a framework within which the empirical studies can be assessed.

An alternative route through which FDI can affect firm and industry performance is if the presence of multinationals induces changes in the behaviour of local firms. These changes can arise in a number of ways. For example, competition from multinationals may induce changes in the scale of local firms, as we saw in Section 3.4. Local firms may acquire foreign technology, either through licensing agreements or through technological spillovers from multinationals. And there may be pecuniary externalities, as with the modelling of linkages in Section 3.4.3. In common with most of the literature we call these effects *spillovers*, noting that the label groups together pecuniary as well as technological effects. Evidence of these spillovers is presented in Section 7.6.

7.1 Aggregate Effects of FDI on Economic Growth: Cross-Country Evidence

If FDI is beneficial to host economies, one might expect that this is reflected in better economic performance by countries that are recipients of large amounts of FDI than by those that are not. One way of looking at this is by cross-country growth regressions, seeing if those countries that get larger investment flows grow faster. Cross-country studies of this type use FDI data, i.e. investment flows as recorded by balance-of-payment statistics, since comparable data on MNEs' activities are not available across sufficiently many countries.

Findings from this approach are quite mixed and rarely conclusive. While there is no empirical support for a relationship between FDI and growth in general terms, there is some evidence of a positive effect when host economies are sufficiently developed to interact with foreign activities. Among a sample of developing countries Blomström et al. (1994b) find that FDI is positively related to growth only for the higher-income ones. Similarly, Borensztein et al. (1998) analyse the effects of FDI flows from industrial countries to 69 developing countries over the last two decades. They find that FDI is an important vehicle for transferring technology and that it has a growth-enhancing effect; however, this holds only if the host country has a minimum threshold stock of human capital. According to this study, this threshold ranges between 0.76 and 1 year of post primary schooling. Some studies find that other factors also affect the aggregate impact of FDI: the level of development of domestic financial markets (Alfaro et al. 2004) or the degree of export orientation of the host economy (Balasubramanyam et al. 1996).

All these results, however, are refuted by another study, Carkovic and Levine (2002). Based on a panel of industrialized and developing countries between 1960 and 1995, this work applies different techniques for dynamic panel estimations than earlier studies, also taking into account problems of reverse causality. The authors find no evidence that FDI affects growth.[3] This also holds when they control for those specific factors discussed above: the level of human capital and income per capita of the domestic economy, the degree of sophistication of domestic financial markets and the degree of trade openness.

Although suggestive, aggregate analysis is fraught with methodological problems. It is very difficult to isolate the effect of FDI in the aggregate. In countries like Ireland (see the case study in Chapter 8), where MNEs employ one every two persons working in manufacturing, FDI has a very strong effect on aggregate dynamics, but in other countries where it plays a less prominent role, the effect of foreign financial flows can be counterbalanced by many other observed and unobserved factors. Moreover, aggregate FDI flows cannot be classified according to their growth potential. FDI in primary resources is likely to have a smaller impact on growth than equivalent investments in high-tech manufacturing or in services like software. Finally, it is not possible to isolate the channels through which FDI affects growth. Is it because foreign activities replace less efficient local resources? Or is it because they enhance the efficiency of domestic activities? To answer these questions we need to revert to firm-level data and to country-specific studies, and this is the approach of the remainder of the chapter.

7.2   Firm Effects: Conceptual Framework

As we remarked in the introduction to this chapter, most studies are micro-oriented, looking at the performance of local and multinational firms. Before reviewing evidence from these studies it is useful to have an analytical framework within which the studies can be located and evaluated. To develop this framework we focus on productivity, although it can be applied to other variables of interest. Suppose that firms have some characteristic (or set of characteristics), x, that determines their productivity, q. Thus, local firms have technology summarized by the function $q = \beta z(x)$, where the function $z(\cdot)$ is increasing in the characteristic and β is an efficiency parameter. Firms are heterogeneous, and the proportion of national firms' total employment that is in firms with characteristic x is given by the density function $n(x)$. The average

---

[3]They use generalized methods of moments (GMM) panel estimators designed by Arellano and Bover (1995) and Blundell and Bond (1998). The problems concerning the estimation of dynamic panels will be discussed extensively in Section 7.3. Campos and Kinoshita (2002) is another paper applying these estimation techniques.

productivity of local firms is then

$$\bar{q}^N = \int \beta z(x) n(x)\, dx, \qquad 1 = \int n(x)\, dx. \qquad (7.1)$$

Multinationals are described in a similar way, but may have a different efficiency parameter; so they have productivity $q = \alpha z(x)$ and for given x are more efficient if $\alpha > \beta$. The distribution of multinationals' employment across firms with different characteristics is $m(x)$, so the average productivity of multinational firms

$$\bar{q}^M = \int \alpha z(x) m(x)\, dx, \qquad 1 = \int m(x)\, dx. \qquad (7.2)$$

For the economy as a whole, a proportion μ of the labour force is in multinationals, and $1 - \mu$ is in local firms, so average productivity is

$$\bar{q} = \mu \bar{q}^M + (1 - \mu)\bar{q}^N. \qquad (7.3)$$

Given this framework, what questions can the researcher ask? The first question is simply to compare averages. Do multinationals, on average, have higher productivity than local firms, $\bar{q}^M > \bar{q}^N$? We will see considerable evidence that this is the case. The differences are driven, at least in part, by the fact that MNEs are generally firms with large firm-specific economies of scale, concentrated in industries rich in intangible assets, R&D, brand image and so on. Thus, MNEs are different from local firms in that they bring in bundles of things which are not available locally, like technologies, market opportunities, capital, management and employment opportunities. Studying MNEs as bundles implies comparing them with local firms, without enquiring into why they are different from local firms. We will call these comparisons of the whole bundle of differences *unconditional* effects.

The second question is, do multinational firms have higher technical efficiency than local firms? In our framework, is $\alpha > \beta$? Answering this requires econometrics that controls for observable firm characteristics, x, in order to isolate the effects of the ownership status. In comparing MNEs and local firms, its focus is understanding whether foreign ownership per se explains differences in performance. This implies controlling for all the other factors x (size, technology, etc.) which may affect performance and which may be correlated to foreign ownership. Some papers merely control for characteristics such as firm size and age, and others take into account the endogeneity of these controls, as well as the endogeneity of multinational status itself. The studies using this approach find evidence that foreign ownership improves performance, but the effect becomes much weaker and in some cases is not significant. We call comparisons based on this the *conditional* approach.

The conditional approach is, in some sense, the proper scientific approach. It identifies parameters of the technology, and hence fundamental differences between local and multinational firms. Despite this, the conditional approach may not provide the answer that is of interest to policy makers: what is the effect of FDI on productivity? The point is simply that a multinational entrant might have characteristic x^* and replace employment in local firms with characteristic $\hat{x}$. If $x^* > \hat{x}$, then multinational entry will raise productivity even if $\alpha = \beta$. The policy maker is interested in the effects on productivity irrespective of whether these arise because $\alpha > \beta$ or because $x^* > \hat{x}$. From a welfare and policy perspective, the reason why MNEs are interesting is precisely that they are different from national firms, as they bring in bundles of things which are not available locally. Essentially, the reason why under the conditional approach there is no evidence of significant differences in performance between MNEs and national firms is that there is not much left which is worth comparing. Thus, trying to isolate the effect of ownership by defining the perfect counterfactual, the one that differs from the foreign firm just for the fact of being domestic, might be irrelevant from the welfare perspective (see Lipsey (2002) on this issue).

The third question the researcher can ask is, how does the presence of FDI affect local firms? These are the 'spillover effects' to which we have already alluded. In our framework, they occur if $\beta = \beta(\mu)$, so that an increasing presence of multinationals in the economy (or perhaps the particular sector or region) directly affects productivity. The numerous studies investigating such effects are discussed in Section 7.6.

Finally, evaluation of the effect of MNEs requires that we identify what national activities shrink in order to accommodate incoming multinationals. The theory models of Chapters 3 and 4 made some progress in that direction, focusing on product market equilibrium and factor market equilibrium, respectively. However, what is needed are models where firms are heterogeneous and, as we saw, work on such models is in its infancy. Empirically, we will see that there are a few studies that use dynamic panel analysis to isolate the appropriate benchmark local firm with which the performance of MNEs can be compared.

7.3 Productivity

The question addressed in this section is whether foreign subsidiaries are more or less efficient than domestic firms. To address this question empirically it is necessary to use firm-level datasets, combining foreign- and domestic-owned firms. Such datasets are country specific and only available for a limited number of countries (UK, USA, Italy and a few others). Our discussion will be largely focused on the UK, where most of the studies addressing this issue have been carried out (Griffith 1999; Griffith and Simpson 2001; Conyon et al. 2002; Girma et al. 2001; Görg and Strobl 2002; Criscuolo and Martin 2003; Harris 2002; Harris and Robinson 2003). These studies use the Annual Census of Production (ACOP) Respondents Data Base (ARD), which contains very detailed information on foreign and local

Table 7.1.   Comparing foreign-owned and national UK based plants (average 1996–2000).

	Foreign owned	National
Number of observations	3499	161 234
Value added/employee	44.61	27.98
Output/employee	151.98	76.52
Employment	485.05	142.09
Capital/employee	98.82	38.23
Intermediate inputs/employees	107.81	50.52

Values in thousands of pounds sterling.
Source: Criscuolo and Martin 2003, table 4.

establishments based in the UK since 1970 (Griffith 1999), and they illustrate many of the important methodological issues well.

As outlined above, comparison of MNEs and domestic firms can be tackled from two different perspectives that we termed the *unconditional approach* and the *conditional approach.*

Unconditional measures

The fact that MNEs are, on average, more productive than local firms can be easily gauged from Table 7.1. This table is reproduced from Criscuolo and Martin (2003) and reports average values for a sample of MNEs based in the UK and of UK national firms drawn from the ARD. Consistent evidence is available from Italian (Benfratello and Sembenelli 2002), US (Howenstine and Zeile 1994; Doms and Jensen 1998) studies and other UK studies (Griffith and Simpson 2001).

Two measures of labour productivity are reported: value added and output per employee. On both accounts MNEs are roughly twice as productive as national firms. But the two groups of firms differ in all the other features taken into account (the *x* factors in the framework of Section 7.2). MNEs are much larger (both in terms of output, employment and value added), they invest more and they use more intermediate inputs per employee. All of these factors are correlated with labour productivity: larger firms exploit economies of scale; the intensive use of other factors of production like capital and intermediates makes production less labour intensive and implicitly raises labour productivity. To be able to say anything on the link between performance and the nationality of ownership we therefore need to control for the effect of these other factors on productivity.

Conditional measures

The next step in comparing the performance of MNEs and local firms is to regress firm-level performance against a dummy variable reflecting the ownership status of the firm and a set of controls, which measure some characteristics of the firm. The general form of this regression (which can be analysed as a panel when both firm, or plant, k and time t observations are available) can be written as follows:[4]

$$\ln(q_t^k) = \alpha + \sum_{i=1}^{n}(\beta_i \mathrm{MNE}_{it}^k) + \sum_{s=1}^{v} \gamma_s X_{st}^k + e_t^k, \tag{7.4}$$

where q_t^k measures performance, usually labour productivity or total factor productivity (TFP). MNE is a variable capturing the ownership of the firm. It can either be constructed as a set of n dummies, each taking the value 1 if firm k is of a given foreign nationality i (US, French, etc.) or as just one dummy ($n = 1$), which takes the value 1 if firm k is foreign owned and 0 otherwise. MNE can be time invariant (then it has no suffix t) or it can vary with time like the other variables. X is a vector of observable characteristics s of the firm. If the dataset is a panel, the error term is given by

$$e_t^k = \rho^k + \psi_t + \varepsilon_t^k,$$

i.e. it is composed of a fixed effect ρ^k, a time dummy ψ_t and an idiosyncratic productivity shock ε_t^k.[5] The fixed effect controls for those time-invariant characteristics of the firm which cannot be directly observed but which influence k's performance (e.g. the management's ability). The time dummy controls for unobservable shocks arising at time t and affecting all firms in the panel (e.g. a devaluation of the exchange rate). The idiosyncratic productivity shock controls for specific shocks arising at time t and just affecting performance of firm k (e.g. firm k is taken over). Such shocks are assumed not to affect productivity in other periods, and thus not to be correlated in time (for example, a takeover affects k's productivity only in the year when k is taken over).

Griffith and Simpson (2001) use equation (7.4) to estimate the relationship between ownership and labour productivity (measured by real value added per worker) for a panel of UK firms between 1973 and 1996. Given that in their estimations the ownership status is time invariant, its effect would be fully captured by the fixed-effect term ρ^k. It is therefore necessary to estimate (7.4) in two steps (see Hsiao 1986). They first run a panel estimation, where they regress labour productivity on the observable characteristics of firms, but excluding the ownership status. They then regress the residual averaged across time, $\bar{e}^k$, from the first step (which includes the fixed effect within the group estimator) on the ownership status of the firm.

---

[4]Panel datasets contain information on samples of firms observed at more than one period in time. Whether data are at the plant or at the firm level has important methodological implications. However, in order to make our argument simpler, in what follows we will use the terms plant, firm and establishment as synonyms.

[5]If equation (7.4) is estimated as a cross-section, then all variables are time invariant, and the error term is e^k.

The results of their baseline estimation are shown in Table 7.2. The top part reports the estimates of the first step and the bottom part those of the second step. Their observable characteristics include size (measured by employment normalized by mean industry employment), age and whether the firm ceases to exist (exits from the sample) in the period analysed. Their ownership variable distinguishes between local firms and five groups of foreign firms: from North America, the European Union, other European countries, Japan, and the rest of the world.

Our main interest is in the second step, which estimates the effect of foreign ownership. The performance premium of foreign firms can be computed from the coefficients of the nationality dummies reported.[6] Foreign firms, from all the groups considered, are more productive than British firms. North American establishments are more productive by 68%, EU ones by 53%, other European plants by 42%, Japanese by 42% and plants from the rest of the world by 77%.

These results are in line with those obtained in other works that estimate various versions of equation (7.4): foreign firms are shown to be systematically more productive in the UK (Davies and Lyons 1991), in other industrialized countries (Globerman et al. (1994) and Doms and Jensen (1998) on the US) and in developing countries (Blomström and Wolff (1994) on Mexico, Sjöholm (1999a) on Indonesia, Kokko et al. (2001) on Uruguay, Haddad and Harrison (1993) on Morocco). These results are obtained independently of the estimation technique (cross-section or panel), the measure of performance used and the number of controls for observed and unobserved heterogeneity.

Therefore, labour productivity in foreign subsidiaries of MNEs is higher than in domestic firms. These estimations, though, are based on a partial measure of productivity, as value added per worker is also affected by the use of other factors of production which are not taken into account by measures of labour productivity.[7] A standard way of also taking into account the effects of other factors of production on productivity is to estimate the TFP instead of labour productivity. Two studies which compare TFP between MNEs and local firms are Griffith (1999) on the car industry in the UK and Benfratello and Sembenelli (2002) on manufacturing in Italy. These studies consider Cobb–Douglas production functions like

$$Y_t^k = A_t^k (K_t^k)^{\alpha 1} (L_t^k)^{\alpha 2} (M_t^k)^{\alpha 3}, \tag{7.5}$$

---

[6]$\exp(\beta) - 1$ is approximately the proportional difference between the national and the foreign firm, where β is the coefficient of the dummy measuring nationality in the log-linear regression.

[7]Griffith and Simpson (2001) also analyse different usage of factors of production between MNEs and local firms. They find that foreign firms in the UK are consistently more capital and skill intensive than national firms. For example, North American establishments are found to invest twice as much per worker as British establishments. Thus, the productivity premium can partly be attributable to differences in skill and capital intensity.

Table 7.2. Differences in real value added per worker between MNEs and local firms.

Dependent variable: ln(real value added per worker$_t^k$)		
$\ln(\text{age}_t^k)$	0.018***	(0.003)
$\ln[(\text{age}_t^k)^2]$	0.0003***	(0.0001)
$\ln(\text{size}_t^k)$	−0.034***	(0.006)
$\ln[(\text{size}_t^k)^2]$	0.001***	(0.0002)
Exit_t^k	−0.094***	(0.022)
Year dummy	Yes	
Within groups fixed effect	Yes	
Observations	131 097	
Dependent variable: $\bar{e}^k$		
North American	0.517***	(0.042)
European Union	0.424***	(0.086)
Other European	0.351***	(0.052)
Japanese	0.496***	(0.132)
Other foreign	0.572***	(0.146)
Observations	13 909	

Notes. Robust standard errors in brackets. ***, Statistically significant at 99% confidence level. All regressions are grossed up to population weights, and weighted by the establishment's employment. Year indicates full set of year dummies; industry indicates full set of 4-digit industry dummies. Size is number of employees normalized on 4-digit industry-year average employment. Exit is a dummy which takes the value 1 in year t if firm k closes down in year t.
Source: Griffith and Simpson (2001).

where Y is output, A is a Hicks neutral productivity shift parameter, K is capital, L is labour and M measures other intermediate inputs. Equation (7.5) can be estimated in its log-linear form as follows:

$$\ln(Y_t^k) = \alpha_1 \ln(K_t^k) + \alpha_2 \ln(L_t^k) + \alpha_3 \ln(M_t^k) + \sum_{i=1}^{n}(\beta_i \text{MNE}_{it}^k) + \sum_{s=1}^{v} \gamma_s X_{st}^k + a_t^k.$$
(7.6)

Total factor productivity is measured by the residual a_t^k (namely, it captures the effect of all those factors affecting output which are not measured by independent variables). This is composed of a time-invariant fixed effect ρ^k, which controls for time-invariant unobservable characteristics of the firm, a time dummy ψ_t capturing common shocks and an establishment-specific idiosyncratic productivity shock ε_t^k. To analyse the effect of foreign ownership in this case we can proceed in two ways. The first is to estimate (7.6) without controlling for the ownership of the firm (assuming $\beta_i = 0$) and then regress the time-averaged residual, $\bar{\hat{a}}^k$, on the ownership status of the firm. This is the same procedure as the one described above. Alternatively, it is possible to include the dummies measuring foreign nationality directly in the estimation (assuming $\beta_i \neq 0$ in (7.6)). Ordinary least squares (OLS) estimates of (7.6) for the UK and Italy based on the latter approach show once more that MNEs have higher TFP than local firms. Thus, even when all measurable factors of production are accounted for by TFP measures of performance, MNEs are still more efficient than local firms. This result holds for both the UK and Italy, where the foreign-ownership premium varies between 1.7 and 7%. Note that even though foreign firms keep being more productive than local ones, once all factors of production are accounted for, their productivity premium declines drastically (it was between 32 and 77% in studies using labour productivity).

However, OLS or panel estimates of TFP still fall short of explaining the order of causality between the nationality of ownership and performance (see Griffith (1999) and Benfratello and Sembenelli (2002) for detailed accounts of the econometric problems of estimating production functions comparing foreign and domestic firms). The first issue is that TFP estimates should be carried out in a dynamic setting. In fact, there could be path dependence in performance, in that present performance is affected by past performance; it is therefore necessary to also take this factor into account if we want to isolate the effect of ownership. The second problem is that the results observed could still be driven by other variables, which are correlated with foreign ownership and performance and which are not included in X^k or (in the case of panel) which are not time invariant and therefore controlled for by the fixed-effect estimator. The third caveat is that the inputs included in the TFP, capital and also labour, are often subject to measurement errors. The fourth problem is that the estimates reported consider the nationality of ownership as an exogenous factor and do not take into account problems of simultaneity: foreign firms may appear to be more productive because foreign investors acquire the more productive firms, not because they become productive as a consequence of a foreign takeover. In other words, the evidence reported up to now supports a statistical association between foreign ownership and productivity, but not a causal link.

Some recent papers (Griffith 1999; Harris 2002; Harris and Robinson 2003; Benfratello and Sembenelli 2002) use econometric techniques that partly or fully take into account these problems. To deal with path dependence, they study a dynamic version of (7.6), which includes lagged productivity as a regressor. To deal with the effects of unobservable factors they instrument all the explanatory variables with their lagged values, by using GMM system estimators.[8] By instrumenting it is also

---

[8]The most widely used GMM estimators are by Arellano and Bond (1991, 1998) and the system estimator by Blundell and Bond (1998, 2000). When the Arellano–Bond estimator is used, time-invariant unobservable factors are taken into account by first differencing all the variables. Further reading of these papers is also useful for understanding the conditions under which it is appropriate to used lagged values as instruments.

possible to take care of the simultaneity between ownership and performance, but this can be done only if some firms in the sample change ownership status with time (Benfratello and Sembenelli 2002). If the ownership status is time invariant, the ownership status at t is perfectly correlated with lagged ownership status.

When these estimation techniques are used, differences in productivity between the two groups of firms are smaller than in earlier estimations and often insignificant. This result holds for both the Italian and the British studies. In Table 7.3 we report the results of the dynamic OLS and GMM system with instrumental variables estimations for the UK from Griffith (1999).[9]

The coefficients of interest for our purposes are those pertaining to the nationality dummies. Only US and German firms are taken into account in these results, thus the omitted category is domestically owned firms. Implicitly, these coefficients measure the difference in performance between foreign and domestic firms. It can be seen that the coefficient of the dummies capturing US and German nationality are positive and significant in the OLS estimation, whereas in the system estimations the US dummy loses significance. German firms still produce 7% more output than their British counterparts. In contrast, Benfratello and Sembenelli (2002) show that in the case of Italy only US firms have a significant and positive productivity premium.

Other studies on the UK, using similar techniques to control for the endogeneity problem, find controversial results. Girma et al. (2001) analysing a different sample than Griffith (1999) finds a 5.29% TFP differential in favour of foreign firms. Similarly Conyon et al. (2002) compare data of British firms before and after a foreign acquisition. They find that these companies experience a 14% increase in labour productivity after acquisition. Opposite results are found by Harris and Robinson (2002): they find that foreign firms systematically acquire more productive British plants and that productivity declines after acquisition.

Summing up, there is strong and robust evidence that foreign-owned subsidiaries are more productive than domestic firms. What we learn from studies that use the conditional approach is that, even when observed and unobserved heterogeneity and the simultaneity problem are controlled for, there is still in some cases a small positive effect of foreign ownership on performance. The evidence of a causal relation, that foreign ownership per se affects performance, is more controversial, although some of the studies reviewed find that foreign ownership per se does appear to cause better performance.

However, as discussed earlier, the conditional approach controls for all those other factors that come along with foreign ownership and make foreign firms different from domestic ones. These factors may of themselves be of value to the domestic economy, for example, having newer and larger firms. The bottom line is then that

---

[9]Note that in Griffith (1999) the ownership status is time invariant, so this paper does not control for the simultaneity of ownership and performance.

Table 7.3.   Foreign ownership and total factor productivity.

Dependent variable output: $\ln(Y_t^k)$

	OLS		System	
Instruments	—		$t - 3, Dt - 2$	
$\ln(L_t^k)$	0.396***	(0.027)	0.393***	(0.082)
$\ln(L_{t-1}^k)$	−0.307***	(0.026)	−0.249***	(0.074)
$\ln(K_t^k)$	0.061**	(0.024)	−0.002	(0.097)
$\ln(K_{t-1}^k)$	−0.045*	(0.023)	−0.054	(0.094)
$\ln(M_t^k)$	0.547***	(0.023)	0.471***	(0.048)
$\ln(M_{t-1}^k)$	−0.398***	(0.026)	−0.167**	(0.068)
$\ln(Y_{t-1}^k)$	0.749***	(0.019)	0.502***	(0.078)
USA	0.013**	(0.006)	0.024	(0.019)
Germany	0.038*	(0.023)	0.068*	(0.036)
Sargan (P-value)	—		0.092	
CRS (P-value)	0.179		0.394	
m1	0.000		0.000	
m2	0.157		0.923	

Notes. Robust standard errors in brackets. ***, Statistically significant at 99% confidence level; **, statistically significant at 95% confidence level; *, statistically significant at 90% confidence level. The sample is an unbalanced panel of 414 establishments from 1980 to 1992 with 3259 observations; system estimates are GMM with instrument indicating the dating of instruments used for right-hand side variables; numbers in brackets are one-step robust standard errors from DPD; Sargan is the P-value from a test of the validity of the over-identifying restrictions for the GMM estimators; CRS is the P-value from a Wald test for constant returns to scale; m1 and m2 are the P-values from tests for first- and second-order serial correlation (see Arellano and Bond 1991, 1998); we omit reporting estimates obtained using minimum distance estimator and imposing the common factor restrictions, as reported in Griffith (1999).
Source: Griffith (1999, Table 12, p. 436).

foreign firms induce a favourable composition effect on average performance, both because their attributes and inputs are different from those of domestic firms and because they use their inputs slightly more efficiently.

7.4   Factor Markets

A concern in the popular debate on MNEs is the behaviour of these firms in the labour market. MNEs are often accused of paying workers in developing countries too little (the sweatshop problem), either compared with local conditions or with what they could do given the profits they make. The public debate is also concerned over whether foreign firms create or deprive host economies of their skilled labour. Additionally, MNEs are often accused of being volatile, responding rapidly to output and factor price shocks by laying off workers and transferring their activities else-where. The first two of these issues are addressed in this section, and the volatility issue in Section 7.5.

Wages

As argued by Lipsey in his extensive survey of the home and host countries effects of FDI, 'it is rare to find a study of FDI and wages in any host country that does not find that foreign owned firms pay higher wages, on average, than at least privately owned local firms' (Lipsey 2002b, p. 20).

Part of this may be due to multinationals employing higher-skilled labour than local firms and skills being often imperfectly measured. But there are also reasons why multinationals might pay higher wages for identical workers (Lipsey 2002b; Scheve and Slaughter 2003). First, there could be reasons related to the fact that monitoring workers in foreign countries is more difficult than at home. If MNEs transfer part of their proprietary knowledge to their foreign subsidiaries (technolo-gies, procedures, etc.), they probably want to minimize the risk that this proprietary knowledge gets dissipated through frequent labour turnover. Foreign firms may want to avoid losing workers who have accumulated firm-specific skills and who are costly to replace. They may also seek to build reputations as good employers in order to improve the quality of job applicants, as well as the job tenure of current workers. This may be particularly relevant if a problem of asymmetric information in the labour market means that foreign firms know less about the characteristics of local workers than do local firms. Second, high wages may be compensating differ-entials for other disadvantages of multinational employment. One possibility is that MNEs could be perceived by employees as more volatile employers, willing to hire and fire rapidly, than are local companies. Employees consequently demand a risk premium. Third, MNEs may face different government regulations. Regulations in host countries could segment labour markets and force foreign firms to face a higher cost of labour. Finally, there could be a complex set of issues to do with compara-bility of pay across countries. Internal fairness policies could induce MNEs to even out the wage gaps between employees based in different locations, thus avoiding excessive geographical disparities. External pressure, e.g. from NGOs, could work in the same direction.

On the other hand, the argument against MNEs paying higher wages is essentially one, that MNEs being large employers, especially in developing countries, might enjoy a monopsonistic position or have strong bargaining power vis à vis workers in the local economy.

The methodological problems related to the empirical analysis of whether MNEs pay different wages than national firms are essentially the same as those discussed above (see Lipsey (2002) for a thorough discussion of this), thus they will not be mentioned again in this section, which, rather, will focus on the most important findings in the available literature.

Almost all empirical studies on this matter conclude that MNEs pay higher wages than local firms. Evidence of this for advanced countries is mostly based on US and UK data. Studies in the US find that MNEs pay wages between 10 and 15% higher than local firms, depending on the period and the industry considered (Lipsey 1994; Feliciano and Lipsey 1999). Studies based on UK data find similar results; the wage premium paid by MNEs varies between 6 and 26%, according to study (Griffith and Simpson 2001; Oulton 1998; Girma et al. 2001; Driffield and Girma 2002). In the US case, the wage gap is not always robust when the effects of co-variates like size or industry distribution are also controlled for. In contrast, for the UK, wage gaps are persistent even when such controls are included, and also when they are estimated with techniques controlling for endogeneity. For example, Conyon et al. (2002) analyse a sample of UK establishments that change nationality of ownership in the period observed and find that wages increase by 3.4% after the acquisition by foreign investors and decline by 2.1% after the acquisition of foreign-owned companies by domestic investors.

The evidence on developing countries also reports that MNEs pay higher wages than local firms. Plant-level studies on Cote d'Ivoire, Morocco and Venezuela report wage premiums which vary widely, between 10 and 260% (Aitken et al. 1996; Harrison 1996; Haddad and Harrison 1993). Also, other studies on Indonesia report a positive wage gap between 12 and 50% (Lipsey and Sjöholm 2001). Again, these results are robust to the inclusion of various controls and estimation techniques.

This evidence is only based on the comparison between MNEs and domestic firms, and does not provide an answer to the question of whether MNEs pay workers acceptable wages (the sweatshop debate) with respect to their level of profits. However, it tells us that MNEs offer better paid employment opportunities than the alternatives available in the domestic economies.

As argued, one remaining problem related to the evidence that MNEs pay higher wages, is that workers' ability and skills are generally imperfectly measured. Thus, part of the wage gap could be explained by unmeasured skill differentials. We therefore now move to the analysis of whether MNEs are likely to employ workers with better skills than local firms.

Skills

We saw in Chapter 4 that the impact of FDI on domestic factor prices depends in part on the skill intensity of FDI relative to the local activity that would have taken place in the absence of FDI. While simple models might suggest that the movement of unskilled-labour-intensive activities to developing countries tends to reduce the skill premium, the analysis of Chapter 4 indicates how this depends on whether the

FDI is unskilled labour intensive relative to alternative activities in the host country (and not just unskilled labour intensive relative to activities in the home country).[10]

This is an empirical issue, but unfortunately the evidence is scant. Feenstra and Hanson (1997) analyse the impact of FDI on the demand for skills in *maquiladoras* in Mexico. Specifically, they study the impact of FDI on the wage share of skilled labour between 1975 and 1988, using state-specific two-digit industry-level data. They find that FDI can account for over 50% of the increase in the share of skilled labour in total wages in the late 1980s, in those regions where FDI had concentrated. This implies that FDI is intensive in the use of skilled labour, relative to other Mexican activities.

As for advanced countries, the evidence is controversial. Blonigen and Slaughter (2001) carried out a study of the effects of inward investments on US wage inequality based on industry-level data. They find that the activities of MNEs have not contributed significantly to within-industry skill upgrading. Rather, when focusing on Japanese investments, they find that their share in industry-specific activities is correlated with lower demand for skills. Arguably, the role of FDI is disguised by the fact that the studies of both Feenstra and Hanson and Blonigen and Slaughter use industry- rather than firm-level data.

A study based on firm-level data is Griffith and Simpson (2001) on the UK. It finds that MNEs employ a larger proportion of skilled workers than local firms in the UK. However, this result could partly be driven by the possibility that foreign investors buy relatively skill-intensive firms. Indeed, Almeida (2003), working with a sample of Portuguese firms and controlling for endogeneity in the choice of firms acquired, finds that the causal relationship goes in the opposite direction. By observing labour demand and wages of workers of different skills before and after foreign acquisition, she finds that foreigners 'cherry pick' domestic firms to be acquired, choosing those with a more educated labour force. These firms are already very similar to foreign firms before being acquired.

The evidence, then, is that skilled workers are more likely to be concentrated in MNEs. Anyway, this finding holds especially for developing countries like Mexico. In advanced economies like the US there is not much of a difference in the skill intensity of foreign-owned and national activities, particularly within the same industry.

A slightly different issue is whether MNEs train their employees more than local firms. This issue is again related to the evidence that MNEs pay higher wages than national firms. If firm-specific training is more productive in foreign firms, their workers will benefit more from training and they will have a steeper wage profile, and consequently a wage premium growing over time. On this matter we only have

---

[10] In Chapter 9 we will discuss this issue extensively from the point of view of the home country.

evidence for developing countries. Görg et al. (2002) test this prediction for a sample of firms in Ghana, where they use a dataset matching firms and employee data. They find that while there are no differences in starting wages between workers in domestic and foreign firms who receive training, the latter experience higher wage growth after training. This is consistent with findings from other developing country studies reported in Blomström and Kokko (2003).

7.5 Employment Volatility

A problem that is widely discussed in the globalization debate is whether the exposure of economic activities to international shocks, because of trade and FDI, increases the volatility of output, employment and wages (Rodrik 1997).[11] Here, we are not particularly concerned by aggregate volatility, but rather by whether someone finding a job in an MNE faces more volatile working conditions than if he or she were working in a local firm. MNEs are often accused of being ready to close their foreign plants more frequently and more readily than local firms. But beyond anecdotal evidence, the issue is not clear-cut. As the argument is both important and technically challenging, we deal with it quite extensively. In this section we discuss the main analytical issues and in the next one we report some empirical results. Why then should MNEs be more volatile employers than national firms? There are two main mechanisms. One is that the two groups of firms could face a different exposure to exogenous technology or price shocks which would shift their downward-sloping labour demand schedules. The other is that MNEs and local firms may adjust their levels of employment differently to an equal change in the home wage rate. Thus the elasticity of labour demand, hence the slope of their labour demand schedule, could differ.[12] Let us take these two mechanisms in turn.

Are MNEs more or less exposed than local firms to exogenous shocks? There are no clear theoretical predictions here. As MNEs operate in more than one market, they are more likely to be hit by a shock than national firms. However, it all depends on whether shocks are positively or negatively correlated across countries. In the former case, the risk is higher, and in the latter it is lower—multinationality offers diversification.

As for the reactions of the two groups of firms to shocks, four main factors are important. The first one is whether the relationship between employment in the host

---

[11] For evidence of the relationship between labour demand elasticity and globalization see Slaughter (2001) and Faini et al. (1999). It has also been investigated in the context of dramatic changes in trade regimes in a number of developing countries. This approach has been followed, using plant-level data, by Krishna et al. (2001) for Turkey and Fajnzylber and Maloney (2001) for Chile, Colombia and Mexico, finding, however, no support for the conjecture of more-elastic labour demand in response to trade liberalization.

[12] At the firm level, the elasticity in absolute terms is the percentage decline in the quantity of labour demanded as a consequence of a 1% change in wages.

country and factors of production in other locations is one of substitutability or complementarity. For example, if there is substitutability between labour at home and in other foreign subsidiaries, then an increase in wages in one location, say in China, will cause a larger reduction in employment in China for MNEs than for national firms, as they can easily replace Chinese labour with labour elsewhere. In contrast, if there is complementarity, the impact of a cost increase in China on Chinese labour is mitigated by the fact that this is only a share of the total costs of an MNE, even though this increase in costs gets transmitted to other locations too. In principle, we expect that substitutability is more likely to arise for HFDI with plants performing the same activity in different locations and complementarity for VFDI, where plants carry out just one or a few stages of the whole production process. In Chapter 9 we estimate cross price elasticities between employment at home and employment in foreign subsidiaries and we find support for this prediction.

A second factor is that being less committed towards the countries hosting their subsidiaries, MNEs bargain from a privileged position with (national or local) governments and unions, thus sometimes obtaining exceptions on hiring and firing practices and being more resilient to political and social pressures.[13]

Moreover, and this is the third factor, the elasticity of labour demand is also a function of product demand elasticity. International economic integration is expected to increase competition in the product market and raise product demand elasticity, which in turn translates into more elastic labour demands. Indeed, at the industry level, the presence of MNEs could bring along more competition in the product market: average product demand elasticity would increase for all competitors in that market. But, if the market is not perfectly competitive and MNEs have a larger market share than national firms, their perceived demand could be more rigid than the one of national firms. The more so if MNEs have large intangible assets, like strong brands or exclusive technologies, granting them monopolistic advantages in any market.

Fourth and finally, we should note that MNEs may employ different factors of production than national firms, and this may affect labour demands, generally making them more rigid. We have seen earlier that MNEs are relatively skill intensive compared with local firms. As labour demand of skilled workers is generally less elastic to changes in wages (Hamermesh 1993), average labour demand will be more rigid for MNEs. MNEs are also more capital intensive. If the share of labour in total production costs is lower (as the share of capital is higher), also labour elasticity is

---

[13]There is evidence, for instance, that MNEs have managed in a number of countries to bargain wages at a more decentralized level compared with domestic firms (Katz 1993; Ehremberg 1994). Moreover, in some countries and regions (e.g. export processing zones) less stringent hiring and firing rules have been granted to MNEs with the purpose of attracting FDI. For theoretical models of wage bargaining between unions and multinationals, see Mezzetti and Dinopoulos (1991) and Zhao (1998).

lower. Intuitively, MNEs react proportionally less than national firms to changes in wages, because labour is less important for their activities.

To illustrate this issue better it is useful to follow and introduce a simple formalization. Let us first see how exogenous shocks and demand elasticity combine in generating volatility in employment and wages. We follow Scheve and Slaughter (2003) and Fabbri et al. (2003) on this. Define $\hat{\alpha}^k$ as the proportionate shift in labour demand due to an exogenous random shock to prices and technology affecting firm k. Note that shocks may differ between types of firms. Define η_S as the wage elasticity of the labour supply faced by firm k and assume η_S to be the same for all type of firms; η_{LL}^k is the labour demand elasticity of firm k. It can be shown that the resulting percentage changes in wage and employment are

$$\hat{w}^k = \left(\frac{\eta_{LL}^k}{\eta_{LL}^k + \eta_S}\right)\hat{\alpha}^k \quad \text{and} \quad \hat{L}^k = \left(\frac{\eta_S \eta_{LL}^k}{\eta_{LL}^k + \eta_S}\right)\hat{\alpha}^k. \tag{7.7}$$

The derivation of (7.7) is reported in the appendix to this chapter. We can measure volatility in terms of the variance of wage and employment. This is given by

$$\text{var}(\hat{w}^k) = \left(\frac{\eta_{LL}^k}{\eta_{LL}^k + \eta_S}\right)^2 \text{var}(\hat{\alpha}^k), \quad \text{var}(\hat{L}^k) = \left(\frac{\eta_S \eta_{LL}^k}{\eta_{LL}^k + \eta_S}\right)^2 \text{var}(\hat{\alpha}^k). \tag{7.8}$$

The central point emerging from (7.8) is that the volatility of wage and employment for people working in firm k depend on both the exogenous shock $\hat{\alpha}^k$ faced by k and the wage elasticity of k's labour demand.

We now need to discuss labour demand elasticities. Using the Hicksian decomposition of labour demand we obtain

$$\eta_{LL}^k = \left(\frac{w}{L^k}\right)\left(\frac{\partial L^k}{\partial w}\right) = S_L^k(\sigma_{LL}^k + \phi^k). \tag{7.9}$$

The derivation of (7.9) can be found in the appendix. The wage elasticity of demand for labour is the percentage change in employment, following a 1% change in wages, with $\eta_{LL}^k < 0$. w is the wage rate, L^k employment in firm k and S_L^k is the share of labour in total production costs. Note that η_{LL}^k can be decomposed into two terms. The first term, $\sigma_{LL}^k < 0$, is the elasticity of substitution between labour and other factors of production. It captures the extent to which the firm substitutes labour with other factors of production as a consequence of an increase in wages. (It is also sometimes defined as the constant-output labour demand elasticity.) The second term, ϕ^k, reflects the price elasticity of demand for the output of firm k. It captures the fact that an increase in wages raises the price of output and reduces the quantity sold. Both effects are larger the larger the labour share S_L^k on total production costs.

The components of (7.9) provide the theoretical underpinning of the factors presented above to explain why MNEs have different elasticity than national firms.

Insofar as MNEs face lower costs of hiring and firing than domestic firms (thus a lower cost of substituting labour in the host country with imported inputs), their elasticity of substitution σ_{LL}^k will be higher in absolute terms: any percentage change in wages will generate a proportionally larger percentage change in employment than in local firms (first and second factors). The second component is related to market power. The more MNEs have market power compared with local firms, the more rigid is their product demand (the smaller is ϕ in absolute terms) and consequently the smaller is the effect of this second component on total labour demand elasticity (third factor). Finally, if MNEs use less labour in production than local firms (the labour share is smaller), then the effects of the elasticities of substitution and of output on labour demand will be smaller for any given change in wages (fourth factor).

There is one further issue that needs to be discussed before we move to the empirical evidence. The concept of elasticity captures the *extent* of the labour demand adjustment: how many workers are laid off if the wage rises. However, another fundamental concept is the *speed* of adjustment, how long it takes for a firm to adjust to its desired level of employment. The speed of adjustment may be affected by frictions in the labour markets, by the way firms organize their activities, and by the type of employees they use. These factors may differ between MNEs and national firms: for example, differences in firing and hiring costs affect both the speed and the extent of the adjustment.

The speed of adjustment can be captured by entering lagged employment L_{t-1}^k as a determinant of labour demand at t. In other words, employment at t is partly determined by employment at $t-1$: the relationship between employment and its lag can be expressed formally as follows:

$$\frac{L_t^k}{L_{t-1}^k} = \left(\frac{L_t^{k*}}{L_{t-1}^k} \right)^{\lambda_i},$$

where L_t^{k*} is the desired employment of firm k at t and λ^k, with $0 \leqslant \lambda^k \leqslant 1$, captures the frictions faced by firm k in adjusting employment to its desired levels. The closer to 1 is λ, the faster is the adjustment of firm k. Having set up the analytical apparatus, we can now move to the empirical analysis.

The evidence

Slaughter (2001), working with a panel of industry data from 1961 to 1991 for the United States, finds that labour demand elasticities for production workers have been rising with time. In contrast, the elasticity of demand of non-production workers is stable. He then tests whether these trends can be associated with the effects of trade and of MNEs' activities at the industry level. He finds that this is not the case: the dynamics of labour demand elasticity is essentially captured by a time trend which controls for technical progress.

Slaughter's analysis, however, examines average industry trends and does not provide any evidence of whether MNEs behave differently from local firms. The only empirical works directly addressing this issue are Barba Navaretti et al. (2003) and Fabbri et al. (2002). We start with the former. This paper works with a large panel of firms based in 11 European countries between 1993 and 2000. It estimates the following constant dynamic labour demand function derived from a Cobb–Douglas production function:

$$\ln(L_t^k) = \gamma_0 + \gamma_1 \ln(L_{t-1}^k) - \gamma_2 \ln(w_t) + \gamma_3 \ln(Y_t^k) + \gamma_4 \ln(r_t) + \gamma_5 T + \varepsilon_{it}, \quad (7.10)$$

where L_t^k is employment in firm k at time t, Y_t^k is real output, r_t the real rental cost of capital, w_t real wages and T a time trend to control for (Hicks-neutral) technical progress. Two things should be noted from (7.10). The first is that coefficient γ_2 captures $S_{L\sigma_{LL}}$, the short-run constant output wage elasticity of labour demand (this is so, given that output Y enters directly as a determinant of labour demand). The second is that the coefficient γ_1 captures how far employment at t is explained by its lagged value. If γ_1 is constrained to vary between 0 and 1, then $1 - \gamma_1$ measures the speed of adjustment. The closer it is to unity the faster the adjustment, with instantaneous adjustment if $1 - \gamma_1 = 1$.

By interacting each explanatory variable with the usual dummy MNE^k, which captures if firm k is foreign or nationally owned (in this case MNE is strictly dichotomous), Barba Navaretti et al. (2003) measure two sets of relevant coefficients, one for MNEs and one for local firms for the 11 countries analysed.[14] These are reported in Table 7.4.

The results reported are quite striking. First, MNEs adjust much faster than local firms: virtually instantly, as if there were no frictions. The coefficient for the speed of adjustment of MNEs is close to unity for all the sample countries (Belgium has the minimum value of 0.8), and always higher than for local firms. Second, MNEs adjust less than local firms: for any given change in the wage rate, the change in employment is smaller. Indeed, their short-run wage elasticity is always smaller in absolute terms than for local firms. Namely, people who work in an MNE are less likely to be laid off, but if it happens it happens fast.

The role of the speed of adjustment has received little attention in the literature. The fact that MNEs are perceived as volatile could have to do more with their ability to react quickly, rather then with the extent of their adjustment. However, the result that the wage elasticity is lower for MNEs needs to be qualified. Barba Navaretti et al. (2003) cannot control for the skill composition of the work force. MNEs probably

---

[14]To avoid the effect of unobserved heterogeneity and endogeneity, (7.7) is estimated in first differences, using the Arellano–Bond estimator and also controlling for size and sector effects.

Table 7.4. Speed and extent of labour demand adjustment:
a comparison between local firms and MNEs.

	Speed of adjustment $(1 - \gamma_1)$		Short-run wage elasticities (γ_2)	
	Local firms	MNE	Local firms	MNE
Belgium	0.09	0.80	−0.53	−0.45
Denmark	0.32	1.07	−0.74	−0.43
Spain	0.36	0.98	−1.06	−0.73
Finland	0.78	1.03	−0.42	−0.54
France	0.69	1.00	−0.91	−0.73
Germany	0.52	0.92	−0.88	−0.71
Italy	0.59	1.00	−0.96	−0.90
The Netherlands	0.23	0.86	−0.58	−0.47
Norway	0.85	0.97	−0.75	−0.68
Sweden	0.55	1.01	−0.31	−0.50
United Kingdom	0.13	0.92	−0.46	−0.43

Source: Barba Navaretti et al. (2003, Table 3, p. 716).

have a lower elasticity because they are relatively skill intensive. Would this result change if measured for homogeneous groups of workers?

Fabbri et al. (2002) compare labour demand elasticity for foreign- and domestic-owned firms based in the UK, spanning the years between 1973 and 1992. Their study is based on the ARD (see above) and they can distinguish between production and non-production workers. As predicted, they find that non-production workers face a lower constant output labour elasticity than production workers. In line with Barba Navaretti et al. (2003) they also find that for much of the period observed, MNEs have a more rigid labour demand than that of local firms, for both skilled and unskilled workers.

These results are consistent with other works which use an alternative approach to the study of volatility. They analyse the likelihood of plant shutdown and whether it differs between national and domestic firms. Plant shutdowns are just a component of workers' layoffs, but in the case of MNEs they could be relatively important. A paper by Girma and Görg (2002) examines this issue for the UK electronics and food industry between 1980 and 1993.[15] They find that a foreign takeover reduces the lifetime of the acquired plant in both industries under study. Also, Fabbri et al.

---

[15]They estimate a standard hazard model and they control for endogeneity using instrumental variables and constructing a matched sample of firms. By use of the matching technique it is possible to construct a counterfactual of national firms 'matching' the sample of foreign ones in a way that the two groups of firms differ just in the feature under study, namely the nationality of ownership. For a discussion of matching techniques of sample construction, see Blundell and Costa Dias (2000, 2002).

(2002) find a similar result for a general sample of manufacturing firms in the UK. However, they notice that these results hold only when other variables affecting the likelihood of survival are included in their estimations as controls. Without controls their results are reversed: MNEs survive longer and are less likely to shut down. This is once more the problem discussed above—whether conditional or unconditional effects are important. MNEs are bundles of things which make them different from national firms. What matters is that MNEs survive longer, independently of the reason why this is so.

Summing up, the little evidence available does not at all support the view that MNEs are more volatile than national firms. Rather, they are more likely to preserve their employees following labour demand shocks. True, MNEs adjust more rapidly, but the policy maker should be more interested in the overall loss of jobs rather than the speed at which they are lost.

7.6　Multinationals and Local Firms

Up to now we have been dealing with composition effects of MNEs in host economies. In this section we focus on the effects of MNEs on domestic activities; for example, do MNEs cause local firms to become more efficient? Although MNEs may engender economy-wide effects, here we strictly focus on their effects on local firms. This issue, which is normally analysed under the heading of spillovers (or external effects), has attracted much attention in the literature since the early 1960s. The first author to systematically include spillovers among the possible consequences of FDI was MacDougall (1960), who analysed the welfare effects of foreign investment. Other early contributions were provided by Corden (1967), who looked at the effects of FDI on optimum tariff policy, and Caves (1971), who examined the industrial pattern and welfare effects of FDI. The general heading of spillovers does not do justice to the complex mechanisms through which MNEs affect local economies. In what follows we discuss these mechanisms. We then move to reviewing the empirical evidence.

Effects on domestic activities: analytical issues

Multinational and local firms interact in a variety of ways. They may trade directly with each other—the supply of inputs or new technologies. They will typically compete in product and factor markets, and these markets may be imperfectly competitive, so profits are shifted and market structure may change. And there will be non-market interactions between firms—externalities. All of these channels may be associated with changes in the measured efficiency of local firms. To understand potential effects we outline four mechanisms through which they are transmitted: market transactions; technological externalities; pecuniary externalities; pro-competitive effects.

Market transactions.   Transfer of proprietary assets from MNEs to national firms could take place on the market, i.e. through transactions deliberately negotiated between the parties. In Chapter 5 we discussed at length why and when MNEs may decide to carry out these transactions with local firms rather than internalize them in a parent–subsidiary relationship. The transfers may take the form of licensing agreements for particular technology, or be part of a package of upgrading associated with supply of inputs, assembly or marketing. For example, Lall (1980b), on the basis of a case study of foreign truck manufacturers in India, finds that local suppliers were getting deliberate and explicit support from downstream MNEs in many areas.

Technological externality.   Alternatively, these mechanisms could be external to an explicit transaction, with transfers taking place through externalities that do not bring any direct return to the MNE. The literature deals extensively with these spillovers from MNEs: Blomström and Kokko (1998), Lipsey (2002), Görg and Greenaway (2001), Hanson (2001) are useful surveys of this issue.

There are many channels through which spillovers get diffused. Sometimes these are difficult to foresee: managers of MNEs playing golf with managers of national firms. In other cases they are unpredicted consequences of explicit contracts. We have discussed in Chapter 5 how contracts are often incomplete, as they cannot take into account all contingencies and transactions taking place in the relationship between MNEs and local firms. When MNEs and local firms interact explicitly, more information and technological flows may transit between the two than foreseen by their contractual relationship. For example, local assemblers could learn much more about the technology of the components they assemble than MNEs wish them to. Think of the use of reverse engineering in the early development stages in Japan and other East Asian countries.

This inability to write complete contracts is a reason why MNEs sometimes prefer to carry out such transactions internally, by way of their own subsidiaries. But even to internalize all transactions may not be enough to prevent externalities. MNEs' employees could move to local firms bringing along what they have learned. For example, Caves (1996) reports that the inter-firm mobility of managers has contributed to the spread of specific management practices from Japan to the US. Gerschenberg (1987) reports that the mobility of highly trained managers from MNEs to local firms was instrumental to the diffusion of know-how to local firms.

Pecuniary externality.   MNEs may also affect the domestic economy because of network and aggregation effects. Their presence and their demand could generate investments in activities or goods, the production of which is characterized by economies of scale. An example is the development of public goods, like infrastructure, universities, training, etc. Public investments in these areas cannot be cost effective unless there is a sufficiently large demand. Equally, as discussed in Chap-

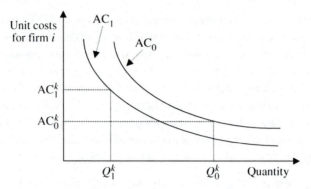

Figure 7.1.   Spillovers and crowding out. *Source:* Aitken and Harrison (1999).

ter 3, MNEs could lead to investments in private goods not available before, for example, the development of input supplier industries, also providing better quality inputs at lower prices to locals. There is widespread evidence that MNEs, by making use of local suppliers, have expanded both output and quality of these producers (Katz 1969; Behrman and Wallender 1976; Reuber et al. 1973).

By the same token, the agglomerative effects caused by FDI could also create diseconomies to local firms, for example, if growing demand raises the price of local factors of production (e.g. labour). As we will see in the next chapter, the massive inflows of FDI to Ireland brought about both positive and negative pecuniary externalities.

Pro-competitive effects.   MNEs also increase competition in domestic markets. If these are imperfectly competitive, their presence may force local firms to reduce their margins and become more efficient. However, in industries with economies of scale, the reduction of the market share of local firms forces them up their downward-sloping average cost curve, away from their minimum efficient scale. Sometimes, MNEs may force less efficient local firms to exit.

Negative competitive effects can more than offset favourable technological externalities. Aitken and Harrison (1999) provide a useful and simple illustration of this problem in the short term. Take an imperfectly competitive market with fixed costs of production. Local firms face a downward-sloping average cost curve, like AC_0 in Figure 7.1. Assume there are no MNEs. Firm k produces Q_0^k at an average cost AC_0^k. Now imagine that more efficient MNEs enter. If their marginal costs are lower, they will produce more than local competitors, taking away part of the local demand from them. All the same, some of their superior efficiency spills over to average local firms, so their AC schedule shifts down to AC_1. As a consequence of these two combined effects firm k will produce less ($Q_1^k < Q_0^k$) at higher average costs ($AC_1^k > AC_0^k$), even if positive spillovers have taken place.

Aitken and Harrison's analysis is of relevance when MNEs compete in the same output market of domestic firms. Otherwise, when MNEs are export oriented, the product market competition described does not take place.

Effects on domestic activities: evidence

MNEs may, in principle, have both positive and negative effects on local firms. Unfortunately, empirical studies do not provide a clear resolution of this ambiguity. Notwithstanding the very large number of studies on this matter, it is also difficult to detect a clear answer from the empirical literature. Results are not robust to changes in methodology, countries and samples.

The only clear message that emerges is that the likelihood of positive effects on the domestic economy depends on specific factors: the size of the technological gap between MNEs and the economic activities in the host country; the extent of vertical linkages between MNEs and local firms; the nature of competition in the industry; the geographical proximity between MNEs and local firms. For this reason, it is difficult to detect generalized positive effects on domestic activities. We will return to this later; now let us first step back and discuss the empirical strategies used to address this issue.

Most empirical studies have focused on the productivity of local firms. To estimate the effects of MNEs on the productivity of local firms, we can use a generalized version of equation (7.6) (see, for example, Aitken and Harrison 1999; Haskel et al. 2002):

$$\ln(Y_t^k) = \sum_{s=1}^{n}(\alpha_s B_{st}^k) + \beta \text{MNE}_t^k + \upsilon \text{MNESECTOR}_t^K$$
$$+ \varphi(\text{MNE}_t^k * \text{MNESECTOR}_t^K) + \sum_{s=1}^{m} \gamma_s X_{st}^k + a_t^k. \qquad (7.11)$$

This equation expresses the output of firm k at time t as a function of n factor inputs (now summarized in vector B, rather than listed separately as in equation (7.6)) and a number of other terms. The firm-specific term MNE_t^k controls for the productivity effect of k's ownership, exactly as we saw in equation (7.6) (although for simplicity we now assume that $i = 1$, firms are either national or foreign owned). Spillovers are captured first by the variable MNESECTOR_t^K, which measures the presence of MNEs in the same industry as firm k (industry K); it is generally the share of MNEs in industry K activities such as employment, sales, or value added, etc. The variable MNESECTOR_t^K sometimes also enters interacted with the firm-specific MNE dummy, MNE_t^k. The idea is that spillovers may affect local and multinational firms differently. Thus, if $\upsilon > 0$ (meaning there are spillovers), then if $\varphi > 0$ spillovers mostly affect other foreign firms, while if $\varphi < 0$ they benefit mostly domestic firms. Other factors are summarized in the vector X_{st}^k. Many variations of equation (7.11) are available in the literature. For example, the specification (7.11) assumes that spillovers are intra-industry; some studies have analysed inter-industry effects. Equations like (7.11) have also been analysed at the sectoral level (in which case all firm-specific variables are dropped), as a cross-section (in which case the time dimension t is dropped) and finally as a panel.

The outcomes of these estimations have been found to be strongly biased by the methodologies used. This can be clearly seen in Table 7.5, which is derived from Görg and Greenaway (2001) and lists 31 empirical papers on spillovers, grouped by the type of country analysed (developed, developing and transition). The table also indicates the level of aggregation of the study (industry- or firm-specific), the methodology used (cross-section or panel) and the sign of the estimated spillover effect. Earlier studies are essentially based on cross-sectional data and almost always find a positive effect of MNEs on productivity. This is even more so when industry rather than firm data are used. Thanks to the availability of larger datasets and the development of new econometric techniques, more recent papers use panel datasets. In this case the estimated effect is either negative or undetermined. Noticeable exceptions are two studies on the UK. Haskel et al. (2002), in a recent paper on UK manufacturing between 1973 and 1992, find robust evidence of positive spillovers: a 10% increase in foreign presence in a UK industry raises the TFP of that industry's domestic plant by about 0.5%. Griffith et al. (2003) investigate if there is convergence in TFP towards the technological frontier at the establishment level in the UK. They find that MNEs constitute a large share of the firms operating at the efficiency frontier, and that they contribute to productivity growth through technology transfers. They also find that increased foreign presence raises the speed of convergence towards the technological frontier.

The fact that results are strongly influenced by the methodology used is also confirmed in a paper by Görg and Strobl (2002), who find econometrically a strong statistical association between techniques and results.

The bad news is that from the methodological point of view panel analysis is much more accurate than cross-sections, which are likely to give biased results. The problems are exactly the same as those faced when comparing MNEs and national firms. In cross-sections it is not possible to follow firms in time and to observe outcomes arising after a time lag. It is not possible to control for the effect of unobservable factors, which could be correlated to both performance and ownership. Finally, it is not possible to control for the endogeneity of productivity and ownership. Cross-sections using sectoral data find that performance is correlated to the presence of MNEs, possibly because foreign investors prefer to invest in high productivity sectors, rather than work to boost the productivity of laggards. With such data the direction of the causal link cannot be explored.

Table 7.5. The analysis of spillovers: methodology and results.

	Author(s)	Country	Year	Data	Aggregation	Result
	Developing countries					
1	Blomström and Persson (1983)	Mexico	1970	CS	Industry	+
2	Blomström (1986)	Mexico	1970/1975	CS	Industry	+
3	Blomström and Wolff (1994)	Mexico	1970/1975	CS	Industry	+
4	Kokko (1994)	Mexico	1970	CS	Industry	+
5	Kokko (1996)	Mexico	1970	CS	Industry	+
6	Haddad and Harrison (1993)	Morocco	1985–89	Panel	Fm & Ind.	?
7	Kokko et al. (1996)	Uruguay	1990	CS	Firm	?
8	Blomström and Sjöholm (1999)	Indonesia	1991	CS	Firm	+
9	Sjöholm (1999a)	Indonesia	1980–91	CS	Firm	+
10	Sjöholm (1999b)	Indonesia	1980–91	CS	Firm	+
11	Chuang and Lin (1999)	Taiwan	1991	CS	Firm	+
12	Aitken and Harrison (1999)	Venezuela	1976–89	Panel	Firm	−
13	Kathuria (2000)	India	1976–89	Panel	Firm	?
14	Kokko et al. (2001)	Uruguay	1988	Cs	Firm	?
15	Kugler (2001)	Colombia	1974–98	Panel	Industry	?
	Developed countries					
16	Caves (1974)	Australia	1966	CS	Industry	+
17	Globerman (1979)	Canada	1972	CS	Industry	+
18	Liu et al. (2000)	UK	1991–95	Panel	Industry	+
19	Driffield (2001)	UK	1989–92	CS	Industry	+
20	Girma et al. (2001)	UK	1991–96	Panel	Firm	?
21	Girma and Wakelin (2000)	UK	1988–96	Panel	Firm	?
22	Girma and Wakelin (2001)	UK	1980–92	Panel	Firm	?
23	Harris and Robinson (2003)	UK	1974–95	Panel	Firm	?
24	Barry et al. (2001)	Ireland	1990–98	Panel	Firm	−
25	Barrios and Strobl (2002)	Spain	1990–94	Panel	Firm	?
26	Dimelis and Louri (2001)	Greece	1997	CS	Firm	+
27	Haskel et al. (2002)	UK	1973–92	Panel	Firm	+
28	Griffith et al. (2003)	UK	1980–92	Panel	Firm	+
	Transition countries					
29	Djankov and Hoekman (2000)	Czech Rep.	1993–96	Panel	Firm	−
30	Kinoshita (2001)	Czech Rep.	1995–98	Panel	Firm	?
31	Bosco (2001)	Hungary	1993–97	Panel	Firm	?
32	Konings (2001)	Bulgaria	1993–97	Panel	Firm	−
		Poland	1994–97			?
		Romania	1993–97			
33	Damijan et al. (2001)	Bulgaria,	1994–98	Panel	Firm	? or −, +
		Czech Rep.,				only for
		Estonia, Hungary,				Romania
		Poland, Romania,				
		Slovakia, Slovenia				

Source: Extended and updated from Görg and Greenaway (2001).

Notes. (i) Data: 'CS' denotes cross-sectional data, while 'Panel' denotes use of combined cross-sectional time-series data in the respective analysis. (ii) Aggregation: use of either Industry- or Firm-level data in the analysis. (iii) Result: regression analysis finds a '+' (positive and statistically significant), '−' (negative and statistically significant), '?' (mixed results or statistically insignificant) sign on the foreign presence variable.

When we compared MNEs and local firms, cross-section estimations with few controls provided useful statistical associations. This is not the case for the analysis of spillovers. If local firms belonging to sectors with many foreign investors are found to be more efficient than those in sectors with few foreign investors, this could have nothing to do with the presence and the role of foreign firms.

The fact that in general terms there is no robust statistical evidence on the existence of spillovers does not mean that these spillovers are completely absent. Favourable effects may emerge under special circumstances and between groups of firms with some particular characteristics. In what follows we discuss four specific circumstances that have been shown to have an effect on spillovers. These are the technological and the geographical proximity between local firms and MNEs, the extent of their vertical linkages and the competitive features of the product market.

Technological proximity.   The level of technology of the activities carried out by MNEs influences the amount of spillovers to local firms. Across countries, spillovers are not likely to arise in poor countries. MNEs start being beneficial to domestic activities at higher steps of the income and technological ladders, from middle-income countries onward. Few local firms in the poorest countries are in direct competition with foreign MNEs, and few of these countries possess the technical skills needed to absorb modern technologies.

Across industries, spillovers are larger in industries where MNEs are widely present and when locals are able to interact. This rule seems to be valid both in developing and developed countries. An abundance of good engineers is a key factor generating technological spillovers in Bangalore, Dublin and Silicon Valley alike. In some other countries spillovers could be especially large in traditional industries, because here is where locals have sufficient capabilities to interact with foreign firms.

This result emerges consistently from several studies. Blomström et al. (1994a) examine the role of the host country's overall development level as a determinant of spillovers. Their comprehensive cross-country study of 101 economies suggests that spillovers are concentrated in middle-income developing countries, while there is no evidence of such effects for the poorest developing countries. Similarly, Balasubramanyam (1998) concludes that FDI can be a powerful instrument of development, but only in the presence of a threshold of human capital, well-developed infrastructure facilities and a stable economic climate. Thus, 'FDI is a rich country's good' (p. 18) and only the most advanced developing countries are able to benefit from FDI. He also finds that the type and the amount of technology imported by MNEs vary systematically with host country characteristics. These imports seem to be larger and more technology intensive in countries and industries where the educational level of the local labour force is higher and where local competition is tougher (Blomström et al. 1994a; Blomström and Kokko 1995).

The evidence from these cross-country studies is in line with findings of several works based on industry- or firm-specific data for individual countries. As a consequence of the competitive pressure of MNEs, local firms become more productive, but this only happens in sectors where best-practice technology lies within their capability. In contrast, when the gap is too great, there are no significant transfers of modern technology. This is the finding of Haddad and Harrison (1993) in a test of the spillover hypothesis for Moroccan manufacturing during the period 1985–89 (on this also see Blomström (1986)).

Examining data for Mexican manufacturing, Kokko (1994) finds that spillovers are positively related to the host economy's capacity to absorb them. Similar findings for the Uruguayan manufacturing sector are reported in Kokko et al. (1996). Their study suggests that weak technological capability at the firm level may be an obstacle for spillovers. Kathuria (1998, 2000, 2001) in various studies of the Indian economy suggests that the indirect gains from MNEs are not automatic. Rather, they depend to a large extent on the efforts of local firms to invest in learning and R&D activities. No evidence was found of spillovers to low-tech Indian companies.

This story also works for developed countries. Perez (1998), in a study of UK industries, and Cantwell (1989), who investigates the responses of local firms to the increase in competition caused by the entry of US multinationals into European markets between 1955 and 1975, argue that positive technology spillovers did not occur in all industries. According to Cantwell, 'the technological capacity of indigenous firms... was the major factor in determining the success of the European corporate response' (p. 86) to the US challenge. More specifically, Cantwell suggests that the entry of US affiliates provided a highly beneficial competitive spur in the industries where local firms had some traditional technological strength. In contrast, local firms in other industries were forced out of business or pushed to market segments that were ignored by MNEs.

Görg and Strobl (2001a, 2002) show that the presence of foreign companies in the Irish economy has a life-enhancing effect on indigenous firms and plants in high-tech industries, where MNEs are indeed concentrated and where a very large and concerted public/private effort to upgrade local capabilities was carried out (see Chapter 8). Similarly, studies on the UK by Girma et al. (2001) and Girma and Wakelin (2000, 2001) find evidence of spillovers only in skill-intensive industries. Using firm-level data, they find that local firms benefit less from the presence of MNEs, the further they are from the productivity frontier. Sembenelli and Siotis (2002) in their study on a Spanish panel between 1983 and 1996 find that MNEs generate larger and faster positive spillovers on local firms in R&D-intensive sectors than in non-R&D-intensive ones.

Anyway, the relationship between technological distance from MNEs and the productivity of local firms is likely to be non-linear. Beyond a technological threshold, some studies find evidence of catching up, in that laggards grow faster than firms closer to the frontier (Griffith et al. 2003; Castellani and Zanfei 2003; Peri and Urban 2002).

Geographical proximity.   Another important factor is that voluntary or unintended transfers of technology are smaller the larger the geographical distance between the transferor and the receiver. The literature on technological spillovers has shown in a quite uncontroversial way how these decline with distance (see Jaffe et al. 1993). The assumption that spillovers are local for foreign investments is therefore quite reasonable. It is more likely that employees from MNEs move to local firms based in the same location of the MNE rather than elsewhere. It is also likely that firms with vertical linkages locate nearby.

Unfortunately, the evidence on FDI is once more controversial. Within one country, FDI does not seem to affect differently national firms located nearby than those further away. The paper by Aitken and Harrison (1999) on Venezuela mentioned above keeps finding that FDI has no positive effects on national firms, independently of the geographical proximity between the two groups of firms. In contrast, Girma and Wakelin (2000, 2001) on the UK find that spillovers are larger when MNEs are located in the same region and sector as national firms. However, as argued above, these spillovers are only significant for firms with a low technology gap with respect to MNEs.

Vertical linkages.   Effects on domestic firms are especially likely to occur when there are vertical linkages between local firms and MNEs. These effects have been found to be particularly strong towards upstream local suppliers, less so towards downstream assemblers. Lall (1980b) argues that MNEs deliberately support suppliers in various ways: by helping them in setting up production facilities; by providing technical assistance to raise product quality; by assisting them in purchasing raw materials; by training employees and managers.

In his case study of truck manufacturers in India, Lall finds evidence of all such channels of support. Similar results have been found by various other case studies based on different developed and developing countries (Behrman and Wallender 1976; Watanabe 1983a,b; Reuber et al. 1973). A recent World Bank study on Latvia (FIAS 2003) reports that 82% of the MNEs operating there have at least one local supplier of intermediates. Accordingly, 36% of Latvian firms supplying MNEs reported that they were receiving assistance from their customers.

By studying a large panel of firms in Lithuania in the period 1996–2000, Smarzynska (2003) finds evidence of spillovers from MNEs to their upstream suppliers. She finds that productivity of national firms is positively related to their links with MNEs as customers. In contrast, local firms do not benefit from MNEs when these are competitors or suppliers of inputs (forward linkages). Aitken and Harrison (1999) instead do not find positive effects arising from backward linkages in their Venezuelan sample.

Competition in the product market. The question of competition in the product market has rarely been explored in the literature, as it raises complex methodological problems. As discussed in the previous section, the basic idea is that the entry of MNEs in the product market forces local firms to react and increase efficiency. The entry of MNEs is defined as pro-competitive in this case. However, the pro-competitive entry of MNEs dampens profit margins, even when this entry is efficiency enhancing in the longer run. Thus, a decline in profit margins does not necessarily lead to the crowding out of local firms. It is anyway extremely challenging to disentangle these two effects (spillovers and increased competition), which take place at the same time with opposite effects on profit margins.

Sembenelli and Siotis (2002), in their study of Spanish firms discussed earlier, try to disentangle the pro-competitive and the spillover effects. They find that especially in non-R&D-intensive sectors the entry of MNEs dampens the profit margins of local firms in the short run, to give way to efficiency-enhancing effects in the longer run. Thus, MNEs have a pro-competitive effect on local firms. Following their entry, the profit margins of local firms decline initially, but then, thanks to efficiency gains, they grow again in the longer run. In R&D-intensive sectors spillover effects dominate, as argued above.

Kokko (1996) analyses the effects of competition in Mexican manufacturing with a similar approach. He argues that efficiency-enhancing effects from competition are not determined by the presence of foreign firms alone, but rather by the interactions between foreign and local firms. Hence, it is possible that spillovers are larger when a few foreign MNEs stir up a previously protected market than when foreign affiliates hold large market shares but refrain from competing hard with local firms. In fact, in some cases, a large presence of foreign firms may even be a sign of a weak local industry, where local firms have not been able to absorb any productivity spillovers at all and have therefore been forced to yield market shares to the MNEs.

Analysing the operations of foreign and domestic firms in Mexican manufacturing, Kokko (1996) finds support for these hypotheses. The labour productivity of foreign and local firms appears to be jointly determined. Moreover, competition from foreign affiliates seems to have an independent efficiency-enhancing effect on the productivity of local firms, independently from the size of their share of economic activities.

Our review has focused on the effects on productivity. Another issue concerning product markets is whether MNEs generate market access spillovers, helping local firms to enter export markets. Also, we have not touched upon the broader effects of MNEs on factor markets, and particularly on wages. Both issues face the same methodological problems of the analysis of the efficiency effects and the evidence of the few studies available is not yet conclusive. We therefore do not deal with these two further effects here and instead we refer the interested reader to the comprehensive surveys of Görg and Greenaway (2001) and Lipsey (2002) that cover both aspects extensively.

7.7   Conclusions

This chapter examines the effects of MNEs in host countries. It follows two separate lines of inquiry. The first is to examine if MNEs are different from local firms. We define this effect as the composition effect. Insofar as MNEs are different, their entry changes the average performance and behaviour of local economies. The second one is to look at the effects of MNEs on domestic activities, mostly on local firms.

On the first account we find that MNEs are indeed very different from local firms. They are larger, more efficient, they pay higher wages and employ more skilled personnel. This is so because MNEs bring to host countries a bundle of characteristics that are not necessarily available locally: technologies, brands, management procedures, market access and so on. Also, it could be so because foreign investors cherry pick the best firms. The challenging problem from the methodological point of view is trying to single out the strict causal effect of foreign ownership on performance. This implicitly requires stripping the bundle from all features other than the nationality of ownership, essentially examining what would have happened to a local firm that becomes foreign owned compared with what would have happened if it had stayed local. When adopting these stringent econometric techniques, differences between foreign and domestic firms are small and not always significant. However, foreign firms are still found to perform better in some cases and never worse than local firms.

We also examine extensively the issue of whether MNEs behave differently from local firms in the labour market. We find that they pay higher wages than local firms, even after controlling for skill differences and for firm-specific factors. We also checked if jobs in MNEs are more volatile, and find that this is not the case. MNEs adjust faster than local firms to shocks affecting labour demand, but they react less, varying employment less for any given change in the wage rate.

The last part of this chapter deals with the external effect of MNEs on domestic activities. These arise as unintended technological and pecuniary externalities or as intended transactions with local firms. The evidence on this ground is controversial and difficult to generalize. Results are not very robust to changes in methodology and samples. The bottom line is that it is quite difficult to find general effects, perhaps because external effects only arise under specific circumstances: when there are effective transactions between MNEs and local firms, better if among equals. Positive effects are also more likely if local firms have vertical linkages with MNEs, better when they are suppliers to their foreign counterparts, and when local and foreign firms operate in nearby locations. Finally, we find that in certain cases MNEs have a pro-competitive effect on local firms: they lower their profit margins, but they enhance their efficiency in the longer run.

To complement this general review of the host country effects of MNEs, it is useful to focus in detail on one country study. In the next chapter we present a case study of Ireland, the European country which has been most successful in attracting FDI and where FDI has completely changed the landscape of the domestic economy.

Appendix

Derivation of Equation (7.7)

The measures of volatility in wages and employment reported in equation (7.7) can be derived as follows. Assume the following generic production function $Y = AL^\beta K^{1-\beta}$, where Y is real output, A is a technological parameter and $0 < \beta < 1$, implying decreasing returns to labour. If we are in the short term, K, capital, is constant and for simplicity we normalize it to 1. Profit maximization implies equating wages (w) to the value of the marginal product of labour: $w = \beta p A L^{1-\beta}$, where p is the price of output. We can then derive labour demand as

$$L^D = \left(\frac{w}{\beta p A}\right)^{1/(1-\beta)} = \left(\frac{w}{\alpha}\right)^{-\eta_{LL}}. \tag{A7.1}$$

where $\alpha = \beta p A$ is a labour demand shifter capturing price and technology shocks and $\eta_{LL} = 1/(1 - \beta)$ is the absolute value of the labour demand elasticity. We assume a generic labour supply: $L^S = w^{\eta_S}$. Then, by equating labour demand and supply we get

$$w = \alpha^{\eta_{LL}/(\eta_{LL}+\eta_S)}. \tag{A7.2}$$

By totally differentiating (A7.2), dividing both sides by w and including superscript k, we obtain the percentage changes in wages for firm k as

$$\hat{w}^k = \frac{dw^k}{w^k} = \left(\frac{\eta_{LL}^k}{\eta_{LL}^k + \eta_S}\right)\hat{\alpha}^k. \tag{7.7a}$$

Similarly, by totally differentiating labour supply and dividing both sides of it by L, we obtain the percentage change of labour as

$$\hat{L}^k = \frac{dL^k}{L^k} = \eta_S\frac{w^k}{dw^k}.$$

If we then substitute w^k/dw^k from (A7.3), we obtain

$$\hat{L}^k = \left(\frac{\eta_S\eta_{LL}^k}{\eta_{LL}^k + \eta_S}\right)\hat{\alpha}^k. \tag{7.7b}$$

Derivation of the Decomposition of Labour Demand Elasticity (7.9)

For expositional reasons we have so far assumed that capital is constant and that the price of output is an exogenous parameter, not affected by wages. Consequently, output is also unaffected by wages. This is not realistic, as labour and capital (and also other factors not considered here) are substituted to some degree in the longer term and because prices are set endogenously in relation to marginal costs and thus to wages. Therefore, changes in the wage rate affect labour demand both directly, and indirectly, via the impact on marginal cost, prices and then output. This is the meaning of the decomposition of the labour demand elasticity presented in (7.9). To derive it, we need to introduce a long-term production function where capital is no longer constant. We start by deriving the decomposition at the industry level and we will then make it firm specific. Consider an industry with firms using a constant returns-to-scale technology, behaving competitively on factor markets and facing an infinitely elastic supply curve. For simplicity, and without loss of generality, assume that two factors of production are used: labour and capital. Given the assumption of constant returns to technology, the generic labour demand L^D when both labour and capital are used as inputs is

$$L^D(w, r, Y) = l(w, r)Y[p(w)],$$

where r is the rental rate of capital, l is labour per unit of real output Y and $l_w < 0$. The desired level of output by each firm is found on the product demand function and is negatively related to its own price: $Y = Y(p)$, $Y_p < 0$. In turn p is a function of wages. Thus, under such conditions, wages affect labour demand both directly, and indirectly, via the impact on output. The total impact of wage changes on labour demand is measured by the total labour demand elasticity η_{LL}. This is given by

$$\eta_{LL} = \frac{\partial L^D}{\partial w}\frac{w}{L^D} = L_w^D\frac{w}{L^D} + L_Y^D\frac{\partial Y}{\partial p}\frac{\partial p}{\partial w}\frac{w}{L^D}. \tag{A7.3}$$

The first term in the above expression is the constant-output labour demand elasticity, and the second term captures the impact on labour demand via the change in output. The constant-output labour demand can be expressed as $L_w w/L^D = s_L \sigma_{LL}$, where s_L is the share of labour costs on the value of output and σ_{LL} is the Allen–Uzawa substitution elasticity between labour and capital. As for the second term in expression (A7.3), the following transformations can be implemented. First, from the assumption of constant returns to scale, $L_Y = l(w, r)$. Second, from the definition of output demand elasticity, $\partial Y/\partial p = \phi Y/p$, where ϕ is the output demand elasticity. Finally, from perfect competition prices equal marginal costs, i.e. $p = \partial C/\partial Y = c$. Using Shephard's Lemma and constant returns to scale one obtains $L^D = \partial C/\partial w = c_w Y$. It follows that

$$\frac{\partial p}{\partial w} = \frac{\partial C/\partial Y}{\partial w} = c_w = \frac{L^D}{Y}.$$

Using the above results and the definition for the output demand elasticity

$$\phi = \frac{\partial Y}{\partial p} \frac{p}{Y},$$

we obtain

$$L_Y^D \frac{\partial Y}{\partial p} \frac{\partial p}{\partial w} \frac{w}{L^D} = l\phi \frac{Y}{p} \frac{L^D}{Y} \frac{w}{L^D} = \frac{wL^D}{pY}\phi = s_L\phi.$$

Thus, the total labour demand elasticity is

$$\eta_{LL} = s_L(\sigma_{LL} + \phi). \tag{A7.4}$$

Following Fabbri et al. (2003), under the assumption of imperfect competition, (A7.4) can be used to approximate the perceived labour demand elasticity of firm k:

$$\eta_{LL}^k = s_L^k(\sigma_{LL}^k + \phi^k). \tag{7.9}$$

8

FDI and the Host Economy:
a Case Study of Ireland

The Irish boom of the 1990s saw the country come to be dubbed 'the Celtic Tiger'. Ireland's level of real national income per head rose from less than 65% of the EU average at the beginning of the 1990s to achieve rough parity by the decade's end, while the net job creation rate over the boom period exceeded even that of the US, traditionally the world's 'job creation dynamo'.[1] The boom was fuelled at least in part by a strong increase in FDI inflows. Even before the 1990s Ireland had been the most FDI-reliant economy in the EU. Now almost 50% of Irish manufacturing employment is in foreign-owned firms. This compares with an average of 19% for the other 11 EU member states for which data are given in Table 8.1. The importance of FDI is further reflected in the high level of inward FDI per head of population in Ireland, for which data are also presented (on the relationship between various FDI measures, see Lipsey (2001)). The key foreign sectors in Ireland are pharmaceuticals, electronics and computer software. By the late 1990s nine of the top ten pharmaceutical companies in the world—including such names as Glaxo, Johnson and Johnson, Pfizer and Merck—had operations in Ireland. Almost half of the country's foreign multinationals are in the information and communications technology field, including market leaders such as IBM, Intel, Hewlett-Packard, Dell and Microsoft. Each of the top ten independent software companies in the world has significant operations in Ireland, which is, according to the OECD Information Technology Outlook 2000, the world's largest exporter of software goods. Foreign presence is also significant in Teleservices and in the International Financial Services Centre in Dublin.

Ireland therefore represents an obvious choice as a case study on FDI-related issues. Why was the country so successful in attracting foreign investment? What are the characteristics of the investments that were attracted? And what was the

---

[1] These national income figures use GNP rather than GDP to exclude the profits earned by foreign firms in Ireland.

Table 8.1.   Share of foreign affiliates in manufacturing employment, and inward FDI stock.

	Share of foreign affiliates in manufacturing employment (1998)	FDI inward stock (USD) per head of population (2000)
Ireland	47.5	16 486
France	27.8	4 550
Sweden	21.1	8 649
The Netherlands	19.7	15 871
Austria	18.6	3 383
Belgium	18	
Luxembourg	46.3	
Belgium and Luxembourg		35 108
UK	17.8	8 183
Finland	15.9	4 517
Italy	11.5	2 001
Portugal	7.3	2 683
Germany	6	5 615
Spain	n.a.	3 624
Greece	n.a.	2 180
Denmark	n.a.	9 843

Notes. Share of affiliates in manufacturing employment comes from OECD (2001a, Tables C.4.1 and C.4.2.1); note that the databases from which these tables are derived give very different results for some countries, such as France and Norway; results reported here are those that appear to be most consistent with OECD (2001b). FDI Inward Stock data comes from the UNCTAD (2001) World Investment Report.

contribution of the FDI boom to the transformation of the economy? These three broad issues are addressed in turn in the following sections.

8.1   Ireland's Success in Attracting FDI

Ireland only emerged from protectionism in the 1960s, about a decade later than most of the rest of Western Europe. National income per head in the 1960s remained at around 60% of the EU average. Integration into the EU—membership in 1973, and deeper integration following the completion of the Single Market programme in 1992—naturally meant that the combination of low wages, a favourable corporation tax regime and good market access made Ireland an attractive location for multinational export platform activities. EU accession and the development of the Single Market coincide with the two main booms in foreign investment. The number of jobs in foreign-owned industry grew by almost 40% between 1973 and 1980 and by another 40% between 1987 and 1999, the era of the Single Market and the worldwide high-tech boom.

Table 8.2. Proportions of manufacturing employment in foreign-owned firms accounted for by firms of various nationalities.

	1972	1986	1999
USA	19	50	61
UK	46	17	10
Rest of EU	26	23	20

Source: Census of Industrial Production, various years.

Table 8.3. Proportion of gross output exported.

	1986	1991	1999
EU firms, of which:	61	61	69
UK	n.a.	43	55
Non-EU, of which:	95	95	95
USA	n.a.	96	96
Total foreign industry	83	86	92

Source: Census of Industrial Production, various years.

Even before accession, however, the character of FDI inflows had changed. Most foreign firms operating in the economy in the 1950s, under protectionism, were low-tech UK-owned companies and, as tariff jumpers, were naturally oriented towards the Irish home market. The introduction in the late 1950s of a zero tax rating on profits derived from manufactured exports led to firms from Continental Europe and the US adopting Ireland as an export platform. Foreign industry in the economy at the time of EU accession consisted therefore of two quite separate groups: the older (primarily British) firms which had set up under protectionism and the newer (primarily US and German) firms which were explicitly export oriented. The importance of the first group inevitably declined thereafter; as indicated in Table 8.2, the share of British-owned establishments in total foreign-sector manufacturing employment fell from 46% in 1972 to 10% in 1999, while that of US establishments rose from 19% to 61% over the same period.

The trend in export orientation followed suit, as the Irish operations of the British establishments which dominated in the pre-accession era were (and continue to be) much less export oriented than the US establishments that came to dominate after accession. By 1986 foreign industry was exporting 83% of gross output and this share has continued to rise, reaching 92% of gross output by 1999 (see Table 8.3).

The technological orientation of foreign industry also changed. Only 12% of foreign employment in 1974 was in high-tech sectors, as defined by the OECD, while 65% was located in low-technology sectors. By 1999 these figures stood at 56% and 24%, respectively.

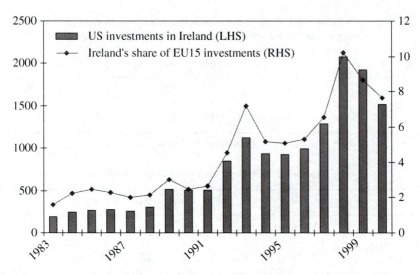

Figure 8.1. Investment by US manufacturing companies in Ireland (millions US$, 1996 prices). *Source:* US Department of Commerce, Survey of Current Business (various issues).

By the 1980s Ireland had become well established as a European production base for US multinationals. It was therefore well positioned to capture increased FDI inflows when US corporate strategy began to respond to the forthcoming Single European Market in the late 1980s and early 1990s. This period, which overlapped with the worldwide boom in high-tech activities, saw US investments in Europe increase substantially, and Ireland captured a growing share of these investments, as reported in Figure 8.1.[2]

Arguably, much of the FDI boom upon EU accession was to be expected as part of the integration of a relatively low wage economy into the large EU market. There were equivalent FDI booms in Spain and Portugal following their accession in the 1980s. By the mid 1990s, however, the share of foreign industry in these economies began to stabilize, at much lower levels than in the Irish case.[3] What was it about Ireland that made it so attractive to inward investors? We discuss some of the major factors in turn.

---

[2]As to why the Irish share should have risen, MacSharry and White (2000, Chapter 10) describe how restrictive public procurement policies on the part of some of the larger member states offered a strong incentive to multinational firms to locate there rather than in Ireland. These practices were outlawed under the Single Market initiative.

[3]Table 8.1 shows that foreign industry accounts for almost 50% of manufacturing employment in Ireland and less than 10% in Portugal, where the definition of foreign ownership is restricted to plants with more than 50% of capital owned by foreign firms. Equivalent figures for Spain are difficult to establish. However, survey evidence suggests that foreign firms comprise around 30% of employment in large firms, and are likely to comprise a much smaller fraction of employment in smaller firms.

8.1.1 Relevant Features of the Irish Economic Environment

Two policy aspects have been especially important in explaining the growth of FDI in Ireland: the corporation tax regime and the activities of Ireland's Industrial Development Agency (IDA). We discuss these first and then consider some other factors that are also likely to have been of importance.

Corporation tax

Ireland's movement towards free trade began in earnest with the signing of the Anglo-Irish Free Trade Agreement, to take effect in 1966, and culminated in Ireland's accession, along with Denmark and the UK, to the then European Economic Community in 1973.

Even before EU accession, however, the zero corporate profits tax rate on manufactured exports, which had been introduced in the late 1950s, had induced substantial change in the economy. The share of manufactured exports in total merchandise exports rose from 19% in 1959 to 35% in 1971. Nearly half of manufactured exports at the time of EU entry were estimated to have come from firms established since the zero tax rate was introduced.

The change was also reflected in Ireland's revealed comparative advantage. Before the tax change, Ireland had an export comparative advantage, at the SITC 1-digit Section level, only in two sectors: Food and Live Animals, and Beverages and Tobacco. These accounted for almost two-thirds of exports. By the time of EU accession, these sectors' share in total exports had fallen to around one-half, while Chemicals had grown from less than 0.5% of exports to some 6%. Ireland had gained an export comparative advantage in both Chemicals and, to a much smaller extent, Manufactures Classified by Material (SITC 6, which includes Textiles, Clothing and Footwear) (see Lipsey 2003). The firms established under the new tax regime also contributed to a substantial diversification of exports markets, with the UK share of manufactured exports falling from 83% in 1959 to 58% in 1972.

The value of the tax regime to these newly entering firms may be discerned from the diversification of export activity away from the UK and towards the then six-country EEC—whose share rose from 6% to 16% over this same period—even though in the years preceding accession Ireland faced an average (post Kennedy Round) nominal tariff of over 9% on EEC-bound industrial exports.

Ireland, upon accession, was the EU member state with the lowest effective corporate tax rate, and this continues to be the case to date.[4] Given the importance of

---

[4]Ireland also offers grants and other incentive packages to firms, subject to EU state-aid limits. The country is ranked close to the EU mid-point in terms of state aid as a percentage of GDP. Aid granted to foreign firms came to 0.29% of GDP in 1990, declining to 0.16% of GDP by the year 2000. A satisfactory outcome of a cost–benefit analysis is a necessary though not sufficient condition for a project to receive financial assistance (Barry et al. 2003c).

Table 8.4.   EU corporation tax rates, effective and nominal.

	Average effective tax rate on US MNCs (1992)[a]	Average effective tax rate on US MNCs (1997)[b]	Top rate of corporation tax on manufacturing (1997)
Ireland	5.8	9.1	10
Finland	15.8		28
Sweden	16.7	20.6	28
The Netherlands	17.9	17.2	35
UK	19.3	24.9	31
Luxembourg	21.6		32
France	22.8	29	42
Portugal	25.3		36
Spain	25.33	24.6	35
Belgium	25.9	27.4	39
Germany	28.9	33.7	45
Denmark	31.0		34
Italy	32.56	41	37
Austria	32.58		34
Greece	33.4		35

Source: [a]Altshuler et al. (2001); [b]Desai et al. (2002b).

US FDI in Ireland, Table 8.4 reports measures of the average effective corporation tax rates on US investments in 1992 and 1997, while the third column shows the maximum nominal tax rates for 1997.[5]

A low corporation tax environment offers multinational firms an incentive to shift profits to the low tax location via transfer pricing. Some prima facie evidence for this is provided by Honohan and Walsh (2002). They contrast reported net output per worker in foreign-dominated sectors in Ireland with the EU average figures, illustrating that the gaps between the two can be very large, as seen in Table 8.5.[6] Transfer pricing distorts much of the trade and output data on the Irish economy. Irish economists therefore prefer to focus on employment when discussing the role

---

[5]The effective tax rate measures the ratio of the sum of foreign income taxes to the sum of net income and foreign income taxes in each country. Rates are constructed in this way, rather than as a percentage of taxable income, in order to capture the effects of differences in tax base definitions, special investment incentives such as accelerated depreciation and other important aspects of tax systems that are not reflected in statutory tax rate differences. Various other cross-country measures of effective rates are also available. While the ranking of some countries changes with the different measures, Ireland invariably comes out with the lowest effective rate in the EU.

[6]Productivity per worker, even accounting for transfer pricing, nevertheless remains substantially higher in foreign than in indigenous industry in Ireland, and overall productivity per worker in manufacturing is higher than in the UK. This compares with a situation in 1968 when Irish net output in manufacturing was 20% below the UK level.

Table 8.5. Indications of possible transfer pricing:
net output per worker, 1999, millions of Irish pounds.

Industry	Nace code	EU average	Ireland	Sectoral share of manufacturing employment in Ireland (%)
Computers	30	104	169	8
Electronic components	32.10	104	230	3.4
Organic and basic chemicals	24.14, 24.4	163	848	5.2
Software reproduction	22.3	64	728	2.5
Cola concentrates	15.85, 15.88, 15.89	90	1015	0.9

and importance of foreign industry. This practice is also followed in the present chapter.

The role of the Industrial Development Agency (IDA)

Ireland was one of the first countries in the world to adopt an FDI-based development model, and the IDA consequently has amassed a huge amount of experience in the international competition to attract FDI.[7] The history of the organization is related in the book *The Making of the Celtic Tiger* (2000) by former Finance Minister and EU Commissioner Ray MacSharry and former IDA Managing Director, Padraic White, from which the following account is largely drawn.

The introduction of Export Profits Tax Relief gave the IDA a distinctive investment incentive with which to market Ireland as a location for foreign companies. Perhaps not surprisingly, given that its major focus was on job creation, the organization in its early years did not discriminate in favour of any particular type of FDI. This changed in the 1970s when the IDA shifted from what MacSharry and White call the 'scatter gun' approach to one more akin to a 'rifle shot'. The current modus operandi can be summarized as follows. First, the sectors and subsectors experiencing international growth, and that are thought to provide a good fit for Ireland's resources and development aims, are identified. These sectors, of course, change over time in line with developments in the international economy and in the country's factor endowments. The strongest companies in these targeted subsectors are then identified, and are approached with a view to persuading them to locate in Ireland. The type and value of incentives required to attract such companies also changes over time, of course. The agencies simultaneously have an influence in the

---

[7]This means it has been much in demand as a consultant in training development agencies in other countries. Sometimes this has had unintended consequences. The IDA, for example, helped design Costa Rica's strategy to attract FDI. Costa Rica later went on to beat Ireland, Malaysia and Mexico in the competition to attract a major new Intel semiconductor facility.

upgrading of the human capital and physical infrastructure required to facilitate the country in its aim of ascending the ladder of comparative advantage. This brings them into realms not traditionally recognized as lying within the industrial policy remit, a point which is developed further below. It is clear, however, that they are much more than simply national marketing agencies.

The traditional focus on labour-intensive industries was reversed in the early 1980s with the decimation of the man-made fibres sector in the wake of the oil shocks and the growing difficulties of maintaining a vibrant textiles, clothing and footwear sector. The agencies started to focus on the high-tech sectors which were enjoying strong international growth and which could be induced to invest in the Irish economy. Substantial employment creation, it was felt, could arise through backward linkages, obviating the need to focus on labour-intensive sectors whose long-term commitment to the Irish economy was likely to be precarious. Furthermore, it was felt that the most technologically advanced firms should be targeted, as these were likely to have the greatest chance of long-term success in the marketplace.

The IDA prides itself on having made judicious choices as to which sectors to target. Electronics, computer software and segments of biotechnology and healthcare were targeted in the early 1980s.[8] The IDA electronics division, for example, used a see-through model of a computer to identify components, and then systematically canvassed foreign companies involved in the production of 14 individual components, including keyboards, hard disks, cables, computer mice and sub-assemblies.

The IDA, furthermore, has always laid great emphasis on 'flagship projects' in each sector, in the belief that this will make the subsequent attraction of less high-profile firms easier. Thus in the late 1980s a major effort was made to attract Intel, the world leader in the manufacture of microprocessors for computers and electronic devices. Despite having sales of almost $1 billion in Europe, the company at the time had no production facilities within the EU. Ireland was one of seven European countries under consideration by Intel. At the final stage, even when Ireland had emerged as the frontrunner, the company remained worried about the country's ability to provide sufficient numbers of engineers with the requisite experience. An example of IDA ingenuity reveals how Ireland eventually won out. The organization commissioned interviews with over 300 Irish engineers with the appropriate experience. Even though most of these were working in the US at the time, it was able to report to Intel that over 80% of them had expressed a willingness to return to Ireland if offered a good career opportunity with a quality company.

Further examples abound of how far IDA influence extends within the Irish system. The story is told of how in the late 1970s the organization noticed a huge

---

[8]MacSharry and While (2000, p. 273) suggest, however, that IDA interest in these sectors had been growing since the late 1960s.

looming disparity between electronics graduate outflows and its own demand projections, based on ongoing negotiations with foreign companies. The situation was resolved through an inter-agency initiative to immediately institute 14 one-year conversion courses to furnish science graduates with electronics qualifications, alongside 58 new or expanded courses in electrical engineering. 'The story of such a rapid response by the educational authorities to industry's needs is so rare internationally that the IDA relayed it to prospective investors many times', MacSharry and White note. 'It offered reassurance that Ireland would deliver the skills needed.'

MacSharry and White also provide details of the IDA's role in the transformation of the country's telecommunications infrastructure. 'Some two decades ago', they write, 'the phone system was the weak link in the IDA's marketing efforts to attract foreign investment. . . . When the IDA sought to raise the issue directly with the Department of Posts and Telegraphs the response was hostile. . . Any sentence beginning with the proposition that "the Department should consider" was dismissed as improper interference.' Shortly thereafter control of the system was wrestled from the department's hands and a new state agency was established to run the service on a commercial basis. It put together a huge investment package to develop a digital-based network. 'The [IDA] could now target a new range of industries where first-class international telecommunications was a key factor', MacSharry and White write. 'These ranged from software development to call centres, customer support and data-related services. For the IDA, these knowledge industries became a major new source of job creation.'

The insights contained in these stories lead MacSharry and White to believe that it will be difficult for equivalent agencies elsewhere to emulate IDA successes. Amongst the factors they mention in this regard are the traditional resistance of Foreign Affairs Ministries to allow other government agencies with a substantial foreign presence to emerge, and a failure to provide such agencies with a clear development mandate. This makes it difficult for the agencies to secure effective funding and develop sufficient clout within the public-sector bureaucracy.

Skill levels of the Irish workforce

Executives of foreign-owned companies rank the availability of appropriate skills as one of Ireland's important advantages. Ireland has been successful in implementing a science-based education strategy which enhances its attractiveness to foreign firms. This might appear surprising at first sight as Ireland still lags behind the OECD average on most measures of educational attainment, though this is compensated for to some extent by lower wages.[9]

---

[9] According to the US Department of Labor, the average hourly compensation cost for a manufacturing-sector production worker in Ireland in 1999 was $13.3, compared with $16.4 in the UK, $18.3 in France,

Table 8.6.   Percentage of population aged 25–34 classified
by educational attainment, 1998, by age group.

	At least upper secondary	At least tertiary B (diploma level)	At least tertiary A (degree level)
Ireland	67	29	16
OECD	72	25	16

Source: OECD (2002).

Note: Percentage completing at least tertiary B includes those completing at least tertiary A.

When one looks at educational attainment by age group, however, a more complex picture emerges, as outlined in Table 8.6. Ireland lags behind the OECD mean along all dimensions for cohorts aged 35 and older. Amongst the younger age group 25–34, however, while Ireland continues to lag behind in terms of the proportion of the cohort that has attained at least upper secondary education, it has converged on the OECD average in terms of attainment of at least a university degree or equivalent, and has surpassed the OECD in terms of the proportion attaining third-level diplomas or their equivalent. This extra Irish throughput in tertiary education is largely concentrated in the scientific area. UNESCO (1998) data reveal that 40% of Irish tertiary graduates are in the fields of natural sciences, agriculture and engineering, compared with an EU average of only 28%.

While these relatively recent educational developments cannot explain earlier FDI inflows to Ireland, they do play a role, discussed further below, in explaining how Ireland has moved progressively upwards in terms of the technological orientation of its foreign sector.

One further related factor concerns the age profile of the population. Incoming corporations are likely to be interested primarily in younger workers. An extensive supply of such workers may therefore be of importance. While such demographic conditions may be considered unfavourable when the labour market is in disequilibrium and unemployment is high, the situation may be judged more favourably when there is a plentiful supply of FDI. In this regard, Ireland's demographic situation may be classified as uniquely favourable at present and for the near future, with stronger growth rate projections for the working age population than in the case of any other EU or CEE economy.

Agglomeration and herding

Agglomeration and demonstration effects have also been argued to have contributed to Ireland's ability to attract FDI. Krugman (1997), focusing on the classic Marshallian external economies, as discussed in Chapter 6, mentions the availability

---

$20.6 in the Netherlands, and $27.2 in Germany. The only EU countries with lower labour costs than Ireland were Greece, Spain and Portugal.

of high-quality specialist services in Ireland and of a pool of workers with requisite skills, and mentions the likelihood that technological spillovers have also been important, given the clustering of high-tech industries in the country. On demonstration effects he notes that 'firms considering opening production facilities in other countries... face uncertainties about how well the operations will actually run. In these circumstances firms have a strong incentive to observe each other's decisions and (experiences).... And this mutual observation can cause a tendency for investment to concentrate in a few destinations, over and above the usual external economy arguments.' In this respect Barry and Bradley (1997) note that surveys of executives of newly arriving foreign companies in the computer, instrument engineering, pharmaceutical and chemical sectors indicate that their location decision is now strongly influenced by the fact that other key market players are already located in Ireland. The role of agglomeration and demonstration effects in Ireland has been explored econometrically by Barry et al. (2003b), to be discussed further below.

Factors of particular relevance to US corporations

Ireland has proved to be a particularly attractive location for US corporations. There are a number of factors to be considered in this regard: its status as an English-speaking country, its geographic location between Europe and the US, and the cultural connections between Ireland and the Irish-American business community.

It is difficult to disentangle the first two issues, as both the UK and Ireland share a common language with the US, and both also straddle the Atlantic divide. Both countries furthermore have the highest levels of US FDI relative to GDP in the EU, providing prima facie evidence in favour of these hypotheses.

Krugman (1997) expands on the importance of Ireland's geographical location. While recognizing that conventional transport costs are of declining importance as an influence on plant location, the importance of customized service still means that for certain products European markets are still likely to be served from a European base. Ireland's relatively low wage costs and favourable tax treatment of profits make it attractive as a European export platform. Furthermore, locations that are easily accessible by top management will also tend to be preferred.

Ireland has been growing in importance not just as a base from which US companies export to the EU but also as a base from which they export back to the US. Thus, while in 1995 9.5% of the output of US firms based in Ireland was exported to the US, a level around which it had hovered since the early 1990s, this proportion then rose progressively to reach 17.6% by 1999 (see Figure 8.2).[10] Presumably this

---

[10]Görg (2000), furthermore, shows that 44% of US imports to Ireland in 1994 were of the 'inward processing' type, meaning that they were processed in the EU and then re-exported to destinations outside the EU (including the US). This was by far the highest proportion for any EU country, and also represented by far the largest increase (of roughly 20%) over the period since 1988.

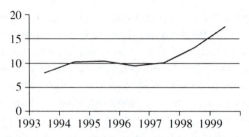

Figure 8.2.   Proportion of US firms' exports bound for the US.
Source: Irish Census of Industrial Production (various issues).

is as a result of the increasing globalization of US firms interacting with the types of factors—geographic, linguistic and fiscal—already seen to operate in Ireland's favour. It is also indicative of a growing share of VFDI in the total.

One also occasionally encounters the argument that Ireland may be an attractive location for US corporations because of links with Irish-American board members. This hypothesis is difficult to test. It was clearly important in the early days, as illustrated by MacSharry and White's account of how the Pfizer Corporation was first attracted to Ireland in the late 1960s. The dominant influence behind the company's decision to locate in Ireland at that time was an Irish emigrant who held one-third of the company's shares. Once the Irish industrial development process got underway, however, the importance of such links has appeared to decline in significance.

General business environment

There are other aspects of the general business environment that are also likely to be of importance. These include labour market conditions, the quality of public infrastructure, and the efficiency of the public administration system.

Wage costs remain low in Ireland relative to most other EU countries, while the incidence of industrial disputes has fallen to very low levels since the late 1980s.[11] Ireland's public infrastructure, which was seriously deficient two decades ago, has also improved substantially with the aid of EU structural funds, particularly in the telecommunications field (Burnham 1998).

Recent work on the Central and Eastern European transition economies has identified administrative corruption as an important impediment to FDI flows. The Internet Center for Corruption Research ranks Ireland in 2002 as ahead of only France, Portugal, Italy and Greece in the EU15 in terms of perceptions of corruption amongst business people and risk analysts. Allegations of corrupt practices in Ireland invari-

---

[11] US Bureau of Labor Statistics data on hourly compensation costs for production workers in manufacturing show that Ireland remains lowest in the EU after Portugal, Greece and Spain. On the incidence of strike activity see Barry (2000).

ably revolve around sectors other than manufacturing, however. Thus it might not represent as serious an impediment to FDI inflows as it appears to at first glance.

8.1.2 Empirical Studies of the Importance of these Various Factors

There is widespread agreement on the empirical importance of effective corporation taxes in influencing FDI activity. One recent study by Slaughter (2003), which focuses on US FDI in Europe, takes a number of other factors into account as well. He shows that European countries that are richer per capita, have larger markets, lower taxes and are closer to the US receive larger amounts of US FDI in all industries, while EU membership appears particularly significant for Manufacturing and Financial Services FDI. Countries with lower per-capita income, and therefore presumably lower wages, are found to attract a higher mix of manufacturing, an industry for which labour costs are relatively important. He also shows that US affiliates are oriented more towards export-platform activity than local sales in smaller markets, and that US multinationals tend to concentrate a region's production in low-tax countries. These findings help explain why Ireland—as a small, low-tax, relatively low-wage western-seaboard EU member state—has achieved such success as a manufacturing export platform for US multinational corporations.

Other studies that focus on the impact of corporation taxes include Altshuler et al. (2001), who also concentrate on the location decisions of US firms, and Gropp and Kostial (2000), who consider total FDI inflows and outflows. Both studies control for exogenous country characteristics such as GDP and GDP per capita, and for differences in national trade policies, while Gropp and Kostial also control for differences in the macroeconomic environment across countries.

The results of such studies can be used to analyse the implications of corporation tax harmonization within the EU, for example. Altshuler et al.'s (2001) estimates of the tax elasticity of US FDI flows suggest that the stock of US manufacturing investment in Ireland is 70% higher than it would have been if Ireland had a tax rate equal to the next lowest EU rate. The effect is even more dramatic, of course, if comparison is made with the average EU tax rate. Gropp and Kostial (2000) come to a similar dramatic conclusion. They find that about 80% of Ireland's net FDI inflow would disappear if rates were harmonized at the average EU level. Not surprisingly, Irish governments have formed coalitions with several other EU member states to resist such harmonization proposals.

Barry et al. (2003b) focus more narrowly on the role of agglomeration and demonstration effects in drawing US firms to Ireland. Their estimates of the number of foreign firms entering a particular sector in Ireland at a particular date find that both agglomeration and endowment effects are positive and significant. The agglomeration effect appears to be larger than the demonstration effect for high-tech sectors, while both effects appear to be equally important for low-tech sectors. Both agglomeration and demonstration effects appear to be particularly strong for firms of the same nationality (i.e. US firms), while the importance of flagship projects also emerges clearly.

Overall, however, the inauguration of the Celtic Tiger era is likely to have resulted from the simultaneous alignment of a whole constellation of positive factors, internal and external, each of which is likely to have played a role in increasing Ireland's FDI inflows (Barry 2000). No study has as yet successfully accounted for the relative contribution of each factor, however. The only work to attempt an empirical evaluation of a full range of factors—including education, industrial strategy, the Single Market, the EU Structural and Cohesion Funds, social partnership and the resolution of the country's long-lasting fiscal crisis—is forced to the conclusion that 'the sources of the "Irish miracle" of the last decade are not entirely clear' (de la Fuente and Vives 1997).

8.2   Characteristics of FDI Inflows to Ireland

What are the main characteristics of Ireland's inward FDI? For data reasons our main focus is on the manufacturing sector. Before discussing this, however, we will allude to the relatively little that is known about foreign ownership in the Irish services sector.

According to OECD (2001a), employment in affiliates of foreign companies comprised almost 14% of services sector employment in Ireland. This is a higher proportion than in any of the other 10 EU countries for which data are reported, apart from Belgium. These foreign-owned enterprises accounted for 89% of service-sector exports, an even greater proportion than the 86% of manufactured exports accounted for by their counterparts in that sector. The scale of this contribution is illustrated by the fact that Ireland is reported to be the third largest services exporter per capita in the world, after Hong Kong and Singapore, and is the world's largest exporter of software.

In the year 2000, computer services comprised 32% of Irish service exports, followed by Tourism and Travel at 16% and Financial Services at 12%. One notable contributor in the latter segment is the International Financial Services Centre. Founded in 1987 and subject at the time to a special low corporation tax rate, it has grown to become one of Europe's largest off-shore financial centres, employing around 8500 people and managing funds worth over $150 billion.

In discussing the characteristics of Ireland's foreign-owned industry below, however, data constraints require that we focus exclusively on manufacturing-sector FDI.[12]

---

[12]Most of the data presented below are drawn from the Irish Censuses of Industrial Production, supplemented by data from the state agency Forfás.

Table 8.7. Characteristics of Irish (I) and
foreign-owned (F) industry in selected sectors, 1999.

Sector		A	B	C	D	Percentage distribution of exports			
						E	F	G	H
Food, Beverages and Tobacco	I	48	15.8	11	35	37	38	4	21
	F	166	24.5	43	74	29	46	3	22
Pulp, Paper, Printing	I	31	20.5	40	13	65	19	7	9
	F	168	23.2	29	95	20	67	4	9
Chemicals	I	36	19.8	65	43	27	59	6	8
	F	93	23.8	84	98	10	41	23	27
Electrical and Optical	I	39	16.2	66	44	29	30	33	8
	F	281	18.4	52	92	20	47	20	14

A, Employees per plant; B, Average wage (thousands of Irish pounds); C, Imports as share of materials purchased; D, Exports as share of gross output; E, UK; F, Other EU; G, US; H, Rest of the World.
Source: Census of Industrial Production.

8.2.1 Characteristics: Firm Size, Productivity, Skills and Wages, R&D and Training

As will be seen below, the bulk of Ireland's foreign industry is located in sectors such as Chemicals and Electrical and Optical Equipment, while domestic industry is disproportionately located in Food and Paper and Printing. As Table 8.7 illustrates, however, sectoral differences do not tend to determine the differences in firm characteristics that we now report.

Foreign firms operating in Ireland are generally substantially larger than Irish indigenous firms, and are more capital intensive. The average foreign firm employs six times as many workers as an indigenous firm and has a capital–labour ratio 2.3 times higher.

With regard to workforce characteristics, foreign industry employs a higher proportion of skilled workers, pays higher wages both on aggregate and to industrial workers, and spends more on training per employee. The average wage paid by foreign industry is 1.3 times that paid by indigenous industry. In part this is accounted for by higher average skill levels in the sector. Administrative and technical staff comprise 16% of employment across all manufacturing, but account for 25%, 20% and 19%, respectively, in such foreign-dominated sectors as Chemicals, Electrical and Optical, and Drink and Tobacco. The average wage of industrial workers in these sectors is 1.3, 1.9 and 1.4 times the average across all manufacturing industries.[13]

---

[13] It is unclear, however, due to data deficiencies in this area whether these differences in skills and wages refer to industry or to ownership characteristics.

Training expenditures per employee in foreign firms are five times the levels prevailing in indigenous firms while R&D expenditures per employee are one and a half times greater. All of these findings correspond to those emerging more generally across the world economy, as reported in Chapter 7.

8.2.2 Trade Orientation

The average foreign firm operating in Ireland exports 92% of gross output, compared with the indigenous average of 31%. Thus Ireland serves primarily as an export platform for the foreign companies which use it as a production location. US firms are the most export oriented, exporting 96% of gross output, while German firms export 92% and UK firms only 55%.

Furthermore, while the UK is more important than Continental Europe as a destination for indigenous exports, for which these locations account for 40% and 35%, respectively, the situation is reversed for aggregate foreign industry; 18% of overall foreign-industry exports go to the UK while almost 50% goes to the rest of the EU.

Foreign industry is also more globalized in terms of the sourcing of inputs. 57% of inputs used by foreign industry are imported compared with a figure of only 27% for indigenous industry. This element of Irish economy expenditures is therefore lower for foreign firms, as are total Irish economy expenditures (by around one-third).

8.2.3 Sectoral Distribution of Manufacturing-Sector FDI Inflows

Table 8.8 identifies the sectoral distribution of employment in indigenous and foreign firms in Ireland. We see that foreign industry predominates in Office and Data Processing, Medical and Optical Equipment, Telecommunications and Electrical Equipment, and Chemicals and Pharmaceuticals. Most of these foreign-dominated sectors are classified as high-tech by the OECD while most indigenous employment is in low-tech sectors (see Table 8.9).

The differences in developments over time in the technology levels of foreign and indigenous industry depicted in Figures 8.3 and 8.3 are striking. Indigenous industry remains almost as strongly excluded from the high-tech sectors as it was in 1974, while foreign industry has been becoming increasingly oriented towards the high-tech sectors.

There are a number of possible explanations for the differences in sectoral composition of foreign and indigenous firms and for these differential developments over time. We now discuss these issues.

The role of corporation tax and transfer pricing

While clearly influencing total FDI inflows, a low rate of corporation tax also influences the types of sector an economy attracts. Transfer pricing arises where arm's-length trading prices are difficult to establish. This is particularly the case for R&D-

Table 8.8. Sectoral distribution of employment in indigenous and foreign industry, 1999.

	Share of indigenous employment	Share of foreign employment
Food	26	6
Drink and Tobacco	1	4
Textiles	6	3
Wood and Products	4	1
Paper and Printing	13	6
Chemicals (less Pharmaceuticals)	2	10
Pharmaceuticals	1	5
Rubber and Plastics	5	3
Non-Metallic Minerals	7	1
Metal Products	9	3
Machinery and Equipment	6	5
Office and Data Processing	2	14
Electrical Machinery and Apparatus	4	8
Radio, TV and Communications	1	10
Medical and Optical Equipment	2	12
Transport	4	4
Miscellaneous	6	2
Total	100	100

Table 8.9. Shares of indigenous and foreign employment in sectors classified by level of technology.

	Low-tech	Medium-tech	High-tech
Indigenous	74	16	10
Foreign	24	20	56

and advertising-intensive sectors, since these factors make it difficult to locate the exact source of value added.[14] According to Davies and Lyons's (1996) categorization, such advertising and R&D-intensive sectors accounted for over 65% of foreign employment in Irish manufacturing in 2000, up from 45% of a much smaller base in 1973.[15]

---

[14] Pharmaceuticals, for example, are typically made from relatively cheap bulk chemicals which, when combined together, yield highly profitable final products. It is difficult to determine the exact proportion of profits that arises from what takes place in the pharmaceutical firm's Irish factories.

[15] Their increasing share can be ascribed either to changes in factors other than the tax rate, such as the increasing stock of human capital, or to the increase in the elasticity of FDI flows with respect to corporation tax rates that Altshuler et al. (2001) document.

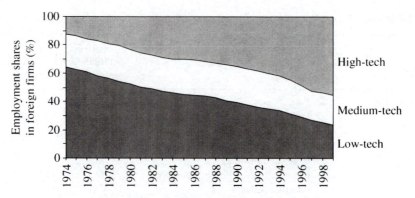

Figure 8.3.   Technology mix of foreign firms.

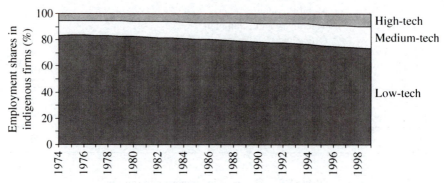

Figure 8.4.   Technology mix of indigenous firms.

Industrial targeting and the development of human capital and physical infrastructure

In discussing earlier the role that the industrial development agencies have played in Ireland, we outlined the industrial targeting practices that they have followed, pointing out their increasing focus on such sectors as pharmaceuticals and electronics. This can clearly have had an independent influence on the resulting sectoral distribution of foreign industry in Ireland. Furthermore, such a sectoral redistribution into high-tech sectors would not have been possible had the economy continued to lag as far behind as it did earlier in terms of physical infrastructure and human capital.

Central versus peripheral industries

A slightly different perspective emerges from recent results in the field of empirical economic geography. Midelfart-Knarvik et al. (2000) isolate the 12 industries in the EU (out of a total of 36) which were most spatially concentrated in the early 1970s (C) and the 12 industries which were most dispersed (D). They then divide the

Table 8.10. Shares of Irish manufacturing employment in particular groups of sectors.

Ireland	1973–76	1993–96
CC	9.5	14.2
CD	11.1	21
DC	19.3	11.6

concentrated sectors into those that retained their concentrated status into the mid 1990s (CC) and those which had become more dispersed (CD), and equivalently divide the dispersed sectors into those that remained amongst the most dispersed in the mid 1990s (DD) and those that had become more concentrated (DC).

The sectors which have remained amongst the most concentrated include ones such as Motor Vehicles and Aircraft, which, as seen in Chapter 2, are characterized by strong plant-level economies of scale. The dispersed industries which have become more concentrated tend to be low-tech low-skill-intensity sectors such as Textiles, Clothing and Footwear. These have shifted primarily to the periphery of the EU.

The main sector of interest to us is the group which had been concentrated, primarily in the EU core, in the early 1970s and which has become more dispersed—the CD group. These industries, which include Office and Computing Machinery, Professional Instruments, Radio TV and Communications, and Machinery and Equipment, all have relatively high skill intensities, medium as opposed to high plant-level economies of scale and relatively low transport costs. This makes them suitable for relocation to high-skill peripheral regions.

Table 8.10 depicts the changing importance of these various groups of sectors in the Irish case. Ireland has developed particularly successfully into all of the CD sectors, as has Finland (with the exception of Professional Instruments in the latter case). Thus Irish industrial growth has been based precisely on those sectors which have become more dispersed over time.[16] Had Ireland targeted sectors such as Aerospace and Motor Vehicles, sectors found not to have become more mobile, the chances of success would have been much poorer. The failure of the Potez aerospace venture, long supported in Ireland by the development agencies, and the similar fate of the DeLorean automobile venture in Northern Ireland are illustrative in this regard.[17]

This is not to suggest that industrial targeting on the part of the Irish authorities did not help, simply that it does not provide the full story. Targeting would have

---

[16] Of the 21% of Irish manufacturing employment located in these sectors in the mid 1990s, furthermore, 77% was in foreign-owned companies.

[17] It is not clear, however, that these categories—CC, CD and DC—would necessarily contain the same sectors worldwide as they do in the case of Europe. While Lipsey (2000) points out that US investments in East Asia tended to be in the sectors identified as 'CD' in Europe, Japanese foreign investments tended to locate in somewhat different sectors.

helped capture these sectors for Ireland rather than having them go elsewhere, and the development agencies played a crucial role in advertising Ireland's advantages, in convincing potential investors that apparent difficulties could be overcome, and in capturing the important 'flagship projects' which are of importance in cluster development.

Comparative advantage?

A final question concerns whether the sectoral distribution of foreign employment in Ireland can be related to the economy's underlying comparative advantage. Revealed comparative advantage (RCA) analysis is frequently used to predict the sectoral effects of increasing openness. The standard indicator of RCA measures the share of sector h in country i's exports, relative to the share of sector h in the exports of the countries with which trade is to be liberalized.

Barry and Hannan (2002) have analysed Ireland's RCA with current and future EU member states prior to the country's EU accession in 1973. To surmount transfer pricing problems, which at the time would have been particularly prevalent in the foreign-owned Chemicals sector, their RCA measures are based on employment rather than export data. They found that Ireland had a strong revealed comparative *disadvantage*, in employment terms, in two aggregate sectors: Chemicals and Metals and Engineering. Nevertheless, a mere several years after accession the country had specialized strongly *into* these two sectors. Thus they argue that RCA does not determine the sectors into which FDI will flow, nor, for countries which experience strong FDI inflows, will it accurately predict the direction of structural transformation of the economy.

Lipsey (2003) offers a useful comment on this, arguing that

> Exports depend not only on the factor endowments and advantages of the country as a geographical entity, but also on the firm-specific advantages of the firms producing there. By severely restricting inward FDI before 1959, Ireland cut itself off from the knowledge and skills, including the knowledge of world markets, possessed by foreign firms. Ireland had other factor endowments needed for manufacturing exports, but not this one. Once it opened up to FDI inflows, that deficiency was removed. The missing link for manufactured exports was supplied by the foreign firms, and Ireland's comparative advantage was transformed.

A further revealing insight is given by Lipsey (2000), who notes that the sectoral specialization of US multinationals tends to reflect US comparative advantage as much or more than that of the host country.

8.3 FDI and the Development of the Irish Economy

To what extent is the success of the Irish economy over the course of the 1990s attributable to FDI? This is a multifaceted question. We discuss it first in terms of the structural development of the economy, where FDI is seen to have contributed to Ireland's growing similarity to the core EU economies. Next we consider the impact that foreign presence has had on indigenous industry, and analyse its impact on employment volatility. Finally, we attempt to evaluate its contribution to the remarkable growth performance achieved over the course of the 1990s.

8.3.1 FDI and Structural Convergence

The richer EU countries share many structural characteristics that distinguish them from the poorer EU member states. These include high shares of human-capital-intensive services employment, large firm size, high shares of modern manufactures in aggregate exports, high levels of intra-industry trade and high R&D expenditures as a proportion of GDP. Ireland in the 1970s and 1980s resembled the other 'cohesion economies'—the traditionally poorer EU states of Greece, Spain and Portugal—in these respects. By the end of the 1990s it had come to bear a stronger resemblance to the richer member states. Barry (2002a) charts the role of the country's foreign sector in this structural transformation. Chapter 4 showed how under various circumstances (but not always) an inflow of FDI can engender a process of skill upgrading and structural transformation in the host country.

Production structure

The Krugman index has come to be widely used in recent times as a measure of the *dissimilarity* in production structures between one region and another, or between one region and a group of others (Krugman 1991a).[18] To surmount transfer-pricing issues, we look as usual at employment rather than output.

The sectoral structure of domestically owned industry in Ireland is found to be quite dissimilar to that of the richer 'core' EU economies, while the addition of foreign industry is found to increase the similarity substantially. Irish domestic industry has been growing more similar to that of the core economies over time, however, in contrast to what has, for example, been happening in Spain. This arguably arises as a

---

[18]The index measures

$$\sum_k \text{abs}\left[v_i^k(t) - \sum_{j \neq i} v_j^k(t) \right],$$

where $v_i^k(t)$ is the share of industry k in country i's manufacturing employment and $\sum_{j \neq i} v_j^k(t)$ is this industry's share in other countries. The index measures the absolute values of the differences between these shares, summed over all industries k. It has a value of 0 if the country has an industrial structure identical to that of others, and attains a maximum value of 2 if it has no industries in common with the other countries under discussion.

consequence of the impact of Ireland's large stock of foreign industry on the sectoral structure of indigenous industry. Görg and Strobl (2002), for example, show that foreign presence increases the entry rate of Irish indigenous manufacturing firms in the same sector, while Görg and Strobl (2003b) show that foreign presence increases the indigenous firm survival rate in high-tech sectors.

The structure of the market services sector in Ireland has also been affected by FDI. Economic geographers Keeble et al. (1988) noted a significant difference in the structure of the services sector between core and periphery, with the former having a higher share of producer services relative to consumer services.[19] Even by the late 1980s Ireland had come to resemble the core in this regard, which Keeble et al. interpreted as evidence of a successful industrial strategy.

The most human-capital-intensive segment of services is the Financial, Insurance, Real Estate and Business Services (FIRE) component. The richer EU countries' shares in total FIRE employment exceed their shares in aggregate employment, with the opposite being the case for the cohesion countries. The gap between the two is diminishing over time, however, with Ireland displaying the smallest gap between a cohesion and a core economy. Midelfart-Knarvik et al. (2000) argue that part of the reason for the increasing dispersion of 'FIRE' services across the EU is that seven of the eight industries most intensive in the use of these services became more dispersed between 1970/73 and 1994/97. Two-thirds of all employment in these industries in Ireland is in foreign firms.

These various indicators of increasing similarity in production structure might be taken to reflect a convergence in factor endowments, driven by the imports of capital and technology typically associated with FDI.

One final measure of production structure concerns enterprise size. The cohesion countries have a larger share of enterprises (in private non-primary sectors) among the micro size class and a smaller share among the large size class. Alone of the four cohesion countries, Ireland has reversed its position in this regard over the 10 years from 1988. In this the impact of foreign industry is straightforward. As pointed out earlier, the average foreign manufacturing firm in Ireland employs six times as many people as the average indigenous firm.

Trade structure

Even as recently as the 1970s, exports from the EU cohesion countries remained concentrated in natural resource-based and traditional sectors, with only very small shares of exports accounted for by modern industry.[20] By 1998 modern industry had

---

[19] Producer services are defined as Transport, Communications and Banking and Financial Services, while consumer services are largely Distribution and Catering.

[20] Natural resource-based sectors are food, live animals, drink and tobacco, and crude materials such as wool. Traditional industry consists of 'basic manufacturing' (which includes rubber, paper and tex-

increased its share in the exports of each periphery economy. Again by far the most dramatic increase is seen in the Irish case, where the share of the modern sector overtook that of the UK. This change in trade structure is again driven by Ireland's foreign sector, which accounts for around 85% of all Irish exports and exports five times more from modern than from traditional sectors.

Modern industry tends to be more complex than traditional or natural-resource-based industries, and the complexity of a sector tends to be reflected in a high share of intra-industry trade. Chemicals and Machinery record the highest intra-industry trade (IIT) levels (and are amongst the sectors known to be most conducive to FDI, as Table 1.6 shows). In 1970, the four cohesion countries plus Finland (the next poorest of the current EU15 at the time) had the lowest shares of manufacturing-sector IIT in the EU15. Ireland has progressively caught up to the EU average in the interim.

R&D activity

One further measure of structural convergence concerns R&D activity. Ireland has now achieved the same levels of business-sector R&D relative to GDP as characterize other small relatively rich nations such as Denmark and the Netherlands. In Ireland, however, foreign firms over the 1980s and 1990s consistently accounted for over 60% of this expenditure, and are also responsible for the bulk of the increase.

8.3.2 Impact on Indigenous Industry

Foreign presence can have both positive and negative effects on indigenous firms, as discussed in Chapters 3 and 7. Negative effects can arise when both groups compete either in product or in factor markets, while positive effects might include productivity spillovers or increased demand arising, for example, from sub-supply activities on the part of indigenous firms.

There is little product-market competition between indigenous and foreign firms in the Irish case. Firstly, since the foreign-owned sector is almost completely export oriented, there is little product-market competition on the home front. Secondly, the sectoral origins of foreign and domestic exports are quite different. Over 80% of foreign-company exports came from the Chemicals and Electrical Equipment sectors, which account for only a little over 10% of indigenous exports. Thirdly, the export destinations of foreign and domestic firms are quite different, with the bulk of foreign-sector exports shipped to EU countries other than the UK while most domestic-firm exports go to the UK. This suggests that the dominant form of crowding out will come through the labour market.

---

tiles) and 'miscellaneous manufactures' (which includes furniture, clothing and footwear, etc.). Modern industry consists of chemicals plus machinery and transport equipment.

The size and productivity of the foreign-owned sector in Ireland clearly affects wages at the macroeconomic level, leading to a crowding out of lower productivity sectors and firms. At the microeconomic level, there is some unpublished evidence that foreign presence may reduce average wages and productivity in certain indigenous firms by bidding up the relative price of skilled labour and encouraging these firms to substitute towards less skilled workers.

Now let us consider possible positive interactions between foreign and indigenous firms. Take input–output linkages first. The Irish state agency, Forfás, regularly publishes an Irish economy expenditures survey which distinguishes between indigenous and foreign firms. Based on these data, Barry et al. (1999) show that real Irish economy expenditures per employee (a measure of backward linkages) rose by around 50% between 1983 and 1995 for both types of firms.[21] Notwithstanding the fact that Irish economy expenditures per employee are lower for jobs in foreign-owned industry, the employment that the latter creates is estimated to be higher because of the greater share of spending directed towards services, in contrast to the case of indigenous firms for whom the bulk of spending goes on materials. A ballpark estimate of around 100 service sector jobs is suggested and 10 indigenous manufacturing jobs created via backward linkages per 100 foreign-sector manufacturing jobs.

Of course, these interactions between upstream and downstream sectors can impart an important dynamic to the economy, as seen in Chapters 3 and 7. Foreign multinationals create additional demand for domestically produced intermediates which, in the presence of economies of scale, can lead to a decrease in average costs and an increase in firm entry. The resulting fall in the price of intermediates can in turn induce entry into the final-goods sector. Görg and Strobl (2002) provide empirical support for these effects in the Irish case, demonstrating that indigenous-firm entry is positively affected by foreign-firm presence in the same sector and in industries downstream of that sector.

Foreign presence can also give rise to technological spillovers, a topic explored for the Irish case by Görg and Strobl (2003b). They posit that technological spillovers will reduce the recipient firm's average production costs, yielding a positive effect on the firm's survival rate. Controlling for the fact that multinationals tend to locate in high-productivity sectors, they find that foreign presence does indeed have a life-enhancing effect on domestic firms, though only in high-tech sectors.[22] They find

---

[21] Irish economy expenditures consist of wages paid and Irish materials and services purchased, along with the profits earned by domestic firms and the profits tax paid by foreign firms operating in Ireland. While backward linkages per unit of output are low for the foreign sector, Rodriguez-Clare (1996) argues that it is backward linkages *per job* that is the more relevant measure.

[22] This result appears to apply only to smaller domestic firms, for whom sub-supplying to foreign firms is more important.

no such evidence for domestic low-tech plants, speculating that this may be due to a lack of absorptive capacity on their part.

The impact of foreign presence on the entry rate of Irish indigenous manufacturing firms may also be related to their role as 'incubators' for new entrepreneurs. A recent study of the Irish indigenous software sector, for example, finds that one-third of entrepreneurs had worked in foreign firms immediately before the start-up of the new firm, while two-thirds had worked in foreign firms at some stage in their careers (O'Gorman et al. 1997). The study also argues that foreign firms in Ireland have been an important source of demand, with a requirement for high standards, in the early stages of new indigenous start-ups.

8.3.3 *Impact on Employment Volatility*

With the bursting of the high-tech bubble in the early years of the new millennium, concern began to be expressed that Ireland may have become overly specialized in a narrow range of foreign-owned sectors that are highly vulnerable to fluctuations in the world economy.

Two different analytical approaches to this issue have been taken. Görg and Strobl (2003a) find that foreign plants are more likely to exit in the face of adverse circumstances than indigenous plants are, when other firm and industry-specific characteristics are controlled for.[23] Barry and Kearney (2002) argue, however, that controlling for firm and industry characteristics obfuscates the issue. If employment numbers in the heavily foreign-dominated sectors were very volatile, for example, even if this were due to sectoral rather than ownership effects, it would suggest that foreign presence could heighten economic instability.

Barry and Kearney bring the tools of portfolio theory to bear on the issue. Given that the high employment growth sectors in Ireland are also relatively volatile, a mean-variance efficiency frontier can be graphed, representing the lowest variance that various 'national portfolios of industries' can achieve for any given levels of employment growth.[24] While the expansion of the foreign sector in Ireland has increased overall volatility, the analysis nevertheless shows that it has brought the Irish economy closer to this efficiency frontier, given its employment growth, which

---

[23] They also find that new jobs in foreign companies that do not exit are more persistent than jobs in equivalent indigenous plants.

[24] Several conceptual differences between a portfolio of stocks and a country's industrial structure must be addressed, however. First, industrial structure cannot be changed as easily as a portfolio of financial assets. In the Irish case, however, this question arguably raises fewer problems than it does elsewhere, because the country's foreign-owned sectors have been largely established as a result of specific policy instruments. A second difference is that an investor's choice of portfolio does not influence the returns and variances of the individual stocks. With inelastic factor supplies, however, high growth in some sectors will inevitably imply low growth (or decline) in others. Again, however, this raises fewer problems in the Irish case, because both the Irish labour market and the Irish capital market are amongst the most open in the world.

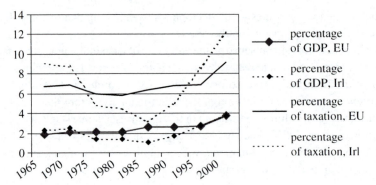

Figure 8.5. Corporation tax receipts expressed as a proportion of GDP and of total tax revenue, Ireland and the EU, 1965–2000. *Source:* OECD Revenue Statistics, 1965–2001.

is higher than for the national sector. Furthermore, the foreign sector, though more volatile than indigenous industry, acts as a 'hedge' in the national portfolio because of a negative covariance between employment growth in the two sectors. Thus overall volatility is reduced below what it would have been had only the lower-volatility domestic sector been present in Ireland.

8.3.4 Impact on Tax Receipts

Notwithstanding the low effective tax rate, the high level of profits recorded in Ireland ensures that corporation tax receipts as a proportion of total tax revenue have been higher than the EU average in recent years, while, expressed as a proportion of GDP, the 3.8% recorded for 2000 is at the same level as the EU average (see Figure 8.5). Furthermore, the vast bulk of corporation taxes paid by the manufacturing sector is known to come from foreign-owned industry.

8.3.5 Impact on Growth

There are two alternative theories of why the Irish economy took off in the 1990s. The first of these, the 'delayed convergence' hypothesis, tends to downplay the importance of the expanded FDI inflows of the period, while the second, the 'regional boom' perspective, views them as crucial.

The delayed convergence hypothesis, which underpins the analysis of Honohan and Walsh (2002), for example, argues that the boom of the 1990s simply made up for several decades of Irish underperformance. The underperformance of the 1960s and 70s is ascribed to Ireland's failure to drop its trade-protectionist stance and increase educational throughput until about a decade after the rest of Western Europe. Most of the 1980s in turn was written off by the struggle to rein in the public debt and re-establish control over the government finances.

The alternative hypothesis, proposed by Krugman (1997), holds that the period of extraordinary growth should be more appropriately thought of as a 'regional boom', since the Irish labour market is extraordinarily open. Wages in such an economy will be largely determined by the levels prevailing elsewhere, and the primary response to shocks will come through labour migration rather than wage adjustment.[25]

The regional perspective focuses attention on the economy's export base, as services employment, both public and private, arises largely to service that base. The bulk of Ireland's exports, of course, arises from the foreign-owned sector. This suggests an important distinction between the policy implications of the two hypotheses. The regional perspective proposes that, while orthodox policies may be necessary for regional growth, they are unlikely to be sufficient. The policies identified as crucial in the delayed convergence story remain crucial, but the sine qua non here is the corporation-tax-based and IDA-led industrialization strategy.[26]

The importance of FDI for growth in Ireland surfaces in a study by FitzGerald and Kearney (2000), who explore the issue via simulations of a macroeconometric model of the Irish economy. As the bulk of FDI inflows to Ireland comes from the US, Irish GDP growth is strongly correlated to US growth. The elasticity of Irish GDP with respect to US GDP increased during the 1990s because of FDI. To explore the role of the increased FDI inflows, therefore, FitzGerald and Kearney (2000) leave the elasticity of Irish with respect to US GDP unchanged at its 1990 level, to generate a picture of how the Irish economy might have looked had the increased inflows not been forthcoming.

This simulation shows a reduction by 1998 of over 17% of GDP relative to the benchmark, amounting to a reduction in the per-annum growth rate of around two percentage points. Numbers of people employed would have been 12–15% lower by the late 1990s, as would the level of skilled wages. Emigration would have replaced the substantial immigration that actually characterized the period. Unskilled wage rates in the model are fixed by the level of unemployment benefits and, with no unskilled migration, unskilled unemployment would have been almost five percentage points higher by the end of the period.

---

[25]This regional perspective bears a resemblance to the model that Blanchard (2002) proposes in his comments on Honohan and Walsh (2002). He suggests that Ireland has behaved more like the so-called AK endogenous growth model than the Solow model of convergence theory. Small improvements in competitiveness, or a shift towards the production of more capital-intensive goods (which has been associated with Ireland's increased FDI inflows), can have large effects on growth in such a framework.

[26]Thus Markusen (1988) shows that a regional economy needs to subsidize the use rather than the training of skilled labour, which is one of the things low corporation taxes do. Subsidizing training will effectively subsidize foreign economies via emigration.

While it is clear that the specification of FDI is overly simplified in these simulations, they nonetheless serve as an illustration of the possible importance to the Irish economy of the increased FDI inflows of the period.[27]

8.4   Concluding Comments

Having discussed at length the reasons for Ireland's success in attracting FDI and the role that FDI has played in the country's economic development, it is worthwhile considering some possible threats to the country's continued success in these respects. We will consider two: a movement towards corporation tax harmonization within the EU, and the increased competition for FDI that will arise with Eastern enlargement of the union. We conclude with a discussion of embeddedness, an important issue about which surprisingly little appears to be known as yet.

It is clear that even though proposals for tax harmonization across the EU have been blocked by a coalition of member states that includes Ireland, there is nothing to prevent individual countries reducing their corporation tax rates towards the Irish level, as indeed has been happening over the last decade or so (IFS 2000). The studies discussed earlier suggested that the corporation tax harmonization could lead to a reduction in Irish inward FDI of between 50 and 80%. While these are likely to err on the high side, as they do not take account of other favourable factors, such as the English-language environment and the efficiency of the Irish industrial development agencies, the effects would undoubtedly be dramatic.

Even if current EU member states do not move further in the direction of harmonization, several of the Central and Eastern European EU accession states have watched the Irish experience closely and have learned some valuable lessons. Thus both Hungary and Estonia have adopted corporation tax rates far below the EU average, and Poland is set to reduce its rate progressively.[28] The more advanced candidate countries, furthermore, have skill levels that appear similar to Ireland's, while labour costs are very much lower. The Irish experience also suggests that productivity and R&D rankings may be more appropriately regarded as *endogenous* variables, reflecting success or failure at attracting FDI, rather than *exogenous* variables that determine the likelihood of success or failure in this regard. Upon accession, a number of the new EU states will have equally easy, if not greater, access to the high-income markets of Western Europe and are likely to enjoy an equally

---

[27] The theoretical 'regional boom' models of Dascher (2000) and Barry (2002b), which are set up with Irish conditions in mind, show that labour inflows will dry up and the boom come to a halt once housing stocks and other infrastructural elements become congested. This certainly happened in Ireland over the course of the 1990s as evidenced by house price inflation of over 10% per annum.

[28] IFS (2000) notes the negative correlation between corporation tax rates and country size in the EU. (Effective) corporation tax rates are also negatively correlated with the level of development and a measure of peripherality.

stable macro policy environment and equivalent regulatory and public administration systems. Thus Ireland could well face a substantial increase in competition for FDI.[29] Against this, however, Dunning (1997a,b) showed that earlier enlargements and previous bouts of trade liberalization have increased the overall levels of FDI in the EU.[30]

Would indigenous industry be strong enough to take up the slack if Ireland's foreign industry were to disappear precipitously? This might be assured were the Irish labour market truly a national market, in which case such an adverse shock would reduce wages or otherwise induce sufficient efficiency-enhancing changes that new firms and new industries would eventually emerge. With an open labour market, however, the result could mean a resumption of emigration rather than equilibrating changes in wages, entrepreneurship and management and work practices.

The strength of Ireland's foreign sector tends to mask ongoing structural weaknesses in indigenous industry. These manifest themselves across a number of relevant dimensions: export orientation, vulnerability to sterling fluctuations, and technological and R&D levels. Indigenous manufacturing firms export less than one-third of their output, a figure lower than the manufacturing export-output ratios of seven of the eight EU countries for which OECD (2001a, Table C2.2.1) presents data. They are also much more dependent on the UK market. Only 26% of indigenous employment is in medium- or high-tech sectors (compared with a figure of 76% of foreign-sector employment) and they account for only a small proportion of R&D and training expenditures. The sector accordingly has a very poor record in developing patentable processes or inventions.

Irish-owned multinational firms, furthermore, are disproportionately located in non-traded sectors such as Construction and Paper and Packaging and do not exhibit the type of 'created asset' intensity (derived from R&D and strong product differentiation) that Dunning et al. (2001) find for Korean or Taiwanese multinationals, while Irish indigenous overseas mergers and acquisitions in high-tech sectors are concentrated on the US and tend to be directed toward 'technology sourcing'. This can possibly lead to a downsizing of domestic R&D facilities and a reduction in domestic high-skill employment (Barry et al. 2003a).

Thus it seems crucial for Irish development that the country retain its foreign-owned industry. A harmonization of tax rates would force the country to rely instead on factors such as the quality of infrastructure and the educational system. The country is clearly deficient in the former at least, finishing last among the 30 countries

---

[29] It is important to bear in mind, from our earlier discussion of Midelfart-Knarvik et al. (2000), that the foreign sectors which have contributed most to Irish growth remain the internationally mobile ones.

[30] Unlike in the case of Southern Europe, furthermore, there are as yet no indications that FDI has been diverted away from Ireland. Hungary's growing strength in the Office and Data Processing sector, for example, has displaced countries other than Ireland from the sectoral value-added chain (Barry and Curran 2004).

surveyed in the World Competitiveness League tables for 2003 in terms of infrastructural planning. To the extent to which Ireland's attractiveness as a location for FDI is primarily ascribable to the corporation tax regime, then, the country might be deemed more vulnerable to other countries' actions (such as tax harmonization) than are economies that are less reliant on FDI.

This brings us to the under-researched issue of *embeddedness*. What factors can ensure that multinational companies which choose a location for one set of reasons remain even when these initial conditions change? In other words, how easily might the agglomeration and demonstration effects discussed earlier be unwound? The high capital–labour ratios associated with foreign investment in Ireland might be thought to increase embeddedness, though the rapid rate of depreciation of capital in high-tech sectors would diminish this effect. So too does the international mobility of more highly skilled labour (Krugman 1993).

Embeddedness depends to some extent on 'competition within companies', i.e. on competition between the plants which a company has set up in various locations. An Irish example is provided by the pharmaceuticals company Bristol Myers Squibb. Local management saw the dangers inherent in having a local plant that was primarily engaged in bulk production, as it would be open to strong competition within the company from lower-cost locations in poorer countries. In response to this the Irish management strove to develop the local operation into an important research facility (Durkan 2002).

In focusing on the importance of location to the individual firm, the study of embeddedness draws together the field of economic geography and the analysis of the multinational firm. How do we measure the contribution of the local plant to technological development within the organization? Cantwell and Piscitello (2002), in addressing this issue, suggest that interactions between innovation systems in different locations may prove to be as important in certain circumstances as competition between locations.

9

Home Country Effects of Foreign Direct Investment

Debates on the effects of MNEs are generally focused on host countries, studying foreign subsidiaries of MNEs in the countries where they operate. We reviewed these host country effects in the previous two chapters. Here, we focus on the effects in home countries: what happens in domestic economies when national firms become increasingly multinational?[1]

As is the case for host countries, popular feelings on the home effects of MNEs are mixed. People take national pride when their MNEs do well in Fortunes' ranking of the largest firms in the world, but they worry when they see their companies closing domestic plants and opening up new ones in cheap-labour countries. Feelings are mixed because the issue is intricate. This chapter is devoted to understanding the economics underlying this debate. We discuss the various home effects of foreign investments and we review the available empirical evidence of their importance. We address the following questions. What is the effect of outward FDI on production and employment at home? What is the effect on the skill mix and hence relative wages? Does FDI lead to technology upgrading by firms? What is net effect on the productivity of firms?

As shown in the theoretical chapters, host and home effects are often jointly determined. For example, if unskilled-labour-intensive activities are transferred to a foreign country, the average skill intensity of the remaining home activities will rise. For expositional reasons, however, in what follows we isolate home effects, as if they were a partial equilibrium problem, and discuss their interrelation to host effects only when strictly necessary.

We start this chapter with a brief discussion of the main home country effects. We then review the empirical evidence and address each of the questions listed above.

---

[1] In this chapter we use the term 'multinational' and the abbreviation 'MNE' to indicate the home activities of multinationals (headquarters, home plants, etc.). We also use the term 'national firms' to indicate nationally owned firms operating in the home country. Note that in Chapters 7 and 8 we used the abbreviation 'MNE' to indicate foreign subsidiaries of multinationals.

We will show that in general outward FDI strengthens rather than damages home economies.

9.1   What are the Effects? Setting the Issues

The main concern for countries where MNEs are based is that outward FDI causes production and employment that would have taken place in the home country to instead take place abroad, reducing home economic activity. In terms of immediate impact this is generally true, but the researcher's task is to go beyond the immediate impact and establish the wider and longer-term effects on the firm's activities and the home economy as a whole.

The first issue we investigate is the effect of FDI on home output and employment. In principle, these may either increase or decrease, depending on whether home and foreign activities are complements or substitutes. Take vertical investment (VFDI), which relocates stages of production previously carried out at home. We have seen in Chapter 4 that, for some values of trade costs and factor prices, activities shift from one country to another, reducing home value added. However, in the longer term these effects could be reversed if MNEs gain market shares because of the cost savings induced by VFDI: the remaining home activities may then get strengthened. As for HFDI, we have shown in Chapter 3 that it reduces domestic plants' exports and therefore output when home and domestic products are substitutes. But, to the extent that foreign plants use inputs or other complementary products from home plants, domestic output will rise. Also, increasing numbers of foreign plants raise the demand for headquarter services at home, those activities characterized by firm-level economies of scale. These output and employment effects are reviewed in Section 9.2.

The second issue is the composition of inputs used in home country activity. Investing abroad may cause a change in the composition of inputs used in production at home and particularly a relative decline in the demand for unskilled labour. We have seen in Chapter 3 that the HFDI model does not provide clear predictions of the sign of the changes in factor demands in home and host countries. Skill intensity at home could possibly increase because of an expansion of activities such as headquarter services and R&D, but little can be said on changes at the plant level. The VFDI model, instead, predicts that the relative demand for skills and capital are likely to rise in high-income home countries, as labour-intensive activities are transferred to cheap-labour countries (see Section 4.4).[2] If home activities become more skilled and capital intensive, this change might impinge on income distribution, as changes in factor demand affect relative factor prices. VFDI is an important

---

[2] Remember from Chapters 4 and 7 that the effects in host cheap-labour countries is instead ambiguous and that VFDI does not necessarily bring about factor price convergence.

component of the fast-growing process of outsourcing and fragmenting production. This process, along with technological progress, is a driver of the increasing relative demand for skilled labour and the consequent rising wage gap between skilled and unskilled employment, e.g. in the US (Feenstra 2003). Changes in factor intensities will be discussed in Sections 9.2 (labour) and 9.3 (skills).

The third important question addressed in the literature is whether outward investment has any impact on technological upgrading and R&D activities at home. Indeed, foreign subsidiaries can be effective channels for transferring technological knowledge at home, particularly when based in locations with a high density of high-tech activities. For example, electronics firms gain from having a presence in Silicon Valley. On the other hand, we have argued in Chapter 5 that MNEs are often very concerned about depleting their proprietary technologies by investing in other counties and by interacting with foreign partners. We discuss this issue in Section 9.4.

These three factors, besides being relevant per se, also affect the productivity of home activities and their contribution to real income. To the extent that there are firm-level economies of scale, foreign expansion may raise the efficiency of the firm. However, if plant-level economies of scale are more important, contraction of home activities may reduce productivity. As argued in Chapter 4, the change in the composition of inputs used in production might enhance the efficiency of the production process, as plants relocate to specialize in activities intensive in the use of factors which are abundant and relatively cheap in foreign countries. Finally, technological sourcing creates opportunities for technological upgrading and for improving products and production processes. We look at the evidence of the effect of outward FDI on the productivity of firms at home in Section 9.5.

Evaluation of these effects requires, of course, benchmarking against an appropriate counterfactual: what would have been the size, the skill intensity, the efficiency of home firms had they not invested abroad and turned themselves into MNEs? Consider an industry where production can be fragmented between components and assembly. The threat of foreign competition may mean that retaining integrated production in the home country is not an option. The choice is between fragmenting and preserving some home production, or not producing at all. For example, a clothing producer in the UK could face the alternative of transferring labour-intensive stages of production to a cheap-labour country or not producing at all. Thus, even though the UK firm has to lay off workers, the alternative is complete closure. This alternative is, of course, hypothetical and, if the firm fragments, will not be observed. However, as argued in Chapter 7, relatively accurate proxies of the counterfactual can be constructed through conditional comparisons of MNEs and national firms based on appropriate econometric techniques.[3] We will see how this has been applied in the context of productivity in Section 9.5.

---

[3] When looking at host economies the event under study was arrival of a foreign multinational, so

Finally, we should note that spillovers—effects which are external to the firm—are important for home as for host country. All the channels creating technological and pecuniary externalities in host economies are at work in home economies too: links to suppliers and customers, movements of employees from MNEs to national firms, demand for infrastructure and so on. Unfortunately, this is an area where more research effort is needed, since, to the best of our knowledge, there are no studies available on external effects.

9.2   Foreign Production and Domestic Activities: Substitutes or Complements?

The main concern from the perspective of a country with a net outflow of FDI is the effect of these investments on the scale of economic activities. Most contributions analysing the effects of foreign investment at home focus on whether foreign output and jobs substitute for or complement domestic output and jobs. We will see that FDI in general strengthens economic activities at home. This holds particularly for VFDI to developing countries, contradicting the general belief that these investments engender a permanent loss of jobs and value added.

Output and trade

The empirical literature analysing the effects on output focuses on the relationship between foreign production and exports from the home country. Overall, it does not find that foreign output substitutes for the home output of MNEs. Rather, exports from MNEs home operations complement the activities of their subsidiaries based in foreign countries.

Examples of studies finding this relationship of complementarity are the papers by Lipsey and Weiss (1981, 1984) on the activities of US multinationals. They estimate exports from home plants as a function of foreign affiliate sales and different control variables, such as GDP and the distance between home and host countries. They find evidence of complementarity both within industries and individual firms. Thus, an increase in foreign affiliate sales is typically associated with an increase in exports by the home operations of the multinational. Similar evidence is also found by a number of studies on Japanese (Lipsey et al. 1999, 2000) and European multinationals.[4]

The basic problem with these studies is that the determinants of FDI often coincide with the determinants of exports. We have seen in Chapter 6 that the same gravity

the unconditional comparison of this firm with local firms was of interest. From the standpoint of the home economy the event is becoming multinational (or expanding multinational activity), and we seek to establish how this affects remaining home country activities of the firm.

[4]Swedenborg (1979, 1985, 2001) and Blomström et al. (1988) on Swedish MNEs. Fontagné and Pajot (2002), Chédor and Mucchielli (1998) and Chédor et al. (2002) on French MNEs. Bajo-Rubio and Montero-Munoz (2001) on Spanish multinationals. Pfaffermayr (1996) on Austrian MNEs.

equations explain trade and FDI flows alike. This problem of endogeneity has been controlled for by employing various instrumental-variable techniques in papers by Svensson (1996), Blomström et al. (1988), Grubert and Mutti (1991) and Clausing (2000). These studies confirm that FDI and export flows are complementary, and that they never find a relationship of substitution.

These general findings can be qualified when using firm-level data that classify foreign affiliates on the basis of the type of their activity (production of goods or provision of services) and the stage of production they carry out (production of intermediates or assembly of final goods). Two good examples of these studies are Head and Ries (2001) and Blonigen (2001). Head and Ries (2001) use a panel dataset containing 932 Japanese manufacturing firms over a 25-year period. For the complete sample they confirm the earlier result of complementarity between FDI and exports. The relationship, however, varies across firms. In particular, as expected, they find substitution when firms are not vertically integrated and assembly facilities in foreign countries are not supplied by intermediates produced at home. Their results are confirmed by the study by Blonigen (2001). Using data on Japanese production of automobile parts and consumer products in and exports to the US, he finds that both complementarity and substitution effects may arise, depending on the nature of the relationship between parents and foreign affiliates. For example, Japanese investment in car assembly in the US is complementary to exports of auto parts from Japan. In contrast, auto parts FDI in the US substitutes for auto parts exports from Japan.

Summing up, in general terms a relationship of complementarity between foreign output and export emerges from most studies. However, when the activities of foreign affiliates can be classified as vertical and horizontal, complementarity appears to hold for VFDI. In the case of HFDI some studies find evidence of substitutability. These results are in line with the theoretical predictions.

Employment

A second line of research looks at the effect of wages in different countries on employment by multinationals. The main question asked is, how do changes in foreign wages affect employment in home operations?[5]

Most studies on this subject share the common finding that there is a price complementarity between employment in foreign subsidiaries in cheap-labour countries and home employment. To illustrate this point, consider a UK clothing multinational with a plant at home and one in China. What is the effect of a wage decline in China on employment in the UK plant? Studies would typically find a positive (sometimes insignificant) effect.

---

[5]See Section 7.4 for a discussion of the effects of changes in national wages on foreign affiliates of MNEs.

In contrast, we can find evidence in the literature of price substitutability of labour between plants based in countries with similar factor costs. Assume that the UK firm also has a plant in Malaysia. Employment in Malaysia would decline following the decline in China's wages relative to Malaysia. Or, if it had a plant in France, employment in the UK would decline following a decline in French wages relative to the UK.

However, we should emphasize that these findings are derived from studies analysing the marginal effect of changes in foreign wages on employment at home, i.e. conditional on the multinational having already invested abroad. Most of the studies dealing with this issue take this approach. They look at the relationship between labour in existing plants and, as we will see below, they are unable to take into account or isolate the effects of new investments. This can be a problem, as the nature of the relationship changes once the investment takes place. Consider once more our example of the UK firm and imagine it has not yet invested in China. When the firm initially opens up a subsidiary in China, it transfers a labour-intensive stage of production there. Then, Chinese output (value added) and labour will *substitute* for UK output and labour. This is indeed what the model of VFDI in Chapter 4 postulates. However, once the Chinese plant has been set up, then Chinese labour and the remaining UK labour are complements, as they perform two complementary stages of the production process. A decline in Chinese wages makes the whole firm more competitive and its total output increases, including UK output. The increase in UK output also brings about an increase in UK employment.

We will start our discussion by looking at works estimating labour demand at home conditional on the firm having already invested. We will then discuss the implications of lifting this assumption.

We discuss three papers that follow the same methodology to study US (Brainard and Riker 1997b), Swedish (Braconier and Ekholm 2000) and European (Konings and Murphy 2001) multinationals.[6] We especially focus on Brainard and Riker (1997b), the first of these studies, which is based on firm-level data for a panel of foreign affiliates of US MNEs between 1983 and 1992.

These studies derive a comprehensive labour demand function for a plant located in a given country i. The plant is part of MNE k, which is a multiplant firm producing global output using factors of production in different countries. By estimating labour demand, it is possible to derive cross-wage elasticities to see how employment of the plant located in i is affected by changes in wages in another country j, where k has another plant. Depending on the study, i can either be the home country (to study

---

[6]An earlier study by Slaughter (1995) is based on the same methodology, but using the Bureau of Economic Activity (BEA) industry-level data on US manufacturing multinationals in the 1980s. Slaughter finds that total industry-wide domestic employment and total overseas affiliate employment are complementary, but only weakly so.

the relationship between employment at home and in other foreign subsidiaries), or the country where another foreign plant is based (to study the relationship between employment in different subsidiaries belonging to the same multinational). Brainard and Riker (1997b) focus on the relationship between affiliates. Anyway, labour demand of affiliates based in a high-skill country is a good proxy for the labour demand of parent companies at home, given that most MNEs are based in high-income countries.

Labour demands are conditional on firms having already invested abroad and chosen their investment location. In other words, the question addressed is, *once* a domestic firm has foreign subsidiaries in given countries, how do changes in foreign wages affect its labour demand at home?

These studies focus on short-run labour demands; therefore, labour is the only factor of production. They are also unable to control for the skill composition of the labour force at the firm level. Thus, there is no explicit distinction between skilled and unskilled labour and skilled and unskilled wages. The only distinct characteristic of labour is its geographical location.

A very simple production function of MNE k may be represented in the following form:

$$y^k = F(L^{Ik}, \ldots, L^{Jk}, \ldots) \quad \text{for } J = 1, \ldots, n \text{ and } J \neq I, \tag{9.1}$$

where L^{Ik} and L^{Jk} are employment in plant I of MNE k located in country i (which can be home or any other country where a given plant is based) and J is one of the other n plants of MNE k located in a country j different from i. On the basis of the standard theory of production with several inputs, it is then possible to infer how changes in the wage rate in all locations j affect the demand for labour in location i (taking factor prices as exogenous).

To control for the possibly different relationship between employment in countries with different factor endowments (price complementarity: UK and China) and in countries with similar factor endowments (price substitutability: UK and France), Brainard and Riker (1997a) define two groups of countries, those whose national average schooling was less than six years in 1985 (low-skill countries) and those whose average schooling was more than six years (high-skill countries). The former correspond to developing countries and the latter to high-income ones. Then, each firm I faces two different average foreign wages, W_{d}^{Ik} and W_{s}^{Ik} for countries with, respectively, different and similar factor endowments to country i.[7]

---

[7] An average foreign wage for affiliate I of MNE k is $W^{Ik} = \sum_{j=1}^{n} \omega^{Jk} W_j$. This is the weighted average of country-specific wages (industry/country specific in some studies) in the j locations. ω^{Jk} is the share of affiliate J's production capacity in total k's foreign production capacity.

Assuming profit-maximizing behaviour, it is possible to derive a reduced-form log-linear labour demand function for affiliate I of MNE k at time t:

$$\ln(L_t^{Ik}) = \alpha_0 + \alpha_1 \ln(W_{it}) + \alpha_2 \ln(W_{dt}^{Ik}) + \alpha_3 \ln(W_{st}^{Ik})$$

$$+ \alpha_4 \ln D_{it} + \alpha_5 \sum_{j=1}^{n} \ln(D_{jt}) + e_t^{Ik}, \quad (9.2)$$

where W_{it} is average wage in country i where I is located, and W_{dt}^{Ik} and W_{st}^{Ik} are average foreign wages for countries with different and similar factor endowments to i. D_{it} and D_{jt} control for the effects of aggregate consumer demand in countries i and j at time t and e_t^{Ik} is an error term. Since the sum $\sum_{j=1}^{n} \ln(D_{jt})$, measuring the size of the global market, only varies with respect to time, Brainard and Riker (1997b) capture this effect by using time dummies.

It is now possible to analyse whether workers in different locations are price substitutes or price complements within the multinational firm. This depends on the signs of the α_2 and α_3 coefficients. The previous expression being log-linear in the variables, these coefficients are cross-price elasticities of labour demand. As argued, we expect α_2 to be negative (locations with different factor endowments and complementary activities) and α_3 to be positive (locations with similar factor endowments and substitute activities). Brainard and Riker (1997b) carry out two separate ordinary least-squares (OLS) estimations of (9.2), one when Is are located in high-skill-abundant countries and one when they are in low-skill-abundant countries. Their results are reported in Table 9.1.

Results are as expected. In both estimations α_3 is positive and α_2 is negative. Both coefficients are always significant. In words, the labour of affiliates located in high-income countries is the price complement of labour of other affiliates in developing countries and the price substitute of labour of other affiliates in high-income countries. The opposite can be observed for the labour of affiliates located in developing countries.

The results of Brainard and Riker (1997b) are consistent with those of the other two studies based on the same methodology. These also explicitly analyse the relationship between foreign subsidiaries and the parent company. They are also more careful in controlling for the problem of endogeneity, which typically affects the relationship between employment and wages in the estimation of labour demand. Braconier and Ekholm (2000) carry out a firm-level study of Swedish MNEs between 1970 and 1994. They find a relationship of substitutability between parent employment in Sweden and employment in affiliates based in other high-income locations, while there is no relationship with employment in affiliates located in low-wage countries.

Their findings are also partly confirmed by Konings and Murphy (2001), on the basis of a dataset of over 1200 European MNEs and their affiliates within the EU and

Table 9.1. Estimation of labour demand.

Dependent variable: $\ln(L_t^{Ik})$

| | Affiliate I located in a | |
	high-income country	developing country
Local wage	−0.755***	−0.366***
	(0.120)	(0.1)
Wage of other affiliates in	0.154***	−0.225***
high-income countries	(0.057)	(0.080)
Wage of other affiliates in	−0.185***	0.170**
developing countries	(0.049)	(0.075)
Local aggregate demand	0.828***	0.426***
	(0.073)	(0.028)
Constant	0.044***	0.02
	(0.011)	(0.03)
R^2	0.462	0.209
Number of observations	9174	3677

Source: Brainard and Riker (1997b, Table 4).
Note: OLS estimations are for a pool of all affiliates in manufacturing industries. It includes firm/country fixed effects. Heteroskedasticity robust standard errors into brackets with ***, ** and * denoting significance at the 1%, 5% and 10% levels, respectively.

in Central and Eastern Europe in the period 1994–98. Once more, they find evidence of price substitution effects between labour at home and in foreign subsidiaries in other high-income countries. An average decline of 10% in the wage costs in foreign subsidiaries is associated with a decline in employment at home of 1.5–2% on average. However, substitution mainly takes place when foreign subsidiaries are located within the EU, and less so with those in cheap-labour Central and Eastern European countries.[8]

Other studies have analysed this issue by estimating labour demands conditional on output in the multinational firm. For example, Brainard and Riker (1997a) derive labour shares from translog cost functions for a panel of US MNEs between 1983 and 1992. This includes the sample of US foreign affiliates just discussed and their parent companies. Therefore, they directly analyse the relationship between employment in subsidiaries and in parent companies. Their results are consistent with those reported above. They find that employment in US parents responds modestly to changes in

---

[8]Note that their dataset does not include subsidiaries outside the EU and Eastern Europe, so they cannot take into account the complete set of cross elasticities between locations.

foreign wages, and strong substitutability between affiliates based in countries with similar factor endowments.[9]

All the studies discussed so far analyse short-term labour demands. MNEs often take time to adjust actual labour demand to their desired level. The sign and the magnitude of the relationship between domestic and foreign employment may change as MNEs gain experience in foreign markets. Long-term changes and labour adjustment costs can only be captured by estimating dynamic labour demands. Bruno and Falzoni (2003) do so by using industry-level data on US MNEs (for the period 1982–94) and they estimate short- and long-run cross-wage elasticities conditional on home output. Also their results are consistent with those of the other papers analysed. The relationship between home employment in US MNEs and employment in their subsidiaries in Latin America gets reversed from the short to the long run. While in the short run there is evidence that the two are price substitutes, in the long run home and foreign labour are complements. Home and foreign labour are instead always substitutes when US subsidiaries are based in Europe.

As argued above, the studies discussed so far are unable to capture the one-off effect of the initial investment. They only look at the relationship between existing plants and locations. Unfortunately, very few studies look at the impact of new investments. Barba Navaretti and Castellani (2003) address this issue for Italy by comparing employment dynamics in national firms and in firms investing abroad for the first time. After carefully constructing a benchmark of national firms, following a methodology similar to the one that will be outlined in detail in Section 9.5, they do not find evidence that the employment dynamics of investing firms is significantly different from the one of non-investors.[10] This implies that even if employment declines in firms that open up new plants, this decline is not larger and sometimes smaller than what it would have been if these firms had not invested abroad. Thus, if compared with accurate counterfactuals, foreign investments, even to developing countries and even labour-saving ones are paradoxically a good strategy to preserve home employment.[11]

This result is important and partly reassuring, given the widespread fear that jobs in high-income countries get exported to developing countries through FDI. It is also in line with the evidence of output reported in the previous subsection.

---

[9]Blomström et al. (1997) and Lipsey et al. (2000) carry out a descriptive analysis of the relationship between employment at home and output in foreign subsidiaries, controlling for home output, for cross-sections of US, Swedish and Japanese MNEs. Their results are not fully conclusive.

[10]They use a propensity score matching technique.

[11]Brainard and Riker (1997b) also carry out one estimation where they control for wage changes corresponding to affiliate start-ups. They find results in line with their earlier ones.

9.3 Skill Intensity

The opening up of foreign plants could also affect the way in which things are produced at home. As foreign factors of production become available, optimal factor proportions at home may change. We have just discussed labour intensity. If labour is not homogeneous, outward FDI also affects the composition of home employment between skilled and unskilled labour. We argued that the relocation of activities may change the division of labour within the multinational firm, leading, for instance, to a concentration of skilled-labour-intensive activities at home. If this change leads to a more efficient use of resources, efficiency and profits at home will rise. Also, if MNEs account for a large share of economic activity in the home country a relative increase in their demand for skilled labour will affect the broader distribution of income.

Indeed, the analysis of the effects of FDI on the demand for skills is nested in the broader debate on the sources of the increasing wage gap between skilled and unskilled workers since the 1980s, especially in the US.[12] The question is whether this pattern is related to trade-induced changes in the specialization of high-income economies, following growing imports from countries abundant in unskilled labour. The standard Heckscher–Ohlin model predicts that a skill-abundant country opening to trade with economies abundant in unskilled labour will experience a fall in the relative price of unskilled-labour-intensive goods. This will reduce the wage of unskilled labour and raise the wage of skilled labour (the Stolper–Samuelson theorem). It will also cause the structure of the economy to become increasingly specialized in skill-intensive goods (the Heckscher–Ohlin–Samuelson theorem).

The evidence for the US is not consistent with these predictions. According to Berman et al. (1994), just a small part of the increase in the demand for skilled workers can be accounted for by shifts in output between industries. Rather, most of it is related to within-industry changes. Also the Stolper–Samuelson theorem does not seem to apply. The price of unskilled-intensive products like garments rose during the 1980s and the 1990s relative to the price of skill-intensive products like computers (Lawrence and Slaughter 1993).

One reason for this apparent inconsistency is that trade effects were operating within industries as firms fragmented their production (Feenstra and Hanson 1996, 1997).[13] If firms in high-income countries fragment their production process and outsource to cheap-labour countries, this leads to a within-industry change in specialization and in the demand for skills. This process can therefore partly account

---

[12] See Feenstra (2003, Chapter 4) for a thorough survey of this debate. In continental European countries with highly regulated labour markets this pattern took the form of an increasing gap in unemployment rather than in wages between the two groups of workers.

[13] The other reason is, of course, technical progress.

for the increasing relative demand for skills. As argued in Chapters 1, 6 and 7, there is widespread evidence of a large increase in North–South trade of intermediates in the 1990s (Hummels et al. 2001; Ng and Yeates 1999). Part of this broad process of outsourcing is being carried out via VFDI (Hanson et al. 2001).

Chapter 4 provides a theoretical backing to this pattern and shows that vertical investment may lead to an increase in the relative demand for skilled labour in high-income countries. This prediction is consistent with cursory and anecdotal evidence. In general terms, headquarters' activities are more skill intensive than production. Headquarters provide specialized services to foreign affiliates in skill-intensive areas such as R&D, design, marketing, finance, strategic management. Also, unskilled-labour-intensive activities tend to move where labour is cheap.

The econometric works addressing this issue follow the same methodology as studies analysing the broad effect of trade in intermediate inputs. These works derive a demand for relative skilled labour from industry- or firm-specific production functions and examine whether international activities measured in various ways affect this demand.

Three studies focus directly on the activities of MNEs: Slaughter (2000) on the US; Hansson (2001) on Sweden; and Head and Ries (2002) on Japan. In a cost-minimization setting, these papers derive simple short-run labour demands from translog cost functions, based on the assumption that only two factors of production—skilled and unskilled labour—can vary, whereas capital is assumed to be fixed in the short term. The derivation of labour demands from translog cost functions is carried out in the appendix. Skill upgrading is measured as an increase in the wage share of non-production (skilled) workers. Measures of the degree of internationalization of the firm are added to the basic specification as demand shifters. To test for the role of FDI, the measures of internationalization capture the importance of the multinational activities of the firms.

The generic empirical specification tested is the following:

$$\mathrm{SH}^k_{St} = \beta_0 + \beta_1 \ln w^k_{Ut} + \beta_2 \ln w^k_{St} + \beta_3 \ln \frac{K^k_t}{Y^k_t} + \beta_4 \ln Y^k_t + \beta_5 \mathrm{MNE}^k_t + e^k_t, \quad (9.3)$$

where SH^k_{St} is the skilled-labour share of the total wage bill in home country i for firm k (or industry h if the analysis is carried out at the industry level); w^k_{St} and w^k_{Ut} are skilled and unskilled wages in the home country at time t; K^k_t is capital; Y^k_t is output or value added. MNE^k_t measures the importance of multinational activities for firm k at time t. It is usually proxied by the ratio of overseas employment (value added or sales) to national employment (value added or sales). The important coefficient is β_5; when significant, if it is positive, other things being equal, MNEs cause skill upgrading, if it is negative, skill downgrading. The final e^k_t is an error term.

The results of the estimations of (9.3) crucially depend on whether the analysis is carried out using industry- or firm-level data. In the former case, no significant effect has been found, whereas in the latter the effect of MNEs is always found to be positive and significant.

Slaughter (2000) focuses on the role of US MNEs and uses an industry-year panel from 1977 to 1994.[14] He tests whether the transfer of production stages from US parents to foreign affiliates has contributed to US skill upgrading within industries. Slaughter checks different measures of 'production transfer' within MNEs, all based on industry-specific ratios between the activities of foreign subsidiaries of US MNEs and total domestic activities in the United States. He finds no statistically significant evidence that the activities of foreign subsidiaries influence the demand for skilled labour at home.

Head and Ries (2002) address the effect of overseas production on home skill intensity for Japanese MNEs. As they also use firm-level data over the period 1971–89, they can directly observe the skill intensity of the MNEs' home activities. Table 9.2 presents some of Head and Ries's (2002) estimations of equation (9.3) on industry- and firm-level data.[15] When Head and Ries aggregate firm data at the industry level and perform regressions similar to those of Slaughter (2000), they also find that foreign production has no effects on skill intensity at home (the coefficient of MNE_t^k is insignificant in regressions 1 and 2).[16] Moving to firm-level data, their empirical results change dramatically. Foreign production is found to have a positive and significant effect on domestic skill intensity (regressions 3 and 4).

These effects also depend on the skill abundance of the host country. When they include the income of the host country in their estimations (not reported in Table 9.2), Head and Ries show that the positive effect of overseas activities on skill intensity at home is larger, the larger the share of foreign employment in subsidiaries based in low-income countries.

The econometric evidence shown by Hansson (2001) for Swedish multinationals confirms the findings of Head and Ries (2002). Hansson uses firm-level data and classifies outward FDI by country of destination (OECD versus non-OECD). He finds that in the 1990s, the relocation of activities to non-OECD regions has contributed to the skill upgrading of the home activities of Swedish manufacturing MNEs. The rise of FDI to Eastern European countries after 1993 had an especially large effect. As in the other studies just mentioned, industry-level estimations do not show any statistically significant effect of FDI on skill upgrading in Sweden.

---

[14]The panel is based on the Bureau of Economic Analysis (BEA) dataset on US manufacturing multinationals and on NBER manufacturing productivity database.

[15]Differently from specification (9.3), wages are not included as regressors. Following Berman et al. (1994), Head and Ries maintain the assumption that there is no exogenous variation in wages across industries and include year dummies to capture year-to-year changes in the wage levels faced by all firms (see also Feenstra 2003).

[16]However, differently from Slaughter (2000), they find a negative and statistically significant sign for both scale and capital intensity.

Table 9.2. Offshore production and skill upgrading in Japanese manufacturing MNEs.

Dependent variable: log of non-production share of the wage bill (SH_{St}^k)

Unit of observation	Industries		Firms	
	First differences		Industry-fixed effects	Firm-fixed effects
Method	(1)	(2)	(3)	(4)
$\ln(K_t^k/Y_t^k)$	-2.49^{***}	-1.81^{***}	-7.92^{***}	-4.10^{***}
	(0.38)	(0.35)	(0.17)	(0.13)
$\ln(Y_t^k)$	-3.83^{***}	-3.51^{***}	0.86^{***}	-3.18^{***}
	(0.47)	(0.45)	(0.08)	(0.16)
MNE_t^k	-1.14	-1.81	1.11^{***}	3.01^{***}
	(1.02)	(1.20)	(0.23)	(0.18)
Residual	0.07	0.16	6.76^{***}	12.52^{***}
change	(0.16)	(0.19)	(0.53)	(0.32)
N	1584	1584	19 845	19 845
R^2	0.08	0.06	0.154	0.262
Root mean square error	1.008	1.183	11.782	5.58

Source: Head and Ries (2002, Table 3).

Notes. In specification (1) all regressors are weighted by the industry's share of the total manufacturing wage bill as in Slaughter (2000). Standard errors in parentheses with ***, ** and * denoting significance at the 1%, 5% and 10% levels, respectively. Sample period runs from 1971 to 1989. MNE is the ratio of overseas to home employment.

Overall, the results of these studies seem to support the idea that FDI and particularly vertical FDI to cheap-labour countries has a positive effect on the skill intensity of MNEs' activities in the home country. However, the foreign activities of multinationals fail to explain aggregate industry effects, i.e. the average skill upgrading in manufacturing sectors observed in advanced investing countries.

9.4   Technological Sourcing

Another important issue is the effect of FDI on technological upgrading at home. MNEs are generally assumed to invest abroad to exploit some advantage that gives them competitive leverage to compensate for the higher costs of opening a new plant. It is, however, possible that the reverse pattern is also at work. As technological knowledge is concentrated geographically (Jaffe et al. 1993), MNEs with no particular competitive advantage may locate their plants in knowledge-intensive areas to acquire new technologies and skills directly or by way of spillovers. Theoretical models by Fosfuri and Motta (1999), Neven and Siotis (1995) and by Siotis (1999) show that laggard firms may use foreign investments to acquire location-specific knowledge.

Much empirical and anecdotal evidence supports this view that technological sourcing is an important determinant of FDI. This evidence was discussed in Chapter 6. If MNEs invest to source foreign knowledge, how does this knowledge impact on productivity? Results are mixed. Braconier et al. (2001) use firm-level panel data on a sample of Swedish MNEs to assess the impact of foreign R&D spillovers channelled through outward and inward FDI. Their idea, which builds upon the pioneering work on trade-induced R&D spillovers by Coe and Helpman (1995), is that the larger the inward and outward activities of multinationals and the larger the R&D stock of the partner country, the larger the spillovers from foreign R&D to domestic operations. Consequently, an investing firm is expected to benefit from R&D spillovers the more it invests in R&D-rich countries. For each MNE k belonging to industry h and with subsidiaries in country(ies) j, Braconier et al. (2001) derive an outward FDI weighted measure of the foreign R&D stock that may generate spillovers as

$$\text{OFDI}^{kh} = \sum_j \frac{L_j^{kh}}{L_j^h} S_j^h, \tag{9.4}$$

where L_j^{kh}/L_j^h is the employment of firm k in industry h in country j over total employment in h in country j and S_j^h is the stock of R&D investments of country j in sector h. They then look at how this foreign R&D stock is related to the productivity of the parent operations of the MNE, controlling for other sources of technological learning like the R&D investments of the firm itself and the R&D intensity of inward investments in industry h. They find no evidence of R&D spillovers induced by technological sourcing.

Pottelsberghe de la Potterie and Lichtenberg (2001) use a similar methodology, but they analyse aggregate inward and outward FDI flows for 13 OECD countries between 1971 and 1990. Their findings are that a country's productivity is increased by outward investments when it invests in R&D-intensive countries. Inward investments, on the contrary, channel no spillovers to the host economy.

Finally, Branstetter (2000) takes a more focused approach and examines if the patenting activities of a sample of Japanese firms are influenced by their foreign operations in the US. He finds that a US presence does increase Japanese firms' propensity to patent. The idea here is that R&D spillovers directly affect technological upgrading, besides for their overall effect on the productivity of the firm.

9.5 Effects on Productivity: Comparing MNEs and National Firms

All the factors analysed so far combine in affecting productivity of the home activity of MNEs. This section is devoted to analysing this productivity effect. Differently from the evidence discussed up to this point, here we compare MNEs and national firms. Is there evidence that domestically based MNEs perform better than 'national' firms—those that have not become multinational?

We therefore proceed in three steps, analogous to those in Section 7.2. First, does the unconditional comparison—simply looking at average measures of productivity for MNEs and national firms—reveal differences? Second, conditional comparisons; once we control for observable differences in characteristics such as firm size, does the productivity gap persist? Third, and most importantly, is it possible to identify a causal relationship between becoming multinational and changes in performance?

It is especially important here to isolate the causal effect of foreign investments on productivity. When looking at host economies the event under study was the arrival of foreign multinationals, so conditional and unconditional comparisons of these firms with local firms was of interest. In the analysis of home economies the event under study is the departure of activities that could have been or were previously carried out at home, so comparing MNEs with national firms is not particularly interesting per se. Here, the relevant question is what happens to the remaining home activities of MNEs compared with what would have happened had firms not become MNEs. As argued in Chapter 7, conditional comparisons of MNEs and national firms provide an indirect way of carrying out this counterfactual analysis, if appropriate techniques controlling for endogeneity are used.

The causal relationship is, of course, the most difficult one to identify empirically. In the preceding section we outlined some mechanisms through which becoming MNE may change firms' performance, but it is also likely that causality runs in the opposite direction. To what extent is the case that firms become more efficient because they are MNEs, or is it simply that efficient firms self-select into becoming MNEs? Firms that have large intangible assets, in the form of brand image or technology, are precisely those that are likely to become multinational (Chapters 3 and 5). Helpman et al. (2004) show in a model with heterogeneous firms, that high-productivity firms are the most likely to become multinational. Additionally, more profitable firms may find it easier to finance foreign investments than do smaller or less profitable companies.[17]

---

[17]Note that the sunk cost of setting up a new foreign subsidiary may create hysteresis. If profits from foreign operation are stochastic, firm-, industry- or time-specific, shocks to the demand of foreign products or to the marginal costs of foreign production may reduce the profitability of foreign operations. Firms, may, however, decide not to close down their foreign plants in a given period, even when foreign profits are negative, to avoid facing a new setting-up fixed cost if the subsidiary is expected to be profitable in the future. Other things being equal, each year a firm is more likely to have a foreign subsidiary if the subsidiary was already in place the previous year. Accordingly, Pennings and Sleuwagen (2002) in their analysis of the determinants of alternative modes of restructuring (exit, downscaling and relocation to a third country) for a sample of Belgian firms find that relocating is more likely than the other two options when firms are already MNEs (the sunk cost of relocation is likely to be lower) and when their profits

Table 9.3. Comparing foreign-owned plants, national UK-based plants and home plants of UK multinationals (average 1996–2000).

	Foreign owned	National	Home plants of UK MNEs
Number of observations	3499	161 234	2919
Value added/employees	44.61	27.98	36.98
Output/employees	151.98	76.52	105.3
Employment	485	142	475
Capital/employees	98.82	38.23	65.41
Intermediate inputs/employees	107.81	50.52	69.76

Values in thousands of pounds.
Source: Criscuolo and Martin (2003, Table 4).

We look at the unconditional and conditional comparisons in the next subsection, and then at causality in Section 9.5.2. Unfortunately, there are few firm-level studies comparing MNEs and national firms in home countries, mostly because of a lack of comprehensive datasets combining information for national and multinational firms. This is particularly so when we seek to use time series data to identify causal effects.

9.5.1 Are MNEs More Productive Than National Firms?

We start by comparing some basic features of national firms and of home activities of MNEs. Table 9.3, derived from Criscuolo and Martin (2003), provides evidence for the UK. It partly reproduces Table 7.1, with an additional column, which reports average values for the home plants of UK MNEs. These have higher labour productivity (value added and output per employee) than national plants, and are also larger and use more capital-intensive technologies. Essentially, their characteristics lie between those of national firms and foreign multinationals.

We now move on to test if these differences in performance still hold when we control for differences in technology and for other observable factors. The basic equation to be estimated has the same general form as (7.4):

$$\ln(q_t^k) = \alpha + \beta \text{MNE}_t^k + \ln \sum_{s=1}^{v} \gamma_s X_{st}^k + e_t^k, \tag{9.5}$$

where q_t^k measures productivity, MNE_t^k is a dummy that takes value 1 if firm k is an MNE at time t, X is a vector of observable firm-specific characteristics s and e_t^k is an error term. Note, however, that differently from (7.4), MNE_t^k now indicates whether firm k owns foreign subsidiaries, not whether the firm is itself a foreign

---

are higher on average. See also Helpman et al. (2004) on the prediction that only the most efficient firms will be investing abroad.

Table 9.4.   Differences in total factor productivity between MNEs and national firms.

Dependent variable: $\ln(q^k)$	
MNE^k	0.158*** (0.021)
$\ln(\text{size}^k)$	0.042** (0.009)
Sector dummies	Yes
Number of observations	1587
R^2	0.09

Standard errors in brackets.
*, 90% significance; **, 95% significance; ***, 99% significance.

subsidiary. Also, MNE_t^k is a dichotomous variable and we do not take into account the number and size of k's subsidiaries, nor the countries in which they operate.

We follow Barba Navaretti and Castellani (2003) to estimate equation (9.5) for a sample of Italian firms observed between 1993 and 1998.[18] The productivity measure is total factor productivity (TFP) and size is measured by total employment in home plants.[19] For simplicity equation (9.5) is estimated as a cross-section of average 1993–98 values (thus t is invariant). MNEs are all firms with at least one foreign subsidiary in at least one year between 1993 and 1998. For firms which are MNEs, productivity refers only to their home activities (this dataset has firm-level and not plant-level observations). National firms are strictly domestically owned. The controls include the size of the firm and sector dummies. The results of the estimations are reported in Table 9.4.

We find that the domestic activities of MNEs in our sample are on average 17% more productive than are national firms with no foreign subsidiaries, even after controlling for size and the sector of the firm. These results are consistent with the average characteristics of UK MNEs reported in Table 9.3.

However, these results simply report a statistical association, even though conditional on a set of other observable characteristics of the firm. How can we isolate

---

[18]The sample includes a balanced panel of 1587 firms, observed between 1993 and 1998. Of these, 1119 are national firms with no foreign subsidiaries during the whole period, 321 are firms with foreign subsidiaries during the whole period and 147 are firms which opened their first foreign subsidiary in the period observed. National firms are drawn as a random sample from the total population of Italian firms. The dataset, put together by the Centro Studi Luca d'Agliano, merges the Reprint dataset on Italian FDI, constructed by the Politecnico di Milano and the Amadeus dataset, containing de-consolidated balance sheet and other data of Italian firms.

[19]TFP is obtained as the residual from a log-linear Cobb–Douglas production function (see equation (7.3)). A GLS-AR(1) estimator is used, allowing for autocorrelated productivity (AR(1)). As noted by Baltagi and Griffin (1997) this estimator has some desirable properties compared with the GMM-IV estimator for dynamic panels proposed by Arellano and Bond (1991) when response parameters (i.e. output elasticities of the various factors of production in this case) are characterized by heterogeneity.

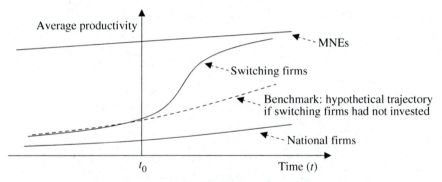

Figure 9.1.   Average productivity trajectories in home plants.

empirically the impact of the MNE status on performance from the fact that those more productive firms self-select into investing abroad?

9.5.2   *Self-Selection or Performing by Investing? From Statistical Association to Causal Inference*

In order to try to separate self-selection from causality, we look at what happens to firms that change status, becoming MNEs by opening their first foreign subsidiary. This approach is in line with the works discussed in Chapter 7 that analyse the change in performance patterns of firms acquired by foreign investors (Conyon et al. 2002; Harris and Robinson 2002). It also draws on the methodologies used in recent studies that have examined the link between exporting and performance (Bernard and Jensen 1999; Clerides et al. 1998; Aw et al. 2000; Castellani 2002; Delgado et al. 2002; Girma et al. 2002; Kraay 1999). The problem of the exporter is similar to the problem of the investing firm. Entering a new foreign market involves fixed costs: gathering information on the market, setting up distribution networks, adapting products to foreign specifications and so on. Such activities will be more profitable for more efficient firms.[20] At the same time, exporting is expected to cause learning effects and improve efficiency.

Following Clerides et al. (1998) in Figure 9.1, we draw hypothetical productivity trajectories for three types of firm (solid lines): those which have a foreign subsidiary during the whole period observed (MNEs), those which never have a foreign subsidiary in the period observed (national firms), and those which open their first foreign subsidiary in t_0 and therefore switch status from national to multinational (switching firms).

The existence of a productivity premium for MNEs, as estimated in (9.5), tells us that these firms have higher average productivity than national firms. Thus, their

---

[20]Helpman et al. (2004) find that US MNEs have higher labour productivity than US non-MNE exporters. Both groups of firms are more productive than national firms which are neither MNEs nor exporters.

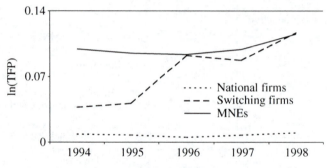

Figure 9.2.   Home productivity trends.

average productivity trajectory is assumed to always lie above that of national firms. If there is self-selection, switching firms are more productive than other national firms before investing. Consequently, we assume their trajectory to lie above that of national firms even before the investment. If productivity improves because of the investment, then the trajectory of switching firms gets steeper in the aftermath of the investment, converging to the MNEs' trajectory.

Do the data from the panel of Italian firms described above match these trajectories? In Figure 9.2 we report the 1994–98 trends for productivity. Switching firms open their first foreign subsidiary between 1993 and 1997. The match between the two figures is quite remarkable. The three groups of firms rank as expected: national firms are at the bottom and MNEs at the top. Switching firms are in the middle. These firms are already doing better than national firms at the beginning of the period analysed, suggesting that investing firms are self-selected among the high-performing ones. But, in addition, their productivity trajectory gets steeper when they start investing, supporting the hypothesis that firms benefit from their foreign activities.

Let us go back to Figure 9.1 for a moment. This figure is useful to understanding why we need to derive an appropriate counterfactual to isolate the causal effect of the investment. Comparing solid lines—and the real trajectories in Section 9.2— is equivalent to the unconditional comparisons discussed in Section 9.5.1. If we compare the average switching firm with the average national firm, we do not know whether the former performs better because of the investment or because it was performing better anyway, even before the investment. Alternatively, if we just focus on the trajectory of switching firms and observe that it improves after the investment, we would not know if this is because of the investment or because of other events that took place in t_0 that affect the performance of all firms and that we cannot observe (e.g. an exogenous shock to aggregate demand).

Now, the dotted line draws the hypothetical trajectory that would have been followed by switching firms if they had not invested: this is our benchmark. What we need to find out is whether there is indeed a gap after the investment between the trajectory of switching firms (level of productivity) and this dotted line. Or, equally, whether the slope of the trajectory (rate of growth of productivity) becomes steeper than that of the dotted line after the investment. In this case the improvement in performance could only have been caused by the investment. As the dotted line cannot be observed, it can be proxied by identifying a counterfactual of national firms that is as similar as possible to switching firms, besides for having invested abroad in t_0.

This, in essence, is what econometric techniques controlling for observed and unobserved heterogeneity and for endogeneity do. There are various techniques for doing so and we have discussed them in Chapter 7. As an illustration, here we use GMM Arellano–Bond estimators where all variables are instrumented with their lagged values.[21]

We just focus on two groups of firms, switching and national ones. Thus, we exclude from our estimations those firms which are MNEs during the whole period. We relate productivity at time t of firm k, q_t^k, to a switch from national to MNE made by firm k in the previous period as follows:

$$\ln(q_t^k) = \alpha_0 + \alpha_1 \ln(q_{t-1}^k) + \beta_1 \text{MNE}_{t-1}^k + v_t^k, \tag{9.6}$$

where q_{t-1}^k is productivity at $t-1$; MNE_{t-1}^k is a dummy variable that takes value 1 if firm k has opened its first foreign subsidiary in $t-1$ and becomes a multinational for the first time, and is zero otherwise; v_t^k is an error term. We include lagged productivity to control for the effects of past productivity on performance at t.

The Arellano–Bond GMM estimator implies estimating (9.6) in first differences. This controls for time-invariant unobservable characteristics, which get wiped out by first differencing. In Table 9.5 we report results for one estimation of (9.6).

The results in Table 9.5 are consistent with the expectation that firms that invest abroad perform better in the aftermath of the investment than firms which remain national. The coefficient of the variable measuring the change in status, $\Delta \text{MNE}_{t-1}^k$, implies that productivity grows faster and is higher in level after the investment than for the benchmark of national firms. The coefficient is not significant in this estimation, probably because Arellano–Bond estimations might yield slightly biased results given the relatively short time series of this panel (maximum of three periods). However, alternative estimations for the same Italian sample, based on propensity score matching techniques, find significant evidence that, because of the investment,

---

[21]Our results should be taken as strictly illustrative, as Arellano–Bond estimations might yield slightly biased results given the relatively short time series of this panel (maximum of three periods).

Table 9.5. The effect of investing abroad on performance at home.

Dependent variable: $\Delta \ln(q)_{it}$	
	AB-GMM
$\Delta \ln(q_{t-1}^k)$	0.367** (0.113)
$\Delta \mathrm{MNE}_{t-1}^k$	0.079 (0.072)
Constant	−0.001 (0.002)
Number of observations	3692
Number of firms	1291
Sargan (P value)	15.17
m_1	−4.58**
m_2	0.74

Note: all estimations are carried out in first differences using the Arellano–Bond GMM estimator; *, 90% significance; **, 95% significance. See footnote to Table 7.3 on the tests performed.

the rate of growth of productivity at home is 4.9% higher for switching firms than for the counterfactual of national firms (Barba Navaretti and Castellani 2003).[22]

Thus, we find descriptive evidence that firms investing abroad are the best performers in terms of productivity in the sample, even before the investment. We also find econometric evidence that investment abroad causes a further improvement in performance; certainly, we find no evidence that it causes a worsening of performance.

We should underline that these results should be taken with a certain degree of care—the evidence reported is based on the case of one country as there is no other evidence available on this issue. It is, however, suggestive of how the effects of outward investments on the home activities of MNEs should be addressed empirically.

9.6 Conclusions

In this chapter we have analysed the home effects of outward FDI. This problem has a different perspective than the one of analysing host effects. Here, activities move out from the home country, and the real concern is whether this move strengthens or weakens the remaining economic activities at home. As a consequence of this difference in perspective, the analysis of the home effects is more careful in understanding

---

[22]These estimations are not introduced here as they would be beyond the scope of this chapter. Also, two-stage least-squares estimates of (9.6) with instrumental variables and carried out in first difference give a significant 19% premium in TFP growth for switching firms. However, two-stage least-squares estimates provide weaker controls for endogeneity than Arellano–Bond estimators and propensity score matching.

what happens within the MNE, in the home activities of the MNE: whether foreign employment substitutes for domestic employment; whether production technologies change; whether traditional skills and competencies get dissipated, and so on.

The evidence summarized in this chapter bends much more on the positive side than on the negative one: all together foreign investments are more likely to strengthen than to deplete home activities. We find that foreign output and employment do not substitute for domestic ones, particularly, and against conventional wisdom, when investments are carried out in cheap-labour countries. There is also evidence of technological upgrading at home, as MNEs become more skill intensive and sometimes manage to acquire foreign technological knowledge from their foreign subsidiaries. Comparing firms investing abroad and national firms just operating in the home country, we find that investing abroad enhances the productivity path of investing firms, which gets steeper after the investment, compared with the path of non-investing firms.

Thus, if national firms invest abroad and become MNEs, on average this is good for the home economy. This evidence counters the claims of many that the transfer of production stages elsewhere, particularly to cheap-labour countries, could be damaging for domestic economies.

However, research on home country effects is limited, compared with that on host countries, mostly because of lack of data. For example, we have no studies analysing the spillovers of outward investments outside investing firms on the rest of the home economy. As argued, these can be large. This is an important gap that future research should soon try to fill up.

Appendix. Derivation of Empirically Testable Demands for Relatively Skilled Labour

The empirical literature has largely employed the translog cost function to examine the sources of increased demand for skilled labour. The reason for this choice lies in the flexibility of this functional form, allowing for cross-factor substitutability or complementarity. A detailed discussion of the econometric issues that are involved in implementing the translog cost function specification in the estimation of demands for factors of production may be found in Berndt (1991, Chapter 9).

The translog cost function may be written as

$$\ln C = \alpha_0 + \sum_{g=1}^{G} a_g \ln w_g + \sum_{z=1}^{Z} \beta_z \ln x_z + \frac{1}{2} \sum_{g=1}^{G} \sum_{b=1}^{B} \gamma_{gb} \ln w_g \ln w_b$$

$$+ \frac{1}{2} \sum_{z=1}^{Z} \sum_{v=1}^{Z} \delta_{zv} \ln x_z \ln x_v + \sum_{g=1}^{G} \sum_{z=1}^{Z} \phi_{gz} \ln w_g \ln x_z, \quad (9.7)$$

where w_g denotes the wages of the optimally chosen inputs $g = 1, \ldots, G$, and x_z denotes either the quantities of the fixed inputs or outputs $z = 1, \ldots, Z$.

If we apply the following restrictions, the translog cost function is homogeneous of degree one in the prices of inputs:

$$\sum_{g=1}^{G} a_g = 1, \qquad \gamma_{gb} = \gamma_{bg}, \qquad \sum_{g=1}^{G} \gamma_{gb} = \sum_{z=1}^{Z} \phi_{gz} = 0.$$

The conditional factor demands are not linear in the parameters, but the factor shares are linear in parameters. Then logarithmically differentiating the above cost function with respect to wages and then employing Shephard's Lemma, we obtain cost share equations of factor g of the form

$$\frac{\partial \ln C}{\partial \ln w_g} = \frac{w_g}{C} \frac{\partial C}{\partial w_g} = SH_g = \alpha_g + \sum_{b=1}^{I} \gamma_{gb} \ln wb + \sum_{k=1}^{K} \phi_{gz} \ln x_z. \qquad (9.8)$$

This set of linear equations can then be estimated over time and/or across industries to obtain the coefficients γ and ϕ. Given that x_z may denote any shift parameter it can also be used to measure any structural factor pertaining to the international activities of the firm or the industry, like export share, share of imported inputs or an index of multinational activity. Equation (9.8) is the general form of (9.3).

10

Policy Implications and Effects

The theoretical and empirical analyses presented in earlier chapters of this book reveal that FDI affects economies in many ways. Inward investments are often welcomed as they generate employment and may lead to increased demand for domestic intermediates. Such activities by foreign MNEs could also imply transfer of technology to local firms and improved skills to the labour force, and could work as a catalyst for the development of domestic industries, e.g. supplying intermediate products to the MNEs. However, there are also effects that may not be considered positive for the host country. A significant share of the FDI takes the form of mergers or acquisitions, and when a domestic firm is bought by an MNE there are often fears that the foreign owners could act in ways that are not necessarily in accordance with national interests.

Outward FDI could also have positive and negative effects on the home country. The 'export of jobs' argument emphasizes that outward FDI reduces domestic employment, and hence is negative for the home country. On the other hand, it is often claimed that the alternative could be worse, as without such 'outsourcing' the whole activity may close down. The fact that firms are able to fragment their production makes them able to move the parts of the production for which the home country does not have a comparative advantage to other countries, and in this way strengthen the basis for the parts of the production process that remain in the home country.

Whether one effect or the other dominates, it is quite clear that many countries care about the FDI flows, and that they design policy with actual and potential MNE behaviour in mind. The existence of MNEs affects the basis of many economic policies. Tax policies, for example, will have to take into account the international mobility of capital and firms. When assessing trade policies governments should be aware of the fact that a significant share of foreign supply does not appear as trade but rather through foreign subsidiaries. Countries do not only adjust existing, general policies to reflect the fact that MNEs are important, they also apply policies that are more directly aimed at affecting MNEs.

In this chapter we will look at various aspects of policies in relation to MNEs and FDI, structuring the discussion around three questions.

   (i) Does the existence of FDI and MNEs affect the effectiveness and the optimal design of general policies such as tax or trade policy?

  (ii) Should countries design special policies to influence FDI flows?

 (iii) Is there a need for international policy coordination or cooperation to avoid harmful policy competition?

10.1 The Impact of FDI on Economic Policy

The fact that MNEs have production activities in many countries, together with the potential mobility of their production between countries, influences the effectiveness and the optimal design of various types of economic policy. For example, the effectiveness of tax policy is reduced if multinationals are able to transfer price, shifting profits between countries. The consequent impression that multinationals cannot be held to account by national governments is a major source of resentment. Policy may also create incentives for multinationals to relocate their activities. This shapes the design of tax policy, and may also have a bearing on many other policy areas, including trade policy, labour market policy, competition policy and policy towards the protection of intellectual and other property rights.

    This section will look at two of these areas in some detail. The first is tax policy, and the second trade policy.

10.1.1 Tax Policies

There are a number of important questions in relation to taxation with capital mobility and multinationals. We will focus on three key issues in this section: the choice of tax principle, problems related to transfer pricing, and the question of special tax treatment of MNEs, including the effects of corporate taxes on the location of MNEs.

Principles of capital taxation

When the tax base becomes mobile, several problems arise. Should factors of production with different degrees of mobility be taxed differently? In which country should income be taxed? How should taxes paid in other countries be treated? Does the choice of tax system matter for the location and size of the tax base?

    The general theory of optimal taxation says that there should be an inverse relationship between tax rates and the elasticity of supply of the tax base, as this would minimize the distortions caused by the taxes. Hence, for efficiency reasons factors in inelastic supply should be taxed more heavily than factors for which the supply is more sensitive to price changes. In the international context, the rule would imply that the tax burden should be shifted towards the more immobile factors. As capital is often regarded as the most mobile factor, this suggests a shift of taxes away from capital and towards labour, land and other relatively immobile factors. In the remainder of this section, we critically evaluate this argument, looking at both the theory and the evidence.

A fundamental issue is the long-standing debate on the relative merits of source- or residence-based taxation (see Haufler (2001) for a thorough review). Under the source-based system, firms' profits are taxed by the country in which the investment is made. Under the residence principle, taxes are levied on the ultimate recipients of profits, i.e. where the capital owner lives.

The residence-based principle has a number of advantages over the source based. To investigate this let r_i and t_i be pre-tax return and the tax rate in country i, and let us focus on two countries, home (h) and foreign (f). Under the residence principle a resident in the home country receives post-tax return $r_f(1 - t_h)$ from a foreign investment and $r_h(1 - t_h)$ from a domestic investment. It is immediately apparent that variations in tax rates (given pre-tax returns) do not distort the choice of where the investment is made—the same tax rate is paid, providing the residence of the income recipient does not change. An increase in tax rates at home might be distortionary insofar as it encourages emigration of income recipients or discourages saving. But from the perspective of returns to a multinational of locating investments in different countries, the residence-based system is neutral. Notice also that, if there is perfect capital mobility, then a residence-based system achieves world efficiency in the allocation of capital. Capital flows will respond to pre-tax returns, r_i, and portfolio equilibrium will be attained when these have been equalized in all countries, $r_f = r_h$. The marginal product of capital is therefore the same in all countries, so there is no efficiency gain from further reallocations of capital around the world.

In contrast, the source-based principle gives a resident in each country post-tax return $r_f(1 - t_f)$ from an investment in foreign and $r_h(1 - t_h)$ from an investment in home. Evidently, tax rates do now distort the investment decisions of the resident of a particular country. Thus, an increase in t_h will cause investment to be diverted from home to foreign. If there is perfect capital mobility, then, in the long run portfolio equilibrium, it will be the case that $r_f(1 - t_f) = r_h(1 - t_h)$, implying that, if $t_h > t_f$, then $r_h > r_f$. Capital outflow will continue until the home marginal product of capital rises to a level correspondingly greater than that in foreign.

Faced with these potential capital flows, how will governments set tax rates under the source-based principle? If the home economy is small relative to the foreign and there is perfect capital mobility, then optimum capital taxation is zero. The intuition is that the supply price of capital to the home economy is $r_f(1 - t_f)$, the post-tax return on any investment in foreign; by offering a net return at or above this level, the economy can secure capital inflows, and below it will have outflow. Productive efficiency requires that the marginal product of capital at home be equated with this supply price, so $r_h = r_f(1 - t_f)$. Combining this with the portfolio equilibrium condition, $r_f(1 - t_f) = r_h(1 - t_h)$ establishes that $t_h = 0$. This result is modified if the country in question is a large one, or if the capital mobility is not perfect. A large country can influence the world market rate of return to capital. Hence, there may be a terms-of-trade effect of capital taxation: by taxing capital imports it can force down the price it has to pay for capital. If capital mobility is not perfect, there may be some room for national differences in rates of return, although the distortionary effects of capital taxation on the location of investments will remain, except in the limiting case where there is no capital mobility. Application of the source-based principle therefore suggests that, as capital becomes increasingly mobile, so there will be downwards pressure on rates at which capital is taxed.

Despite the theoretical advantages of residence-based taxation, in practice most countries use some kind of source principle. This is primarily because there are a number of practical problems related to applying the residence principle. Bilateral tax treaties[1]—focusing on the danger of double taxation—normally give the host country a right to tax incomes that originate within its territory, while the home country has two options: it can either exempt foreign-earned income from domestic taxation, or it can grant a tax credit for foreign-paid taxes. The former implies that capital income is taxed according to the source principle. The latter implies a residence principle, provided that a full tax credit is granted (including a tax refund, if foreign taxes exceed the domestic tax rate). However, a system with tax credits gives the host country strong incentives to increase the tax rates, while the residence country may end up with no net revenue from taxing capital. This follows directly from the fact that the host country knows that any tax burden it puts on the firm will be refunded, fully or partly, by the home country of the capital owner. Hence, high tax rates need not have negative effects on the firm's decisions. If the countries behave non-cooperatively, there are several possible outcomes, depending on the exact situation: there may be no non-cooperative Nash solution, or equilibria with either no capital trade or zero tax rate for capital (see Haufler (2001) for details).

Furthermore, there are problems of enforcement. How do tax authorities get information about income abroad? When should the foreign income be taxed—when it is earned, or when it is repatriated? We will not address any such problems. The idea here is simply to illustrate that increased international mobility—be it of capital, firms or maybe people—creates new challenges for the tax system.

Empirically, there seems to be some common trends in the tax reforms in many countries over the last 10–15 years (see Haufler 2001): (i) most of the reforms are of the tax-rate-cut-cum-base-broadening type; (ii) tax rates for capital income have been reduced below those for labour income; and (iii) there has been an international convergence of effective marginal tax rates for capital. All of these elements may

---

[1] Bilateral tax treaties are usually based on the recommendation of the OECD model double taxation convention (OECD 1977).

be seen as a reflection of the increased mobility of capital, even if the reforms have not changed the system from source- to residence-based taxation.

Taxation of MNEs

The discussion up to this point has been concerned with an abstract concept of mobile capital. How does this relate to taxation of MNEs? MNEs are in general affected by the tax systems of both home and host countries, and also by tax treaties that may exist between the countries. Various aspects of the tax system matter for the location decision as well as in determining the scale of activities in a location. Although tax systems are often quite complex and with detailed rules that may be of great importance for the individual firm, in general terms two key features are of particular relevance: the tax rate and the tax base. The tax rate determines how hard taxable income is taxed, while the tax base—which is a function of allowances, deductions, valuations of assets, and so on—determines what the taxable income is.

As mentioned above, there have been significant tax reforms in many advanced countries over the last two decades. Most of these reforms seem to share the same overall features: lowering the tax rates, and broadening the tax base. Devereux et al. (2002a) study tax reforms in 18 industrialized countries over the period 1982–2001, and show that statutory corporate income tax rates have gone down in all but three countries over the period.[2] The weighted average tax rate has been reduced from approximately 50% to around 35% for these countries. Devereux et al. (2002a) further find that the present discounted value of allowances decreased over the same period for most of the countries in their study, indicating a broadening of the tax base.

While a lower tax rate is an advantage for firms, a broader tax base tends to work in the opposite direction. So what is the net effect for firms? A summary measure often used to show the combined effects for firms' incentives of changes in tax rates and allowances is the *effective tax rate*. The effective tax is like a 'flat tax rate' equivalent of a more complex system. The effective *marginal* tax rate (EMTR) captures the investment incentives for a marginal project, while the effective *average* tax rate (EATR) gives a similar measure for average income of a plant or a firm. Devereux et al. (2002a) study the development of EMTR and EATR over the 20-year period, and conclude that while the weighted average of EMTR has remained fairly stable (but with significant country variation), the EATR has gone down in all but two countries. Furthermore, EATR has typically fallen more for highly profitable projects.

How does the corporate tax system affect MNEs? Devereux et al. (2002a,b) emphasize that it is important to distinguish between the effects of EMTR and EATR

---

[2]Tax rates increased slightly in Italy and Spain, and were unchanged in Ireland. Ireland, however, had the lowest tax rate of all countries both in 1982 and in 2001, following a very significant corporate tax reduction in 1981.

when it comes to international mobility. EMTR plays a key role in determining the net marginal return to capital; hence, if we look at capital as a continuous variable, where the optimum level is determined from a 'marginal return equal to marginal cost' condition, EMTR is the relevant tax rate. In the section on capital taxation above, t_i would typically be the effective marginal tax rate of country i. If, on the other hand, we look at the location decisions of MNEs, these are normally discrete choices; it is about where to locate an entire plant or project if you have a number of potential locations to choose between. In such a case, it is not the marginal but the average return that matters. Then it also follows that the relevant tax measure is the EATR, not the EMTR. The MNE wants to know how the tax system of country i affects the overall profitability of locating the project in the country, and that is exactly what EATR intends to measure.

Hence, for the location decision of an MNE, EATR is what matters. When deciding on the level of investment or activity in a given location, on the other hand, EMTR is important as well. So how have the changes in tax systems over the last 20 years affected multinationals? Devereux et al. (2002a) observe that the fact that the EATR has been falling—and more so the higher the profitability of the projects—may be related to the presence of MNEs. If countries want to attract highly profitable, mobile firms, the observed changes in the tax system may be one way of doing so. And if profitable firms have become more mobile over the last 20 years, that may help explain the changes in the tax systems in many countries.

The key question in taxation of MNEs is the extent to which multinational behaviour, in particular, their location decisions, is actually affected by tax policy. As we saw in Chapter 6 many factors are important in influencing MNEs' choices. Tax is one of these, although so too are factors that are driven by government expenditures, for example, infrastructure and education. There is therefore a trade-off between taxes and the public services that the firms feel they get in different locations, and the overall efficiency of the government may matter more than just the tax levels.

Whether taxes actually matter for the choice of location of MNEs is basically an empirical question. There is a large literature that tries to address these questions.[3] Although earlier works like Brainard (1997) and Wheeler and Mody (1992) find that tax differentials had a negligible effect on FDI flows, the broad consensus emerging from several more recent studies is that taxes matter for the choice of location. Hines (1999), in his survey of empirical studies, concludes that the 'econometric work of the last 15 years provides ample evidence of the sensitivity of the level and location of FDI to tax treatments.' The conclusion follows from both time-series and cross-section studies, and from a wide range of model specifications. However, due

---

[3] See Section 6.6 for a review of some of these contributions.

to data availability, almost all of the evidence is based on US data, either outflows from the US to various countries or inflows to the US or states in the US from different countries. For outflows, the key questions analysed are whether and to what extent differences in host country tax rates affect the location and level of US FDI. For inflows both variation in corporate taxes at the state level in the US and differences in the home country's treatment of taxes paid abroad (tax credits versus tax exemption) are potential determinants of FDI. Investments from countries that grant tax credits for foreign taxes should be less sensitive to variation in foreign taxes than investments from countries with a tax exemption system. According to Hines (1999) the overall evidence of the influence of taxes on FDI is convincing, and he even states that an elasticity of FDI with respect to taxes of -0.6 is a typical result of much of the literature. There is, however, need for more research to establish how various tax regimes affect the form of FDI (greenfield, M&A, joint ventures, etc.) and how the tax sensitivity of FDI influences the formation of domestic tax policies.

Devereux and Griffith (2002), in their summary of empirical studies, reach a more cautious conclusion. Although taxes matter for location decisions, they claim that there is little consensus on how strong the tax effects are. This is in particular so because different studies differ substantially in their approach and methodology. While a few studies focus on the discrete choice of location, and emphasize that the effective average tax rate (EATR) is the relevant tax parameter for this choice, other studies use data on marginal tax rates, either to analyse the investment levels of existing foreign operations, or to lump together the location choice and the decision on activity levels.

Devereux and Griffith (1998) is one of the papers that does look at the locational choice as such. In their analysis of the choice of location for US firms between the UK, France and Germany—conditional on having chosen to locate in Europe— they conclude that there is strong evidence that the effective average tax rates play a significant role. The effects are country specific, but as an example they estimate that a one percentage point fall in the UK EATR would increase the probability of a US firm choosing to locate in the UK by around 1%.

The location of an MNE's research and development (R&D) activities may be of particular interest, as such activities may have the most important externalities. A few studies look at the mobility of R&D units, and the impact of tax treatment on the location of R&D. Bloom and Griffith (2001) conclude that R&D is footloose and moves easily in response to cross-country changes in tax treatments. Hines (1999) also finds that taxes are important for the location of R&D activities.

The effects of the tax rates on the location of MNEs cannot be studied in isolation, as the decisive factor is often the tax treatment in one location relative to the tax levels and regimes of other potential locations. To the extent that the location of production of MNEs is sensitive to relative tax rates, countries may find it tempting to try to attract MNEs by cutting taxes. If all countries do so, then there is a 'race to the bottom', with low corporate tax rates in all countries. The question of international interactions of tax policies will be discussed in Section 10.3.

Tax havens

A special case often mentioned in relation to multinationals is the role of tax havens. A tax haven would be a country with no or only nominal taxes for foreign investments. These are normally very small countries, and the idea must be to attract foreign activities through a very generous tax system. The countries often have little else to offer, except for the tax rules. For firms the attraction of tax havens is, of course, the chance of lowering the overall tax burden. To achieve tax reductions of any importance, however, the tax haven must be the source of a significant share of the firms' income. In addition, the firms must be sure that the income is not taxed elsewhere as well. Unless the firms are willing to move a large share of their activities to such countries, this involves transferring income from elsewhere in the company to the subsidiary in the tax haven. The unit in the tax haven could be the headquarters, an R&D activity, or simply a financial activity; and the transfer of income could be more or less legal.

A key question is whether such tax havens are harmful, in the sense that they distort capital flows and undermine other countries' abilities to tax capital. OECD, in its ongoing project identifying harmful tax practices (see, for example, OECD 2001c), says that four conditions should be met for a tax haven to be harmful: there should be no or very low taxes, a lack of exchange of information, lack of transparency, and no substantial activities in the country. These conditions clearly show that, for tax havens to be harmful, the activities should involve tax evasion or tax avoidance. Thus they probably do not concern standard practices of MNEs.

Transfer pricing

Transfer pricing constitutes a specific tax problem linked to multinationals. Transfer pricing is about the fact that MNEs are able, through the prices they set on internal transactions, to move earnings between subsidiaries. To the extent that income is taxed differently in different countries, the MNEs can thus affect their overall tax burden by moving their income between countries. There is ample evidence that such transfer pricing actually takes place.

There are several ways of dealing with the problems of transfer pricing, but none of them are perfect. We will only mention some of the most common solutions, without going into details.

One obvious solution to the transfer-pricing problem is to try to get rid of transfer pricing. One could, for example, require that transactions within an MNE should take place at market prices—so-called arm's-length transactions (this would be in accordance with OECD guidelines (see OECD 1997)). For transactions where relevant market prices exist, this is a viable solution. However, there are at least two major problems. One is that for quite a lot of transactions comparable market prices are not available. And, secondly, it would be very difficult to monitor all transactions and ensure that such a rule is followed. The MNEs would have strong incentives to make any transaction look like a very special one, without a relevant market price to apply. Alternative solutions imply various ways of calculating what the 'correct' price of the transfer should be, in cases where there are no comparable market prices. However, similar problems arise for such methods.

A second solution to the transfer-price problem is to change the tax system to reduce the effects of transfer pricing, e.g. by taking into account all profits made by an MNE, irrespective of where the profit is reported. One possible scheme is what is called formula apportionment, where the tax base is the global profits made by the MNE, and where the split of the tax base between different jurisdictions follows some kind of predetermined rule. As an example, employment or activity shares in different countries could form the basis for splitting the overall profits into tax bases in each country. With such a system, the firms would only have limited opportunities to manipulate their tax burden, since moving income around would not help. They could still influence the taxes by moving real activities between countries, but that would be a more expensive type of adjustment, and it is less likely to be done for tax reasons only.[4]

There is a huge literature, both theoretical and empirical, on transfer pricing. (For a recent survey see Gresik (2001). Hines (1999) reviews the empirical evidence.) We need not go into that here; our purpose is simply to illustrate that multinationals and the globalization of economic activities constitute new challenges for tax policies. There may be a need for new and better monitoring systems, or there may be a need for revising the tax systems, and maybe introducing supranational measures for taxation of such enterprises.[5]

10.1.2 Trade Policies

Trade policies play an important role as a determinant of FDI, as discussed in Chapter 6. In the case of horizontal FDI (HFDI) one would expect the FDI flows to increase with trade barriers, while with vertical FDI (VFDI) trade liberalization

---

[4]See, for example, Nielsen et al. (2004) for a discussion of formula apportionment as a way of dealing with transfer pricing. They emphasize that transfer pricing could be used for both tax and strategic reasons. While formula apportionment reduces the use of transfer pricing for tax purposes, there may still be strategic reasons for firms to use transfer prices to affect the competitive position in various markets.

[5]Haufler and Schjelderup (2000) analyse the optimal taxation in the presence of FDI and transfer pricing, and find that such phenomena could be one of the motivations for the recent 'tax-rate-cut-cum-base-broadening' reforms of corporate taxation in most OECD countries.

would normally lead to more FDI. In either case, trade policies matter for FDI. However, FDI also matters for trade policies. Both the incentives for using trade policies and the effects of such policies are affected by FDI.

Trade policies are normally used to secure domestic rents or employment. In some cases trade policies may improve national welfare (optimal tariffs), but more often it helps some domestic interest groups at the expense of other domestic groups. In the latter case, the actual policy choices follow from a political-economy process where those who gain from protection have strong political impact. FDI may alter both the effects of protection and the political-economy process. We will not go through all possible cases here, only mention some examples (for a more thorough discussion see Barba Navaretti et al. (2001)).

The presence of multinationals means that some of the domestically earned rents will not necessarily end up in 'national pockets', simply because foreigners own part of the production facilities. And unless the government wants to help the foreign firms, this may reduce the motives for protection. Furthermore, the mobility of firms may affect the actual rents generated by protection. If, for example, the purpose of protection is to increase market shares and shift profits to domestic firms in an imperfectly competitive market, then mobility may change the outcome. As a consequence of protection foreign firms may well choose FDI and local production rather than trade, and if that happens domestic firms experience tougher competition rather than protection.[6] This is as we saw in the Chapter 3 analysis of the effects of HFDI. Entry of foreign firms may crowd out local producers, so tariffs may lead to inward FDI displacing both imports and some production by local firms.

Outward FDI may also have an impact on the choice of trade policies. If outward FDI and production facilities in other countries generate imports to the home country, trade barriers could hurt one's own multinationals, and that may not be the intention. This is seen most clearly in the context of VFDI and production networking. As we saw in Chapter 4, this fragmentation of production and location of different parts of the production process in different countries occurs to take advantage of local cost conditions or local expertise. The profitability of fragmentation requires that relative factor prices differ significantly between regions, and that trade, transaction and monitoring costs of shipping parts and components between locations are not too high. Trade policies play an important role here. With high trade barriers, international fragmentation would simply not be profitable, while low trade costs and stable trade relations, on the other hand, typically encourage networking, in particular, if these conditions apply between countries with significant differences in factor prices.

---

[6]Haaland and Wooton (1998) give an example of how protection through anti-dumping measures may actually lead to tougher domestic competition due to inward FDI.

The reduction in trade costs and the improvement in trade conditions that we have seen over the 1990s, may thus help explain the growth in VFDI over the same period. In Chapter 6 it was indicated that while HFDI seems to dominate in much of the empirical research based on data from 1980s and early 1990s, there is reason to believe that the relative (and absolute) importance of VFDI has increased since the mid 1990s. This could at least in part be explained by the development in trade policies, with a trend toward freer trade and more open markets.

A very good example of how changes in trade and market conditions may give new opportunities for production networking is the development between Central and Eastern European countries (CEECs) and the EU. With geographical proximity and very significant differences in relative factor prices, the relationship between CEECs and the EU should be ideal for production fragmentation and networking. While high trade costs and lack of a long-term commitment to stable market conditions in CEECs previously prevented such VFDI, the development towards market economies with a strong commitment to market integration with the EU opens up new opportunities. And there are also clear indications that such networking has indeed grown over the 1990s. Kaminski and Ng (2001), for example, show that the importance of what they label 'production fragmentation exports' (exports of parts and components) from CEECs to the EU increased significantly for most countries between 1993 and 1998; for several countries the share of such trade more than doubled. They also note, however, that there are clear differences between CEECs; the first-tier accession countries show stronger growth in production networking trade than other CEECs. This tells us that close market integration and long-term commitments may be important for production networks, and thus for VFDI.

A further case where trade costs matter is what is sometimes called export-platform FDI. With regional free-trade areas, external producers may choose to set up production facilities in one inside country to service the whole of the free-trade area. Export-platform FDI could be vertical or horizontal, perhaps depending on rules of origin, relative trade costs, etc. For such a solution to be profitable, a combination of high external trade costs and low internal costs, are necessary. American firms producing in Ireland for the entire EU market is one example of such export-platform FDI.

From this brief discussion it should be clear that trade policies matter for FDI, and that the existence and the cost of FDI matter for the formulation of trade barriers. Trade liberalization between fairly different countries would in particular improve the conditions for VFDI.

10.2 FDI Incentives

The fact that so many countries design specific policies towards FDI is an indication of the perceived importance of such investments. Over time there has been a shift in policy stance in many countries, from barriers towards FDI to more liberal policies or even direct incentives to attract FDI. UNCTAD (2001) reports a significant number of explicit changes in policies towards FDI in recent years, and almost all of these are shifts towards more liberal regimes. UNCTAD (2001) also discusses the very strong growth in the number of bilateral investment treaties (BITs); over the 1990s the number of BITs worldwide increased from around 400 to almost 1950, reaching 2100 by the end of 2001. This is a clear indication of the importance that both host and home countries attach to FDI.

Direct incentives to attract FDI comprise several different policy measures (see Section 10.2.3); hence, it is almost impossible to collect a comprehensive database that could tell how important such incentives are in various countries or regions, or how they have developed over time. Country studies, however, including that of Ireland reported in Chapter 8, indicate that incentive schemes are quite significant in many cases, and that the magnitude and importance of these may have increased over time. In UNCTAD (1996) an attempt is made to give a more complete picture of the range and importance of FDI incentives. The report shows that financial incentives were offered in 59 of the 83 countries reviewed. Some of these are very significant; to give only a few examples, government financial incentives for a car plant in Portugal amounted to more than 250 000 dollars per employee in the early 1990s, Alabama offered more than 160 000 dollars per employee for a Mercedes-Benz plant, and Newcastle-upon-Tyne subsidized a Siemens plant with approximately 50 000 dollars per employee in the mid 1990s. UNCTAD (1996) also reports an increase in the use of fiscal incentives from the 1980s to the 1990s, and in 59 of 67 countries for which data were available, other incentives, like subsidized infrastructure and services, and technical support, were in use. Hence, both anecdotal and more-comprehensive evidence reveal that financial and other incentives are used in very many countries to attract FDI; some of these are of a very significant magnitude, and there is a clear indication that the importance of such schemes have increased over time.

Previous chapters of the book have discussed the host country effects—positive and negative—in theory and in practice. The question we address in this section is whether the existence of such effects is a reason for special policies designed to attract foreign investments. Should countries offer subsidies or other incentives to foreign firms to encourage inward FDI? Do the policies we actually observe enhance national welfare in the host country, or should we look for other reasons for such policies?

Hanson (2001) discusses the key question of whether countries should promote FDI. Theoretically, this is a question of identifying market failures and assessing whether policies could in principle be a remedy to these market failures. Empirically, it is necessary to check both if there is a basis for active policies and if the policies in question work. How important are market failures such as externalities? And how do host country policies actually affect the locational choice of the foreign firms?

It is important to notice that policies should be related to a market failure. Potential benefits of FDI are not sufficient reasons to warrant active policies. With well-functioning markets all benefits would be realized through the market equilibrium, and there would be no added net gains from active policies to attract or promote FDI. This is, of course, nothing but the general insight from economics; policies have a role to play to correct for market failure, but in the absence of such market failures the market provides us with the welfare-maximizing equilibrium. In this respect there is no difference between FDI policies and other policies like, for example, industrial policies or investment policies.

Without market failures, policies could, of course, still have an impact on the equilibrium; both the locations of MNEs and the activity level will typically be affected by host (and home) country policies. And when activities are affected, so are income levels and income distribution. Hence, it is not difficult to understand that policies may be asked for even in the absence of market failures; the difference is only that such policies cannot be defended on welfare grounds. There must be other reasons, typically best understood in a political-economy framework.

When analysing policies towards inward FDI it is thus useful to distinguish between two categories: welfare-improving policies, and other, political-economy based, policies. The first category includes cases where various market failures imply that policies may have a role to play to achieve optimum solutions. Externalities (positive or negative) are typical examples, as policies may be called for both to achieve efficiency and to overcome coordination problems in the market. But policies could also be welfare improving if, for example, there are unemployed resources in the economy. In such cases, FDI policies would hardly be the first-best policies, but they could be second best.

The second category includes all policies stemming from the effects of FDI on special interest groups. In some cases domestic groups may feel threatened by inward FDI—for example, if such FDI implies tougher competition for domestic firms, or maybe foreign control over important activities or resources—while in other cases domestic interests may benefit significantly from FDI. In either case, if those who are affected have strong political impact, policies may be introduced even if they do not increase overall welfare. Both barriers towards FDI and incentive schemes may appear as a consequence of such a political-economy process.

10.2.1 Welfare-Improving Policies

In this section we will briefly sketch how policies may have a role to play in cases where there are potential overall welfare gains from inward FDI, but where market failures prevent the gains from being realized. We do not intend to give a complete catalogue of cases in which policies may be warranted, but rather show some examples.

Most studies emphasize spillovers and externalities both as important sources of overall gains from FDI and as a potential reason for special policies to attract such investments (see, for example, Hanson 2001; Devereux and Griffith 2002). With positive externalities from inward FDI to the domestic economy—be it direct spillovers or pecuniary externalities—there are typically potential overall gains for the host economy, and since not all of the gains accrue to the foreign firm, policies may be called for to ensure that the benefits are realized.

However, even if positive externalities can justify active policies to attract FDI, a number of caveats need to be mentioned. First of all, the question of externalities and spillovers is an empirical one: how important are such effects? The evidence seems to be fairly mixed, as discussed in Chapter 7 (see also Hanson 2001; Devereux and Griffith 2002). The importance of externalities varies between industries; in addition, host market conditions seem to matter for the effects. Secondly, even if externalities exist, it is not necessarily easy to identify the right firms or industries for support. And, as we shall see below, if industries without such externalities are subsidized, the overall effect for the host economy would be to reduce welfare. Thirdly, although it is not difficult in theory to specify cases where a subsidy may help, the empirical studies indicate that a broader range of host country policies and conditions—like education, general investment conditions, the legal system and so on—may be more important than specific support in ensuring attractiveness for and benefits from foreign FDI. Finally, once specific policies to attract FDI are considered, the question of policy competition between countries arises. Policy competition will be discussed in Section 10.3 below.

With all these qualifications in mind, let us take a brief look at why policies to attract FDI in certain cases may play a role in ensuring positive welfare effects for the host country. Building on Markusen and Venables (1999) and Haaland and Wooton (1999), let us think of an economy with a modern and a traditional sector. The traditional sector produces homogeneous goods using labour as input and with decreasing returns to labour (maybe because of a specific factor in the sector). The modern sector could be modelled in many different ways; however, the common feature would be that the sector reveals pecuniary externalities, with several firms or subsectors linked together through an input–output structure, and with increasing returns to scale and imperfect competition in at least some of the subsectors. In such a setting, the size of the modern sector matters for the overall productivity and profitability of the sector. A small sector may have too low productivity to survive; it may lose in the competition for domestic inputs, or it may lose when facing international competition in output markets. In either case, a small sector may disappear entirely. Once the sector reaches a certain size—a critical mass—it becomes productive enough to be competitive both in domestic factor markets and in foreign output markets. And with external economies of scale, the process may be self-reinforcing; so, when critical mass is achieved, the sector continues to grow.

Where does FDI fit into this picture? FDI typically takes place in the modern sector, and as soon as the size of the sector matters, such investments may contribute to a process that improves overall productivity and competitiveness. Markusen and Venables (1999) study several different cases where there are backward and forward linkages between firms in upstream and downstream industries, and where FDI could take place in the upstream or downstream industry. They focus on the productivity and competition effects for local firms interacting with foreign-owned plants, and show how FDI in certain cases can work as a 'catalyst' for the development of domestic industry. Haaland and Wooton (1999) focus on one particular case, where FDI is in the final-goods sector, and with the productivity of domestic intermediate-goods producers being positively affected by the size of the downstream, final-goods sector. In this particular model, as well as in several of the cases studied in Markusen and Venables (1999), the number of and the activity level in foreign-owned plants matter for the overall productivity and profitability of the modern sector. And in such a setting, policies to attract FDI may have a role to play.

A simple diagram can illustrate the main points (Figure 10.1). Assume for simplicity that labour is the only variable input, and let L^0 be labour demand from the traditional sector. L^0 exhibits decreasing returns to scale. L^M is labour demand in the modern sector; due to external economies of scale based on one or more of the mechanisms mentioned above, the marginal product of labour in the modern sector is increasing with the activity level in the sector. It should be emphasized that since the economies of scale are external to the firm, each firm would experience a normal, downward-sloping labour demand schedule. However, the more firms there are in the modern sector, the higher this demand curve for each firm will be. Hence, any one firm could not on its own capture the benefits of economies of scale by increasing its activity level; it is only through the interaction of firms that the positive scale effects appear.

To be specific, assume that there are n (identical) firms in the modern sector, each producing x units of output, using l units of labour. The productivity of labour, $a(l, n)$, depends on the firm's own activity level as well as on the number of firms in the industry, so each firm's total output is

$$x = la(l, n) \quad \text{with} \quad \frac{\partial a(l, n)}{\partial n} > 0.$$

The relationship between the firm's productivity and its own employment level may take many forms. Productivity may be independent of l, or it may, for example, be hump-shaped, in which case $\partial a / \partial l$ is positive for low levels of l, and negative for higher levels. In any case, however, an increase in the number of firms gives an

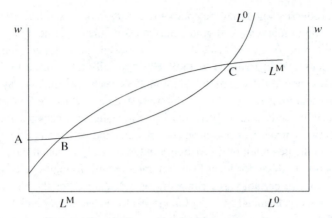

Figure 10.1. Multiple equilibria.

upward shift in the marginal product in all firms, due to the external economies of scale. If the aggregate production and employment in the modern sector are labelled X^M and L^M, respectively, we have

$$X^M = nx = nla(l, n) = a(l, n)L^M.$$

Hence, when the industry expands through an increase in the number of firms, n, the average productivity of labour goes up. In terms of the aggregate demand for labour from this industry, this implies that the higher the employment is, the more the industry is willing and able to pay for the workers. As the marginal product of labour exceeds the average product, however, the industry's demand of labour will be given by the value of the average product of labour, rather than the value of the marginal product.[7] Thus, in Figure 10.1, the L^M curve is given by $p^M(X^M/L^M) = p^M a(l, n)$. For the traditional sector, on the other hand, the labour demand curve, L^0, measured from the right-hand side of the diagram, is given by the value of the marginal product of labour in that sector; i.e. $p^0 \partial X^0 / \partial L^0$. The size of the box is equal to the total labour supply; hence when the two curves intersect we have full employment, i.e. $L^0 + L^M = \bar{L}$.

Figure 10.1 shows possible labour market equilibria in this economy. There are actually three possible equilibrium outcomes in this model. In A all resources are used in the traditional sector. This is a stable equilibrium; in the sense that attempts to start activities in the modern sector would fail. The sector would be too small and with too low labour productivity to be able to compete for the labour force. This is true as long as we are to the left of B, the point where the modern sector is big enough to offer a wage rate that can match the traditional sector. B is an equilibrium; but an

---

[7] If the firm were to pay a wage equal to the value of the marginal product, this would be higher than the value of the average product; thus it would incur a loss.

unstable one, since any small change in the activity level would lead the economy to move away from B. A small reduction in the modern sector would start a process in which the sector may disappear. A small increase in the modern sector beyond B would make it attractive for more labour to move from the traditional to the modern sector, and this process will go on until the economy reaches point C. C is a stable equilibrium in this model.

Hence, we have a situation with multiple equilibria, and with a clear welfare ranking of the equilibria from the host country's point of view. C is obviously better than A (or B) as the wage rate is higher, and the increase is only partly offset by the reduced return to specific factors in the traditional sector. However, the market outcome may not give C as the result. If the economy starts out with a small modern sector, A is a more likely equilibrium. Individual firms or investors would have no incentive to invest in the modern sector if the economy is close to A; yet as soon as a sufficient number of firms actually enter, other firms would have incentives to follow. To move the economy from A to C requires coordination of the decisions of a sufficient number of investors, and policies may have a role to play to initiate this process. If FDI is potentially important in the modern sector, one way of moving the equilibrium away from A would be to encourage more foreign firms to establish production in the country. Once a sufficient number of firms have established plants, the rest would be an automatic process. Both domestic and foreign firms would experience growth in labour productivity and they would demand more labour, until C is reached.

In this setting, policies may matter. A subsidy to one or several foreign multinationals could convince them that they should invest in the modern sector in this country, and if sufficiently many do that, the economy moves from equilibrium A to C, with clear welfare gains over and above the cost of the subsidy.

Figure 10.2 illustrates the effects of a subsidy to the modern sector. The direct effect is to increase the marginal and average value of employment for firms in the modern sector; hence, for any level of L^M, firms are willing to pay a higher wage due to the subsidy. This gives existing firms incentives to increase productions and new firms incentives to start up; with positive externalities, increased activity levels may induce more firms to enter the sector, and we get a cumulative process. Depending on the initial equilibrium, such subsidies could have quite different effects on the economy.

If the economy starts out from an equilibrium like C, with a significant modern sector, the subsidy would shift the equilibrium to C', implying that the modern sector increases even further. Is this good or bad for the economy as a whole? Apparently, the sector becomes 'too big', since the marginal value of labour in the traditional sector exceeds the wage rate that the modern sector would be willing to offer net of subsidies. However, as mentioned above, with economies of scale, L^M does not

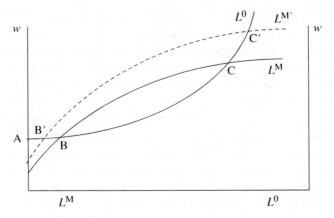

Figure 10.2. Modern sector subsidy.

reflect the marginal value of labour in the modern sector. The wage rate offered by
the increasing-returns sector is determined by the average return to labour in that
sector, which is lower than the marginal return due to the economies of scale. Hence,
we know that the marginal value of labour in the modern sector is higher than the
L^M curve, implying that the optimal scale of production is higher than C. For this
reason, a small subsidy can be welfare improving, even in an economy that starts
out with a significant modern sector. (See Norman and Venables (2004) and Orvedal
(2002) for a discussion of this question.)

   If the economy starts out with a very small or non-existing modern sector—close
to point A in the model—the effects of the subsidy could be very different. In such a
case, the subsidy could induce some firms to enter the modern sector in this country,
and once a sufficient number of firms have entered, the cumulative process will
move the economy to the new, stable equilibrium C'. In terms of welfare, we know
that C is better than A for the economy; and that the optimum scale is larger than the
production in C. C' may be higher or lower than the optimum scale, depending on
the size of the subsidy. However, there must obviously be cases in which national
welfare is higher in C' than in A. In such cases, the welfare gain appears because
the subsidy leads to a shift from one possible equilibrium to another. The subsidy
acts as a coordination device for the firms in the sector, or as a 'catalyst' to start off
the cumulative process.

   Hence, to sum up, subsidies may have two roles to play in a sector characterized
by external scale economy—to help overcome two types of market failures in such
an economy. First, due to economies of scale marginal revenue exceeds the average
revenue, and policies may be needed to achieve the optimum scale of production.
Secondly, externalities imply that there is a coordination problem in such a market,

and policies may act as a coordination device. Depending on the initial situation, one or both of these effects may be relevant.

The analysis in Figure 10.2 could apply to any subsidies to the modern sector; it is not explicitly about FDI incentives. However, as mentioned above, inward FDI often plays an important role in the initial phase of a modern sector; hence, applying this to FDI policies seems particularly relevant. If the FDI subsidies induce some foreign firms to establish production, linkages effects to domestic upstream firms as well as to other foreign firms could start off a cumulative process as described above. UNCTAD (2001) emphasizes in particular such linkages effects of inward FDI.

This is one example of a setting where direct policies to attract foreign investments may be called for. There are clearly many other examples. Fumagalli (2003) focuses on direct productivity spillovers from FDI to domestic firms, and shows how countries with a low initial level of productivity may have a lot to win from attracting FDI, and that such low-productivity countries should typically be willing to offer the highest subsidies to get such investments.

Another important area relates to market failures in the labour market. With labour-market rigidities and unemployment, the effects of inward FDI could be to increase overall employment in the host economy. If the alternative is to remain unemployed, this is clearly a gain for the country. A first-best policy towards such a market failure should obviously be directed towards the labour market. However, as a second-best tool, subsidizing inward FDI could improve national welfare (see, for example, Haaland et al. 2002). Barros and Cabral (2000) show that in such a setting FDI incentives can be welfare improving even in cases where there is policy competition between potential host countries.

10.2.2 Policies Based on Political-Economy Processes

Without market failures of the kind discussed above, policies of the type studied in the previous section would not be welfare improving. A simple example is sufficient to illustrate the point. Figure 10.3 shows the effects of subsidies (or other support) in a two-sector economy where the subsidized sector does not exhibit (external) economies of scale (so the labour demand curve L^M is downward sloping). In this case there is a unique, initial, equilibrium in A, and the effects of the subsidies would be to move this equilibrium to B. It is easy to show that the costs of such a subsidy will have to exceed the benefits in this case, and the efficiency loss for the economy as a whole is given by the triangle ABB$'$ in Figure 10.3. In general terms this follows from the fact the market equilibrium (A) would give an efficient allocation of resources in this economy. Subsidizing one of the sectors (M) then implies that this sector becomes too large.

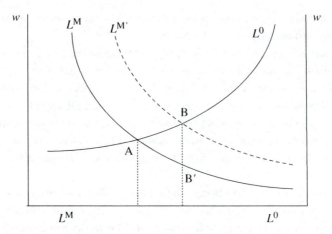

Figure 10.3.   Losses from a subsidy.

However, the fact that the overall welfare effects are negative does not imply that everyone would lose from such policies. In this simple case workers gain from the subsidies, as the general wage rate goes up. In addition, the overall surplus in the modern sector increases, since the increased revenue from the subsidy is only partly offset by higher wages. Hence, firms and factors specifically linked to the modern sector benefit from the policy, while other sectors as well as taxpayers lose. Other sectors (sector 0 in the model) lose because they have to pay more for the workers; taxpayers lose because the subsidy must be financed through increased taxes.

Of course, the political economy of decision taking means that policies may well be chosen even if they do not maximize national welfare. This is not the place to discuss political-economy issues in general but the issue is illustrated by our example. Workers and other factors specifically demanded by the modern sector may have an incentive to use their political influence to lobby for support. This could be support in general, or it could be a campaign to improve the conditions for inward FDI in this sector. And whereas it may be difficult to lobby for direct subsidies to your own sector in many countries, it seems much easier to gain general acceptance for the need to secure good conditions for inward FDI. Such policies may benefit both the foreign investor and the domestic agents in the modern sector, and together they may form a strong political coalition.

10.2.3   Policy Instruments

There is little doubt that incentive schemes are used in many countries and regions. Lots of examples—some of which were referred to at the beginning of Section 10.2— show that countries offer substantial incentives to attract FDI. UNCTAD (1996) classify policy incentives for FDI in three main categories: fiscal incentives, financial incentives and other incentives.

Fiscal incentives include various types of direct or indirect subsidies or tax reliefs. They differ in their base and in how they are implemented. Thus, according to UNCTAD (1996) fiscal incentive schemes could be profit based, capital investment based, labour based, sales based, value added based, import based, export based or based on particular expenditures. They could appear as permanent or temporary tax reductions, investment allowances, tax deductions, exemptions from import duties or export duties, and so on. Financial incentives include a number of measures related to the financing of new foreign investments or operations. The most common financial incentives are government grants (direct subsidies) to cover capital, production or marketing costs; government credits at subsidized rates, government equity participation and government insurance at preferential rates. Other incentives comprise a wide range or measures that could give advantages to foreign firms. Subsidized infrastructure or services, special market preferences or preferential treatment on foreign exchange are examples mentioned in the UNCTAD report.

Hence, there are a number of seemingly quite different policy schemes directed towards attracting FDI. However, even if there is a wide variety in terms of the specific schemes, for the purpose of understanding the motives for and effects of policies, the simple analysis of a subsidy sketched above is sufficient. Any of these incentives would have as a main effect that they would reduce expected costs and increase expected profits for a potential FDI project in the country in question. It could be mainly directed towards the initial start-up costs, or it could be in terms of reducing operating costs. For a potential investment, however, the decisive factor would be how the policies affect the overall expected net present value of the project.

10.2.4 Do Incentive Schemes Work?

Assessing the effectiveness of incentive schemes in practice is a controversial and difficult area, in which different studies have produced quite different conclusions. Based on an overview of several surveys, UNCTAD (1996) concludes that incentives seem to play a minor role relative to other factors—such as market size, production costs, skill levels, political and economic stability and regulatory framework—in MNEs' choice of location. However, the impact of incentives is not negligible; in particular, in the choice between relatively similar countries, incentives may be decisive for the choice of location.

Hanson (2001) looks at the effects of incentives in three case studies—two automobile plants in Brazil and an electronics plant in Costa Rica. For the automobile plants, generous incentive schemes, including both direct subsidies and long-term tax breaks, were offered to attract the plants to different states in Brazil. And the incentives worked, in the sense that they actually influenced the final location. For Intel's production of semiconductors in Costa Rica, on the other hand, general conditions—like political and economic stability, supply of professional and technical operators, ease of imports and exports, and so on—were the decisive factors.

Hanson also tries to assess whether the subsidies were worthwhile from the states' point of view. In his framework, there would be positive effects for the host country if the FDI implies spillovers and linkages to local firms, or benefits to local consumers, whereas there could be negative effects if the FDI crowds out domestic firms from factor or goods markets. In all three case studies, he concludes that there is little evidence of positive effects for the host countries; the firms seems to rely primarily on foreign firms for their intermediates, and thus do not interact very much with local firms. Furthermore, the products are not primarily for the local market, so the local consumers do not benefit. For the Brazilian cases, in particular, Hanson concludes that policy competition between states resulted in substantial extra burdens for taxpayers, without really contributing to state or national welfare. In the case of Costa Rica, the net benefits are also moderate; however, as Costa Rica did not offer much in the way of direct subsidies, the problems were less pronounced there.

In a detailed survey of the case of Intel in Costa Rica, Larrain et al. (2000) come to a different conclusion. They find that Intel's establishment has had significant positive effects on the Costa Rican economy, not only in terms of production and trade, but also through externalities, e.g. through the labour force and the education system. Although Intel's presence has implied increased labour costs for existing firms, the benefits seem to outweigh these additional costs. For the nation, the tax exemption that is given to Intel as a firm in an export processing zone (EPZ) could represent a negative fiscal effect. However, again this study finds that the positive effects dominate. Moran (2001) reviews and discusses a number of cases of FDI in developing countries and economies in transition. He concludes that the benefits of foreign investments dominate in a large majority of the cases reviewed, and furthermore that policies often play a vital role for success. He emphasizes in particular the possible need for policies to overcome the coordination problems in cases with learning-by-doing and external economies of scale. However, Moran also points to the negative effects of policy competition between both developing and developed countries, and the danger of growing protection through local content requirements and anti-dumping measures in many countries. Hence, although policies may be called for to ensure the positive effects of inward FDI, there is clearly a need for international policy coordination (see Section 10.3).

It may seem like a puzzle that apparently similar studies come to different conclusions with regard to the net benefits or costs of FDI projects, as in the case of the two studies of Intel's investments in Costa Rica. However, this may simply illustrate the fact that these are complicated mechanisms. Welfare gains are, for example, to a large extent related to externalities and linkage effects between firms, and it is not obvious how one should measure such effects given the available data. While

Hanson claims that there is fairly moderate interaction between Intel and domestic firms, and hence little reason to expect strong linkages effects, the study by Larrain et al. refers to a survey that indicates significant linkages and externalities. Furthermore, both studies point to the potential crowding out of local firms due to pressure in the local labour market for skilled workers. However, in the latter study this is regarded more as a temporary problem, as the supply of technicians and engineers is increasing as a consequence of Intel's establishment.

UNCTAD (2001) emphasizes very strongly the importance of linkages between foreign and domestic firms to ensure host country benefits. In spite of a large number of examples and case studies, however, the report says that it is difficult to find comprehensive evidence on the degree of (backward) linkages between foreign and domestic firms. The pattern of interaction between firms seems to a large extent to be specific to each industry and country, rather than to show common features. However, policies also matter; many countries have special programmes to promote linkages between foreign firms and domestic industry, and according to UNCTAD (2001) such programmes may be of great importance. In general terms, however, the report identifies some important requirements for successful policies: strong political commitment, clear and coherent lines of goals and responsibility, and effective private–public partnerships.

It is, in short, difficult to find solid evidence of the effects of specific types of policies or incentives. Most studies end up emphasizing the general economic and political environment as the most important prerequisite for beneficial foreign investments. In addition, however, there may be scope for policies more specifically directed towards multinationals—both to attract the investments and to promote the interaction between foreign and domestic firms. Success (or failure) cannot be related to one or a few policy parameters; it is the overall political and economic conditions that matter. Policies are still important, but more in terms of how they contribute to the totality of the 'package' than as individual elements. Ireland is often mentioned as a success story when it comes to benefiting from inward FDI; our discussion of Ireland in Chapter 8 confirms the conclusion that success follows from the combined effect of a wide set of economic and political conditions. It is not possible to point to a simple 'formula' for success.

10.3 Policy Competition and Policy Coordination

There is plenty of evidence of countries using policy to attract FDI. Even if such policies yield benefits for the host country, they may have wider implications, not necessarily beneficial. For example, one country's gain may be another country's loss. Furthermore, if location choices are distorted by incentives, it is quite possible that 'investment diversion' occurs, so that the selected location is not—from the standpoint of world welfare—the most efficient choice. And once countries start competing for FDI, then the non-cooperative game between them may lead to a prisoner's dilemma outcome, in which potential benefits from hosting investment are competed away. In this section we explore these issues, first by looking at policy competition between jurisdictions, and then at the case for regulating such competition.

10.3.1 Policy Competition

If an MNE's choice of location is determined by active policies and incentive schemes rather than by the underlying market conditions in the successful country, then the outcome may be inefficient. And if several countries try to use active policies to attract the same inward FDI, it results in policy competition between countries. In many cases such policy competition may be harmful for the participating countries and for the world as a whole. However, there are also cases in which policy competition could lead to an efficient solution.[8] For example, policy competition to ensure transparency and viable market conditions to foreign investors is certainly welfare enhancing. Rather than discussing policy competition in relation to specific types of policy (taxation, policy reform, subsidies, etc.) in detail, however, we will address the question in more general terms.

A very simple model illustrates some of the effects of policy competition for FDI. Assume that there are N potential host countries for a given FDI project. The profits to the MNE of the project, if located in country i, are Π_i (which could be positive or negative, depending on market conditions and opportunities for the firm). B_i denotes the expected benefit for country i if the project takes place there, and we take B_i as a given value for each country. These benefits could come from agglomeration effects or technology transfers, or, as in the model of policy competition of Barros and Cabral (2000), from employment effects.

In the absence of policy, the project clearly goes to the country in which the private returns, Π_j, are highest; label this as country m with returns Π_m. What happens if a single country can choose to use a subsidy (others, by assumption, not subsidizing)? The country receives net benefits from attracting the project as long as $B_j > 0$. To attract the project it has to pay a subsidy at least as large as $\Pi_m - \Pi_j$; it will choose to do so providing $B_j > \Pi_m - \Pi_j$, so there remains some benefit after payment of the subsidy. Several points are noteworthy about this outcome. First, there is a transfer of resources from the taxpayer in country j to the MNE. Second, one country's gain is another's loss, as country m loses the benefit it was receiving, B_m. And, third, world efficiency may be reduced by this diversion of investment. The aggregate benefits of the project locating in country m or country j are $B_m + \Pi_m$ and $B_j + \Pi_j$, respectively, and it is quite possible that the former exceeds the latter.

---

[8]This discussion is, of course, also closely related to the question of tax competition for capital; for a survey of such tax competition, see Wilson (1999).

What happens if there is policy competition, and two or more countries try to attract the same investment? A simple two-stage game illustrates possible outcomes. Assume that at stage 1 countries decide simultaneously on their subsidy schemes, and at stage 2 FDI takes place in one of the countries and the associated benefits and costs are realized. The result of this game is straightforward. The country that offers the highest total return to the firm wins the game. The maximum subsidy a country is willing to offer is B_j (the whole of the surplus), in which case the return to the firm would be $B_j + \Pi_j$. The firm goes to whatever country has the highest value of $B_j + \Pi_j$, although the actual subsidy this country pays may be somewhat lower, just outbidding the subsidy offered by the next-best location.

Two main conclusions follow directly from this. First, as before, there is a transfer of resources from the taxpayer to the MNE. This is seen most starkly in the case in which all countries are symmetric, i.e. all have the same values of B_j and Π_j. Competition then causes the subsidy to be raised to the maximum possible level, B_j. One of the countries will get the investment, but at such a high subsidy rate that there are no net benefits left to the country—a quite extreme prisoner's dilemma. In this case all the gains of the project are transferred to the foreign investor.

Second, the policy competition brings about the project location which is, from the standpoint of the world, welfare maximizing.[9] The reason is simply that without subsidies (or with completely harmonized subsidies) location is determined solely by private returns, Π_j, whereas in the policy game location is determined by total returns, $B_j + \Pi_j$. Policy competition can therefore be beneficial in the sense that overall world welfare may be higher in an equilibrium with policy competition than in a case with zero subsidies.

This result is, of course, dependent on all the potential host countries having welfare-maximizing governments, and being able to use subsidies and the maximum subsidy they are willing to pay being equal to the national benefit, B_j. However, policies do not always follow from welfare maximization alone; as we have seen above, political-economy processes with strong special interest groups often imply that policies to attract FDI are chosen even if they do not maximize national welfare. In such cases, as well as with other types of market failure, policy competition may very well be harmful not only in terms of redistributing income from the host countries to the MNEs, but also in terms of actually leading to an inefficient

---

[9] See Barros and Cabral (2000) for derivation of this result in a more fully specified model. Haaland and Wooton (1999) study policy competition with a model similar to that in Figures 10.1 and 10.2, with external economies of scale in the modern sector and policies to attract FDI in that sector. Their results show that, even in cases where inward FDI gives significant overall gains to the economy, the successful host country may end up with such expensive incentive schemes that there are no net benefits left in the country. In such a setting, all the benefits are transferred to the foreign multinational. Haaland and Wooton (2002) study a case where the important dimensions of country heterogeneity are industry risk and labour market flexibility.

allocation of FDI between countries. Countries with strong lobbies for inward FDI could, for example, win the subsidy game, even if the overall benefits of the project are higher in other locations.

In conclusion, the outcome of policy competition may simply be a transfer of funds from government to firms with, in equilibrium, no effect on the location of firms. However, if it interacts with some other market or policy failure, it can move location in either an efficiency-increasing way (e.g. where welfare-maximizing governments internalize some market failure) or an efficiency-decreasing way (e.g. if subsidies are determined by lobbies that happen to be stronger in countries in which the activity does not have a comparative advantage).

Of course, which case applies is an empirical matter. Although it is not easy to find hard evidence on the actual welfare implications of policy competition, there are at least clear indications that policy competition does take place. For FDI incentives, there is no comprehensive database that could help us assess the degree of policy competition. However, more anecdotal 'evidence' indicates that such competition is important in many cases and that it probably results in incentive schemes that are too generous. The examples from UNCTAD (1996), referred to above, show that quite often several countries compete for the same FDI projects, and the winning country tends to end up with very high levels of subsidy. To mention only one of the examples, when the financial incentives to a car plant in Portugal amounted to more than 250 000 dollars per employee in the early 1990s, there is good reason to believe that this is not an efficient solution.

It is easier to find solid data and evidence for tax competition. Devereux et al. (2002b) address the question of whether countries compete over corporate tax rates. As discussed in Section 10.1.1, they note that theoretically there are at least two relevant models, depending on what the mobile variable factor is—firms or capital. If countries compete for mobile firms, as would typically be the case with FDI, the effective average tax rate is what matters. The reason is simply that in such a case the relevant decision is a discrete choice of whether to locate a plant in one country or another. For that choice it is not the marginal tax rates or the structure of the tax system that matter; the decisive factor is the overall average tax burden in different countries. If, on the other hand, we focus on mobile capital in the more traditional sense—where a small change in the expected rate of return in a country implies a marginal shift in the capital flows to that country—the relevant tax parameter is the effective marginal tax rate. After clarifying these theoretical differences, Devereux et al. (2002b) empirically test the degree of competition in corporate taxes, using data from 21 large industrialized countries for the period 1983–99. The paper concludes that there is ample evidence that countries compete over firms, i.e. for FDI, through the average tax rate, while the evidence for competition for capital through the marginal tax rates is more mixed.

10.3.2 *Policy Coordination*

Given these findings, is there a case for limiting competition between jurisdictions? Is the best reply, as suggested by Hanson (2001), 'to seek international cooperation between governments to prevent multinationals from extracting all gains associated with their presence in the economy'?

In general there are three distinct types of argument that could call for international policy coordination:[10]

  (i) avoidance of the prisoner's dilemma in the policy competition game;

 (ii) commitment to avoid bad outcomes of domestic policy games;

(iii) international harmonization to increase transparency and reduce transaction costs.

The first argument follows from the analysis of the preceding subsection. If policy competition reduces or eliminates overall benefits that would otherwise accrue to one of the potential host countries, then at least some of the countries would be better off if there was a binding agreement not to use such policies. A policy competition game may lead to a prisoner's dilemma, where it is difficult to reach the common best solution, even if all countries know that they would be better off with no subsidies or tax preferences. In general, we know that non-cooperative solutions are not efficient for such policy games; there is a need for international cooperation to ensure efficient outcomes.

However, it is not necessarily easy to see what such an agreement should look like, given that individual countries may have strong incentives to use active policies no matter what the other countries do. Only binding international agreements can ensure a more efficient result. For trade policies, the GATT system (and now the WTO) plays this role. We do not so far have a similar, multilateral system for investment policies.

The second reason for policy coordination is to tie the hands of governments faced with domestic lobbies. For example, if barriers or incentive to inward FDI are introduced for political-economy reasons, the policy could be motivated to protect domestic producers at the expense of consumers. Nicoletti et al. (2003) argue that broader policy barriers, particularly anti-competitive domestic regulations and restrictive labour market arrangements, restrain FDI flows in the OECD area as much as explicit FDI restrictions. Hence, an international policy agreement, limiting the possibilities for protecting local producers, could be welfare improving.

Focusing on developing countries, Hoekman and Saggi (1999) also emphasize how international coordination of investment policies could provide an important

---

[10]See Hoekman and Saggi (1999) for a discussion of several reasons for policy coordination.

signal to potential investors that the political environment is stable and policy commitments are credible in the host country. Such issues are of special significance when it comes to investments. An FDI is a long-term commitment to engage in economic activities in a country, and among the key factors in deciding whether or where to invest would be the expectations about future market conditions and political conditions. International coordination and agreements may be one way of reducing the uncertainty; in particular, for countries with a history of unstable political conditions.

Finally, an argument for policy coordination is that it could reduce transaction costs and make all policies more transparent and coherent. The wide set of national and bilateral policy regimes that exists today could in itself be a barrier to investments that would otherwise be efficient and beneficial for the parties involved. From the MNEs' point of view, the question of transaction costs and transparency, and maybe also common rules for performance requirements (local content, export requirements, technology transfers, and so on) are among the most important potential benefits of a multilateral agreement on investments. However, Nunnenkamp and Pant (2003) claim that although transaction costs may be significant and important, it is not necessarily the case that a multilateral investment agreement would help very much. The reasoning is partly that national and regional differences in regulatory regimes will remain even if a multilateral agreement is agreed upon; and partly that a lot of the transaction costs—like differences in language, culture, politics and the general business climate—cannot be regulated through an agreement.

Although stable and transparent investment conditions would improve global welfare, reduce the cost of investing abroad and thus favour FDI flows, policy coordination is in fact quite difficult to achieve. As we argue in what follows, the failure so far of all attempts to introduce multilateral rules on investments show how a common framework is unlikely to be accepted and implemented by parties with very asymmetric positions in the matter, like developing and high-income countries.

10.4   International Governance of Investment Regimes

We have now outlined many of the theoretical arguments and much of the empirical evidence on policy towards FDI. What practical steps forward can be made at the international level, both to regulate the activities of governments, and to regulate the activities of firms themselves?

10.4.1   The International Coordination of Government Policies

While there has been a good deal of concern about the effects of policy competition, most of the practical work on policy towards international investment has been directed to reforming regulatory environments to make their treatment of FDI more transparent and less discriminatory. To some extent this has gone on in regional integration agreements (like the EU and NAFTA) and in the multilateral system (particularly in the GATS, TRIPS and TRIMS agreements). However, the main action has been in bilateral investment treaties (BITs). As noted above, there has been a very strong growth in the number of such bilateral treaties over the 1990s—rising from less than 500 to more than 2000.

UNCTAD (1999a) shows that most of these treaties have much in common. The aim of the investment agreements is generally to eliminate restrictions on foreign investments, remove discrimination against foreign enterprises and protect against government actions such as nationalization or expropriation.

Most BITs have some elements in common (see UNCTAD 1999a, Box 5), including the following.

- Fair and equitable treatment.

- Most favoured nation (MFN) treatment, subject to some exceptions.

- National treatment, subject to qualifications and exceptions. Typically, exceptions could be related to specific industries, or specific types of policies, such as incentives and taxation.

- Guarantee of free transfer of payments related to the investment.

- Conditions for host country expropriation—should be for public purposes, non-discriminatory and accompanied by compensation.

- Dispute settlement provision, both state-to-state (all agreements) and investor-to-state (growing number of agreements).

From this list it should be clear that the main elements of BITs are about eliminating barriers to FDI and ensuring transparency, stability and discipline concerning expropriation, rights to transfer and so on. According to UNCTAD (1999a) there is little known about the actual use made of BITs by countries or investors in international arbitration. The main impact is through signalling an attitude towards FDI. Hence, BITs form an important element of the standard investment climate for any country interested in attracting FDI.

In terms of our list of reasons for international policy coordination and agreements in the previous section, it seems quite clear that the existing agreements are more about elimination of loss-making policies (for political-economy reasons) and the creation of credible policy commitment than about regulating international externalities or policy competition. The fact that the bulk of the bilateral investment agreements involve developing countries indicates that international agreements may be an efficient way of signalling commitment and stability. However, the genuine need for coordination in relation to international externalities is not yet covered in the international agreements.

The scope for a multilateral investment agreement should in principle be all the elements discussed above, and in particular the parts that have to do with international externalities and policy competition. However, there is good reason to believe that at least in the initial phase, an agreement will look more like the bilateral ones— limiting barriers and creating transparency and stability of investment conditions. And if that is true, the question is whether it is more efficient to do this in a multilateral agreement than in the huge set of bilateral agreements that exist today.[11] In the longer run, however, it should also be an aim to cover investment incentives and the danger of harmful policy competition in such an agreement.

As mentioned above, existing WTO agreements go some way towards regulating policies of relevance for FDI. However, the focus of these regulations is trade, not investments as such. The agreement on TRIMs (trade-related investment measures) limits the use of, for example, local content requirements, trade balance and foreign exchange clauses, or export controls, but it does not cover domestic policies towards investments. The rules on subsidies and countervailing measures ban the use of export subsidies and other incentives linked to trade performance; but the rules do not cover investment incentives in general. And the agreement on TRIPs (trade-related intellectual property rights) is about non-discriminatory rules for protection of copyrights, patents, geographical indicators, industrial design and so on. Finally, the GATS agreement includes 'commercial presence' as one mode of cross-border supply of services. All of these agreements are of great importance in relation to FDI and the activities of multinationals; yet, they do not coordinate investment policies as such, nor do they regulate the activities of multinational firms.

Lately, there has been much discussion about a possible multilateral agreement for FDI extending beyond actual WTO regulations, but negotiations on the matter have so far been quite a failure. An OECD initiative to establish a Multilateral Agreement on Investments (MAI) failed a few years ago. More recently, the issue of an investment agreement is on the agenda for the present WTO round (initiated in Doha, November 2001). At the time of completing this book, however, the status for negotiations on an investment agreement is not clear. Such negotiations were to be initiated at the fifth WTO Ministerial Conference in Cancun, Mexico, September 2003, but no consensus was reached there. Many developing countries are fiercely opposed to such an agreement. According to many commentators, their opposition even to start negotiations was the main reason why the Ministerial Conference, which was dealing with several trade-related issues, failed to reach any agreement at all.

---

[11] See Nunnenkamp and Pant (2003) for an assessment of what can be achieved in a multilateral framework relative to the set of bilateral and regional treaties that are in place today. They argue that although limiting policy competition and the use of subsidies and incentives could be an important task for a multilateral agreement, such an agreement seems difficult to achieve and difficult to enforce.

10.4.2 The Regulation of Multinational Firms

The growth of FDI and the increasing importance of multinationals are among the key features of the current wave of globalization. Hence, it is no wonder that a substantial share of the arguments of the anti-globalization movements is directed towards multinationals and the lack of regulations of multinationals. Without going into the debate over the good or not-so-good consequences of globalization as such, it should be quite clear that there is a growing need for supranational regulation of the behaviour of 'supranational' firms. Even if in principle the various parts of an MNE's activities are covered by national laws and regulations in the country where the activities take place, international coordination or cooperation is called for to make sure that the regulations are sufficient and efficient from a global perspective.

There are a number of policy areas where the need for some kind of international regulation of MNEs applies. Some of these have been discussed above. Tax policy is a prime example of an area where international cooperation is necessary, for several reasons: to avoid harmful policy competition, to limit the possibilities of tax avoidance, and to facilitate the enforcement of national tax rules. Although some international cooperation exists, a lot remains to be done, both in terms of binding international agreements and in terms of reformulation of national policies to adapt to the multinationality of firms (see Gordon and Hines (2002) for a thorough discussion of international taxation issues.)

Investment incentives have many of the same features as tax policies, and again international cooperation should include rules to avoid harmful policy competition (see Section 10.3.2).

Competition policy plays an important role in regulating the behaviour of firms in many countries. While less than 40 countries had competition laws in 1980, almost half of the countries in the world had such laws by 2003 (see UNCTAD 2003). The purpose of such policies is to limit the concentration of economic power and to avoid the abuse of strong market positions. The instruments at hand for the competition authorities are linked to merger controls, and to the detection and regulation of anti-competitive actions. With internationalization of markets and firms, however, the nature of competition and anti-competitive behaviour changes, and the instruments of national competition authorities may not be sufficient or adequate. On the one hand, internationalization of markets may imply tougher competition and hence less need for domestic regulations in many industries. On the other hand, the strong growth in cross-border mergers and acquisitions and the trend towards huge multinational enterprises may imply an international concentration of economic power of unprecedented magnitude. While the former effect of internationalization may call for a reorientation of domestic competition policies, the latter shows the need for supranational policies.

With the strong growth in international mergers and acquisitions, the scope for assessing and controlling M&As should have an international focus. Cross-border M&As obviously need to be assessed on more than a national basis, but even domestic M&As may have important repercussions in international markets. With regard to anti-competitive behaviour—cartels, market-sharing arrangements, etc.—the international dimension is also important. Even if internationalization as such increases the market size and the number of potential competitors, it does not help much if a few dominating firms can control or share the whole market. Traditional measures of dominance used by competition authorities, such as the market shares of large firms in the domestic market, are, however, not necessarily good indicators of market power in an integrated, international market. If the market in question is truly international and integrated, domestic market shares do not really matter, as competition and price setting would not be confined to that market. In many countries, in particular small ones, it is in fact argued that a strong position with high market shares in the home market is a prerequisite for domestic firms to survive on the international arena, and competition authorities are urged to allow such large market shares, as the firms would not be able to exploit any market power. If, on the other hand, large market shares in one sub-market stem from an implicit market-sharing arrangement amongst the suppliers, a more lax competition policy is a problem. And the same may be true if the markets are in fact not as integrated as one is led to believe. In all these examples, there is clearly a need for supranational competition authorities to assess the overall competitive situation in national and international markets. This is particularly the case if the enforcement of national competition rules becomes less strict to reflect internationalization of markets. Otherwise, MNEs (and other big firms) can exploit their market power both in national and international markets.

On a regional basis, the need for a supranational competition authority has been recognized and to some extent implemented. The European Union has an active competition authority at the union level working together with the national authorities; and other regional integrations, like MERCOSUR, follow the same path. Globally, however, there is still no common ground for competition regulations. Bilateral or regional international investment agreements do normally not include clauses on competition, even if there is a close link between cross-border FDI, and in particular M&As, and competition questions. And in relation to WTO and international trade, competition policy is among the so-called Singapore issues, in line with investment policies and a few other areas.[12] Although these issues in principle are part of the Doha round of WTO negotiations, as argued in Section 10.4.1 there is strong opposition, in particular from developing countries, against including such new pol-

---

[12]These issues were first raised as possible policy areas to include in the WTO framework at the Ministerial Conference in Singapore in 1996; hence the name Singapore issues.

icy areas under the WTO. And at the Ministerial Conference in Cancun, Mexico, in September 2003, no agreement to continue negotiations on such issues was reached.

A related question is about the relationship between the protection of intellectual property rights (IPR) and competition. To the extent that IPR protection becomes more international, as it does through the TRIPS agreement, it also has a potential effect on competition. The TRIPS agreement includes clauses recognizing the potential danger of reduced competition, but there are no direct measures to tackle the problem. Hence, unless there are forceful competition authorities, the balance may well be in favour of granting IPR and accompanying market power to multinationals on an international basis, without being able to control their market power.

Another important area, where the growing importance of MNEs may play a role, is that of environmental policy. Some environmental problems—like CO_2 emissions and global warming or CFC gases and the ozone layer—are truly global problems, and need global solutions. Other environmental problems are more local, and the optimum policy response is then at the local level. In either case, however, the presence of MNEs may play an important role, in particular in cases where adequate environmental policies are not in place. MNEs typically have a high degree of mobility and flexibility, and can adjust quickly and strongly to local market conditions. Differences in environmental policies between countries or regions may thus give rise to significant changes in the pattern of production and trade. Countries with less-strict regulation may attract inward FDI, which would in turn add to the environmental problem. This may clearly represent a problem; however, it is not always obvious what the solution should be. If the environmental problem in question is a trans-border or global one, there is obviously a need for international or global policies. Each individual country cannot decide on its own policies if the consequences of 'wrong' policies affect everyone. If, on the other hand, the environmental problem is a local one, it is not clear whether the international community should be given the right to dictate different policies from the one the local authorities have chosen. Even if it is evident from the foreigners' point of view that the environmental policy should be more restrictive, it need not be so according to the standards of the local government.

The current status of environment regulations gives a mixed picture. For global environmental issues, like global warming or ozone layer problems, the need for global solutions is clearly recognized. The Montreal protocol has been successful in limiting the emission of CFC gases, while for the Kyoto protocol on greenhouse emissions, it remains to be seen how successful the implementation will be. The fact that the US has decided not to ratify the agreement is a major setback; perhaps this shows the influence that big companies have over policies? For other environmental questions, there have been several initiatives to include environmental clauses in the

WTO agreements; however, the opposition has been and is strong, and so far there are no significant elements of environmental regulation in the WTO negotiations.

Labour standards is another area where there has been a demand for supranational regulations as a reflection of the growth of MNEs. The lack of appropriate regulation of labour standards in many developing countries and the poor labour market conditions in such countries are matters of great concern. The potential interaction between labour standards and trade and investment makes this a particularly sensitive issue in the globalization debate. There are several concerns relating to workers both in developing and industrialized countries. Does trade (and FDI) lead to exploitation of workers in developing countries? Does 'social dumping' by developing countries harm workers in industrialized countries? And do trade and foreign investments put labour standards under pressure in both developing and developed countries? (See CEPR (2002) for a more complete discussion.) Concerns like these have been fuelled by examples of child work, low pay and other violations of 'normal' minimum labour standards by MNEs and subcontractors for MNEs in some developing countries. However, in general terms, it is far from obvious that more open markets with increased trade and activities by MNEs harm workers in developing countries. On the contrary, there is good reason to believe that the conditions offered by foreign MNEs are often better than the alternative opportunities for the workers in question.

No matter whether MNEs in general imply higher or lower labour standards, the strong concerns about labour market conditions and the possibilities of exploitation of workers are real ones. Hence, there is a need for supranational rules and regulations. The International Labour Organization (ILO) has as its main objective the promotion of decent working standards and adequate regulations in the member countries. ILO's core conventions on the freedom to collective bargaining, the abolition of child work, the elimination of forced or compulsory labour and the elimination of discrimination in respect of employment or occupation are ratified by a large majority of the member countries, and should contribute to the goal of decent labour standards in all countries. However, it is obvious that a lot remains in terms of implementation in many countries.

In 2002 the ILO established the World Commission on the Social Dimension of Globalization with the objective of identifying policies that could reduce poverty, foster growth and employment, widen opportunities for decent work, and make the globalization process more inclusive. The Commission will also assist the international community towards greater policy coherence in order to advance both economic and social goals in the global economy. Hence, the background and objectives of the World Commission reflect the growing recognition of the need for international policy coordination and regulation to ensure beneficial effects of globalization for all people. The commission is due to report on its progress and results early in 2004.

The inclusion of labour standards and labour market conditions has been one of the hot topics in recent WTO debates. While a number of industrialized countries demanded that minimum labour standards should be part of a new WTO agreement, this has been strongly opposed by developing countries, claiming that such clauses would represent a more or less hidden protection of producers and workers in the industrialized regions. The issue of linking trade liberalization and labour standards was one of the major obstacles to reaching agreement on launching a new WTO round in the WTO Ministerial Conference in Seattle in 1999. In Doha two years later, the new round was launched without the inclusion of labour market clauses.

The current position seems to be that the ILO is the right arena for international agreements on labour standards and labour conditions; there is, however, close cooperation between the WTO and the ILO on these issues. Questions of decent work conditions worldwide are, of course, not only about trade and the activities of multinationals; these are general questions of great importance. Nevertheless, the increased importance of multinationals and the tighter economic integration between countries and regions highlight very strongly the international dimension of labour standards and decent labour market conditions. Without a common understanding of the importance of such issues, the process towards more open and integrated markets may be a difficult one.

10.5   Concluding Remarks

In this chapter several policy issues of importance for international investments and the activities of multinational enterprises have been discussed. The aim has been to highlight the two-way relationship between policies and MNEs. On the one hand, a wide range of policies play a role in forming the overall economic environment for the MNEs. Taxation, labour market conditions, trade policies, environmental regulations, competition policies, investment incentives and so on all matter for the MNE's choice of location as well as the decisions on the type and size of activities in various locations. The high degrees of mobility and flexibility characterizing MNEs imply that decisions on location and activity levels are typically sensitive to international differences in policy regimes or to changes in policies over time. Empirical studies confirm that MNEs do adjust to differences in tax regimes, and that labour market conditions and investment incentives play a role. However, it should be clear that what matters is the overall conditions in a location, not each policy area in isolation.

The other aspect discussed in this chapter is the impact of FDI and MNEs on policy formation. The existence and growing importance of multinationals represent a challenge for policy makers both nationally and internationally. Nationally, the tighter economic integration and the increased mobility of firms and activities call for a reorientation of policies in many countries. In a more competitive environment, having a good mix of policies is a key element in attracting economic activities; while the consequences of 'bad' policies become more pronounced. While difficult to implement, the need for international policy coordination and cooperation is increasingly clear. For a number of areas domestic policies are no longer sufficient; international coordination or supranational regulations are called for to ensure that international markets work in an efficient and beneficial way.

11
Conclusions

During the time taken to write this book, the process of globalization has come under serious attack from some sections of society. At the same time, negotiations on global agreements to liberalize trade have encountered increasing difficulties and, after the failure of the WTO ministerial meeting in Cancun, have probably now come to a standstill. In some industrialized countries claims that national industries are threatened by trade and by outsourcing are getting louder, even within government and policy circles. This turmoil is not just to do with trade, but also with multinational firms. They are constant targets of anti-globalization movements. Paradoxically, one of the main issues on which Cancun failed is the harmonization of the rules governing foreign firms in host economies. Individual countries, particularly developing ones, prefer to deal with MNEs on their own ground, and while competing to attract foreign resources they nevertheless fear undue influence of foreign capital.

The reasons why we wanted to write a book on multinationals became clearer as this globalization backlash was developing. We wanted to provide some firm ground for a crucial and little-understood aspect of the globalization debate. A considerable volume of research in the last 20 years has shed light on the role played by multinationals. But the outcome of this research still needed to be surveyed and analysed within a coherent framework, in order to provide an answer to critical questions like, What are multinationals? Why do they arise? What effects do they have on host and home economies? We believe that this book provides an answer to many of these questions, in a way that can satisfy academics and lay people alike. We show that many fears derive from a poor understanding of what multinationals are and what they do. Multinationals are a fundamental and efficient component of a globalized world, not an enemy within. In these conclusions we argue why we believe this is the case by summarizing the main lessons emerging from the book.

Multinationals are not just giant corporations. The traditional identification between multinationals and giant corporations is blurred. Although it is impossible to be a giant corporation without being a multinational, the opposite is not true. Any firm organizing its activities in more than one country is a multinational. These are often medium-sized firms. In this book we have been telling tales about world giants like IBM or Coca-Cola and rather unknown players, like Calzaturificio Carmens in Padua, Italy, with sales of around 100 million euros. Being multinational corresponds to a common way of organizing economic activities across different locations, an option available to many firms in high-income economies and also in developing ones.

Mobility of firms not capital. Foreign direct investments (the investments of multinationals) are long term if compared with highly mobile capital flows, like portfolio investments or bank credits. They cover the cost of starting or buying and then running foreign plants or other activities, and are best thought of as movements of firms, rather than movements of capital. The key difference is that firms bring in their own very distinctive bundle of capabilities. Whether a loan is granted by Citicorp or by Crédit Agricole does not make much difference. But whether a foreign direct investment is carried out by Renault or by Monsanto makes a great difference. Indeed, each firm is a unique bundle of factors, competencies and procedures which get transferred to foreign operations. Consequently, different investments might have quite substantially different effects on the host and home economies.

Variety of motives. The heterogeneity in the characteristics of multinationals is mirrored in the variety of reasons why firms become multinationals. The standard explanation of why firms invest abroad is rooted in the idea of firm-level economies of scale. Some firms develop assets, defined as intangible assets, like a brand name or a new technology. Their benefits can be spread in a non-rival way, firm-wide, across several plants. The brand name of Coca-Cola benefits Coca-Cola plants in the US as well as in Ghana. These intangible assets are a source of increasing returns to scale and market power. Thus, they produce a natural association between multinationals and giant corporations. Then, why is a medium firm like Calzaturifico Carmens a multinational? Because firms also invest abroad for reasons other than the international exploitation of market power, and by so doing are able to save on costs of production and distribution. They go abroad to gain market access, to look for cheap factors of production, to source specific technologies, and to exploit externalities which are location specific. These investment motives can be pursued by relatively small firms that implement flexible and fragmented operations across several countries.

How to organize production in a globalized economy. The largest part of FDI has been intended primarily to serve host country markets. In some cases these investments arise to circumvent trade barriers and are boosted by protectionism. However, firms are increasingly seeking to organize their production to benefit from the advantages that globalization and a freer trading environment have created. People think that the world is globalized because there are many multinationals around. True, but things also work in the opposite direction: there are many multinationals because the world is globalized. We show in this book that being multinational is often the optimal way to operate in an integrated global economy. To understand this point we need to compare trade and foreign investment flows. The surge of multinationals in the 1990s is intertwined with the process of trade liberalization at the global and regional level. International competition induces firms to reduce production costs and to tap cheap factors of production around the world. But the activities of multinationals often require and generate trade. Thus, they can be carried out only if trade costs are low. Calzaturificio Carmens would not set up a plant in Serbia if it were unable to import finished products back to Europe cheaply.

Internal or external operations. Foreign operations do not necessarily need to be carried out by wholly owned foreign subsidiaries. In many circumstances they can be carried out in looser ways, through arm's-length contracts and agreements with local firms. Examples of these agreements are licensing contracts to produce a component or to assemble a finished good, and agency contracts to market a given product. These agreements are often a cheaper option than setting up a foreign subsidiary. A considerable share of international activities is carried out in this way, and this share would be even larger were it not for market failures that often prevent these agreements from functioning efficiently. For example, a multinational owning an exclusive technology may fear that a licensing contract could lead to a dissipation of its proprietary knowledge. In that case, setting up a foreign subsidiary is an optimal choice because alternatives that would be cheaper, and perhaps more beneficial to local economies, are often unviable.

Efficiency gains to the global economy. Organizing activities across the border works. There are complementarities between the capabilities of firms and the characteristics of countries that can be effectively achieved by international investments. MNEs are invariably found to perform better than national firms in home and host economies alike. Such firms are able to expand by becoming multinational, applying their higher productivity to a wider range of inputs. Multinationals are on average larger than other firms, they do more R&D, they use more skilled personnel. We find consistent and robust evidence of this when comparing the activities of multinationals in both home and host countries to those of national firms.

Global benefits mostly translate into local benefits. If multinationals are more efficient than national firms, then the larger the share of world activity they account for, the more efficient will be world production and the higher world income. However, these global benefits may not necessarily make everyone better off. At the country level it might not always be the case that world gains in efficiency trickle down to improve welfare. Theory tells us that many factors are at play here, and the outcome cannot be predicted easily. It depends on what firms do with their higher efficiency and on how the economy adjusts to their presence.

Outward investments divert national resources to foreign countries. This diversion could impoverish the home countries if it leads to a contraction of activities. But the evidence is that more often than not outward investments strengthen firms, leading to expansion rather than contraction of activities in their home countries. The relocation of labour-intensive activities is a key concern in high-income countries. But in general we find that this is an opportunity for firms to reduce their production costs and remain competitive. Although activities get transferred, they become an element of a strategic process which is governed from home and which strengthens activities that remain in the home country.

Inwards investments may cause profits to be funnelled abroad and local industry to be damaged. But the evidence is generally that crowding out affects only the most inefficient local producers, local resources that are released are put to a better use, and prices decline to the benefit of local consumers. Technology transfer and linkages to local firms can develop, particularly where host countries have sufficient skills and technology to interact with multinationals. When technological and income gaps are too wide, then foreign direct investments are no shortcut to faster income growth.

Convergence or divergence of world income. The nature of the interaction between foreign firms and domestic activities in host countries has long-term implications for the convergence of world income. Foreign investments in developing countries are of particular importance here. These investments provide an important source of capital formation even in very backward economies, and, more importantly, a source of firm-level capabilities that would otherwise be absent. However, the impact on host economies is small if there is little interaction with domestic activities. Consider the creation of human capital, a key ingredient for growth. The evidence is that even in developing countries multinationals employ more educated personnel than the average national firms. If there is no local effort to expand and enhance local skills (e.g. through education policies), the gains are likely to be small. To understand this point, compare two extreme examples: investments in oil extraction in countries like Gabon, Nigeria or Azerbaijan and investments in high-tech industries in Ireland. Oil investments in most oil-producing countries had very limited spin-offs on local activities and on the demand for skilled personnel. Indeed, most activities related to oil extraction require highly skilled services that locals are rarely able to provide. Also, downstream activities like refineries and chemicals are often not efficient in these backward economies, and the largest share of oil is exported raw. In contrast, Ireland is a very good case study of the opposite outcome, and is extensively studied in this book. Ireland is not a developing country but it was quite a low-income one when it joined the EU in 1973. The high-tech American multinationals that invested there in the 1980s and 1990s generated a massive demand for local skills. Irish engineers based abroad moved back home and an explicit policy to enhance higher education in science and technology was launched. This was, of course, to the benefit of the whole Irish economy.

Short- or long-lasting effects. Another problem for long-term income growth is that the presence of multinationals could be short-lived. Their cost of mobility is generally lower than for national firms, as their production is already organized across countries. Thus they could react more and faster to adverse shocks in any location and move their activities elsewhere. The only available evidence of the volatility of multinationals refers to high-income economies. Surprisingly multinationals are found to be less volatile than national firms. They react faster to shocks, but the overall magnitude of their reaction is less than that of national firms. However, this need not be the case for developing countries. Many recent investment flows to developing countries are essentially seeking cheap labour, and many of these investments are concentrated in cheap-labour countries neighbouring large, high-income markets, like Mexico or the Central and Eastern European countries. Also, thanks to these foreign investments, these economies have been able to achieve high rates of growth and important export performances. However, wages rise with income. For these foreign activities to stay in the longer term, other factors of attraction must be developed. Many of these favourite locations of the 1990s are already falling out of favour, as activities move to new locations where labour is cheaper. Particularly worrying are reports that even countries with an obvious locational advantage like Mexico are seeing investments moving away to locations, particularly China, which are much further away from the US but where labour is cheaper. Foreign firms may come and go and their blessing could be deceptively short. For this reason developing countries cannot just rely on cheap labour as a factor to attract foreign direct investments. The strategy followed by Ireland successfully managed to use its initial cost advantage to create long-lasting linkages with foreign investors.

Future research. The final lesson we gather from this book is that there are many promising avenues for future research which have yet to be explored. From the standpoint of theory, it is necessary to study more carefully the determinants and the effects of multinationals when firms are heterogeneous. Most theoretical frameworks are still based on the simplifying assumption of homogeneous agents and theories encompassing heterogeneity are still in their infancy. We have, however, seen how the heterogeneity of firms is a central feature emerging from the empirical study of multinationals. From the empirical point of view, we have as yet little empirical evidence of the patterns of international fragmentation of production. How does this take place? How are activities effectively fragmented between host and home countries? How do patterns of fragmentation evolve with time? It is difficult to carry out these types of analysis since standard datasets, even firm-level ones, contain little information on this. Also, we have no explicit evidence of arm's-length agreements carried out by MNEs and virtually no tests of the circumstances under which they arise instead of foreign subsidiaries. Another issue is that there is still not enough research on home effects. Again, this is due to the fact that firm-level databases focusing on the investing country and combining information on home and foreign activities are still scant.

Summing up, we hope we have been able to provide a coherent framework to present the wide body of literature on the subject of the multinational firm. We also hope this book can shed some light on the obscurities of what is still a very emotional debate. We have noticed that there are still areas which are severely under-researched. To close this gap a joint effort is necessary, involving theoretical analysis, new empirical studies and the development of databases.

Appendix A

Statistical Definitions and Databases on Foreign Direct Investment and the Activities of Multinationals

There are two 'families' of statistics on foreign direct investment (FDI): (i) data on flows and stocks of FDI from balance-of-payment statistics; (ii) data on the activities of multinationals (MNEs). FDI data are from official statistics, are standardized and comparable across countries and available for many countries and years. MNEs' data are mostly collected through ad hoc surveys concerning several aspects of business activities and are available for only a few countries and for a limited number of years.

In this appendix both types of data are presented. Section A.1 is devoted to international statistics on FDI. After a brief overview of technical definitions and guidelines internationally adopted for balance-of-payment accounting, it presents synthetic information on the most important international databases on FDI. Section A.2 examines data on the activities of MNEs. It presents synthetic information on three cross-country databases and on the main country-specific databases.

A.1 International Statistics on Foreign Direct Investment

A.1.1 Statistical Definitions

International guidelines and definitions for the compilation of balance-of-payments and international investment statistics appear in the International Monetary Fund's *Balance of Payments Manual* (IMF 1993) (BPM5) and the OECD's *Benchmark Definition of Foreign Direct Investment* (OECD 1996) (Benchmark). This body of recommendations provides comprehensive and detailed international standards for recording both positions and flows related to FDI. The recommendations cover a wide range of issues, including concepts and definitions, time of recording, collection methods, dissemination, etc.

A list of the most widely used definitions is provided below.

Direct investment is the category of international investment that reflects the objective of a resident entity in one economy (direct investor) of establishing a lasting interest in an enterprise (the direct investment enterprise) resident in another economy. 'Lasting interest' implies the existence of a long-term relationship and a significant degree of influence by the direct investor on the management of the direct investment enterprise. Direct investment involves both the initial transaction between the two entities and all subsequent capital transactions between them and among affiliated enterprises, both incorporated and unincorporated.

A *direct investor* is defined as an individual, an incorporated or unincorporated public or private enterprise, a government, a group of related individuals, or a group of related incorporated and/or unincorporated enterprises which have a direct investment enterprise that is a subsidiary, associate or branch, operating in a country other than the country or countries of residence of the direct investor(s).

A *direct investment enterprise* is defined as an incorporated or unincorporated enterprise in which a foreign investor owns 10% or more of the ordinary shares or voting power of an incorporated enterprise or the equivalent of an unincorporated enterprise. Ownership of 10% or more of the ordinary shares or voting stock is the guideline for determining the existence of a direct investment relationship. An 'effective voice in the management', as evidenced by at least 10% ownership, implies that a direct investor is able to influence, or participate in, the management of an enterprise; absolute control by a foreign investor is not required. Direct investment enterprises may be subsidiaries, associates and branches.

A *subsidiary* is an incorporated enterprise in which

(i) the foreign investor controls directly or indirectly (through another subsidiary) more than 50% of the shareholders' voting power, or

(ii) the foreign investor has the right to appoint or remove a majority of the members of this enterprise's administrative, management or supervisory body.

An *associate* is an enterprise where the direct investor and its subsidiaries control between 10% and 50% of the voting shares.

A *branch* is an unincorporated enterprise that

(i) is a permanent establishment or office of a foreign direct investor;

(ii) is an unincorporated partnership or a joint venture between a foreign direct investor and third parties;

(iii) is land, structures and immovable equipment and objects directly owned by a foreign resident;

(iv) is mobile equipment operating within an economy for at least one year if accounted for separately by the operator (e.g. ships, aircraft, gas- and oil-drilling rigs).

Foreign direct investment flows are made up of three basic components.

- Equity capital: comprising equity in branches, all shares in subsidiaries and associates (except non-participating, preferred shares that are treated as debt securities and are included under other direct investment capital) and other capital contributions such as provisions of machinery, etc.

- Reinvested earnings: consisting of the direct investor's share (in proportion to direct equity participation) of earnings not distributed, as dividends by subsidiaries or associates and earnings of branches not remitted to the direct investor.

- Other direct investment capital (or inter-company debt transactions): covering the borrowing and lending of funds, including debt securities and trade credits, between direct investors and direct investment enterprises and between two direct investment enterprises that share the same direct investor.

More specifically, *foreign direct investment flows* are defined as follows.

- For subsidiaries and associate companies:

    (i) the direct investor's share of the company's reinvested earnings;

    (ii) plus the direct investor's net purchases of the company's shares, debt securities (bonds, notes, money market and financial derivative instruments) and loans (including non-cash acquisitions made against equipment, manufacturing rights, etc.);

    (iii) less the company's net purchases of the direct investor's shares, debt securities and loans;

    (iv) plus the net increase in trade and other short-term credits given by the direct investor to the company.

- For branches:

    (i) the increase in reinvested profits;

    (ii) plus the net increase in funds received from the direct investor;

    (iii) plus inter-company flows, with the exception of certain flows between affiliated banks, affiliated intermediaries (e.g. security dealers), and Special Purpose Entities (SPEs) with the sole purpose of serving as financial intermediaries.

International direct investment stocks (or *positions*) are defined as follows.

- For subsidiaries and associates:

    (i) the market or book (balance sheet) value of shares and reserves attributable to the direct investor;

    (ii) plus loans, trade credits and debt securities credited by direct investors (including determined but not yet paid dividends);

    (iii) less reverse loans, trade credits and debt securities.

- For branches:

    (i) the market or book value of fixed assets, investments and current assets, excluding amounts due from the direct investor;

    (ii) less the branches liabilities to third parties.

Not all countries fully apply these guidelines for data collection. Details on deviations from guidelines and on the level of consistency of the data across countries can be found in the official publications of the organizations supplying the data.

A.1.2   Databases on Foreign Direct Investment

A.1.2.1   UNCTAD Foreign Direct Investment Database

Main characteristics.

Type of data:	Balance-of-payments data
	Inward and outward FDI flows and stocks
Country coverage:	196 countries
Level of aggregation:	By country of origin and of destination
	(with regional aggregations)
	—by industry (only for individual countries)
Time coverage:	Yearly—since 1970 for flows and since 1980 for stocks

Description of the database. UNCTAD's Division on Investment, Technology and Enterprise Development (DITE) compiles worldwide statistics on FDI. The data are presented in two separate products.

(a) *Foreign Direct Investment On-line*, an interactive database accessible on-line presenting the aggregate FDI statistics worldwide, regularly updated.

(b) *World Investment Directory On-line*, an electronic publication presenting detailed and extensive information for individual countries. For each country, FDI flows and stocks are disaggregated by industry and country of origin/destination. A discussion of the sources, definitions and adherence to international guidelines of country-specific FDI data is reported. Data on MNEs' operations (sales, employees, profits, exports, etc.) are also presented (see also Section A.2.1.1).

The main sources for the database on FDI are published and unpublished national official FDI data collected by UNCTAD directly from central banks, statistical offices or national authorities on an aggregated and disaggregated basis. These data are further complemented by the data obtained from other international organizations such as the IMF, the World Bank, the OECD, etc., as well as UNCTAD's own estimates.

Related publications. Other indicators on FDI and MNEs' activities, together with analysis of the trends and determinants of FDI, are available in the *World Investment Report* published yearly by UNCTAD.

Reference website. www.unctad.org

A.1.2.2 OECD International Direct Investment Database

Main characteristics.

Type of data:	Balance-of-payments data
	Inward and outward FDI flows and stocks
Country coverage:	OECD countries
Level of aggregation:	By country of origin and of destination
	(with regional aggregations)
	—by industry
Time coverage:	Yearly—since 1980

Description of the database. The OECD International Direct Investment Database gathers detailed historical statistics on international direct investment to and from the OECD area.

The database developed by the OECD Directorate for Financial, Fiscal and Enterprise Affairs is updated regularly through a joint OECD–Eurostat questionnaire.

The data are based for the most part on balance-of-payments statistics published by the central banks and statistical offices, but also on other sources such as notifications or approvals.

Although FDI statistics are presented according to a standardized format for all Member Countries, there are some limits in data comparability across countries.

Related publications. OECD, *International Investment Statistics Yearbook*, various years, Paris.

Reference website. www.sourceoecd.org

A.1.2.3 Eurostat Foreign Direct Investment Statistics

Main characteristics.

Type of data:	Balance-of-payments data
	Inward and outward FDI flows and stocks
Country coverage:	European Union Countries, Canada, Japan,
	Switzerland and United States.
Level of aggregation:	By country of origin and of destination
	(with regional aggregations)
	by industry (NACE classification Rev. 1)
	—by industry and region
Time coverage:	Yearly—since 1992

Description of the database. Eurostat compiles and publishes data on FDI flows and stocks for the European Union Countries, the Candidate Countries, and some other main industrialized countries.

Data on FDI are a section of the NewCronos database (Domain Theme2/bop/).

Eurostat collects FDI data through a joint OECD–Eurostat questionnaire. Eurostat harmonizes national data and estimates missing or unavailable data for each Member State to build complete EU FDI flows and stocks. Estimates exploit secondary data sources or use knowledge-based modelling techniques.

Related publications. Eurostat, European Union Direct Investment Yearbook, various years.

Reference website. www.europa.eu.int/comm/eurostat

A.2 Financial and Operating Data on Multinational Firms

In this section we present information on datasets on the activities of multinationals. Compared with FDI data, data on the activities of MNEs are much less widely available. France, Germany, the UK and the US produce outward and inward direct investment data collected through their official economic analysis bureaux or central banks by means of mandatory surveys. In other countries data on the activities of MNEs are collected by public and private research institutions for specific research purposes. They are usually based on voluntary surveys which do not cover the entire universe of firms in the country and are supplemented by information gathered from newspapers, annual reports of major firms, official registers and various other ad hoc documentation.

UNCTAD, the OECD and Eurostat have developed or are developing comparable cross-country statistics based on these country-specific databases. We provide a synthetic description of these three datasets. We will then describe the major country-specific databases.

Information on the activity of MNEs can also be gathered from international commercial databases, such as, for example, Dun and Bradstreet (Who Owns Whom database) and Bureau van Dijck (Amadeus database), which contain balance sheet and other information for large samples of firms.[1] These databases include information on the nationality of individual firms' ownership, and it is therefore possible to distinguish between foreign subsidiaries and national firms. They also have partial information on the foreign subsidiaries of individual firms. As they are not specific to the activities of MNEs, we do not cover them in this appendix.

---

[1] The Amadeus database produced by Bureau van Dijck has been widely used in empirical studies. The database consists of company accounts plus other information like employment reported to national statistical offices for European companies for which at least one of the following criteria is satisfied: total turnover or assets of at least $12 million, or total employment of at least 150. The database is organized by country with records for firms within each country. The company records include information on the nationality of the ultimate owner(s) of the company, on whether the company has an ownership stake in a foreign affiliate, and identify affiliates by name and a unique identification number. Companies in all industries are included.

A.2.1 International Compilations of Statistics on the Activities of Multinationals

A.2.1.1 UNCTAD World Investment Directory

Main characteristics.

Type of data:	MNEs' activities data (inward and outward)
Country coverage:	Developed countries and main countries from the following regions: Central and Eastern Europe, Africa, Asia and the Pacific, Latin America.
Level of aggregation:	Data are publicly available by country of origin and of destination, by industry and by industry/region
Time coverage:	Varying across countries

Description of the database. UNCTAD's Division on Investment, Technology and Enterprise Development (DITE) compiles the on-line *World Investment Directory* database providing comprehensive statistics on FDI and the operations of MNEs by country (see also Section A.1.2.1).

Information on each country is available in two formats: a detailed profile, and an 'FDI in Brief', highlighting the most interesting aspects of the profile. Each profile presents 88 country tables that provide extensive coverage of data on both FDI (flows and stocks) and the operations of MNEs (sales, employees, profits, exports, etc.), classified by economic activity and by region, together with listings of the major MNEs in each economy, along with selected financial data.

Statistical definitions and sources, brief discussion and listing of relevant national laws and regulations, information on bilateral and multilateral agreements and a bibliography are also available.

Data on FDI and the operations of MNEs and foreign affiliates are provided essentially as they are reported by national official sources, both published and unpublished. International sources (OECD, IMF, etc.) are also used where no national data are available, as are secondary sources.

Corporate data for major MNEs are based on official national sources, business directories and periodicals, company financial statements and secondary sources. MNEs are usually ranked by sales or assets.

Reference website. www.unctad.org

A.2.1.2 OECD Measuring Globalization Statistics Database

Main characteristics.

Type of data:	MNEs' activities data (inward and outward)
Country coverage:	OECD countries
Level of aggregation:	Data are publicly available by country of origin and of destination and by industry (ISIC Rev. 3)
Time coverage:	1994–99, depending on the country

Description of the database. The dataset reports information by country on a series of financial and operating variables concerning the activity of multinational firms in the main OECD countries, particularly output (or sales), employment, value added, research and exports (inward investment). Recently the database has been extended to cover the activities of OECD multinational firms abroad (outward investment) in manufacturing, and the activities of multinationals in services.

The data refers only to majority foreign-owned (over 50%) firms.

Activities of foreign affiliates are classified into ISIC Rev. 3 industries according to the main activity of the affiliate.

Data are collected through national surveys by the Economic Analysis and Statistics Division of the OECD Directorate for Science, Technology and Industry (STI).

The country sources of the databases are those listed for individual countries in Section A.2.2.

Related publication. OECD (2001b).

Reference website. www.sourceoecd.org

A.2.1.3   Eurostat Foreign Affiliates Trade Statistics (FATS)

Main characteristics.

Type of data:	MNEs' activities data (inward and outward)
Country coverage:	Main European Union countries
Level of aggregation:	Data are publicly available by country of origin and of destination and by industry (NACE classification, Rev. 1)
Time coverage:	Various years between 1996 and 1999

Description of the database. Eurostat, within the framework of Foreign Direct Investment statistics, collects and harmonizes data on the overall activity of foreign-owned companies of EU Member States.

Statistics on foreign-owned affiliates in the reporting EU country are called inward FATS, whilst statistics on foreign affiliates owned by the reporting EU country are simply called FATS.

Data are published in Eurostat's NewCronos database (Domain Theme2/bop/).

The database collects data on the following variables: number of companies, turnover, production value, number of employees, etc.

Data availability varies across EU country, variable and year.

Data are collected through surveys. After a first phase of pilot studies in 1998, Eurostat launched studies to collect data for inward and outward FATS involving an increasing number of countries.

Related publications. Eurostat (2001); Eurostat, Statistics in Focus, Theme 2 and Theme 4, various issues.

Reference website. www.europa.eu.int/comm/eurostat

A.2.2 Main Country-Specific Databases on the Activities of Multinationals

A.2.2.1 France

I. Inward

Main characteristics.

Type of data:	MNEs' activities data
	Firm level
Level of aggregation:	Data are publicly available by industry
	(ISIC Rev. 3)—by country of origin
	—by French region of location
	Access to firm-level data is restricted
Time coverage:	Yearly

Description of the database. Database on foreign-owned firms in France.

Firm-level dataset on firms with a foreign-owned equity share of at least 33.33%, in manufacturing, with 20 or more employees; yearly balance-sheet data.

There are two main sources of data: the 'Ficher des Implantation Etrangère de la Direction du Trésor' (Roll of foreign plants compiled by the Treasury Office), which contains information concerning the identification of every foreign-owned enterprise in France and the 'Ficher de l'Enquete Annuelle d'Entreprise du Ministère de l'Industrie', collecting financial and operating data on all industrial firms with over 20 employees.

The data are available on paper.

Reference. SESSI (various years), L'Implantation Etrangère dans l'Industrie, Paris.

II. Outward

Main characteristics.

Type of data:	MNEs' activities data
	Firm level.
Level of aggregation:	Data are publicly available by industry and
	by country of destination
	Access to firm-level data is restricted
Time coverage:	Yearly (from 1980)

Description of the database. Database on French firms investing abroad and their affiliates.

Data on private companies with 20 or more employees. The database includes financial and operating data on parent firms and affiliates abroad.

Based on LIFI ('liaison financières'), annual mandatory survey developed by the Institute National de la Statistique et des Etudes Economiques (INSEE), and Enquete Implantations, survey developed by the Direction des Relations Economiques Extérieures (DREE).

Reference. INSEE (various years), *Annuaire statistique*. Paris.

A.2.2.2   Germany

I. Inward

Main characteristics.

Type of data:	MNEs' activities data
	Firm level
Level of aggregation:	Data are publicly available by industry
	(ISIC Rev. 3) and by country of origin
	Access to firm-level data is restricted
Time coverage:	Yearly

Description of the database.   Database on foreign-owned companies in Germany.

The data cover all firms in Germany with a foreign equity share of at least 50% and with a book value exceeding €500 000 (for firms with a book value exceeding €5 000 000, the foreign ownership threshold share is 10%).

Data include the main financial variables and details on ownership.

The data are based on reports which German companies and individuals have to submit to the Deutsche Bundesbank once a year according to the Foreign Trade and Payments Regulation.

Reference.   The dataset is published in Deutsche Bundesbank, *International Capital Links*, Special Statistical Publication, various issues.

II. Outward

Main characteristics.

Type of data:	MNEs' activities data
	Firm level
Level of aggregation:	Data are publicly available by industry
	(ISIC Rev. 3) and by country of destination
	Access to firm-level data is restricted
Time coverage:	Yearly

Description of the database.   Database on German companies investing abroad and their affiliates.

The data cover German companies and individuals who, on the reporting date, have direct (primary) or indirect (secondary) holdings of more than 50% of the capital shares or voting rights in an enterprise abroad with a book value of more than €500 000 (for firms abroad with a book value exceeding €5 000 000, the ownership threshold share is 10%).

Information on the main financial variables for affiliates abroad is also reported.

The data are based on reports which German companies and individuals have to submit to the Deutsche Bundesbank once a year according to the Foreign Trade and Payments Regulation.

Reference.   The dataset is published in Deutsche Bundesbank, *International Capital Links*, Special Statistical Publication, various issues. The publication also contains a methodological section. See also Lipponer (2003).

A.2.2.3 Ireland

I. Inward

Main characteristics.

Type of data:	MNEs' activities data
	Firm level
Level of aggregation:	Data are publicly available by industry
	(NACE Rev. 1) and by country of origin
	Access to firm-level data is restricted
Time coverage:	Yearly since 1972

Description of the database. Database on foreign-owned firms in Ireland.

The dataset derives from the *Census of Industrial Production* developed by the Irish Central Statistics Office (CSO).

It includes all foreign-owned firms with at least three employees.

Data include financial and operating variables (including imports and exports).

Reference. The data are published in the *Census of Industrial production*, Irish Central Statistics Office (www.cso.ie).

A.2.2.4 Italy

I. Inward

Main characteristics.

Type of data:	MNEs' activities data
	Firm level
Level of aggregation:	Data are publicly available by industry (NACE Rev. 1),
	by country of origin, by industry and country of origin,
	by Italian region of location
	Access to firm-level data is restricted
Time coverage:	Every two years since 1986

Description of the database. *Reprint Database* on foreign-owned firms in Italy.

Collected by the Department of Economics and Production of the *Politecnico di Milano* with the support of ICE (Italian Trade Commission).

Data on foreign-owned firms in Italy in mining and manufacturing. Data on turnover, value added and employees are reported.

Data are based on surveys and indirect information collected by different sources such as newspapers, industry studies, annual reports of major companies, etc.

Reference. Mariotti and Mutinelli (2003)

II. Outward

Main characteristics.

Type of data:	MNEs' activities data
	Firm level
Level of aggregation:	Data are publicly available by industry
	(NACE Rev. 1), by country of destination,
	by industry and country of destination,
	by Italian region of location
	Access to firm-level data is restricted
Time coverage:	Every two years since 1986

Description of the database. *Reprint Database* on foreign affiliates of Italian firms.

Data on foreign affiliates of Italian firms. Data on turnover, value added and employees are reported.

Reference. Mariotti and Mutinelli (2003)

A.2.2.5 Japan

I. Inward

Main characteristics.

Type of data:	MNEs' activities data
	Firm level
Level of aggregation:	Data are publicly available by industry
	(ISIC Rev. 3) and by country of origin
	Access to firm-level data is restricted
Time coverage:	Yearly

Description of the database. Database on majority foreign-owned firms in Japan. The annual survey on *Trends in Business Activities of Foreign Affiliates in Japan* is carried out by the Enterprise Statistics Division, Research and Statistics Department and the International Business Affairs Division, Industrial Policy Bureau, MITI.

The dataset includes balance sheet data.

Reference. Ministry of Economy, Trade and Industry, *Gaishikei Kigyo no Doko*, various issues.

II. Outward

Main characteristics.

Type of data:	MNEs' activities data
	Firm level
Level of aggregation:	Data are publicly available by industry
	and by country of destination
	Access to firm-level data is restricted
Time coverage:	Yearly

Description of the database. Data on Japanese firms investing abroad and their foreign affiliates.

There are three major sources.

(i) Annual surveys by the Ministry of Finance reporting the number of notifications of investments abroad.

(ii) Annual surveys by MITI collecting data on Japanese investors, foreign affiliates, etc. Benchmark surveys are conducted every four to five years and annual surveys are conducted on small samples. The average coverage of the benchmarks surveys is about 80–90%.

(iii) A list of Japanese firms with investment abroad is collected by a private company.

Reference. Ministry of Economy, Trade and Industry, Wagakuni Kigyo no Jigyo Katsudo, various issues.

A.2.2.6 Sweden

I. Inward

Main characteristics.

Type of data:	MNEs' activities data
	Firm level
Level of aggregation:	Data are publicly available by industry (only according to the principal industrial activity of the affiliate in Sweden; ISIC Rev. 3) and by country of origin
	Access to firm-level data is restricted
Time coverage:	Yearly

Description of the database. Database on foreign-owned companies in Sweden.

Financial and operating data are reported.

Data are based on surveys conduced by ITPS (Swedish Institutes for Growth Policy Studies) in cooperation with Statistics Sweden. In addition to the survey on ownership, these data are also collected from three sources: Statistics Sweden's Central Register of Enterprises and Establishments, Statistics Sweden's Structural Business Statistics, Statistics Sweden's Trade Statistics. Until 2001 the same statistics have been collected by NUTEK (National Board for Industrial and Technical Development).

Reference. ITPS/Statistics Sweden, *Foreign-owned enterprises*, available at www.itps.se.

IIa. Outward

Main characteristics.

Type of data:	MNEs' activities data
	Firm level
Level of aggregation:	Data are publicly available by industry (only according to the principal industrial activity of the enterprise group in Sweden; ISIC Rev. 3) and by country of destination
	Access to firm level data is restricted
Time coverage:	Yearly

Description of the database. Database on Swedish companies investing abroad and their affiliates.

Data cover majority owned foreign affiliates of Swedish firms.

Data are collected through surveys conduced by ITPS (Swedish Institutes for Growth Policy Studies). Until 2001 the same statistics have been collected by NUTEK (National Board for Industrial and Technical Development).

Data collection consists of three main surveys. One carried out every three years on all Swedish groups having employees in subsidiaries abroad; a second one carried out yearly on about 80 large Swedish owned groups in manufacturing and about 40 large groups in service industries having employees in subsidiaries abroad. The third one is an annual survey on about 20 large manufacturing Swedish groups having employees in subsidiaries abroad and it collects data on sales, investment, R&D, etc.

Reference. ITPS/Statistics Sweden, *Swedish-owned enterprises having subsidiaries abroad*, available at www.itps.se.

IIb. Outward

Main characteristics.

Type of data:	MNEs' activities data
	Firm level
Level of aggregation:	Data are publicly available by industry
	(ISIC Rev. 3) and by country of destination
	Access to firm level data is restricted
Time coverage:	The available years are 1965, 1970, 1974, 1978,
	1986, 1990, 1994, 1998

Description of the database. IUI database on Swedish companies investing abroad and their affiliates.

The IUI database is constructed by the Research Institute of Industrial Economics (IUI). It includes manufacturing Swedish companies with 50 or more employees investing abroad.

Data include detailed financial and operating information on Swedish parent companies and on foreign affiliates.

Data are collected through repeated surveys (approximately every four to five years).

Reference. www.iui.se. A description of the database can be found in Braunerhjelm and Ekholm (1998).

A.2.2.7   United Kingdom

I. Inward

Main characteristics.

Type of data:	MNEs' activities data
	Firm level
Level of aggregation:	Data are publicly available by industry
	(SIC 92) and by country of origin
	Access to firm-level data is restricted
Time coverage:	Yearly from 1970

Description of the database. Database on foreign-owned companies in the UK.

Data are derived from the Annual Respondents Database (ARD) of the Office for National Statistics (ONS). This enquiry covers United Kingdom companies engaged in industrial production. It includes all production establishments located in the UK with over 100 employees. Until 1995 separate data for foreign companies are only available for manufacturing.

Detailed financial and balance sheet data reported. The nationality of the ultimate owner of foreign subsidiaries is reported.

Data from 1970 onwards are available in electronic form.

Reference. The aggregate data are published every year by ONS in *Business Monitor— Production and Construction Inquiry, and PACSTAT CD Rom.* A description of the database can be found in Griffith (1999).

II. Outward

Main characteristics.

Type of data:	MNEs' activities data
	Firm level
	Access to firm-level data is restricted

Description of the database. Database on UK firms investing abroad.

Data are derived from the *Annual Survey into Foreign Direct Investment* (AFDI) of the Office for National Statistics (ONS).

Reference. A description of the database can be found in Criscuolo and Martin (2003).

A.2.2.8   United States

I. Inward

Main characteristics.

Type of data:	MNEs' activities data
	Firm level
Level of aggregation:	Data are publicly available by industry
	(ISIC Rev. 3), by country of origin and
	by industry and country of origin
	Access to firm level data is restricted
Time coverage:	Yearly (from 1974)

Description of the database. Database on foreign-owned companies in the US.

Data are collected through Benchmark Surveys and Annual Surveys on US foreign-owned business companies carried out by the Bureau of Economic Analysis (BEA), US Department of Commerce. Mandatory surveys are conducted regularly by BEA under the International Investment and Trade in Services Survey Act. Benchmark surveys (Censuses) were conducted in 1974, 1980, 1987, 1992, 1997 and will continue to be conducted every five years. In non-benchmark survey years, a sample survey is conducted to derive estimates comparable with the benchmark survey data.

Data are on both foreign parent firms and all non-bank foreign-owned affiliates (with a foreign equity share of 10% or more) in the US.

Balance sheet data and data on trade and on intra-firm trade are reported.

Data are separately tabulated for all foreign affiliates and for majority-owned foreign affiliates (MOFA). The foreign parent and ultimate beneficial owner (UBO) of a US affiliate are classified by country.

Coverage of foreign affiliates in the US is complete in benchmark periods.

Reference. The data are electronically released annually and are available at www.bea.doc. gov. For details on the database see Quijano (1990).

II. Outward

Main characteristics.

Type of data:	MNEs' activities data
	Firm level
Level of aggregation:	Data are publicly available by industry
	(ISIC Rev. 3), by country of destination and
	by industry and country of destination
	Access to firm-level data is restricted
Time coverage:	Yearly (from 1977)

Description of the database. Database on US companies investing abroad and their affiliates.

Data collected through Benchmark Surveys and Annual Surveys on US Direct Investment Abroad carried out by the Bureau of Economic Analysis (BEA), US Department of Commerce.

Data are on both parent firms and all foreign business companies where a US citizen owns at least 10% of the equity share directly or indirectly.

Balance sheet data and data on trade and on intra-firm trade reported.

Same data collection method of inward database.

Reference. The data are released electronically annually and are available at www.bea.doc. gov. For details on the database see Mataloni (1995).

Glossary

This glossary defines some keywords used in this book. The definitions reported here may sometimes differ from the official statistical definitions reported in the appendix.[1]

Affiliate or *Subsidiary (foreign)* — Firm owned (totally or partly) by a multinational. Throughout the book the term foreign affiliate or foreign subsidiary is used to define the activity of a multinational operating in a country other than its home country. According to OECD and IMF guidelines, a firm can be defined as a foreign subsidiary if the foreign investor controls more than 50% of the shareholder's voting power or has the right to appoint or remove a majority of the member's of this enterprise administrative, management or supervisory body (see the appendix).

Arm's-length contract — Contractual relationship between two independent firms, e.g. licensing agreements, subcontracting agreements, agency agreements, franchising agreements.

Cost, insurance and freight (CIF) — The cost of a good delivered to the importing country.

Foreign direct investment (FDI) — International investment by a resident entity in one economy (direct investor, parent company, multinational) to acquire or set up a subsidiary (affiliate) in a foreign country and all subsequent capital transactions between the parent company and the foreign subsidiary and among the foreign subsidiaries part of the same multinational (see definition of flows).

> *Flows of FDI* — Capital provided (either directly or through other related enterprises) by a parent company to a foreign affiliate, or capital received by a foreign direct investor from a foreign affiliate. Foreign direct investment flows are made of three basic components: equity capital (parent company's net acquisition of the shares and loans of an enterprise in a country other than its own); reinvested earnings (direct investor's share of affiliates' earnings not distributed); other direct investment capital (inter-company debt transactions, covering the borrowing and lending of funds between direct investors and foreign affiliates and between two foreign affiliates that share the same parent company).

> *Greenfield FDI* — Foreign direct investment involving the creation of an entirely new plant.

> *Horizontal FDI (HFDI)* — Foreign direct investment involving the duplication of part of a firm's activities in a foreign country. It is normally made with the aim of having better and cheaper market access to the host country.

> *Inward FDI* — Foreign direct investment made in a host country.

> *Outward FDI* — Foreign direct investment made by a home country.

---

[1] Some of the definitions used are adapted from Alan Deardorff's on-line Glossary of International Economics: http://www.econ.lsa.umich.edu/-alandear/.

Stock of FDI — Total assets owned by foreign direct investors; real cumulated FDI flows (adjusted by changes in prices or exchange rates, rescheduling or cancellation of loans, debt forgiveness or debt-equity swaps with different values).

Vertical FDI (VFDI) — Foreign direct investment involving the transfer abroad of one or more of a firm's stages of production, generally in order to access low-cost inputs and to use output to supply other parts of the multinational's operations by means of intra-firm exports.

Footloose firm or *activity* or *factor of production* — Firm, activity, factor of production that can move easily across national borders in response to changing economic conditions.

Fragmentation — The splitting of production processes into separate parts to be carried out in different locations, including countries (international fragmentation). See also *outsourcing*.

Free on board (FOB) — The cost of a good, excluding insurance, freight and payments for other services involved in moving the good from the exporting to the importing country.

Holding (company) — Company which owns and controls other companies or firms. It generally provides headquarter services (finance, general strategy, etc.). The headquarter of a multinational would normally be organized as a holding company.

Home country — Country where the multinational firm is headquartered; where the parent company is based.

Host country — Country where a foreign subsidiary of a multinational operates.

Intra-firm trade — Cross-border trade between different units of a multinational (parent company and subsidiaries).

Joint venture — When two or more entities have joint ownership of a firm and none is in the position to exert unilateral control of the firm. In a weaker sense this term is used also to define joint endeavours of two or more entities which do not necessarily involve joint ownership of a firm or other assets, e.g. research joint ventures.

Licensing — Granting of permission, in return for a licensing fee, to use a technology or brand name. See also *arm's-length contract*.

Local firm — Generally used with reference to a host country to define a firm based in that country.

Mergers and Acquisitions (M&As) — A cross-border merger and acquisition is an FDI that involves changing the ownership of an existing enterprise, as opposed to greenfield FDI. There is merger when the foreign investor merges with the firm acquired in the host country.

Multinational firm or *enterprise, company, corporation (MNE)* — A multinational (the term is used as both a noun and an adjective) is a firm which owns a significant equity share of another company operating in a foreign country. Generally, it has headquarters and other activities in one country (home country) and production, marketing, service or other activities in this and other countries (host countries). Headquarters based in the home country are sometimes defined as parent firm/enterprise/company. Activities in the host country are defined as foreign affiliate or subsidiaries. In chapters strictly dealing with host countries we use the general term multinational as a synonym for foreign subsidiaries, in chapters strictly dealing with home countries, as a synonym for headquarters or parent firm.

National firm — A firm that operates in a single country, in contrast to a multinational enterprise.

Outsourcing — The performance of a production activity that was previously done inside a firm or plant outside that firm or plant (Source: Deardorff, Glossary of International Economics). Or, in an international context, 'the geographic separation of activities involved in producing a good (or service) across two or more countries' (Feenstra and Hanson 2001, p. 1). See also *fragmentation*.

Parent firm (or *enterprise, company*) — A parent enterprise is defined as an enterprise that owns assets of other firms in countries other than its home country, usually a substantial share of equity. Used as a synonym for headquarters of a multinational in the home country.

Subcontracting — Delegation by one firm of a portion of its production process, under contract, to another firm, including in another country. See also *arm's-length contract*.

Subsidiary or *Affiliate* — See *affiliate*.

References

Aitken, B. and A. Harrison. 1999. Do domestic firms benefit from foreign investment? Evidence from Venezuela. *American Economic Review* 89:605–618.

Aitken, B., A. Harrison, and R. Lipsey. 1996. Wages and foreign ownership: a comparative study of Mexico, Venezuela, and the United States. *Journal of International Economics* 40:345–371.

Alfaro, L., A. Chanda, S. Kalemli-Ozcan, and S. Sayek. 2004. FDI and economic growth: the role of local financial markets. *Journal of International Economics*, in press.

Allen, F. 1984. Reputation and product quality. *Rand Journal of Economics* 15:311–327.

Almeida, R. 2003. The effects of foreign owned firms on the labor market. IZA (Institute for the Study of Labor) Discussion Paper 785.

Altshuler, R., H. Grubert, and T. S. Newlon. 2001. Has US investment abroad become more sensitive to tax rates? In *International Taxation and Multinational Activity*, ed. J. R. Hines Jr. University of Chicago Press.

Anderson, J. 1979. A theoretical foundation for the gravity equation. *American Economic Review* 69:106–116.

Anderson, J. and E. van Wincoop. 2004. Trade costs. *Journal of Economic Literature* 118:1375–1418.

Antras, P. 2004. Firms, contracts, and trade structure. *Quarterly Journal of Economics*, in press.

Antras, P. and E. Helpman. 2004. Global sourcing. *Journal of Political Economy* 112:552–580.

Arellano, M. and S. R. Bond. 1991. Some tests of specification for panel data: Monte Carlo evidence and an application to employment equations. *Review of Economic Studies* 58:277–297.

———. 1998. Dynamic panel data estimation using DPD98 for GAUSS. Mimeo, Institute for Fiscal Studies, London.

Arellano, M. and O. Bover. 1995. Another look at the instrumental variable estimation of error-components model. *Journal of Econometrics* 68(1):29–52.

Arndt, S. W. and H. Kierzkowski (eds). 2001. *Fragmentation: new production patterns in the world economy*. Oxford University Press.

Aw, B., S. Chung, and M. Roberts. 2000. Productivity and turnover in the export market: micro evidence from Taiwan and South Korea. *World Bank Economic Review* 14(1):65-90.

Bajo-Rubio, O. and M. Montero-Munoz. 2001. Foreign direct investment and trade: a causality analysis. *Open Economies Review* 12:305–323.

Balasubramanyam, V. N. 1998. The MAI and foreign direct investment in developing countries. Discussion Paper EC10/98, Lancaster University.

Balasubramanyan, V. N., M. Salisu, and D. Dapsoford. 1996. Foreign direct investments and growth in EP and IS countries. *Economic Journal* 106:92–105.

Baldwin, R. E. and G. Ottaviano. 2001. Multiproduct multinationals and reciprocal FDI dumping. *Journal of International Economics* 54:429–448.

Baldwin, R. E., R. Forslid, P. Martin, G. Ottaviano, and F. Robert-Nicoud. 2003. *Economic geography and public policy*. Princeton University Press.

Baltagi B. and J. M. Griffin. 1997. Pooled estimators vs. their heterogeneous counterparts in the context of dynamic demand for gasoline. *Journal of Econometrics* 77:303–327.

Barba Navaretti, G. and D. Castellani. 2003. Does investing abroad affect performance at home? Comparing Italian multinational and national enterprises. Centro Studi Luca d'Agliano Development Studies, Working Paper 180.

Barba Navaratti, G., J. I. Haaland, and A. J. Venables. 2001. Multinational corporations and global production networks: the implications for trade policy. Report prepared for the European Commission. Directorate General for Trade, CEPR, London.

Barba Navaretti, G., D. Checchi, and A. Turrini. 2003. Adjusting labour demand: multinational vs. national firms, a cross-European analysis. *Journal of the European Economic Association* 1:708–719.

Barrell, R. and N. Pain. 1999a. Domestic institutions, agglomerations and foreign direct investment in Europe. *European Economic Review* 43:925–934.

———. 1999b. Trade restraint and Japanese direct investment flows. *European Economic Review* 43:29–45.

Barrios, S. and E. Strobl. 2002. FDI spillovers in Spain. *Weltwirtschaftliches Archiv* 138:459–481.

Barros, P. and L. Cabral. 2000. Competing for foreign direct investment. *Review of International Economics* 8:360–371.

Barry, F. 2000. Convergence is not automatic: lessons from Ireland for Central and Eastern Europe. *World Economy* 23:1379–1394.

———. 2002a. Economic policy, income convergence and structural change in the EU periphery. In *Europe and globalisation*, ed. H. Kierzkowski. London: Palgrave-Macmillan.

———. 2002b. FDI, infrastructure and the welfare effects of labour migration. *Manchester School* 70:364–379.

Barry, F. and J. Bradley. 1997. FDI and trade: the Irish host-country experience. *Economic Journal* 107:1798–1811.

Barry, F. and D. Curran. (2004). Enlargement and the European geography of the information technology sector. *World Economy* 27:901–922.

Barry, F. and A. Hannan. 2002. FDI and the predictive powers of revealed comparative advantage indicators. Unpublished manuscript, University College Dublin.

Barry, F. and C. Kearney. 2002. A portfolio analysis of industrial structure. University College Dublin WP03/09.

Barry, F., J. Bradley, and E. O'Malley. 1999. Indigenous and foreign industry. In *Understanding Ireland's economic growth*, ed. F. Barry. London: Macmillan.

Barry, F., H. Görg, and E. Strobl. 2001. Foreign direct investment and wages in domestic firms: productivity spillovers vs labour-market crowding out. Mimeo, University College Dublin and University of Nottingham.

Barry, F., A. Hannan, E. Hudson, and C. Kearney. 2002. Competitiveness implications for Ireland of EU enlargement. University College Dublin WP02/24.

Barry, F., H. Görg, and A. McDowell. 2003a. Outward FDI and the investment development path of a late-industrialising economy: evidence from Ireland. *Regional Studies* 37:341–349.

Barry, F., H. Görg, and E. Strobl. 2003b. Foreign direct investment, agglomerations and demonstration effects: an empirical investigation. *Weltwirtschaftliches Archiv* 139:583–600.

Barry, F., A. Murphy, and B. Walsh. 2003c. *The economic appraisal system for projects seeking support from the industrial development agencies.* Dublin: Forfás.

Beamish, P. 1996. IKEA (Canada) Ltd 1986 (condensed). In *Cases for contemporary strategy analysis,* ed. K. E. Neupert and J. N. Fry. Cambridge, MA: Blackwell Business

Behrman, J. and H. Wallender. 1976. *Transfer of manufacturing technology within multinational enterprises.* Cambridge, MA: Ballinger.

Belderbos, R. A. 1997. Antidumping and tariff jumping: Japanese firms' DFI in the European Union and the United States. *Weltwirtschaftliches Archiv* 133:419–437.

Benfratello, L. and A. Sembenelli. 2002. Foreign ownership and productivity: is the direction of causality so obvious? Centro Studi d'Agliano, Working Paper 166.

Berman E., J. Bound, and S. Griliches. 1994. Changes in the demand for skilled labour within U.S. manufacturing: evidence from the annual survey of manufacturers. *Quarterly Journal of Economics* 109:367–397.

Bernard, A. and J. B. Jensen. 1999. Exceptional exporter performance: cause, effect or both? *Journal of International Economics* 47:1–25.

Berndt, E. R. 1991. *The practice of econometrics: classic and contemporary.* Addison-Wesley.

Blanchard, O. 2002. Comment on Honohan and Walsh. *Brookings Papers on Economic Activity* 1:58–66.

Blomström, M. 1986. Foreign investment and productive efficiency: the case of Mexico. *Journal of Industrial Economics* 15:97–110.

Blomström, M. and A. Kokko. 1995. Policies to encourage inflows of technology through foreign multinationals. *World Development* 23:459–468.

———. 1997a. How foreign investment affects host countries. World Bank Policy Research Working Paper 1745.

———. 1997b. Regional integration and foreign direct investment. NBER Working Paper 6091.

———. 1998. Multinational corporations and spillovers. *Journal of Economic Surveys* 12:247–277.

———. 2003. Human capital and inward FDI. CEPR Discussion Paper 3762.

Blomström, M. and H. Persson. 1983. Foreign investment and spillover efficiency in an underdeveloped economy: evidence from the Mexican manufacturing industry. *World Development* 11:493–501.

Blomström, M. and F. Sjöholm. 1999. Technology transfer and spillovers: does local participation with multinationals matter? *European Economic Review* 43:915–923.

Blomström, M. and E. Wolff. 1994. Multinational corporations and productivity convergence in Mexico. In *Convergence of productivity: cross-national studies and historical evidence,* ed. W. Baumol, R. Nelson, and E. Wolff. Oxford University Press.

Blomström, M., R. E. Lipsey, and K. Kulchycky. 1988. US and Swedish direct investment and exports. In *Trade Policy Issues and Empirical Analysis,* ed. R. E. Baldwin, pp. 259–297. University of Chicago Press.

Blomström, M., A. Kokko, and M. Zejan. 1994a. Host country competition and technology transfer by multinationals. *Weltwirtschaftliches Archiv* 130:521–533.

Blomström, M., R. Lipsey, and M. Zejan. 1994b. What explains developing country growth. NBER Working Paper 4132.

Blomström, M., G. Fors, and R. E. Lipsey. 1997. Foreign direct investment and employment: home country experience in the United States and Sweden. *Economic Journal* 107:1787–1797.

Blonigen, B. 2001. In search of substitution between foreign production and exports. *Journal of International Economics* 53:81–104.

Blonigen, B. A. and R. C. Feenstra. 1997. Protectionist threat and foreign direct investment. In *The effects of U.S. trade protection and promotion policies*, ed. R. C. Feenstra. University of Chicago Press.

Blonigen, B. and M. Slaughter. 2001. Foreign-affiliate activity and U.S. skill upgrading. *Review of Economics and Statistics* 83:362–376.

Blonigen, B. A., R. B. Davies, and K. Head. 2002a. Estimating the knowledge-capital model of the multinational enterprise: comment. *American Economic Review* 91:693–708.

Blonigen, B. A., K. Tomlin, and W. W. Wilson. 2002b. Tariff-jumping FDI and domestic firms' profits. NBER Working Paper 9027.

Bloom, N. and R. Griffith. 2001. The internationalisation of UK R&D. *Fiscal Studies* 22:337–355.

Blundell, R. and S. R. Bond. 1998. Initial conditions and moment restrictions in dynamic panel data models. *Journal of Econometrics* 87(1):115–144.

———. 2000. GMM estimation with persistent panel data: an application to production functions. *Econometric Review* 19:321–340.

Blundell, R. and M. Costa Dias. 2000. Evaluation methods for non-experimental data. *Fiscal Studies* 21:427–468.

———. 2002. Alternative approached to evaluation in empirical microeconomics. Cemmap Working Paper CWP 10/02.

Borensztein, E., J. De Gregorio, and J. Lee. 1998. How does foreign direct investment affect economic growth? *Journal of International Economics* 45:115–135.

Bosco, M. 2001. Does FDI contribute to technological spillovers and growth? A panel data analysis of Hungarian firms. *Transnational Corporations* 10:43–68.

Braconier, H. and K. Ekholm. 2000. Swedish multinationals and competition from high- and low-wage locations. *Review of International Economics* 8:448–461.

———. 2002. Foreign direct investment in Eastern and Central Europe: employment effects in the EU. Mimeo, Stockholm School of Economics (revised version of CEPR Discussion Paper 3052).

Braconier, H., K. Ekholm, and K. H. Midelfart-Knarvik. 2001. In search of FDI-transmitted R&D spillovers: a study based on Swedish data. *Weltwirtschafliches Archiv* 137:644–665.

Braconier, H., P. J. Norbäck, and D. Urban. 2002. Vertical FDI revisited. Working Paper 579, The Research Institute of Industrial Economics (IUI), Stockholm.

———. 2003. Reconciling the evidence on the knowledge capital model. Working Paper 590, The Research Institute of Industrial Economics (IUI), Stockholm.

Brainard, S. L. 1993. An empirical assessment of the factor proportions explanation of multinational sales. NBER Working Paper 4583.

———. 1997. An empirical assessment of the proximity-concentration trade-off between multinational sales and trade. *American Economic Review* 87:520–544.

Brainard, S. L. and D. Riker. 1997a. Are US multinational exporting US jobs? NBER Working Paper 5958.

———. 1997b. US multinationals and competition from low wage countries. NBER Working Paper 5959.

Branstetter, L. 2000. Is foreign direct investments a channel of knowledge spillovers? Evidence form Japan's FDI in the United States. NBER Working Paper 8015.

Braunerhjelm, P. 1994. Regional integration and the locational response of knowledge intensive multinational firms: implications for comparative advantage and welfare of outsiders
and insiders. Dissertation, IUI, Stockholm, Sweden, and The Graduate Institute for International Studies, Geneva, Switzerland.

Braunerhjelm, P. and K. Ekholm (eds). 1998. *The geography of multinational firms*. Kluwer.

Braunerhjelm, P. and R. Svensson. 1996. Host country characteristics and agglomeration in
foreign direct investment. *Applied Economics* 28:833–840.

Braunerhjelm, P., R. Faini, V. D. Norman, F. Ruane, and P. Seabright. 2000. Integration and the
regions of Europe: how the right policies can prevent polarization. *Monitoring European
Integration* 10. CEPR.

Bruce, L. 1987. The bright new worlds of Benetton. *International Management* (November),
pp. 24–35.

Bruno, G. and A. M. Falzoni. 2003. Multinational corporations, wages and employment: do
adjustment costs matter? *Applied Economics* 35:1277–1290.

Burnham, J. 1998. Global telecommunications: a revolutionary challenge. *Business and the
Contemporary World* 2:231–248.

Campa, J. and L. Goldberg. 1997. The evolving external orientation of manufacturing industries: evidence from four countries. NBER Working Paper 5919.

Campos, N. and Y. Kinoshita. 2002. Foreign direct investment as technology transferred:
some panel evidence from the transition economies. *Manchester School* 70:398–419.

Cantwell, J. 1989. *Technological innovation and multinational corporations*. Oxford: Basil
Blackwell.

Cantwell, J. and L. Piscitello. 2002. Corporate diversification, internationalisation and location of technological activities by MNCs in Europe. In *Europe and globalisation*, ed. H.
Kierzkowski. London: Palgrave-Macmillan.

Carkovic, M. and R. Levine. 2002. Does foreign direct investment accelerate economic
growth? University of Minnesota Department of Finance Working Paper.

Carr, D., J. R. Markusen, and K. Maskus. 2001. Estimating the knowledge capital model of
the multinational firm. *American Economic Review* 91:693–708.

Castellani, D. 2002. Export behaviour and productivity growth: evidence from Italian manufacturing firms. *Weltwirtshaftliches Archiv* 138:4.

Castellani, D. and A. Zanfei. 2003. Technology gaps, absorptive capacity and the impact of
inward investments on productivity of European firms. *Economics of Innovation and New
Technologies* 12:555–576.

Caves, R. E. 1971. International corporations: the industrial economics of foreign investment.
Economica 38:1–27.

———. 1974. Multinational firms, competition and productivity in host-country markets.
Economica 41:176–193.

———. 1996. *Multinational enterprise and economic analysis*. Cambridge University Press.

CEPR. 2002. Making sense of globalization: a guide to the economic issues. CEPR Policy
Paper 8.

Chédor, S. and J. L. Mucchielli. 1998. Implantation à l'étranger et performance à l'exportation:
une analyse empirique sur les implantations des firmes francaises dans les pays emergents.
Revue Economique (May).

Chédor S., J. L. Mucchielli, and I. Soubaya. 2002. Intra-firm trade and foreign direct investment: an empirical analysis of French firms. In *Multinational firms and impacts on employment, trade and technology*, ed. R. Lipsey and J. L. Mucchielli, pp. 43–83. Routledge.

Chuang, Y.-C. and C.-M. Lin. 1999. Foreign direct investment, R&D and spillover efficiency: evidence from Taiwan's manufacturing firms. *Journal of Development Studies* 35:117–137.

Clausing, K. 2000. Does multinational activity displace trade? *Economic Inquiry* 38(2):190–205.

Clerides, S., S. Lach, and J. R. Tybout. 1998. Is learning by exporting important? Micro-dynamic evidence from Colombia, Mexico and Morocco. *Quarterly Journal of Economics* 113:903–947.

Coase, R. 1937. The nature of the firm. *Economica* 4:386–405.

Coe, D. T. and E. Helpman. 1995. International R&D spillovers. *European Economic Review* 39:859–887.

Conyon, M., S. Girma, S. Thompson, and P. W. Wright. 2002. The productivity and wage effects of foreign acquisition in the United Kingdom. *Journal of Industrial Economics* 50:83–102.

Corden, W. M. 1967. Protection and foreign investment. *Economic Record* 43:209–232.

Criscuolo, C. and R. Martin. 2003. Multinationals, foreign ownership and productivity in UK businesses. Royal Economic Society Conference 2003, 50.

Damijan, J., B. Majcen, M. Knell, and M. Rojec. 2001. The role of FDI, absorptive capacity and trade in transferring technology to transition countries: evidence from firm panel data for eight transition countries. Mimeo, UN Economic Commission for Europe, Geneva.

Dascher, K. 2000. Trade, FDI and congestion: the small and very open economy. CEPR Working Paper 2526. (Available at http://www.ucd.ie/-economic/workingpapers/2000.htm.)

Davies, S. and B. Lyons. 1991. Characterising relative performance: the productivity advantage of foreign owned firms in the UK. *Oxford Economic Papers* 43:584–595.

———. 1996. *Industrial organization in the European Union.* Oxford: Clarendon Press.

Deardorff, A. V. 1998. Determinants of bilateral trade: does gravity work in a neoclassical world? In *The regionalization of the world economy*, ed. J. A. Frankel. Chicago University Press.

Decoster, G. P. and W. C. Strange. 1993. Spurious agglomeration. *Journal of Urban Economics* 33:273–304.

De la Fuente, A. and X. Vives. 1997. The sources of Irish growth. In *International perspectives on the Irish economy*, ed. A. Gray. Dublin: Indecon. Also available as CEPR Discussion Paper 1756.

Delgado M, J. Farinas, and S. Ruano. 2002. Firm productivity and export markets: a non-parametric approach. *Journal of International Economics* 57:397–422.

Desai, M. A., C. F. Foley, and J. R. Hines. 2002a. International joint ventures and the boundaries of the firm. NBER Working Paper 9115.

———. 2002b. Chains of ownership, regional tax competition and foreign direct investment. NBER Working Paper 9224.

Deutsche Bundesbank. (Various years). *International capital links.* Special Statistical Publication.

Devereux, M. P. and R. Griffith. 1998. Taxes and the location of production: evidence from a panel of US multinationals. *Journal of Public Economics* 68:335–367.

———. 2002. The impact of corporate taxation on the location of capita: a review. *Swedish Economic Policy Review* 9:79–102.

Devereux, M. P., R. Griffith, and A. Klemm. 2002a. Corporate income tax reforms and international tax competition. *Economic Policy* 17:451–495.

Devereux, M. P., B. Lockwood, and M. Redoano. 2002b. Do countries compete over corporate tax rates? CEPR Discussion Paper 3400.

Dimelis, S. and H. Louri. 2001. Foreign direct investment and efficiency benefits: a conditional quantile analysis. CEPR Discussion Paper 2868.

Dixit, A. K. and V. Norman. 1980. *The theory of international trade*. Cambridge University Press.

Dixit, A. K. and J. E. Stiglitz. 1977. Monopolistic competition and optimum product diversity. *American Economic Review* 67:297–308.

Djankov, S. and B. Hoekman. 2000. Foreign investment and productivity growth in Czech enterprises. *World Bank Economic Review* 14(1):49–64.

Doms, M. E. and J. B. Jensen. 1998. Comparing wages, skills, and productivity between domestically and foreign-owned manufacturing establishments in the United States. In *Geography and ownership as bases for economic accounting, studies in income and wealth*, ed. R. E. Baldwin et al., vol. 59, pp. 235–258. University of Chicago Press.

Driffield, N. 2001. The impact on domestic productivity of inward investment in the UK. *Manchester School* 69:103–119.

Driffield, N. and S. Girma. 2002. Regional foreign direct investment and wage spillovers: plant level evidence from the UK electronics industry. GEP Research Paper 2002/04, Globalisation and Labour Markets Programme, Nottingham, Leverhulme Centre for Research on Globalisation and Economic Policy.

Dunning, J. H. 1993. *Multinational enterprises and the global economy*. Addison-Wesley.

———. 1997a. The European internal market programme and inbound foreign direct investment. Part 1. *Journal of Common Market Studies* 35(1):1–30.

———. 1997b. The European internal market programme and inbound foreign direct investment. Part 2. *Journal of Common Market Studies* 35(2):189–223.

———. 1977c. Trade, location of economic activity and the multinational enterprise: a search for an eclectic approach. In *The international allocation of economic activity*, ed. B. Ohlin, P. O. Hesselborn, and P. M. Wijkman. Macmillan.

———. 1981. *International production and the multinational enterprise*. London: Allen & Unwin.

Dunning, J., C. S. Kim, and J. D. Lin. 2001. Incorporating trade into the investment development path: a case study of Korea and Taiwan. *Oxford Development Studies* 29(2):145–154.

Durkan, J. 2002. Foreign direct investment: the case of the electronics and pharmaceuticals industries. In *The Irish economy in transition: successes, problems and prospects*, ed. V. Munley, R. Thornton, and R. Aronson. Oxford: JAI (Elsevier Science).

Ehremberg, R. G. 1994. *Labor markets and integrating national economies*. Washington, DC: The Brookings Institution.

Ekholm, K. 1997. Factor endowments and the pattern of affiliate production by multinational enterprises. CREDIT Research Paper 97/19.

———. 1998. Proximity advantages, scale economies, and the location of production. In *The geography of multinational firms*, ed. P. Braunerhjelm and K. Ekholm. Kluwer.

Ekholm, K. and M. Hesselman. 2000. The foreign operations of Swedish manufacturing firms: evidence from a survey of Swedish multinationals 1998. Papers 540, Industrial Institute for Economic and Social Research.

Ethier, W. J. 1986. The multinational firm. *Quarterly Journal of Economics* 101:805–833.

———. 1992. The multinational firm. In *Imperfect competition and international trade*, ed. G. M. Grossman, pp. 303–324. MIT Press Readings in Economics.

Ethier, W. and J. Markusen. 1996. Multinational firms, technology diffusion, and trade. *Journal of International Economics* 41:1–28.

Eurostat. (Various years). *European Union direct investment yearbook.*

———. 2001. *Foreign-owned enterprises in the EU—results for eight member state.*

Fabbri, F., J. E. Haskel, and M. J. Slaughter. 2002. Globalisation and labour demand elasticities in Britain. Paper presented at the *Adjusting to Globalisation Conference*, University of Nottingham, 28 and 29 June 2002.

———. 2003. Does nationality of ownership matter for labor demands? *Journal of the European Economic Association* 1:698–707.

Faini, R., A. Falzoni, M. Galeotti, R. Helg, and A. Turrini. 1999. Importing jobs and exporting firms? On the wage and employment implications of Italian trade and foreign direct investments flows. *Giornale degli Economisti e Annali di Economia* 58(1):95–135.

Fajnzylber, P. and W. Maloney. 2001. How comparable are labor demand elasticities across countries? World Bank Policy Research Working Paper 2658.

Feenstra, R. 2003. *Advanced international trade: theory and evidence.* Princeton University Press.

Feenstra, R. and G. Hanson. 1996. Globalization, outsourcing and wage inequality. *American Economic Review* 86(2):240–245.

———. 2001. Global production sharing and rising inequality: a survey of trade and wages. NBER Working Paper 8372.

———. 1997. Foreign direct investment and relative wages: evidence from Mexico's maquiladoras. *Journal of International Economics* 42:371–393.

Feenstra, R. C., J. R. Markusen, and A. K. Rose. 2001. Understanding the home market effect and the gravity equation: the role of differentiating goods. *Canadian Journal of Economics* 34:430–447.

Feliciano, Z. and R. Lipsey. 1999. Foreign ownership and wages in the United States, 1987–1992. NBER Working Paper 6923.

FIAS. 2003. Developing knowledge intensive sector, technology transfer, and the role of FDI. Mimeo, Foreign Investment Advisory Services, World Bank, Washington, DC.

FitzGerald, J. and I. Kearney. 2000. Convergence in living standards in Ireland: the role of the new economy. Seminar Paper 134. Dublin: Economic and Social Research Institute.

FitzGerald, R. 1995. *Rowntree and the marketing revolution; 1862–1969.* Cambridge University Press.

Fontagné, L. and M. Pajot. 2002. Relationships between trade and FDI flows within two panels of US and French industries. In *Multinational firms and impacts on employment, trade and technology*, ed. R. Lipsey and J. L. Mucchielli, pp. 43–83. Routledge.

Fosfuri, A. and M. Motta. 1999. Multinationals without advantages. *Scandinavian Journal of Economics* 101:617–630.

Fosfuri, A., M. Motta, and T. Ronde. 1997. Foreign direct investments and spillovers through workers mobility. *Journal of International Economics* 53:205–222.

Fujita, M., P. Krugman, and A. J. Venables. 1999. *The spatial economy: cities, regions and international trade.* MIT Press.

Fumagalli, C. 2003. Competition for FDI and asymmetric countries. *European Economic Review* 47:945–962.

Gerschenberg, I. 1987. The training and spread of managerial know-how: a comparative analysis of multinational and other firms in Kenya. *World Development* 15:931–939.

Girma, S. and H. Görg. 2002. Multinationals' productivity advantage: scale or technology? CEPR Discussion Paper DP3503.

Girma, S. and K. Wakelin. 2000. Are there regional spillovers from FDI in the UK? GEP Research Paper 2000/16, Globalisation and Labour Markets Programme, Nottingham, Leverhulme Centre for Research on Globalisation and Economic Policy.

———. 2001. Regional underdevelopment: is FDI the solution? A semiparametric analysis. GEP Research Paper 2001/11, Globalisation and Labour Markets Programme, Nottingham, Leverhulme Centre for Research on Globalisation and Economic Policy.

Girma, S., D. Greenaway, and R. Kneller. 2002. Does exporting lead to better performance? A microeconometric analysis of matched firms. GEP Working Paper 2002/09, University of Nottingham.

Girma, S., D. Greenaway, and K. Wakelin. 2001. Who benefits from foreign direct investment in the UK? *Scottish Journal of Political Economy* 48(2):119–133.

Glass, A. J. and K. Saggi. 1999. Multinational firms and technology transfer. World Bank Policy Research Working Paper 2067.

Globerman, S. 1979. Foreign direct investment and 'spillover' efficiency benefits in Canadian manufacturing industries. *Canadian Journal of Economics* 12:42–56.

Globerman, S., J. Ries, and I. Vertinsky. 1994. Economic performance of foreign affiliates in Canada. *Canadian Journal Of Economics* 27:143–156.

Gordon, R. H. and J. R. Hines. 2002. International taxation. NBER Working Paper 8854.

Görg, H. 2000. Fragmentation and trade: US inward processing trade in the EU. *Weltwirtschaftliches Archiv* 136:403–422.

Görg, H. and D. Greenaway. 2001. Foreign direct investment and intra-industry spillovers: a review of the literature. GEP Research Paper 2001/37, Globalisation and Labour Markets Programme, Nottingham, Leverhulme Centre for Research on Globalisation and Economic Policy.

Görg, H. and E. Strobl. 2001a. Multinational companies, technology spillovers, and plant survival: evidence from Irish manufacturing. EIJS Working Paper 131, Stockholm School of Economics.

———. 2001b. Multinational companies and productivity spillovers: a meta-analysis. *Economic Journal* 111:F723–F739.

———. 2002. Multinational companies and indigenous development: an empirical analysis. *European Economic Review* 46:1305–1322.

———. 2003a. Footloose multinationals? *Manchester School* 71:1–19.

———. 2003b. Multinational companies, technology spillovers and plant survival: evidence for Irish manufacturing. *Scandinavian Journal of Economics* 105:581–595.

Görg, H., E. Strobl, and F. Walsh. 2002. Why do foreign-owned firms pay more? The role of on-the-job training. IZA (Institute for the Study of Labor) Discussion Paper 590.

Gresik, T. A. 2001. The taxing task of taxing transnationals. *Journal of Economic Literature* 39:800–838.

Griffith, R. 1999. Using the ARD establishment level data to look at foreign ownership and productivity in the United Kingdom. *Economic Journal* 109:416–442.

Griffith, R. and H. Simpson. 2001. Characteristics of foreign-owned firms in British manufacturing. The Institute for Fiscal Studies Working Paper 01/10.

Griffith, R., S. J. Redding, and H. Simpson. 2003. Productivity convergence and foreign ownership at the establishment level. CEPR Discussion Paper 3765.

Gropp, R. and K. Kostial. 2000. The disappearing tax base: is foreign direct investment eroding corporate income taxes? European Central Bank Working Paper 31. (Available at http://ideas.repec.org/e/pgr26.html.)

Grossman, G. M. and E. Helpman. 2002. Integration versus outsourcing in industry equilibrium. *Quarterly Journal of Economics* 117:85–119.

———. 2003. Outsourcing versus FDI in industry equilibrium. *Journal of the European Economic Association* 1(2):317–327.

Grossman, S. and O. Hart. 1986. The costs and benefits of ownership: a theory of vertical and lateral integration. *Journal of Political Economy* 94:691–719.

Grout, P. 1984. Investment and wages in the absence of binding contracts: a Nash bargaining approach. *Econometrica* 52:449–460.

Grubert, H. and J. Mutti. 1991. Taxes, tariffs and transfer pricing in multinational corporate decision making. *Review of Economics and Statistics* 73:285–293.

Haaland, J. I. and I. Wooton. 1998. Anti-dumping jumping: reciprocal anti-dumping and industrial location. *Weltwirtschaftliches Archiv* 134:340–362.

———. 1999. International competition for multinational investment. *Scandinavian Journal of Economics* 101:631–649.

———. 2002. Multinational investment, industry risk and policy competition. CEPR Discussion Paper 3152.

Haaland, J. I., I. Wooton, and G. Faggio. 2002. Multinational firms: easy come, easy go? *Finanzarchiv* 59:3–26.

Haddad, M. and A. Harrison. 1993. Are there positive spillovers from direct foreign investment? Evidence from panel data for Morocco. *Journal of Development Economics* 42:51–74.

Hamermesh, D. S. 1993. *Labor demand.* Princeton University Press.

Hanson, G. 2001. Should countries promote foreign direct investment? UNCTAD G-24 Discussion Paper 9, February 2001.

Hanson, G., Mataloni, R. J., and M. Slaughter. 2001. Expansion strategies of U.S. multinational firms. In *Brookings Trade Forum 2001*, ed. D. Rodrik and S. Collins, pp. 245–282.

Hansson, P. 2001. Skill upgrading and production transfer within Swedish multinationals in the 1990s. CEPS Working Document 163.

Harrigan, J. and A. J. Venables. 2004. Timeliness, trade and agglomeration. Discussion Paper, Centre for Economic Performance, LSE.

Harris, R. 2002. Foreign ownership and productivity in the United Kingdom—some issues when using the ARD establishment level data. *Scottish Journal of Political Economy* 47:318–355.

Harris, R. and C. Robinson. 2002. The effect of foreign acquisitions on total factor productivity: plant-level evidence from UK manufacturing, 1987–1992. *Review of Economics and Statistics* 84:562–568.

———. 2003. Foreign ownership and productivity in the United Kingdom. Estimates of UK manufacturing using the ARD. *Review of Industrial Organization* 22:207–223.

Harrison, A. 1996. Determinants and effects of direct foreign investment in Côte d'Ivoire, Morocco, and Venezuela. In *Industrial Evolution in Developing Countries*, ed. M. J. Roberts and J. R. Tybout, pp. 163–186. New York: Oxford University Press for the World Bank.

Hart, O. 1995. *Firms, contracts, and financial structure.* Clarendon Press and Oxford University Press.

Hart, O. and B. Holmstrom. 1987. The theory of contracts. In *Advances in economic theory*, ed. T. Bewley. Fifth World Congress. Cambridge, MA: Cambridge University Press.

Hart, O. and J. Moore. 1990. Property rights and the nature of the firm. *Journal of Political Economy* 98:1119–1158.

Haskel, J., S. Pereira, and M. Slaughter. 2002. Does inward foreign direct investment boost the productivity of domestic firms? NBER Working Paper 8724.

Hatzius, J. 1997. Domestic jobs and foreign wages: labour demand in Swedish multinationals. CEP Discussion Papers 337, Centre for Economic Performance, LSE.

———. 1998. Domestic job and foreign wages. *Scandinavian Journal of Economics* 100:733–746.

Haufler, A. 2001. *Taxation in a global economy*. Cambridge University Press.

Haufler, A. and G. Schjelderup. 2000. Corporate tax systems and cross country profit shifting. *Oxford Economic Papers* 52:306–325.

Head, K. and J. Ries. 2001. Overseas investment and firm exports. *Review of International Economics* 9(1):108–122.

———. 2002. Offshore production and skill upgrading by Japanese manufacturing firms. *Journal of International Economics* 58:81–105.

Head, K., J. Ries, and D. Swenson. 1995. Agglomeration benefits and location choice: evidence from Japanese manufacturing investments in the United States. *Journal of International Economics* 38:223–247.

———. 1999. Attracting foreign manufacturing: investment promotion and agglomeration. *Regional Science and Urban Economics* 29:197–218.

Helpman, E. 1984. Simple theory of international trade with multinational corporations. *Journal of Political Economy* 92:451–471.

———. 1985. Multinational corporations and trade structure. *Review of Economic Studies* 52:442–458.

Helpman, E. and P. Krugman. 1985. *Market structure and foreign trade*. MIT Press.

Helpman, E., M. J. Melitz, and S. R. Yeaple. 2004. Export vs. FDI with heterogeneous firms. *American Economic Review* 94:300–316.

Hines, J. R. 1999. Lessons from behavioral responses to international taxation. *National Tax Journal* 52:305–322.

Hobday, M. 1995. *Innovation in East Asia: the challenge to Japan*. Cheltenham: Edward Elgar.

Hoekman, B. and K. Saggi. 1999. Multilateral discipline for investment-related policies? Paper presented at the Conference Global Regionalism, Rome.

Honohan, P. and B. Walsh. 2002. Catching up with the leaders. The Irish hare. *Brookings Papers on Economic Activity* 1:1–57.

Horn, H. and J. Levinsohn. 2001. Merger policies and trade liberalisation. *Economic Journal* 111:244–276.

Horn, H. and L. Persson. 2001. The equilibrium ownership of an international oligopoly. *Journal of International Economics* 53:307–333.

Horst, T. 1972. Firm and industry determinants of the decision to invest abroad: an empirical study. *Review of Economics and Statistics* 54:258–266.

Horstmann, I. and J. Markusen. 1987a. Strategic investments and the development of multinationals. *International Economic Review* 28:109–121.

———. 1987b. Licensing versus direct investment: a model of internalization by the multinational enterprise. *Canadian Journal of Economics* 20:464–481.

————. 1992. Endogenous market structures in international trade (natura facit saltum). *Journal of International Economics* 32:109–129.

————. 1996. Exploring new markets: direct investment, contractual relationships, and the multinational enterprise. *International Economic Review* 37:1–20.

Howenstine, N. and W. Zeile. 1994. Characteristics of foreign-owned U.S. manufacturing establishments. *Survey of Current Business* 74:34–59.

Hsiao, C. 1986. *Analysis of panel data analysis*. Cambridge University Press.

Hummels, D. 1999. Have international transportation costs declined? Mimeo, Chicago.

————. 2000. Time as a trade barrier. Mimeo, Purdue University.

Hummels, D., J. Ishii, and K.-M. Yi. 2001. The nature and growth of vertical specialization in world trade. *Journal of International Economics* 54:75–96.

IFS. 2000. *Corporate tax harmonisation in Europe: a guide to the debate*. London: Institute for Fiscal Studies.

IMF. 1993. *Balance of payments manual*, 5 edn. Washington, DC: International Monetary Fund.

INSEE. (Various years). *Annuaire statistique*. Paris.

Jackson, T. and D. Shaw. 2001. *Mastering fashion buying and merchandising management*. London: Macmillan.

Jaffe, A., M. Trajtenberg, and R. Henderson. 1993. Geographic localization of knowledge spillovers as evidenced by patent citations. *Quarterly Journal of Economics* 108:577–598.

Jones, R. W. 2000. *Globalization and the theory of input trade*. MIT Press.

Joskow, P. 1977. Commercial impossibility, the uranium market and the Westinghouse case. *Journal of Legal Studies* 6:119–176.

Kaminski, B. and F. Ng. 2001. Trade and production fragmentation: Central European economies in EU networks of production and marketing. Policy Research Working Paper 2611, The World Bank, DECRG-Trade, Washington, DC.

Kathuria, V. 1998. Technology transfer and spillovers for Indian manufacturing firms. *Development Policy Review* 16:73–91.

————. 2000. Productivity spillovers from technology transfer to Indian manufacturing firms. *Journal of International Development* 12:343–369.

————. 2001. Foreign firms, technology transfer and knowledge spillovers to Indian manufacturing firms: a stochastic frontier analysis. *Applied Economics* 33:625–642.

Katz, H. C. 1993. The decentralization of collective bargaining: a literature review and comparative analysis. *Industrial and Labor Relations Review* 47:3–22.

Katz, J. M. 1969. *Production functions, foreign investment and growth*. Amsterdam: North-Holland.

Keeble, D., J. Offert, and S. Walker. 1988. *Peripheral regions in a community of twelve member states*. Brussels: Commission of the European Communities.

Kim, S. 1998. The rise of multi-unit firms in US manufacturing. NBER Working Paper 6425.

Kinoshita, Y. 2001. R&D and technology spillovers through FDI: innovation and absorptive capacity. CEPR Discussion Paper 2775.

Kogut, B. and Chang, S. J. 1991. Technological capabilities and Japanese foreign direct investments in the United States. *Review of Economic and Statistics* 73:401–413.

Kokko, A. 1994. Technology, market characteristics, and spillovers. *Journal of Development Economics* 43:279–293.

———. 1996. Productivity spillovers from competition between local firms and foreign affiliates. *Journal of International Development* 8:517–530.

Kokko, A., R. Tansini, and M. Zejan. 1996. Local technological capability and spillovers from FDI in the Uruguayan manufacturing sector. *Journal of Development Studies* 34:602–611.

———. 2001. Trade regimes and spillover effects of FDI: evidence from Uruguay. *Weltwirtschaftliches Archiv* 137:124–149.

Konings, J. 2001. The effects of foreign direct investment on domestic firms: evidence from firm level panel data in emerging economies. CEPR Discussion Paper 2586.

Konings, J. and A. Murphy. 2001. Do multinational enterprises substitute parent jobs for foreign ones? Evidence from European firm-level panel data. CEPR Discussion Paper 2972.

Kraay, A. 1999. Exports and economic performance: evidence from a panel of Chinese enterprises. *Revue d'Economie du Developpement* 1–2:183–207.

Kravis, I. B. and R. E. Lipsey. 1982. The location of overseas production and production for exports by U.S. multinational firms. *Journal of International Economics* 12:201–223.

Krishna, P., D. Mitra, and S. Chinoy. 2001. Trade liberalization and labour demand elasticities: evidence from Turkey. *Journal of International Economics* 55:391–409.

Krugman, P. 1991a. *Geography and trade*. Gaston Eyskens Lecture Series. MIT Press and Louvain University Press.

———. 1991b. Increasing returns and economic geography. *Journal of Political Economy* 99:483–499.

———. 1993. Lessons of Massachusetts for EMU. In *Adjustment and growth in the European monetary union*, ed. F. Torres and F. Giavazzi. Cambridge University Press.

———. 1995. Increasing returns, imperfect competition and the positive theory of international trade. In *Handbook of international economics*, ed. G. Grossman and K. Rogoff, vol. 3. North-Holland.

———. 1997. Good news from Ireland: a geographical perspective. In *International perspectives on the Irish economy*, ed. A. Gray. Dublin: Indecon.

Kugler, M. 2001. The sectoral diffusion of spillovers from foreign direct investment. Mimeo, University of Southampton, August.

Lall, S. 1980a. Monopolistic advantages and foreign involvement by US manufacturing industry. *Oxford Economic Papers* 32:105–122.

———. 1980b. Vertical interfirm linkages in LDCs: an empirical study. *Oxford Bulletin of Economics and Statistics* 42:203–226.

Larrain, F. B., L. F. Lopez-Calva, and A. Rodriguez-Clare. 2000. Intel: a case study of foreign direct investment in Central America. CID Working Paper 58. Center for International Development at Harvard University.

Lawrence, R. and M. Slaughter. 1993. International trade and American wages in the 1980s: giant sucking sound or small hiccup? Brookings Papers on Economic Activity: Microeconomics no. 2, pp. 161–226.

Lipponer, A. 2003. A 'new' micro database for German FDI. In *Foreign direct investment in the real and financial sector of industrial countries*, ed. H. Herrmann and R. Lipsey. Springer.

Lipsey, R. E. 1994. Foreign-owned firms and U.S. wages. NBER Working Paper 4927.

———. 2000. Affiliates of US and Japanese multinationals in East Asian production and trade. In *The role of foreign direct investment in East Asian economic development*, ed. T. Ito and A. Krueger. University of Chicago Press.

———. 2001. Foreign direct investment and the operations of multinational firms: concepts, history and data. NBER Working Paper 8665.

———. 2002. Home and host country effects of FDI. NBER Working Paper 9293.

———. 2003. Discussion of EU accession and prospective FDI flows to CEE countries. In *Foreign direct investment in the real and financial sector of industrial countries*, ed. H. Herrmann and R. Lipsey. Springer.

Lipsey, R. E. and F. Sjöholm. 2001. Foreign direct investment and wages in Indonesian manufacturing. NBER Working Paper 8299.

Lipsey, R. E. and M. Weiss. 1981. Foreign production and export in manufacturing industries. *Review of Economics and Statistics* 63:488–494.

———. 1984. Foreign production and export of individual firms. *Review of Economics and Statistics* 66:304–307.

Lipsey, R. E., E. Ramstetter, and M. Blomström. 1999. Parent exports and affiliate activity in Japanese multinational companies, 1986–1992. In *Analytical research based on data from the survey of overseas business activities*, pp. 93–146. Tokyo: Institute for International Trade and Investment.

———. 2000. Outward FDI and parent exports and employment: Japan, the United States, and Sweden. *Global Economic Quarterly* 1:285–302.

Liu, X., P. Siler, C. Wang, and Y. Wei. 2000. Productivity spillovers from foreign direct investment: evidence from UK industry level panel data. *Journal of International Business Studies* 31:407–425.

Lyons, B. 1994. Contract and specific investment: an empirical test of transaction cost theory. *Journal of Economics and Management Strategy* 3:257–278.

MacDougall, G. D. A. 1960. The benefits and costs of private investment from abroad: a theoretical approach. *Economic Record* 36:13–35.

MacSharry, R. and P. White. 2000. *The making of the Celtic tiger, the inside story of Ireland's booming economy*. Dublin: Mercier Press.

Mansfield, E. and A. Romeo. 1980. Technology transfer to overseas subsidiaries by US-based firms. *Quarterly Journal of Economics* 95:737–750.

Mansfield, E., A. Romeo, and S. Wagner. 1980. Foreign trade and US research and development. *Review of Economic and Statistics* 61:49–57.

Mariotti, S. and M. Mutinelli. 2003. *Italia multinazionale 2003*. Rome: ICE.

Markusen, J. R. 1984. Multinationals, multi-plant economies and the gains from trade. *Journal of International Economics* 16:205–226.

———. 1988. Production, trade and migration with differentiated, skilled workers. *Canadian Journal of Economics* 21:492–506.

———. 1995. The boundaries of multinational firms and the theory of international trade. *Journal of Economic Perspectives* 9:169–189.

———. 1997. Trade versus investment liberalization. NBER Working Paper 6231.

———. 2001. Contracts, intellectual property rights, and multinational investment in developing countries. *Journal of International Economics* 53:189–204.

———. 2002. *Multinational firms and the theory of international trade*. MIT Press.

Markusen, J. R. and K. Maskus. 2001. Multinational firms: reconciling theory and evidence. In *Topics in international economics. A Festschrift in honor of Robert E. Lipsey*, ed. M. Blomström and L. S. Goldberg. Chicago University Press.

———. 2002. Discriminating among alternative theories of the multinational enterprise. *Review of International Economics* 10:694–707.

Markusen, J. R. and A. J. Venables. 1996. The increased importance of direct investment in North Atlantic economic relationships: a convergence hypothesis. In *The new transatlantic economy*, ed. M. Canzoneri, W. Ethier, and V. Grilli. CEPR, Cambridge.

————. 1998. Multinational firms and the new trade theory. *Journal of International Economics* 46:183–203.

————. 1999. Foreign direct investment as a catalyst for industrial development. *European Economic Review* 43:335–356.

————. 2000. The theory of endowment, intra-industry and multinational trade. *Journal of International Economics* 52:209–234.

Mas Colell, A., M. Whinston, and J. R. Green. 1995. *Microeconomic theory*. Oxford University Press.

Mataloni, R. J. 1995. A guide to BEA statistics on U.S. multinational companies. *Survey of Current Business*. (Available at www.bea.gov.)

Matouschek, N. 1999. Foreign direct investment and spillovers through backward linkages. CEPR Discussion Paper 2283.

Matouschek, N. and A. J. Venables. 1999. Evaluating investment projects in the presence of sectoral linkages. Draft paper presented at PREM week '99, World Bank.

Mezzetti, C. and E. Dinopoulos. 1991. Domestic unionisation and import competition. *Journal of International Economics* 31:79–100.

Midelfart-Knarvik, K. H., H. G. Overman, and A. J. Venables. 2000. Comparative advantage and economic geography: estimating the location of production in the EU. CEPR Discussion Paper 2618.

Monteverde, K. and D. Teece. 1982. Supplier switching costs and vertical integration in the US automobile industry. *Bell Journal of Economics* 13:206–213.

Moran, T. H. 2001. *Foreign direct investment and development: the new agenda for developing countries and economies in transition*. Washington, DC: Institute of International Economics.

Motta, M. 1992. Multinational firms and the tariff jumping argument. *European Economic Review* 36:1557–1571.

Myerson, R. B. 1991. *Game theory: analysis of conflict*. Harvard University Press.

Neven, D. and G. Siotis. 1995. Technology sourcing and FDI in the EC: an empirical evaluation. *International Journal of Industrial Organization* 14:543–560.

Ng, F. and A. Yeats. 1999. Production sharing in East Asia: who does what for whom and why. World Bank Policy Research Working Paper 2197.

Nicholas, S. 1983. Agency contracts, institutional modes, and the transmission to foreign direct investment by British manufacturing multinationals before 1939. *Journal of Economic History* 43:675–86.

Nicoletti, G., S. Golub, D. Hajkova, D. Mirza, and Y. Kwang Yeol. 2003. Policies and international integration: influences on trade and foreign direct investment. OECD, Economics Department Working Paper 359.

Nielsen, S. B., P. Raimondos-Møller, and G. Schjelderup. 2004. Formula apportionment and transfer pricing under oligopolistic competition. *Journal of Public Economic Theory*, in press.

Norbäck, P.-J. 2001. Multinational firms, technology and location. *Journal of International Economics* 54:449–469.

Norman, V. D. and A. J. Venables. 1995. International trade, factor mobility, and trade costs. *Economic Journal* 105:1488–1505.

————. 2004. Industrial clusters: equilibrium, welfare and policy (CEPR DP 3004). *Economica*, in press.

Nunnenkamp, P. and M. Pant. 2003. Why the case for a multilateral agreement on investment is weak. Discussion Paper 400, Kiel Institute for World Economics.

OECD. 1977. *Model double taxation convention on income and on capital*. Paris: OECD.

————. 1996. *Benchmark definition of foreign direct investment*, 3rd edn. Paris: OECD.

————. 1997. *Model tax convention on income and on capital*. Paris: OECD.

————. 1999. Recent trends in foreign direct investment. *Financial market trends*. Paris: OECD.

————. 2001a. *Science, technology and industry scoreboard: towards a knowledge-based economy*. Paris: OECD.

————. 2001b. *Measuring globalisation. The role of multinationals in OECD economies. Manufacturing and services*. Paris: OECD.

————. 2001c. *The OECD's project on harmful tax practices: the 2001 progress report*. Paris: OECD.

————. 2002. *Education at a glance*. Paris: OECD.

————. 2003a. *International development statistics*. Paris: OECD.

————. 2003b. *Measuring globalisation: the role of multinationals in OECD economies*. Paris: OECD.

O'Gorman, C., E. O'Malley, and J. Mooney. 1997. The Irish indigenous software industry: an application of Porter's cluster analysis. Research Paper 3. Dublin: National Economic and Social Council.

Orvedal, L. 2002. Industrial clusters, asymmetric information and industrial policy. SNF Report 15/02, Bergen.

Ottaviano, G. and A. Turrini. 2003. Distance and FDI when contracts are incomplete. CEPR Discussion Paper 4041.

Oulton, N. 1998. Labour productivity and foreign ownership in the UK. National Institute of Economic and Social Research, Discussion Paper 143.

Pack, H. and K. Saggi. 2001. Vertical technology transfer via international outsourcing. *Journal of Development Economics* 53:389–415.

Pearce, R. D., K. P. Sauvant, and A. Islam. 1992. *The determinants of foreign direct investment: a survey of the evidence*. New York: United Nations.

Pennings, E. and L. Sleuwagen. 2002. The reorganization decisions of troubled firms: exit, downscale or relocate? Vlerick Leaven Gent Management School Working Paper 2002-21.

Perez, T. 1998. *Multinational enterprises and technological spillovers*. The Netherlands: Harwood.

Peri, G. and D. Urban. 2002. The Veblen-Gerschenkron effect of FDI in Mezzogiorno and East Germani. Centro Studi Luca d'Agliano Working Papers 164.

Pfaffermayr, M. 1996. Foreign outward direct investment and exports in Austrian manufacturing: substitutes or complements? *Weltwirtschafliches Archiv* 132:501–522.

Pottelsberghe de la Potterie, B. van and F. Lichtenberg. 2001. Does foreign direct investment transfer technology across borders? *Review of Economics and Statistics* 83:490–497.

Quijano, A. M. 1990. A guide to BEA statistics on FDI in the US. *Survey of Current Business* 70. (Available at www.bea.gov/bea/ail.htm.)

Reuber, G. L., H. Crookell, M. Emerson, and G. Gallais-Hamonno. 1973. *Private foreign investment in development*. Oxford: Clarendon Press.

Rodriguez-Clare, A. 1996. Multinationals, linkages and economic development. *American Economic Review* 86:852–873.

Rodrik, D. 1997. Has globalization gone too far? Institute for International Economics, Washington, DC.

Rugman, A. 1980. A new theory of the multinational enterprise: internationalization vs. internalization. *Journal of World Business* 15(1):23–29.

———. 1985. Internalization as a general theory of foreign direct investment. A reappraisal of the literature. *Welwirtshaftliches Archiv* 116:365–379.

———. 1986. New theories of the multinational enterprise: an assessment of internalization theory. *Bulletin of Economic Research* 38:101–118.

Salant, S., S. Switzer, and R. Reynolds. 1983. Losses due to merger; the effects of an exogenous change in industry structure on Cournot–Nash equilibrium. *Quarterly Journal of Economics* 98:185–199.

Scheve, K. and M. Slaughter. 2003. Foreign direct investment and labor-market outcomes. Paper prepared for the DG ECFIN Workshop, *Who Will Own Europe? The Internationalization of Asset Ownership in the EU Today and in the Future, Brussels.*

Schnitzer, M. 1999. Expropriation and control rights: a dynamic model of foreign direct investment. *International Journal of Industrial Organization* 17:1113–1137.

Sembenelli, A. and G. Siotis. 2002. Foreign direct investment, competitive pressure and spillovers. An empirical analysis on Spanish firm level data. Centro Studi d'Agliano Working Paper 169.

SESSI. (Various years). *L'implantation etrangère dans l'industrie*. Service des Statistique Industrielles, Ministere de l'Industrie, de la Poste et des Telecommunications (SESSI), Paris.

Shapiro, C. 1983. Premiums for high-quality products as returns to reputation. *Quarterly Journal of Economics* 98:659–679.

Shatz, H. J. 2003. Gravity, education, and economic development in multinational affiliate location. *Journal of International Trade and Economic Development* 12(1):117–150.

Siotis, G. 1999. Foreign direct investments, strategies and firms' capabilities. *Journal of Economics and Management Strategy* 8(2):251–270.

Sjöholm, F. 1999a. Technology gap, competition and spillovers from direct foreign investment: evidence from establishment data. *Journal of Development Studies* 36(1):53–73.

———. 1999b. Productivity growth in Indonesia: the role of regional characteristics and direct foreign investment. *Economic Development and Cultural Change* 47:559–584.

Slaughter, M. J. 1995. Multinational corporations, outsourcing, and American wage divergence. NBER Working Paper 5253.

———. 2000. Production transfer within multinational enterprises and American wages. *Journal of International Economics* 50:449–490.

———. 2001. International trade and labor demand elasticities. *Journal of International Economics* 54:27–56.

———. 2003. Host-country determinants of US foreign direct investment into Europe. In *Foreign direct investment in the real and financial sector of industrial countries*, ed. H. Herrmann and R. Lipsey. Springer.

Smarzynska, B. 2003. Does foreign direct investment increase the productivity of domestic firms? In search of spillovers through backward linkages. World Bank WP 2923.

Smith, A. 1987. Strategic investment, multinational corporations and trade policy. *European Economic Review* 31:89–96.

Smith, P. 2001. Patent rights and bilateral exchange: a cross-country analysis of US exports, FDI, and licensing. *Journal of International Economics* 55:411–440.

Svensson, R. 1996. Effects of overseas production on home country exports: evidence based on Swedish multinationals. *Weltwirtschafliches Archiv* 132:304–309.

Swedenborg, B. 1979. *The multinational operations of Swedish firms: an analysis of determinants and effects*. Stockholm: Almqvist & Wicksell.

———. 1985. Sweden. In *Multinational enterprises, economic structure, and international competitiveness*, ed. J. Dunning, pp. 217–248. Wiley.

———. 2001. Determinants and effects of multinational growth: the Swedish case revisited. In *Topics in empirical international economics*, ed. M. Blomström and L. S. Goldberg, pp. 99–131. University of Chicago Press.

Teece, D. 1977. Technology transfer by multinational firms: the resource cost of transferring technological know-how. *Economic Journal* 87:242–261.

———. 1986. *The multinational corporation and the resource cost of international technology transfer*. Cambridge: Ballinger.

The Economist. 2000. Re-inventing the wheel. 22 April, pp. 57–58. London.

Thomas, J. and T. Worrall. 1994. Foreign direct investment and the risk of expropriation. *Review of Economic Studies* 61(1):81–108.

UNCTAD. 1996. Incentives for foreign direct investments. *Current Studies* A30.

———. 1998. *World investment report 1998*. New York and Geneva: United Nations.

———. 1999a. *Trends in international investment agreements: an overview*. New York and Geneva: United Nations.

———. 1999b. *World investment report 1999: foreign direct investment and the challenge of development*. New York and Geneva: United Nations.

———. 2000. *World investment report 2000*. New York and Geneva: United Nations.

———. 2001. *World investment report 2001: promoting linkages*. New York and Geneva: United Nations.

———. 2003. *World investment report 2003*. New York and Geneva: United Nations.

———. 2005. *World investment report 2005. Transnational corporations and the internationalization of R&D*. New York and Geneva: United Nations.

UNESCO. 1998. *World education report*. Paris: UNESCO.

Venables, A. J. and N. Limao. 2002. Geographical disadvantage: a Heckscher–Ohlin–von Thünen model of international specialisation. *Journal of International Economics* 58:239–263.

Watanabe, S. 1983a. Technical co-operation between large and small firms in the Filipino automobile industry. In *Technology marketing and industrialization: linkages between small and large enterprises*, ed. S. Watanabe. New Delhi: Macmillan.

———. 1983b. Technological linkages through subcontracting in Mexican industries. In *Technology marketing and industrialization: linkages between small and large enterprises*, ed. S. Watanabe. New Delhi: Macmillan.

Wheeler, D. and A. Mody. 1992. International investment location decisions: the case of U.S. firms. *Journal of International Economics* 33:57–76.

Williamson, O. 1979. Transaction-cost economics: the governance of contractual relations. *Journal of Law and Economics* 22(2): 233–261.

Wilson, J. D. 1999. Theories of tax competition. *National Tax Journal* 52:269–304.

WTO 1998 *Annual report 1988*, p. 36. Geneva: World Trade Organization.

Yeaple, S. 2000. Three essays on the location decisions of multinational corporations. PhD dissertation, University of Wisconsin.

————. 2003. The role of skill endowments in the structure of US outward foreign investments. *Review of Economics and Statistics* 85:726–734.

Yeats, A. 1998. Just how big is global production sharing. World Bank Policy Research Working Paper 1871.

Zeile, W. J. 1993. Merchandise trade of US affiliates of foreign companies. *Survey of Current Business* October, pp. 52–65.

Zhao, L. 1998. The impact of foreign direct investment on wages and employment. *Oxford Economic Papers* 50:284–301.

Index

Lightning Source UK Ltd.
Milton Keynes UK
UKOW040417220612

194818UK00002B/23/P